The Criminal Code and the Law of Criminal Evidence in Canada Being an Annotation of the Criminal Code of Canada, and of the Canada Evidence Act, with Special Reference to the Law of Evidence and the Procedure in Criminal Courts, Including the...

W. J. Tremeear

null

The Making of Modern Law collection of legal archives constitutes a genuine revolution in historical legal research because it opens up a wealth of rare and previously inaccessible sources in legal, constitutional, administrative, political, cultural, intellectual, and social history. This unique collection consists of three extensive archives that provide insight into more than 300 years of American and British history. These collections include:

Legal Treatises, 1800-1926: over 20,000 legal treatises provide a comprehensive collection in legal history, business and economics, politics and government.

Trials, 1600-1926: nearly 10,000 titles reveal the drama of famous, infamous, and obscure courtroom cases in America and the British Empire across three centuries.

Primary Sources, 1620-1926: includes reports, statutes and regulations in American history, including early state codes, municipal ordinances, constitutional conventions and compilations, and law dictionaries.

These archives provide a unique research tool for tracking the development of our modern legal system and how it has affected our culture, government, business – nearly every aspect of our everyday life. For the first time, these high-quality digital scans of original works are available via print-on-demand, making them readily accessible to libraries, students, independent scholars, and readers of all ages.

THE CRIMINAL CODE

AND THE

LAW OF CRIMINAL EVIDENCE IN CANADA

BEING AN ANNOTATION OF THE CRIMINAL CODE OF CANADA, AND OF THE CANADA EVIDENCE ACT, WITH SPECIAL REFERENCE TO THE LAW OF EVIDENCE AND THE PROCEDURE IN CRIMINAL COURTS, INCLUDING THE PRACTICE BEFORE JUSTICES AND ON CERTIORARI AND HABEAS CORPUS.

SECOND EDITION

BY

W. J. TREMEEAR,

OF THE TORONTO BAR.

TORONTO:
CANADA LAW BOOK COMPANY, LIMITED,
LAW BOOK PUBLISHERS,
32 TORONTO ST.

PHILADELPHIA:
CROMARTY LAW BOOK COMPANY,
1112 CHESTNUT ST.

1908

Canada
223
1908

PREFACE TO THE SECOND EDITION

The re-arrangement of the sections of the Criminal Code by the general revision of the statutes of Canada in 1906, and the many changes made in both the Code and the Canada Evidence Act since the first edition, have created a demand for a new practice book on Canadian criminal law, which I have attempted to supply by this compilation. The annotations in the first edition have been thoroughly revised and supplemented with the decisions reported down to the end of March, 1908. I desire to express my acknowledgments to the members of the Bench and Bar who have from time to time favoured me with their suggestions, which have largely contributed to the improvements of this edition.

W. J. TREMEEAR.

TORONTO, May, 1908.

TABLE OF CONTENTS.

THE CANADIAN CRIMINAL CODE.

PART I.

PRELIMINARY.

PART II.

OFFENCES AGAINST PUBLIC ORDER, INTERNAL AND EXTERNAL.

PART III.

THE PEACE NEAR PUBLIC WORKS.

PART IV.

PART V.

OFFENCES AGAINST RELIGION, MORALS, AND PUBLIC CONVENIENCE.

PART VI.

OFFENCES AGAINST THE PERSON AND REPUTATION.

PART VII.

OFFENCES AGAINST RIGHTS OF PROPERTY AND RIGHTS ARISING OUT OF CONTRACTS, AND OFFENCES CONNECTED WITH TRADE.

PART VIII.

WILFUL AND FORBIDDEN ACTS IN RESPECT OF CERTAIN PROPERTY.

PART IX.

OFFENCES RELATING TO BANK NOTES, COIN AND COUNTERFEIT MONEY.

PART X.

PART XI.

Jurisdiction.

PART XII.

PART XIII.

PART XIV.

PART XV.

PART XVI.

PART XVII.

PART XVIII.

PART XIX.

PROCEDURE BY INDICTMENT.

PART XX.

PUNISHMENTS, FINES, ETC.

PART XXI.

PART XXII.

EXTRAORDINARY REMEDIES.

PART XXIII.

PART XXIV.

PART XXV.

CANADA EVIDENCE ACT.

TABLE OF ABBREVIATIONS OF CANADIAN REPORTS.

A.R. / App. R.	Reports of Court of Appeal of Ontario, 1846-1900.
All.	Allen's New Brunswick, (6-11 N.B.R.) 1848-1866.
B.C.R.	British Columbia Reports, 1882-
Bert.	Berton's New Brunswick, (2 N.B.R.) 1835-1839.
C.C.C.	Canadian Criminal Cases, 1893-
C.L.J.	Canada Law Journal, (new series) 1865-
C.L.T.	Canadian Law Times, 1881-
C.P.	Upper Canada Common Pleas, 1850-1882.
Can. Cr. Cas.	Canadian Criminal Cases, 1893-
Can. Ry. Cas.	Canadian Railway Cases.
Can. S.C.R.	Reports of Supreme Court of Canada, 1877-
Cartw.	Cartwright's Constitutional Cases, 1874-
Chip.	Chipman's New Brunswick, (1 N.B.R.) 1825-1828.
Cochrane	Cochrane's Reports, Nova Scotia, 1859.
Dor. Q.B.	Dorion's Queen's Bench, (Quebec) 1880-
Dra.	Draper's King's Bench Reports, Upper Canada, 1829-1831.
G. & O.	Geldert & Oxley's Nova Scotia, 1866-1875.
Gr.	Grant's Chancery, (Ontario) 1849-1882.
H. & W.	Haszard & Warburton's Prince Edward Island, 1850-1874.
Han.	Hannay's New Brunswick, (12-13 N.B.R.) 1867-1871.
James.	James' Reports, Nova Scotia, 1851-1855.
Kerr.	Kerr's New Brunswick, (3-5 N.B.R.) 1840-1848.
L.C. Jur.	Lower Canada Jurist, 1856-
L.C.L.J.	Lower Canada Law Journal, 1866-1868.
L.C.R.	Lower Canada (Quebec) Reports, 1850-1867.
L.N.	Legal News, (Montreal) 1878-
Man. R.	Manitoba Law Reports, 1884-
Mathieu R.	Mathieu's Quebec Revised Reports.
Mont. L.R.	Montreal Law Reports, 1884-
N.B.R.	New Brunswick Reports, 1825-
N.S.D.	Nova Scotia Decisions, 1867-1874.
N.S.R.	Nova Scotia Reports, 1834-
N.W.T. Rep.	North-West Territories Reports, (old series).
O.R. / Ont. R.	Ontario Reports, 1882-1900.
Old	Oldright's Reports, Nova Scotia, 1860-1867.
Ont. A.R.	Reports of Court of Appeal of Ontario, 1846-
Ont. Elec. R.	Ontario Election Reports, 1891-1900.

O.L.R. .... Ontario Law Reports, 1901-
P. & B. .... Pugsley & Burbidge, New Brunswick, (17-20 N.B.R.) 1877-1881.
P. & T. .... Pugsley & Trueman, New Brunswick, (22 N.B.R.) 1882-1883.
Perrault .... Perrault's Lower Canada Reports, 1726-1759.
Pugs. .... Pugsley's New Brunswick, (14-16 N.B.R.) 1872-1876.
Peters .... Peters' Reports, Prince Edward Island, 1850-1872.
P.E.I. .... Prince Edward Island Reports, 1850-
P.R. .... Practice Reports, (Ont.) 1850-1900.
Pyke. .... Pyke's Reports, Quebec, 1810-1811.
Que. K.B. ...... Quebec Reports, King's Bench, 1901-
Que. L.R. ...... Quebec Law Reports, 1874-
Que. P.R. .... Quebec Practice Reports, 1899-
Que. Q.B. .... Quebec Reports, Queen's Bench, 1892-1900.
Que. S.C. ...... Quebec Reports, Superior Court, 1892-
R. & C. .... Russell & Chesley's Nova Scotia, 1875-1879.
R. & G. .... Russell & Geldert's Nova Scotia, 1879-1882.
R.J.Q., Q.B. .... Quebec Judicial Reports, Queen's Bench, 1892-1900.
R.J.Q., S.C. ..... Quebec Judicial Reports, Superior Court, 1892-
Ramsay & M. ... Ramsay & Morin's Montreal Condensed Reports, 1854.
Rev. Crit. ..... Revue Critique, (Quebec) 1871-1875.
Rev. de Leg. ... Revue de Legislation, (Quebec) 1845-1848.
Rev. Leg. ...... Revue Legale, (Que.) 1869-
Russ. & Ch. .... Russell & Chesley, Nova Scotia, 1875-1879.
Terr. L.R. ...... Law Reports of the North Western Territories, (new series).
Thom. Dec. ...... Thomson's Decisions, Nova Scotia, 1834-1851.
Thom. R. .... Thomson's Reports, Nova Scotia, 1856-1859.
U.C.C.P. .... Upper Canada Common Pleas, 1850-1882.
U.C.L.J. .... Upper Canada Law Journal, (old series) 1855-1864.
U.C.O.S. .... Upper Canada, Queen's Bench Reports, (old series) 1831-1844.
U.C.Q.B. .... Upper Canada, Queen's Bench, 1844-1882.

CASES CITED.

CORRIGENDA.

Page 23, line 12 (date of case cited), for "1895" read "1885."
" 427, line 20 (citation), for "Wiley" read "Riley."
" 583, line 28, correct the name of case cited to read "R. v. Doherty, 3 Can. Cr. Cas. 505."
" 697, correct the second citation of R. v. Buchanan to read "12 Man. R. 190."
" 756, correct date of citation, R. v. Spence, to read "1855."
" 777, correct citation of R. v. Nicholls, to read "10 Cox C.C. 476."
" 877, correct citation of R. v. Hoggard, to read "30 U.C.Q.B. 152."

THE CANADIAN CRIMINAL CODE

AND THE

LAW OF CRIMINAL EVIDENCE

APPLICABLE THERETO.

THE CRIMINAL CODE.

(Revised Statutes of Canada, 1906, Chap. 146 and amending Acts.)

SHORT TITLE.

1. This Act may be cited as the Criminal Code. 55-56 V., c. 29, s. 1. Short title.

Origin.]—The Criminal Code in its present form is a revision and consolidation of the Criminal Code of 1892. That statute went into force on July 1, 1893, and was the first codification of the criminal law of Canada. The Code was modelled after the draft Code formulated by the commissioners appointed to revise the criminal law of England which, however, was not adopted by the British Parliament.

Evidence.]—The Code itself contains many enactments as to the law of evidence in criminal matters. The Canada Evidence Act which follows the Code in this volume is also applicable to prosecutions under the Code. And by sec. 35 of the Canada Evidence Act, the respective laws of evidence in the Provinces of Canada are applicable to proceedings under federal laws, subject to the provisions so made and any other enactments of the federal Parliament.

Legislative power.]—Section 91 of the British North America Act, 1867, embodying the Canadian Constitution, provides that it shall be lawful for the Dominion Parliament to make laws for the peace, order, and good government of Canada, in relation to all matters not coming within the classes of subjects thereby assigned exclusively to the Legislatures of the provinces; and "for greater certainty, but not so as to restrict the generality of the foregoing terms," it is thereby declared that (notwithstanding anything in that Act) the exclusive legislative authority of the Parliament of Canada extends to all matters coming within certain classes of subjects enumerated, amongst which is: (27) The Criminal Law, except the constitution of courts of criminal jurisdiction, but including the procedure in criminal matters.

Section 92 of the same statute provides that in each province the Legislature may exclusively make laws in relation to matters coming within certain other classes of subjects therein enumerated, amongst which is included the following: (14) The administration of justice in the province, including the constitution, maintenance, and organization of provincial courts, both of civil and of criminal jurisdiction, and including procedure in civil matters in those courts.

This latter power has been held to include the power of giving jurisdiction to the provincial courts and to impliedly include the power of enlarging, altering, amending and diminishing the jurisdiction of such courts. R. v. Levinger (1892), 22 O.R. 690. But in R. v. Boucher (1879), Cassels S.C. Dig. 181, Henry, J., of the Supreme Court of Canada, held that to merely add to the existing duties or functions of a police magistrate does not interfere with the constitution, maintenance or organization of the court, even if such office can be called a "court" within the meaning of sec. 92 of the B.N.A. Act, which he doubted. And in R. v. Toland (1892), 22 O.R. 505, it was held that an Ontario statute (sec. 2 of 53 Vict., ch. 18), which authorized police magistrates to try and convict persons charged with forgery was ultra vires of the Provincial Legislature; per MacMahon, J. Enforcing the law against a person charged with the commission of a crime is by the "trial" of the offender and his punishment for the offence. The trial is not connected with the constitution, maintenance or organization of a court but is criminal procedure. Ibid.

The whole domain of crime and criminal procedure is the exclusive property of the Dominion Parliament, and to allow the Parliament of a province to declare that an act which, by the general law, is a crime, triable and punishable as a crime with the ordinary safeguards of the constitution affecting procedure as to crime, shall be something other than or less than a crime, and so triable before and punishable by magistrates as if not a crime, would be destructive of the checks provided by the general law for the constitutional liberty of the subject. R. v. Lawrence (1878), 43 U.C.Q.B. 164, 175, per Harrison, C.J.

But there are many acts not being crimes which are triable before and punishable by magistrates, which, although called offences, are not crimes, and which by the proper legislative authority may be made the subject of summary magisterial jurisdiction, either with or without appeal; but these are not to be mistaken for acts in themselves crimes, and the subject of indictment, and of conviction under indictment, either at the common law or by statute. Such acts as these may by the Provincial Legislature be made the subject of punishment by fine, penalty or imprisonment, when this is done for the purpose of enforcing any law of the province made in relation to any matter coming within any of the classes of subjects exclusively assigned to the Provincial Legislatures. One of the subjects exclusively assigned to the Provincial Legislatures is the right to make laws as to "shop, saloon, tavern, auctioneer and other licenses, in order to the raising of a revenue for provincial, local, or municipal purposes." Ibid.

The passing of a provincial statute, within the powers of the Legislature, cannot in any wise take away from Parliament the right to legislate respecting the same matters, and to prohibit them and to enforce the prohibition by such punishment by way of fine or imprisonment as may be deemed best; or to draw into the domain of criminal law an act which has hitherto been punishable only under a provincial statute. Per Rose, J., in R. v. Stone (1892), 23 O.R. 46, following R. v. Wason, 17 A.R. 221, and R. Hart, 20 O.R. 611.

A provincial statute relating to criminal law passed before Confederation becomes as to that province a part of the criminal law of Canada, and is subject to repeal or amendment by a Dominion statute only. R. v. Halifax Electric Tramway Co. (1898), 1 Can. Cr. Cas. 424 (N.S.).

If it appears that provincial legislation deals with public wrongs and imposes penalties in respect thereof for the enforcement of which all citizens should have an equal interest as distinguished from enactments passed for the protection of a particular class or the regulation of the dealings or business of a certain class, as for example between master and servant, such legislation as to public wrongs is within the exclusive jurisdiction of the Dominion Parliament, although similar legislation as applied to various classes only and not to the public generally would be within provincial jurisdiction as dealing with "civil rights." Ibid.

Section 91, sub-sec. 27 of the British North America Act, 1867, reserves for the exclusive legislative authority of the Parliament of Canada "the criminal law, except the constitution of courts of criminal jurisdiction." It is, therefore, the criminal law in its widest sense that is reserved, and an infraction of the "Lord's Day Act" (Ont.), which in its original form, without the amendment afterwards introduced, was in operation at the time of Confederation, is an offence against the criminal law. Attorney-General (Ont.) v. Hamilton Ry. Co. (1903), 7 Can. Cr. Cas., at page 331 (Imp. P.C.).

Although the Provincial Legislature has the power to constitute courts of criminal law and define the jurisdiction as well territorially as in other respects, the Parliament of Canada has also the power under sec. 101 of the British North America Act to establish Dominion courts, *i.e.*, additional courts for the better administration of the laws of Canada.

The constitution, maintenance and organization of provincial courts of criminal jurisdiction is given to the Provincial Legislature as well as the constitution, maintenance and organization of courts of civil jurisdiction, yet Parliament may in virtue of sec. 101 create new courts of criminal jurisdiction, and enact that all crimes and offences shall be tried exclusively before these new courts. Valin v. Langlois, 3 Can. S.C.R. 1, 5 A.C. 115.

Though the organization of courts of criminal jurisdiction is within the exclusive powers of the Provincial Legislatures, the Parliament of Canada may impose upon existing courts or judicial officers the duty of administering the criminal law, and its action to that end need not be supplemented by provincial legislation. Re Vancini (No. 2) (1904), 8 Can. Cr. Cas, 228, 34 Can. S.C.R. 621.

In the judgment of the Privy Council in Citizens Insurance Company of Canada v. Parsons (1881), 1 Cartw. 265, these secs. 91 and 92 are discussed; and it is there pointed out that no rule can be laid down to define the actual limits of the various powers given to the Dominion and provinces respectively. The powers overlap, and in some instances the provinces can legislate until the subject matter is dealt with as a whole by the Dominion. When this takes place provincial legislation has to give way to the Dominion. R. v. Holland (1900), 4 Can. Cr. Cas. 72, 79, per Drake, J.

A Provincial Legislature may regulate and provide for the course of trial and adjudication of offences against its lawful enactments, although the procedure adopted is analogous to the procedure for criminal offences. R. v. Bittle, 21 O.R. 605.

It has recently been held in the Superior Court of Quebec that sec. 493 of the Quebec statute 62 Vict., ch. 58, punishing incorrigible habitual drunkards with a sentence of six months to one year relates to a matter pertaining to the criminal law and is ultra vires of the Provincial Legislature. Re Beaulieu (1907), 12 Can. Cr. Cas. 346.

The fact that such punishment was to be imposed only upon conviction for a municipal offence within the jurisdiction of a Provincial Legislature conjointly with the habitual drunkenness charged in aggravation thereof, does not validate the additional punishment imposed for the latter cause nor bring it within provincial jurisdiction. Ibid.

Headings.]—The title or heading would not control the meaning of plain language in any of the sections which immediately follow it, but it may properly be looked at in order to determine the sense of any doubtful expression in a clause ranged under the title: R. v. Shand (1904), 8 Can. Cr. Cas. 45, 51; Hammersmith and City R.W. Co. v. Brand (1869), L.R. 4 H.L. 171, at pp. 203, 277; The Queen v. Local Government Board (1882), 10 Q.B.D. 309, at p. 321; Union S.S. Co. v. Melbourne Harbour Trust Commissioners (1884), 9 App. Cas. 365, at p. 369.

Procedure in Ontario.]—Section 599 declares that the practice and procedure in all criminal cases and matters in the High Court of Justice of Ontario, which are not provided for in the Code, shall remain as heretofore.

INTERPRETATION.

Definitions.

2. (*As amended*, 1907.) In this Act, unless the context otherwise requires,—

'Any Act.' 'Any other Act.'

(1) 'Any Act,' or 'any other Act,' includes any Act passed or to be passed by the Parliament of Canada, or any Act passed by the legislature of the late province of Canada, or passed or to be passed by the legislature of any province of Canada, or passed by the legislature of any province now a part of Canada before it was included therein;

'Attorney General.'

(2) 'Attorney General' means the Attorney General or Solicitor General of any province in Canada in which any proceedings are taken under this Act, and, with respect to the Northwest Territories and the Yukon Territory, the Attorney General of Canada;

'Banker.'

(3) 'banker' includes any director of any incorporated bank or banking company;

'Bank note.'

(4) 'bank-note' includes all negotiable instruments issued by or on behalf of any person, body corporate, or company carrying on the business of banking in any part of the world, or issued by the authority of the Parliament of Canada, or any governor or other authority lawfully authorized thereto in any of His Majesty's dominions, or by the authority of any foreign prince, or state or government, and intended to be used as equivalent to money, either immediately upon their issue or at some time subsequent thereto, and all bank bills and bank post bills;

'Cattle.'

(5) 'cattle' includes any horse, mule, ass, swine, sheep or goat, as well as any neat cattle or animal of the bovine species, and by whatever technical or familiar name known, and shall apply to one animal as well as to many;

(6) 'chief constable' includes the chief of police, city marshal or other head of the police force of any city, town, incorporated village or other municipality, district or place, and in the province of Quebec, the high constable of the district, and means any constable of a municipality, district or place which has no chief constable or deputy chief constable; 'Chief constable.'

(7) 'court of appeal' includes, 'Court of Appeal.'

(a) in the province of Ontario, the Court of Appeal for Ontario,

(b) in the province of Quebec, the Court of King's Bench, appeal side,

(c) in the provinces of Nova Scotia, New Brunswick and British Columbia, the Supreme Court in banc,

(d) in the province of Prince Edward Island, the Supreme Court,

(e) in the province of Manitoba, the Court of Appeal,

(f) in the provinces of Saskatchewan and Alberta, the Supreme Court of the Northwest Territories in banc, until the same is abolished, and thereafter such court as is by the legislature of the said provinces respectively substituted therefor;

(g) in the Yukon Territory, the Supreme Court of Canada;

(8) 'copper coin' includes any coin of bronze or mixed metal and every other kind of coin other than gold or silver; 'Copper coin.'

(9) 'deputy chief constable' includes deputy chief of police, deputy or assistant marshal or other deputy head of the police force of any city, town, incorporated village, or other municipality, district or place, and, in the province of Quebec, the deputy high constable of the district; 'Deputy chief constable.'

(10) 'district, county or place,' includes any division of any province of Canada for purposes relative to the administration of justice in the matter to which the context relates; 'District, county or place.'

(11) 'document of title to goods' includes any bill of lading, India warrant, dock warrant, warehouse-keeper's certificate, warrant or order for the delivery or transfer of any goods or valuable thing, bought and sold note, or any other document used in the ordinary course of business as proof of the possession or control of goods, authorizing or purporting to authorize, either by endorsement or by delivery, 'Document of title to goods.'

the possessor of such document to transfer or receive any goods thereby represented or therein mentioned or referred to;

'Document of title to lands.'

(12) 'document of title to lands' includes any deed, map, paper or parchment, written or printed, or partly written and partly printed, being or containing evidence of the title, or any part of the title, to any real property, or to any interest in any real property, or any notarial or registrar's copy thereof, or any duplicate instrument, memorial, certificate or document authorized or required by any law in force in any part of Canada respecting registration of titles, and relating to such title;

'Every one,' 'person,' 'owner.'

(13) 'every one,' 'person,' 'owner,' and other expressions of the same kind include His Majesty and all public bodies, bodies corporate, societies, companies, and inhabitants of counties, parishes, municipalities or other districts in relation to such acts and things as they are capable of doing and owning respectively;

'Explosive substance.'

(14) 'explosive substance' includes any materials for making an explosive substance; also any apparatus, machine, implement or materials, used or intended to be used, or adapted for causing, or aiding in causing, any explosion in or with any explosive substance; and also any part of any such apparatus, machine or implement;

'Form.' 'Section.'

(15) 'form' means a form in Part XXV. of this Act, and 'section' means a section of this Act;

'Indictment.' 'Count.'

(16) (*As amended*, 1907) 'indictment' and 'count' respectively include information and presentment as well as indictment, and also any plea, replication or other pleading, **any formal charge** under section 873A, and any record;

'Intoxicating liquor.'

(17) (*As amended*, 1907) 'intoxicating liquor' means and includes any alcoholic, spirituous, vinous, fermented or other intoxicating liquor, or any mixed liquor a part of which is spirituous or vinous, fermented or otherwise intoxicating, and any such liquor shall be presumed to be intoxicating if it contains more than two and one-half per cent. of proof spirits;

'Justice.'

(18) 'justice' means a justice of the peace, and includes two or more justices, if two or more justices act or have jurisdiction, and also a police magistrate, a stipendiary magistrate and any person having the power or authority of two or more justices of the peace;

(19) 'loaded arms' includes any gun, pistol or other arm loaded with gunpowder, or other explosive substance, and ball, shot, slug or other destructive material, or charged with compressed air and ball, shot, slug or other destructive material; 'Loaded arms.'

(20) 'military law' includes the Militia Act and any orders, rules and regulations made thereunder, the King's Regulations and Orders for the Army; any Act of the United Kingdom or other law applying to His Majesty's troops in Canada, and all other orders, rules and regulations of whatsoever nature or kind to which His Majesty's troops in Canada are subject; 'Military law.'

(21) 'municipality' includes the corporation of any city, town, village, county, township, parish or other territorial or local division of any province of Canada, the inhabitants whereof are incorporated or have the right of holding property for any purpose; 'Municipality.'

(22) 'newspaper,' in the sections of the Act relating to defamatory libel, means any paper, magazine or periodical containing public news, intelligence or occurrences, or any remarks or observations thereon, printed for sale and published periodically or in parts or numbers, at intervals not exceeding thirty-one days between the publication of any two such papers, parts or numbers, and also any paper, magazine or periodical printed in order to be dispersed and made public, weekly or oftener, or at intervals not exceeding thirty-one days, and containing only or principally advertisements; 'Newspaper.'

(23) 'night' or 'night time' means the interval between nine o'clock in the afternoon and six o'clock in the forenoon of the following day, and 'day' or 'day time' includes the interval between six o'clock in the forenoon and nine o'clock in the afternoon of the same day; 'Night.' 'Night-time.' 'Day.' 'Day-time.'

(24) 'offensive weapon' or 'weapon' includes any gun or other firearm, or air-gun, or any part thereof, or any sword, sword-blade, bayonet, pike, pike-head, spear, spear-head, dirk, dagger, knife, or other instrument intended for cutting or stabbing, or any metal knuckles, or other deadly or dangerous weapon, and any instrument or thing intended to be used as a weapon, and all ammunition which may be used with or for any weapon; 'Offensive weapon.' 'Weapon.'

(25) 'Part' means a Part of this Act;

'Peace officer.' (26) 'peace officer' includes a mayor, warden, reeve, sheriff, deputy sheriff, sheriff's officer, and justice of the peace, and also the warden, keeper or guard of a penitentiary and the gaoler or keeper of any prison, and any police officer, police constable, bailiff, constable or other person employed for the preservation and maintenance of the public peace, or for the service or execution of civil process;

'Public department.' (27) 'public department' includes the Admiralty and War Department, and also any public department or office of the Government of Canada, or of the public or civil service thereof, or any branch of such department or office;

'Public stores.' (28) 'public stores' includes all stores under the care, superintendence or control of any public department as herein defined, or of any person in the service of such department;

'Public officer.' (29) 'public officer' includes any inland revenue or customs officer, officer of the army, navy, marine, militia, Royal Northwest mounted police, or other officer engaged in enforcing the laws relating to the revenue, customs, trade or navigation of Canada;

'Prison.' (30) 'prison' includes any penitentiary, common gaol, public or reformatory prison, lock-up, guard room or other place in which persons charged with the commission of offences are usually kept or detained in custody;

'Prize fight.' (31) 'prize fight' means an encounter or fight with fists or hands, between two persons who have met for such purpose by previous arrangement made by or for them;

'Property.' (32) 'property' includes

(a) every kind of real and personal property, and all deeds and instruments relating to or evidencing the title or right to any property, or giving a right to recover or receive any money or goods,

(b) not only such property as was originally in the possession or under the control of any person, but also any property into or for which the same has been converted or exchanged and anything acquired by such conversion or exchange, whether immediately or otherwise,

(c) any postal card, postage stamp or other stamp issued or prepared for issue by the authority of the Parliament of Canada, or of the legislature of any province of Canada, for the payment to the Crown or any corporate body of any fee, rate or duty, and whether still in the possession of the Crown or of any person or corporation;

(33) 'shipwrecked person' includes any person belonging to, on board of, or having quitted any vessel wrecked, stranded or in distress at any place in Canada; 'Shipwrecked person.'

(34) 'stores' includes all goods and chattels, and any single store or article; 'Stores.'

(35) 'superior court of criminal jurisdiction' means and includes, 'Superior court of criminal jurisdiction.'

(a) in the province of Ontario, the High Court of Justice for Ontario,

(b) in the province of Quebec, the Court of King's Bench,

(c) in the provinces of Nova Scotia, New Brunswick, and British Columbia, the Supreme Court,

(d) in the province of Prince Edward Island, the Supreme Court of Judicature,

(e) in the province of Manitoba, the Court of Appeal or the Court of King's Bench (Crown side),

(f) in the provinces of Saskatchewan and Alberta, the Supreme Court of the Northwest Territories, until the same is abolished, and thereafter such court as is by the legislatures of said provinces respectively substituted therefor,

(g) in the Yukon Territory, the Territorial Court;

(36) 'territorial division' includes any county, union of counties, township, city, town, parish or other judicial division or place to which the context applies; 'Territorial division.'

(37) 'testamentary instrument' includes any will, codicil, or other testamentary writing or appointment, as well during the life of the testator whose testamentary disposition it purports to be as after his death, whether the same relates to real or personal property, or both; 'Testamentary instrument.'

(38) 'trade combination' means any combination between masters or workmen or other persons for regulating or altering the relations between any persons being masters or workmen, or the conduct of any master or workman in or in respect of his business or employment, or contract of employment or service; 'Trade combination.'

(39) 'trustee' means a trustee on some express trust created by some deed, will or instrument in writing, or by parole, or otherwise, and includes the heir or personal representative of any such trustee, and every other person upon or to whom the duty of such trust has devolved or come, whether by appointment of a court or otherwise, and also 'Trustee.'

an executor or administrator, and an official manager, assignee, liquidator or other like officer acting under any Act relating to joint stock companies, bankruptcy or insolvency, and any person who is, by the law of the province of Quebec, an *administrateur* or *fidéicommissaire;*

'Trust.' and 'trust' includes whatever is by that law an *administration* or *fidéicommis;*

'Valuable security.' (40) 'valuable security' includes any order, exchequer acquittance or other security entitling or evidencing the title of any person to any share or interest in any public stock or fund, whether of Canada or of any province thereof, or of the United Kingdom, or of Great Britain or Ireland, or of any British colony or possession, or of any foreign state, or in any fund of any body corporate, company or society, whether within Canada or the United Kingdom, or any British colony or possession, or in any foreign state or country, or to any deposit in any savings bank or other bank, and also includes any debenture, deed, bond, bill, note, warrant, order or other security for money or for payment of money, whether of Canada or of any province thereof, or of the United Kingdom, or of any British colony or possession, or of any foreign state, and any document of title to lands or goods wheresoever such lands or goods are situate, and any stamp or writing which secures or evidences title to or interest in any chattel personal, or any release, receipt, discharge or other instrument, evidencing payment of money, or the delivery of any chattel personal;

'Wreck.' (41) 'wreck' includes the cargo, stores and tackle of any vessel and all parts of a vessel separated therefrom, and also the property of shipwrecked persons;

'Writing.' (42) 'writing' includes any mode in which, and any material on which, words or figures, whether at length or abridged, are written, printed or otherwise expressed, or any map or plan is inscribed.

'Part III.' (43) in Part XII. and in Parts XXII., XXIII. and XXIV. of this Act 'Part III.' means such section or sections of the said Part as are in force by virtue of any proclamation in the place or places with reference to which the Part is to be construed and applied; and 'a commissioner' means a commissioner under Part III. R.S., c. 151, s. 1; 55-56 V., c. 29, ss. 3, 92, 383, 420, 460, 519

'A commissioner.'

and 839; 63-64 V., c. 46, s. 3; 1 E. VII., c. 41, s. 11; 6 E. VII., c. 4, s. 4; 6 & 7 E. VII., c. 8; 6 & 7 E. VII., c. 9, s. 1.

Interpretation of criminal statutes.]—Penal statutes must be construed strictly, and where an enactment imposes a penalty for a criminal offence, a person against whom it is sought to enforce the penalty is entitled to the benefit of any doubt which may arise in the construction of the enactment. London County Council v. Aylesbury Dairy Co., [1898] 1 Q.B. 106, 109, Wright, J. R. v. Wirth, 1 Can. Cr. Cas. 231. The rule was thus expressed in Rumball v. Schmidt (1882), 2 Q.B.D. 608, "Where there is an enactment which may entail penal consequences you ought not to do violence to the language in order to bring people within it, but ought rather to take care that no one is brought within it who is not brought within it by express language."

Words are to be construed with reference to their context. Their meaning is to be ascertained by reference to the whole Act including, if necessary, the preamble. Colquhoun v. Brooks (1889), 14 App. Cas. 493. But a section having effect as a substantive enactment is to be first considered, and it is only in a second or last resort that the rest of the statute, or the preamble, or the scheme of governing intention is to be regarded. Spencer v. Metropolitan Board of Works (1882), 22 Ch.D. 142, 162, Jessel, M.R.

Provincial enforcement.]—By the Act of Confederation, the administration of justice in each of the provinces is entrusted to the Provincial Government, and it is therefore the provincial law officers of the Crown whose duty it is to conduct or to supervise, as the case may be, all criminal prosecutions. R. v. St. Louis (1897), 1 Can. Cr. Cas. 141, 145 (Que.); Attorney-General v. Niagara Falls Bridge Co., 20 Grant (Ont.) 34.

Bank-note.]—This definition is taken from sec. 420 of the Code of 1892 where is appeared under the Forgery clauses. A forged paper purporting on the face of it to be a bank note is within the definition, although there be no such bank as named. R. v. McDonald, 12 U.C.Q.B. 543. Even if the illegality of the note would be a defence the onus of proving illegality is upon the prisoner. R. v. Brown, 3 Allen (N.B.) 13.

Constitution of court in Nova Scotia.]—By sub-sec. (*e*) the Court of Appeal for criminal cases in the Province of Nova Scotia is the Supreme Court of Nova Scotia in banc.

The constitution of provincial courts is under the jurisdiction of the provinces, and by the Nova Scotia Judicature Act, R.S.N.S. 1900, ch. 55, sec. 5 the Supreme Court of that province shall consist of seven judges. Three judges may hear civil appeals under the Judicature rules but by Order 66, rule 1, it is expressly provided that these rules shall not affect criminal procedure. Semble, also that the court is sufficiently constituted in banc for the purposes of a court of criminal appeal with three judges. R. v. Ritter, 8 Can. Cr. Cas. 31.

"Count."]—Section 951 of the Code applies to summary trials as well as to trials upon an indictment; and the word "count" as used in secs. 2 and 951, includes an information before a justice for an indictable offence. The King v. Frank Coolen, 8 Can. Cr. Cas. 157.

District or county.]—Where the summary convictions procedure applies, reference should be had to the further definition laid down in sec. 705.

"Everyone," "person."]—"Everyone" is an expression of the same kind as "person," and therefore includes bodies corporate unless the context

requires otherwise. There is no doubt that the expression "every one" is, whether in a legal or popular sense, a wider term than the word "person," Union Colliery Co. v. The Queen, 4 Can. Cr. Cas. 400, 407. In the case of Pharmaceutical Society v. London and Provincial Supply Association, 5 App. Cas. 857, Lord Chancellor (Selborne), said: "There can be no question that the word "person" may, and I should be disposed myself to say primâ facie does, in a public statute include a person in law; that is, a corporation as well as a natural person . . . "That if a statute provides that no person shall do a particular act except on a particular condition, it is primâ facie, natural and reasonable (unless there be something in the context, or in the manifest object of the statute, or in the nature of the subject-matter, to exclude that construction) to understand the legislature as intending such persons, as, by the use of proper means, may be able to fulfil the condition; and not those who, though called "persons" in law, have no capacity to do so at any time, by any means, or under any circumstances, whatsoever."

A corporation is not subject to indictment upon a charge of any crime the essence of which is either personal criminal intent or such a degree of negligence as amounts to a wilful incurring of the risk of causing injury to others. R. v. Great West Laundry Co. (1900), 3 Can. Cr. Cas. 514 (Man.).

Justices.]—The Dominion Parliament has jurisdiction to confer upon justices of the peace appointed under provincial authority jurisdiction to summarily try criminal offences. Rex v. Wipper (1901), 5 Can. Cr. Cas. 17 (N.S.).

Other deadly or dangerous weapons.]—General words are to be given their common meaning unless there is something reasonably plain on the face of the instrument to be construed, to shew that they are not used with that meaning; the mere fact that general words follow specific words is not enough. Parker v. Marchant (1842), 1 Y. & C. 290.

Officials.]—The acts of a de facto officer, assuming to exercise the functions of an office to which he has no legal title, are, as regards all persons but the holder of the legal title, legal and binding. O'Neil v. Attorney-General (1896), 1 Can. Cr. Cas. 303 (S.C. Can.).

The distinction between an officer de jure and an officer de facto is, that an officer de jure is one who has the lawful right or title without the possession of the office, while an officer de facto has the possession and performs the duties under the colour of right without being actually qualified in law so to act. 19 Am. & Eng. Encyc. of Law, 394.

The acts of a justice of the peace, duly commissioned, but who has not qualified by taking the prescribed oath, or who has not the property qualication without which he is prohibited by statute from acting and is declared to be incapable of "being a justice," are sustained as valid if done in a judicial character, and sufficient effect is given to the statute by considering it as penal upon the party acting; and therefore persons seizing goods under a warrant of distress, signed by a justice who had not taken the oaths required, are not trespassers because of the defect. Margate Pier v. Hannam (1819), 3 B. & Ald. 266.

Prize fight.]—An exhibition of fighting with fists or hands to witness which an admission fee is charged to the public and at which it is announced that the stake money will go to the contestant who knocks out his opponent in a stipulated number of rounds is a "prize fight" within sec. 92 of the Criminal Code. Such an exhibition made for gain must be viewed as it appeared or was intended to appear to the public, and it is no defence that the participants had merely feigned to fight. Steele v. Maber, 6 Can. Cr. Cas. 446.

Property.]—The phrase in Code sec. 236 as to lotteries, is "disposing of any property," and this clause of interpretation as to "property" simply states that it includes "every kind of real and personal property." The property need not be "specific property," for it would be an easy evasion if the statute could be got rid of by designating no particular thing, although the winner would be able to exercise his choice among the available prizes offered. Taylor v. Smetten, 11 Q.B.D. at p. 212; R. v. Lorrain (1896), 2 Can. Cr. Cas. 144.

Trade combinations.]—See secs. 496, 497 and 498.

Valuable security.]—It was formerly held that the term "valuable security" meant a valuable security to the person who parted with it on the false pretence, and that the inducing a person to execute a mortgage on his own property was therefore not obtaining a "valuable security." R. v. Brady (1866), 26 U.C.Q.B. 13; R. v. Danger, 3 Jur. N.S. 1011; but the present definition expressly includes any deed, bond, etc., which evidences title.

Defendant was indicted for forging an order for the payment of money, the order being in the following words: "John McLean, tailor, please give M. A. S (defendant) to the amount of $3.50 and by doing you will oblige me, A. McP." It was proved that the signature A. McP. was forged by the prisoner, and prisoner was convicted and sentenced. It was held that this was an order for the payment of money, and not a mere request, and the conviction was affirmed. R. v. Steel (1863), 13 U.C.C.P. 619 (following R. v. Tuke (1858), 17 U.C.Q.B. 296).

The true criterion as to whether a document is an order for payment of money or only a request, is, whether, if the instrument were genuine, and the person to whom it was directed paid it, he could recover the amount from the party by whom the order was given, or charge it to him, for if such be the case it is an order. R. v. Carter, 1 Cox 172; R. v. Ferguson, 1 Cox 241; R. v. Dawson, 3 Cox 220; R. v. Vivian, 1 Den. C.C. 35.

Post card a chattel value.

3. For the purpose of this Act a postal card or any stamp referred to in the last preceding section shall be deemed to be a chattel, and to be equal in value to the amount of the postage, rate or duty expressed on its face in words or figures or both. 55-56 V., c. 29, s. 3.

Valuable security.

4. Valuable security shall, where value is material, be deemed to be of value equal to that of the unsatisfied money, chattel personal, share, interest or deposit, for the securing or payment of which, or delivery or transfer or sale of which, or for the entitling or evidencing title to which, such valuable security is applicable or to that of such money or chattel personal, the payment or delivery of which is evidenced by such valuable security. 55-56 V., c. 29, s. 3.

5. In this Act, unless the context otherwise requires,—

Finding indictment.

(*a*) finding the indictment includes also exhibiting an information and making a presentment;

Possession.

(*b*) having in one's possession includes not only having in one's own personal possession, but also knowingly

(i) having in the actual possession or custody of any other person, and

(ii) having in any place (whether belonging to or occupied by one's self or not) for the use or benefit of one's self or of any other person.

Joint possession.

2. If there are two or more persons, and any one or more of them, with the knowledge and consent of the rest, has or have anything in his or their custody or possession, it shall be deemed and taken to be in the custody and possession of each and all of them. 55-56 V., c. 29, s. 3; 56 V., c. 32, s. 1.

Meaning of expressions in other Acts.

6. In every case in which the offence dealt with in this Act relates to the subject treated of in any other Act the words and expressions used herein in respect to such offence shall have the meaning assigned to them in such other Act. 55-56 V., c. 29, s. 4.

Carnal knowledge.

7. Carnal knowledge is complete upon penetration to any, even the slightest degree, and even without the emission of seed. 55-56 V., c. 29, s. 266.

PART I.

GENERAL.

Application of this Act.

8. Nothing in this Act shall affect any of the laws relating to the government of His Majesty's land or naval forces. 55-56 V., c. 29, s. 983.

This Act not to affect H. M. forces.

9. Except in so far as they are inconsistent with the Northwest Territories Act and amendments thereto as the same existed immediately before the first day of September, one thousand nine hundred and five, the provisions of this Act extend to and are in force in the provinces of Saskatchewan and Alberta, the Northwest Territories, and, except in so far as inconsistent with the Yukon Act, the Yukon Territory. 55-56 V., c. 29, s. 983.

Application of Act to Saskatchewan, Alberta and the Territories.

Application of the Criminal Law of England.

10. The criminal law of England, as it existed on the seventeenth day of September, one thousand seven hundred and ninety-two, in so far as it has not been repealed by any Act of the Parliament of the United Kingdom having force of law in the province of Ontario, or by any Act of the Parliament of the late province of Upper Canada, or of the province of Canada, still having force of law, or by this Act or any other Act of the Parliament of Canada, and as altered, varied, modified or affected by any such Act, shall be the criminal law of the province of Ontario. R.S., c. 144, s. 1.

Criminal law of England applicable to Ontario.

The Quebec Act, 1774.]—The Criminal Law of England was introduced into the Province of Quebec by Royal Proclamation in 1763, and subsequently extended by 14 Geo. III., ch. 83 (Imp.) to what is now Ontario. After the erection of Upper Canada, now Ontario, into a separate province, the Provincial Legislature, after reciting the Imperial Act, 14 Geo. III., ch. 83, passed 40 Geo. 111., ch. 81 in July, 1800, enacted that the Criminal Law of England as it stood on the 17th September, 1792, should be the Criminal Law of Upper Canada. R. v. Malloy (1900), 4 Can. Cr. Cas. 116 (Ont.).

Champerty a criminal offence.]—Champerty is a criminal offence, and a champertous contract will not be enforced by the courts. The English champerty laws were introduced or continued in Ontario and Quebec under the Quebec Act, 1774 (Imp.). Meloche v. Deguire, 8 Can. Cr. Cas. 89; Hopkins v. Smith (1901), 1 O.L.R. 659.

Champerty and maintenance may almost be considered obsolete offences as regards criminal prosecutions therefor. The English Criminal Law Commissioners appointed to draft a Criminal Code, which however never was enacted, recommended that both offences should be abolished, it being considered by them that this law had been used vexatiously in many cases of prosecutions commenced thereunder and not persevered in. Commissioners' 5th Report, pages 34-39.

Criminal law of England applicable to British Columbia.

11. The criminal law of England as it existed on the nineteenth day of November, one thousand eight hundred and fifty-eight, in so far as it has not been repealed by any ordinance or Act—still having the force of law—of the colony of British Columbia, or the colony of Vancouver Island, passed before the union of the said colonies, or of the colony of British Columbia passed since such union, or by this Act or any other Act of the Parliament of Canada, and as altered, varied, modified or affected by any such ordinance or Act, shall be the criminal law of the province of British Columbia. R.S., c. 144, s. 2.

Champerty.]—A bargain by which A., a stranger to B., having no interest recognized by law in a given property, agrees to help B. to recover such property in a court of justice in consideration of getting a portion of the fruits of the suit, is champerty and is an indictable offence by the common law of England. Briggs v. Fleutot, 10 B.C.R. at p. 316.

The criminal law of England on this subject was introduced into British Columbia by the statute R.S.C. 1886, ch. 144, sec. 2.

Criminal law of England applicable to Manitoba.

12. The criminal law of England as it existed on the fifteenth day of July, one thousand eight hundred and seventy, in so far as it is applicable to the province of Manitoba, and in so far as it has not been repealed, as to the Province, by any Act of the Parliament of the United Kingdom, or by this Act or any other Act of the Parliament of Canada, and as altered, varied, modified or affected, as to the Province, by any such Act, shall be the criminal law of the province of Manitoba. 51 V., c. 33, s. 1.

Effect of Act on Remedies.

Civil remedy not suspended.

13. No civil remedy for any act or omission shall be suspended or affected by reason that such act or omission amounts to a criminal offence. 55-56 V., c. 29, s. 534.

No suspension of civil remedy for criminal act.]—This section formerly sec. 534 of the Criminal Code, 1892, has been held in Quebec not to be "criminal law" legislation but legislation dealing with civil rights and therefore ultra vires of the Federal Parliament. Paquet v. Lavoie (1898), 6 Can. Cr. Cas. 314, 7 Que. Q.B. 277.

Semble, the establishment of the English criminal law by the Quebec Act (14 Geo. III. (Imp.), ch. 83) in the Provinces of Ontario and Quebec having been effected by a legislative body having absolute jurisdiction over both civil and criminal law, it must be taken as having introduced in the Province of Quebec the English law with respect to the suspension of civil remedies for criminal wrongs.

The operation of this section is left in doubt by reason of the constitutional questions involved. Can the Dominion Parliament declare that a civil remedy shall not be suspended? Have not the Provincial Legislatures by reason of their exclusive jurisdiction as to civil rights the right to control the suspension of the civil remedy pending the criminal prosecution?

To an action, before the Code, for assault and battery defendant pleaded that before action brought the plaintiff laid an information before a magistrate charging defendant with feloniously, etc., wounding the plaintiff with intent to do him grievous bodily harm, thereby charging defendant with felony; that defendant was brought before the magistrate and committed for trial which had not yet taken place; that the subject of both the civil and criminal prosecutions was the same, and that plaintiff's civil right of action was suspended until the criminal charge was disposed of. Held, on demurrer, that the plea was good; and an order was made staying the civil action in the meantime. Taylor v. McCulloch (1885), 8 Ont. R. 309.

The former rule, excepting in the Province of Quebec, was that on grounds of public policy if it appeared on the trial of a civil action that the facts amounted to felony, the judge was bound to stop the civil proceedings and non-suit the plaintiff in order that public justice might first be vindicated by a criminal prosecution. Walsh v. Nattress, 19 U.C.C.P. 453; Livingstone v. Massey, 23 U.C.Q.B. 156; Williams v. Robinson, 20 U.C.C.P. 255; Pease v. McAloon, 1 Kerr (N.B.) 111. The civil remedy was held to be suspended until the defendant charged with the felony should be either acquitted or convicted thereof. Brown v. Dalby, 7 U.C.Q.B. 162.

Distinction between felony and misdemeanour abolished.

14. The distinction between felony and misdemeanour is abolished, and proceedings in respect of all indictable offences, except so far as they are herein varied, shall be conducted in the same manner. 55-56 V., c. 29, s. 535.

Misdemeanour practice to prevail.]—When a certain practice would have been permissible in case of misdemeanour, and not permissible in case of felony, the practice has been to apply the rule as in cases of misdemeanour, and such is the intention of the Code. R. v. Fox (1903), 7 Can. Cr. Cas. 457.

Prisoner's testimony as witness at another trial—Consent of prisoner's counsel.]—The distinction between felony and misdemeanour having been abolished, the consent of counsel for the accused which before the Code would have been effective in misdemeanours only, is now effective although the offence charged was formerly a felony. And evidence given on the trial of another person including the evidence of the prisoner then called as a witness, may with the consent of the prisoner's counsel be admitted in evidence both for and against the prisoner. R. v. Fox, 7 Can. Cr. Cas. 457 (Ont.).

Felony or misdemeanour.]—A person committed for trial in respect of an indictable offence which was a felony before the Criminal Code, 1892, is not entitled as of right to bail and it is discretionary with the Superior Court exercising habeas corpus jurisdiction to allow or refuse bail in such cases. With respect to indictable offences which were misdemeanours before the Criminal Code, 1892, the accused committed for trial is entitled to bail as a matter of right on habeas corpus. Ex parte Fortier, 6 Can. Cr. Cas. 191.

A provincial statute prior to Confederation, providing for the discharge from imprisonment in default of indictment of an accused person committed for a "felony" will apply equally to cases which were misdemeanours before the abolition by the Criminal Code of Canada of the distinction between felony and misdemeanour. R. v. Cameron (1897), 1 Can. Cr. Cas. 169 (Que.).

Enactments regulating the procedure in courts are usually deemed imperative, and not merely directory. Maxwell on Statutes, 456; Taylor v. Taylor, 1 Ch.D. 426; 3 Ch.D. 145; R. v. Riel (No. 2) (1885), 1 Terr. L.R. 23, 44.

When offence punishable under more than one Act or law.

15. Where an act or omission constitutes an offence, punishable on summary conviction or on indictment, under two or more Acts, or both under an Act and at common law, the offender shall, unless the contrary intention appears, be liable to be prosecuted and punished under either or any of such Acts, or at common law, but shall not be liable to be punished twice for the same offence. 55-56 V., c. 29, s. 933.

What statutory offences indictable.]—When a statute makes that unlawful which was lawful before, and appoints a specific remedy, that remedy may be pursued and no other; and where an offence is not so at common law, but made an offence by Act of Parliament, an indictment will lie where there is a substantive prohibitory clause in such Act of Parliament, though there be afterwards a particular provision and a particular remedy. When a new offence is created by an Act of Parliament, and a penalty is annexed to it by a separate and substantive clause, it is not necessary for the prosecutor to sue for the penalty, but he may proceed on the prior clause, on the ground of its being an indictable offence. R. v. Mason (1867), 17 U.C.C.P. 534.

But by the same unlawful acts a person may be guilty of two separate offences, for both of which he may be convicted. R. v. Smith, 19 O.R. 714; R. v. Handley, 5 C. & P. 565.

But where the defendant may be prosecuted on the same facts under two statutes or laws, for substantially the same offence, a conviction under one law is a bar to a charge under the other: the offender may be tried under either statute, but cannot be tried twice. Wemyss v. Hopkins, L.R. 10 Q.B. 378.

In order to be a bar the issue in the second proceeding must be identical with that in the first one, although the facts may vary, and although the charges formulated may not be the same. R. v. King (1897), 1 Q.B. 214; see notes in 2 Can. Cr. Cas. 497.

Offences at common law.]—Parliament never intended to repeal the common law, except in so far as the Code either expressly or by implication repeals it. So that if the facts stated in the indictment constitute an indictable offence at common law, and that offence is not dealt with in the Code, then unquestionably an indictment will lie at common law; even if the offence has been dealt with in the Code, but merely by way of statement of what is law, then both are in force. Union Colliery Co. v. The Queen, 4 Can. Cr. Cas. 400 (Can.), per Sedgewick, J. So that, for example, a statute which provides a new punishment for an old offence, repeals by implication only so much of the prior law as concerns the punishment, leaving it permissible to indict an offender either under the old law, whether statutory or common, and inflict upon him, upon conviction, the punishment ordained by the new, or under the new statute at the election of the prosecuting power. The offence and punishment, therefore, may be defined by different laws; and so, if a statute simply creates an offence, the common law punishment may by implication be imposed." Bishop on Statutory Crimes, 2nd ed., p. 166.

The common law jurisdiction as to crime is still operative, notwithstanding the Code, and even in cases provided for by the Code, unless there is such repugnancy as to give prevalence to the latter law. R. v. Cole, (1902), 5 Can. Cr. Cas. 330; The King v. Carlile, 3 B. & Ald. 161.

Procedure for offences at common law.]—Section 16 provides that all rules and principles of the common law which render any circumstances a justification or excuse for any act, or a defence to any charge, shall remain in force and be applicable to any defence to a charge under the Code except in so far as they are thereby altered or are inconsistent therewith.

Besides a provision to the same effect the English draft Criminal Code, upon which the Canadian Code was modelled, contained a clause abrogating the common law as regards any possible offences not included in the draft Code, and that seems to have been one of the principal grounds upon which the draft Code was rejected by the British Parliament. No such clause was incorporated in the Canadian Criminal Code and offences at common law may still be prosecuted for in Canada, where the Code neither makes provision to the contrary nor deals with the like offence. But as to matters of mere procedure it is submitted that such provisions of the Code control, in so far as they can be made applicable, the procedure in respect of such common law offences as well as in respect of offences under the Code. Sections 668 to 686, inclusive, headed "Procedure on appearance of accused," purport to deal with preliminary enquiries by justices in any case in which "any person accused of an indictable offence is before a justice whether voluntarily or upon summons, or after being apprehended with or without warrant, or while in custody for the same or any other offence," sec. 668. And although sec. 654 as to informations and the process to compel appearance before a justice is, by its terms, limited to indictable offences against the Code, its provisions may be taken as ancillary only to the more general power contained in sec. 653 to compel the attendance of the person accused of having committed "an indictable offence" within certain territorial limits.

In a recent case the Supreme Court of Nova Scotia held that the Criminal Code of 1892 was intended to make complete and exhaustive provision as to the subjects with which it deals, in so far at all events as its provisions relate to procedure. It is explicitly called a Code by the first section of the chapter in which it is embodied and its utility as a Code will be greatly impaired if it cannot be so considered. R. v. Snelgrove (1906), 12 Can. Cr. Cas. 189. See also the Vagliano Case, [1891] 1 A.C., at p. 144.

Res judicata.]—Where a person has been acquitted by a court of competent jurisdiction the acquittal is a bar to all further proceedings to punish him for the same matter, although a plea of autrefois acquit may not be allowed because of the different nature of the charges. The acquittal on the first charge became res judicata as between the Crown and the accused, and it was not open to the Crown to proceed on the second charge in which a conviction could only be had by the second jury overruling the contrary verdict of the first jury. R. v. Quinn, 10 Can. Cr. Cas. 412, 11 O.L.R. 242.

Justification or Excuse.

Common law rule in force.

16. All rules and principles of the common law which render any circumstances a justification or excuse for any act, or a defence to any charge, shall remain in force and be applicable to any defence to a charge under this Act except in so far as they are hereby altered or are inconsistent herewith. 55-56 V., c. 29, s. 7.

Locality of crime.]—All crime is local, and the jurisdiction over the crime belongs to the country where it is committed. Jefferys v. Boosey (1855), 4 H.L.C. 815, 24 L.J. Ex. 81, per Parke, B.; MacLeod v. New South Wales (1891), A.C., 455, 17 Cox C.C. 341. But if a material part of any crime is committed within the jurisdiction legislation may properly provide for the punishment there of the whole of it: Bishop on Cr. Law, sec. 116.

And offences committed by a subject or citizen within the territorial limits of a foreign state may, by legislation, be made punishable in the courts of the country to which the party owes allegiance, and whose laws he is bound to obey. Wheaton's International Law, sec. 113, re Bigamy Sections, 1 Can. Cr. Cas. 172 (S.C. Can.).

In cases of obtaining goods under false pretences, the crime is complete where the goods are obtained; and, therefore, if the pretences are made within one jurisdiction and the property is obtained in another, the person making the representations must be indicted within the latter jurisdiction. 7 Am. & Eng. Ency. of Law 758; People v. Sully, 5 Parker Cr. Cas. (N.Y.) 142; Skiff v. People, 2 Parker Cr. Cas. N.Y. 139.

On an indictment for obtaining money by false pretences by sending a false return of fees to certain public commissioners, it was shewn that the return was received in Westminster with a letter dated Northampton, together with an affidavit sworn there, and that the commissioners thereupon issued an order upon the treasury to pay certain moneys to the prisoner. It was held by Coleridge, J., that the jury might infer that the documents were posted in Northamptonshire, where the affidavit was sworn, and from which county the letter purported to have been written, and that the prisoner was properly indicted in Northamptonshire for obtaining money by false pretences, the "forwarding" of the false return, etc., being alleged as the false pretence. R. v. Cooke (1858), 1 Foster & F. 64. The last-mentioned case was followed and approved by the Court for Crown Cases Reserved in R. v. Holmes (1883), 15 Cox C.C. 343. It was there held that where a false pretence was made by the prisoner in England by letter there posted to a person in France, and received in France by the latter, in consequence of which the latter sent to the prisoner a cheque drawn in France, but payable in England, which the prisoner cashed in England, an offence was established to have taken place in England, and that the prisoner was properly indicted and convicted there.

Common law jurisdiction.]—The common law is not abrogated by the Code and will still be applicable in cases for which no provision has been made in the Code as well to their prosecution as defence. Even in cases provided for by the Code the common law jurisdiction as to crime is still operative except where there is a repugnancy in which event the Code will prevail. R. v. Cole (1902), 5 Can. Cr. Cas. 330.

Newly settled country.]—Generally speaking, if an uninhabited country be discovered and occupied by English subjects, all English laws then in being, which are the birthright of every subject, are immediately there in force. But this must be understood with many and great restrictions. Such colonists carry with them only so much of the English law as is applicable to their own situation and the condition of an infant colony. Broom & Hadley's Com. 119. At the time of its occupation by English subjects the North-West Territories and the Provinces of Alberta and Saskatchewan would fall within the description of an uninhabited country. R. v. Connor (1885), 2 Man. L.R. 235, 1 Terr. L.R. 4, 13, per Taylor, J.

17. No person shall be convicted of an offence by reason of any act or omission of such person when under the age of seven years. 55-56 V., c. 29, s. 9. Children under seven.

Common law.]—This is in accordance with the common law under which a child under the age of seven years is doli incapax and no evidence was admissible to rebut that presumption. Marsh v. Loader, 14 C.B.N.S. 535.

18. No person shall be convicted of an offence by reason of an act or omission of such person when of the age of seven, but under the age of fourteen years, unless he was competent to know the nature and consequences of his conduct, and to appreciate that it was wrong. 55-56 V., c. 29, s. 10. Children between seven and thirteen.

Children over 14.]—Children after attaining the age of fourteen years are presumed by the law to be doli capaces, and capable of discerning good from evil, and are with respect to their criminal actions subject to the same rule of construction as others of more mature age. 1 Hale 25.

Children between 7 *and* 14.]—Where the offender is between the ages of seven and fourteen, evidence of a mischievous discretion on his part may be given to rebut the presumption of law arising from his tender years, but such evidence must be clear and strong beyond all doubt and contradiction. R. v. Vamplew, 3 F. & F. 520. Two questions are in that case to be left to the jury: (1) Whether he committed the offence; (2) whether at the time he had a guilty knowledge that he was doing wrong. R. v. Owen, 4 C. & P. 236; R. v. Smith, 1 Cox 260; Foster Crown Law 70; Russell on Crimes, 6th ed., p. 115.

It is to be conclusively presumed that a party is physically incompetent to commit an unnatural offence under Cr. Code, sec. 202, if under the age of fourteen, such presumption is not affected by the provisions of this section which refers exclusively to mental capacity to distinguish between right and wrong. R. v. Hartlen (1898), 2 Can. Cr. Cas. 12 (N.S.). But although a minor under fourteen cannot be convicted of sodomy, he may, if the act be committed against the will of the other party, be punished for an indecent assault upon another male person under Cr. Code, sec. 293. Ibid.

By Cr. Code, sec. 298, it is enacted that no one under the age of fourteen can commit the offence of rape.

The leading case of R. v. Brimilow (1840), 9 C. & P. 366, 2 Moody C.C. 122, was decided under the statute 1 Vict. (Imp.), ch. 85, sec. 11, which enacted, "that on the trial of any person for any felony where the crime charged shall include assault, the jury may acquit of the felony and find the party guilty of an assault, if the evidence shall warrant such finding." Brimilow was charged with rape, and on it being proved that he was under fourteen years of age, it was left to the jury to say whether he was guilty of an assault, and on conviction, and a case reserved, it was held that he could, on an indictment for rape, be legally convicted of an assault under that statute.

A boy under fourteen cannot in point of law be guilty of an assault with intent to commit a rape. R. v. Phillips (1839), 8 C. & P. 736, nor of carnally knowing and abusing a girl, although proved that he had arrived at puberty. R. v. Jordan (1839), 9 C. & P. 118, nor of the offence of carnal knowledge of a girl under thirteen. R. v. Waite, [1892] 2 Q.B. 600.

Trial of juvenile offenders.]—See secs. 800 et seq.

Insanity. **19.** No person shall be convicted of an offence by reason of an act done or omitted by him when labouring under natural imbecility, or disease of the mind, to such an extent as to render him incapable of appreciating the nature and quality of the act or omission, and of knowing that such an act or omission was wrong.

Delusions. 2. A person labouring under specific delusions, but in other respects sane, shall not be acquitted on the ground of insanity, under the provisions hereinafter contained, unless the delusions caused him to believe in the existence of some state of things which, if it existed, would justify or excuse his act or omission.

Presumption of sanity. 3. Every one shall be presumed to be sane at the time of doing or omitting to do any act until the contrary is proved. 55-56 V., c. 29, s. 11.

This section of the Code follows the draft Code prepared by the Imperial commissioners, which was never adopted by the British Parliament although largely declaratory of the common law.

Remand for medical examination.]—A remand for eight days for the purpose of a medical examination of the accused as to sanity cannot be made on the mere suggestion of the police officer without bringing the accused personally before the magistrate. Re Sarault (1905), 9 Can. Cr. Cas. 448.

Reserved case.]—A case may be reserved at the instance of the Crown upon a question of law as to whether there was any evidence of insanity to support the jury's verdict of not guilty upon that ground. The King v. Phinney (No. 1) (1903), 6 Can. Cr. Cas. 469.

Indictment notwithstanding insanity.]—A grand jury should not on the ground of the insanity of the accused return "no bill" to an indictment. R. v. Hodges, 8 C. & P. 195. As to procedure on the trial of an indictment where this defence is raised see Code secs. 966-970.

The rule laid down by the judges in reply to a question put to them by the House of Lords, in McNaghten's Case (1843), 4 St. Tr. N.S. 847, 10 Clark & F. 200, 1 Car. & K. 130, was as follows: "Notwithstanding the party accused did the act complained of, with a view, under the influence of insane delusion, of redressing or revenging some supposed grievance or injury, or of producing some public benefit, he is nevertheless punishable, according to the nature of the crime committed, if he knew at the time of committing such crime that he was acting contrary to law; by which expression we mean, the law of the land." And this rule was followed and applied in R. v. Riel (No. 2) (1885), 1 Terr. L.R. 23. Leave to appeal was refused by the Privy Council, 10 A.C. 675, 16 Cox C.C. 48.

The burden of proof of insanity is upon the defence. McNaghten's Case, 10 Cl. & F. 200; Regina v. Stokes, 3 C. & K. 185; Regina v. Layton, 4 Cox C.C. 149. Without evidence to go to the jury, the prisoner cannot be acquitted upon the plea of insanity. If there is in such a case to be any appeal after a conviction, it must be on the ground that the evidence is so overwhelming in favour of the insanity of the prisoner that the court will feel that there has been a miscarriage of justice—that a poor, deluded, irresponsible being has been adjudged guilty of that of which he could not be guilty if he were not deprived of the power to reason upon the act complained of, to determine by reason if it was right or wrong. A new trial should not be granted if the evidence were such that the jury could reasonably convict or acquit. Per Killam, J., in R. v. Riel (No. 2) (1895), 1 Terr. L.R., at p. 63.

One deaf and dumb from his birth, who has no means of learning to discriminate between right and wrong, or of understanding the penal enactments of the law as applicable to particular offences, is by presumption of law an idiot, but if it can be shewn that he has the use of understanding, which many of that condition discover by signs, then he may be tried and suffer judgment, although great caution should be observed in such proceedings: 1 Hale 34; R. v. Berry, 1 Q.B.D. 447.

The proper question to be put to the jury as to the prisoner's state of mind where the defence of insanity is raised is, whether the accused had a sufficient degree of reason to know that he was doing an act that was wrong, but this question should be accompanied with such observations and explanations as the circumstances of each particular case may require. McNaghten's Case, 4 St. Tr. N.S. 931. This is preferable to putting the question generally and in the abstract as to whether the accused at the time of doing the act knew the difference between right and wrong. Ibid.

Proof of insanity.]—Insanity may be proved without medical testimony, and may be inferred from the behaviour of the accused and facts proved. R. v. Dart, 14 Cox C.C. 143. If the accused was deranged shortly before committing the offence and there is no reason for believing that he had recovered his senses in the interim, he should be acquitted. R. v. Hadfield, cited in Collinson on Lunacy, p. 480.

Medical evidence.]—A medical man, conversant with the disease of insanity, and who never saw the prisoner previously to the trial but was present during the whole trial and the examination of all the witnesses, cannot, in strictness, be called as a witness to give his opinion as to the state of the prisoner's mind at the time of the commission of the alleged crime, or his opinion whether the prisoner was conscious at the time of doing the act that he was acting contrary to law or whether he was labouring under any and what delusion at the time, because each of those questions involves the determination of the truth of the facts deposed to, which it is for the jury to decide; and the questions are not mere questions upon a matter of science in which case such evidence is admissible. But where the facts are admitted or not disputed and the question becomes substantially one of science only, it may be convenient to allow the question to be put in that general form, though the same cannot be insisted on as a matter of right. McNaghten's Case, 4 St. Tr. N.S. 932.

But the witness may be asked whether, assuming certain facts sworn to by other witnesses to be true, such facts in his opinion indicate insanity. R. v. France, 4 Cox C.C. 57; R. v. Wright, R. & R. 456; R. v. Searle, 1 M. & Rob. 75.

It is not permissible for counsel to quote in his address to the jury the opinions of medical writers as expressed in medical books, where such opinions have not been referred to in the testimony of the witnesses. R. v. Taylor, 13 Cox C.C. 77.

Dementia through intoxication.]—Though voluntary drunkenness does not constitute an excuse for the commission of crime, yet where the question is whether an act was premeditated or done only from sudden heat or impulse, the fact that the accused was intoxicated is a circumstance proper to be taken into consideration. R. v. Grindley (1819), 1 Russel on Crimes, 6th ed. 144; R. v. Pearson, 2 Lewin 144; R. v. Thomas, 7 C. & P. 817; R. v. Moore, 3 C. & K. 319; R. v. Doody, 6 Cox C.C. 463; but see contra, R. v. Carroll, 7 C. & P. 145 and R. v. Meakin, 7 C. & P. 297. Where the question is whether words have been uttered with a deliberate purpose or are merely low and idle expressions, the drunkenness of the person uttering them is proper to be considered; but if there is really a previous determination to resent a slight affront in a barbarous manner, the state of drunkenness in which the prisoner was ought not to be regarded, for it would furnish no excuse. R. v. Thomas, 7 C. & P. 817, per Parke, B. If the very essence of the crime is the intention with which the act was done, it may be left to the jury to say whether the prisoner was so drunk as not to be capable of forming any intention whatever, and, if so, they may acquit him of the intent. R. v. Cruse, 8 C. & P. 541; R. v. Monkhouse, 4 Cox C.C. 55.

Delirium tremens if it produces dementia rendering the person incapable of distinguishing right from wrong while affected by it is such insanity as will constitute a defence. R. v. Davis, 14 Cox C.C. 563; and see R. v. Baines (1886), cited in Wood-Renton on Lunacy, p. 912.

Feigned insanity.]—The various forms of metal disorders which can be feigned are acute mania, dementia or chronic insanity as distinguished from acute mania, monomania and melancholic. With regard to mania, although it may be simulated, it is a difficult thing to impose upon those acquainted with the disease. It is a physical impossibility for a person of sound mind to present the continual watchfulness, excitement or resistance seen in the true complaint, or to resist the influence of the remedies. In most cases of true mania there are certain premonitory indications associated with and accompanying it—disorders of the digestive functions, headache, sleeplessness, a peculiar form of raving, all of which are absent with the simulator. One important characteristic in true mania is the absence of all feelings of hunger and thirst, and a want of all sense of decency and cleanliness, which cannot be feigned or assumed for any length of time. The reaction following the violence of feigned lunacy must end in sleep, the individual being unable to keep up the deception during the night, while sheer exhaustion compels him to fall asleep. The real maniac continues his ravings during many days and many nights, and seems possessed of abnormal powers of endurance, the restless nights not causing any material difference in his condition, or diminution in his strength. The chief characteristics of monomania are the presence of a false idea or hallucination. The most marked distinction between real and feigned cases of monomania is the condition of the power of reasoning. A real monomaniac cannot be reasoned out of his false ideas, in maintaining which he will set all the principles of logic at defiance, which the imposter would not, from a fear of discovery, venture to do. In true monomania there is no relation between his delusion and anything surrounding him. His ideas are inconsistent, and he is indifferent as to the fact. In the feigner there will exist a desire to modify his delusions and to associate them with what is going on around him, and he is more coherent in his ideas. The imposter will endeavour to force his delusion on others, while the real monomanic rarely alludes to his erroneous views unless when led up to them or questioned thereon, or when the conversation bears upon what is uppermost in his abnormal mind.

20. Except as hereinafter provided, compulsion by threats of immediate death or grievous bodily harm from a person actually present at the commission of the offence shall be an excuse for the commission, by a person subject to such threats, and who believes such threats will be executed, and who is not a party to any association or conspiracy, the being a party to which rendered him subject to compulsion, of any offence other than treason as defined by this Act, murder, piracy, offences deemed to be piracy, attempting to murder, assisting in rape, forcible abduction, robbery, causing grievous bodily harm, and arson. 55-56 V., c. 29, s. 12. Compulsion by threats.

Threats of future injury do not excuse the offence. Stephen's Digest, Art. 31.

As to compulsion of wife see the following sec. 21.

21. No presumption shall be made that a married woman committing an offence does so under compulsion because she commits it in the presence of her husband. 55-56 V., c. 29, s. 13. Compulsion of wife.

Rebutting the presumption.]—The former common law principle that a wife was exempt from liability in certain criminal acts upon the ground of coercion on the part of her husband, did not apply where the wife had committed the offence by her husband's order or procurement, if she committed it in his absence. R. v. Williams (1878), 42 U.C.Q.B. 462. And a plea of compulsion was rebutted by proof that the wife was the more active party, even when the offence was committed in the presence of her husband. Per Gwynne, J., in R. v. Williams (1878), 42 U.C.Q.B. 462; R. v. Howard, 45 U.C.Q.B. 346; R. v. McGregor, 26 O.R. 115.

If, however, there is evidence that the wife acted under the coercion and control of the husband such may still be a defence in certain cases. Brown v. Attorney-General of N.Z., [1898] A.C. 234; R. v. Torpey, 12 Cox 45; R. v. Dykes, 15 Cox 771; R. v. Baines, 19 Cox 524.

Where both husband and wife were jointly indicted for a robbery with violence and the jury found that the wife who had taken an active part in the offence had acted under the coercion of her husband, who had previously planned the crime, the verdict was held equivalent to one of not guilty as to her. R. v. Torpey, 12 Cox 45.

As to a husband or wife being an accessory after the fact in respect of an offence committed by the other of them, see Code sec. 71.

22. The fact that an offender is ignorant of the law is not an excuse for any offence committed by him. 55-56 V., c. 29, s. 14. Ignorance of the law.

Ignorance of law no excuse.]—All persons are bound to know and obey the laws. R. v. Mailloux, 3 Pugsley (N.B.) 493; R. v. Moodie, 20 U.C.Q.B. 399.

Although ignorance of the law is not a defence, it constitutes a ground for an application to the Executive for mercy. R. v. Madden, 10 L.C. Jur. 344.

New offence by statute.]—In Burns v. Nowell, L.R. 5 Q.B. 454, Baggallay, L.J., said: "Before a continuous act or proceeding, not originally unlawful, can be treated as unlawful by the reason of the passing of an Act of Parliament by which it is in terms made so, a reasonable time must be allowed for its discontinuance, and though ignorance of the law may of itself be no excuse for the master of a vessel who may act in contravention of it, such ignorance may nevertheless be taken into account when it becomes necessary to consider the circumstances under which the act or proceeding alleged to be unlawful was continued, and when and how it was discontinued, with a view to determine whether a reasonable time had elapsed without its being discontinued."

Execution of sentence.

23. Every ministerial officer of any court authorized to execute a lawful sentence, and every gaoler, and every person lawfully assisting such ministerial officer or gaoler, is justified in executing such sentence. 55-56 V., c. 29, s. 15.

Execution of process.

24. Every ministerial officer of any court duly authorized to execute any lawful process of such court, whether of a civil or criminal nature, and every person lawfully assisting him, is justified in executing the same.

Gaoler.

2. Every gaoler who is required under such process to receive and detain any person is justified in receiving and detaining him. 55-56 V., c. 29, s. 16.

As to erroneous defective and irregular warrants and process, see secs. 26-29.

Execution of warrants.

25. Every one duly authorized to execute a lawful warrant issued by any court or justice of the peace or other person having jurisdiction to issue such warrant, and every person lawfully assisting him, is justified in executing such warrant.

Gaoler.

2. Every gaoler who is required under such warrant to receive and detain any person is justified in receiving and detaining him. 55-56 V., c. 29, s. 17.

On Sunday.]—By sec. 661 every warrant of arrest authorized by this Act may be issued and executed on a Sunday or statutory holiday.

Seizing certain chattels.]—Under a warrant of arrest on a charge of an indictable offence, articles found in the possession of the accused and in respect of which or with which the offence is believed to have been committed, may be taken possession of by the constable, and detained as evidence in support of the charge. Dillon v. O'Brien, 16 Cox C.C. 245.

Arrest.]—To constitute an arrest the party need not be touched by the officer, it being sufficient if he is commanded to give himself up and does so. 2 Bishop Cr. Law 33.

Execution of erroneous sentence or process.

26. (*As amended,* 1907.) If a sentence is passed or process issued by a court having jurisdiction under any circumstances to pass the sentence or issue such process, or if a warrant is issued by a court, justice, or person having jurisdiction under any circumstances to issue the warrant, the sentence passed or process or warrant issued shall be sufficient to justify the officer or person thereby authorized, to execute the same, and every gaoler and person lawfully assisting in executing or carrying out such sentence, process or warrant, although the court passing the sentence or issuing the process had not in the particular case authority to pass the sentence or to issue the process, or although the court, justice or other person in the particular case had no jurisdiction to issue, or exceeded its or his jurisdiction in issuing, the warrant, or was, at the time when such sentence was passed or process or warrant issued, out of the district in or for which such court, justice or person was entitled to act. 55-56 V., c. 29, s. 18; 6 & 7 E. VII., c. 8.

Origin of enactment.]—Section 26 is in accordance with the report of the Royal Commissioners upon a draft Criminal Code submitted to the Imperial Parliament in the year 1880. The commissioners (Blackburn, Barry and Lush, JJ. and Sir James Fitzjames Stephen, Q.C.), said:

"The result of the authorities justifies us in saying that whenever a ministerial officer who is bound to obey the orders of a court or magistrate (as for instance in executing a sentence or effecting an arrest under warrant), and is punishable by indictment for disobedience, merely obeys the order which he has received he is justified, if that order was within the jurisdiction of the person giving it. And we think that the authorities shew that a ministerial officer obeying the order of a court or the warrant of a magistrate is justified, if the order or warrant was one which the court or magistrate could under any circumstances lawfully issue, though the order or warrant was in fact obtained improperly, or though there was a defect of jurisdiction in the particular case which might make the magistrate issuing the warrant civilly responsible, on the plain principle that the ministerial officer is not bound to enquire what were the grounds on which the order or warrant was issued, and is not to blame for acting on the supposition that the court or magistrate had jurisdiction."

Process irregular on its face.]—Writs issued by a Superior Court, not appearing to be out of the scope of their jurisdiction, are valid, and of themselves, without any further allegation, a protection to all officers and others in their aid acting under them, and that although they be on the face of them irregular or void in form; for the officers ought not to examine the judicial act of the court, whose servants they are, nor exercise their judgment in ascertaining the validity of the process in point of law, but are bound to execute it, and are therefore protected by it. Turner v. Felgate, 1 Lev. 95; Cotes v. Mitchill, 3 Lev. 20; R. v. McGuire, 4 Can. Cr. Cas. 15.

Defective process.]—A search warrant affords absolute justification to the officer executing it if it has been issued by competent authority and is valid on its face, although the warrant may in fact be bad and although it be set aside by reason of a failure to comply with legal requirements. Sleeth v. Hurlbert (1896), 3 Can. Cr. Cas. 197, 25 Can. S.C.R. 620.

A conviction for resisting a sheriff's officer will be supported notwithstanding the fact that the date of the judgment under which it was issued was erroneously stated therein, such an error being an irregularity only and amendable. R. v. Monkman, 8 Man. R. 509.

And a warrant of commitment which is valid on its face is a justification to the constable who executes it, although the imprisonment it directs is not authorized by law. R. v. King, 18 O.R. 566.

The defendant M. laid an information before the defendant J., a justice of the peace, charging plaintiff with obtaining from him a suit of clothes for one W. under the false pretence that she would pay for the same the following week. The information having been sworn to, J. issued a warrant under which plaintiff was arrested. In an action brought by plaintiff claiming damages for false arrest, the Supreme Court of Nova Scotia was divided in opinion. McDonald, C.J., and Ritchie, J., held that the representation that plaintiff would pay for the clothes the following week was not the representation of a fact, either past or present, within the meaning of the Code; and that as the information did not allege that plaintiff had been guilty of any crime, the arrest was illegal and made without any authority; that even if the magistrate were acting bonâ fide, and believed he had jurisdiction, no circumstances were brought to his notice which if true would give him jurisdiction, and his belief on the subject was without ground on which it could be based, and was unreasonable. But in the opinion of Henry, J., and Graham, E.J., the justice having acted with some colour of reason, and with a bonâ fide belief that he was acting in pursuance of his legal authority, was entitled to protection, although he may have proceeded illegally or in excess of his jurisdiction. Mott v. Milne (1898), 31 N.S.R. 372, 35 C.L.J. 81.

Where a person has been illegally taken into custody upon a criminal charge under a defective warrant he may be legally arrested or detained upon that criminal charge on the defect being remedied, without being first set free from the illegal custody and placed at liberty. Southwick v. Hare (1893), 24 O.R. 528.

But a person in illegal custody upon a criminal charge, or supposed criminal charge, cannot, before being liberated therefrom, be legally and properly taken into custody upon civil process—such as a ca. sa.—the reason assigned being that if such an arrest or taking into custody were held to be good, this would enable a plaintiff in a civil proceeding to take an advantage of his own wrong. Re Alfred Eggington, 2 E. & B. 717.

Where a person was convicted of an assault and fined by a magistrate in the county of H., and the magistrate issued a warrant for his arrest for the non-payment of the fine, directed to a constable, who went after the plaintiff and found him in an adjoining county, and the constable told him he had a warrant of commitment for him for his arrest, and at his request allowing him to read it, whereupon the plaintiff said he would go with him, which he did, it was held that what took place constituted an arrest. Aldrigh v. Humphrey (1898), 34 C.L.J. 385 (Ont.).

Sentence or process without jurisdiction.

27. Every officer, gaoler or person executing any sentence, process or warrant, and every person lawfully assisting such officer, gaoler or person, shall be protected from criminal responsibility if he acts in good faith under the belief that the sentence or process was that of a court having jurisdiction, or that the warrant was that of a court, justice or other person having authority to issue warrants, and if it be proved that the person passing the sentence or issuing the process acted as a court under colour of having some appointment or commission lawfully authorizing him to so act, or that the person issuing the warrant acted as a court, justice or other person having such authority, although in fact such appointment or commission did not exist or had expired, or although in fact the court or the person passing the sentence or issuing the process was not the court or the person authorized by the commission to act, or the person issuing the warrant was not duly authorized so to act. 55-56 V., c. 29, s. 19.

Protection from criminal responsibility.]—This section and secs. 28 and 29 deal only with criminal responsibility while in cases to which sec. 26 applies, the sentence or process is a justification both as to civil and criminal responsibility.

28. Every one duly authorized to execute a warrant to arrest, who thereupon arrests a person, believing in good faith and on reasonable and probable grounds that he is the person named in the warrant, shall be protected from criminal responsibility to the same extent and subject to the same provisions as if the person arrested had been the person named in the warrant. Arresting wrong person.

2. Every one called on to assist the person making such arrest, and believing that the person in whose arrest he is called on to assist is the person for whose arrest the warrant is issued, and every gaoler who is required to receive and detain such person, shall be protected to the same extent and subject to the same provisions as if the arrested person had been the person named in the warrant. 55-56 V., c. 29, s. 20. Assisting in such arrest. Gaoler.

See note to sec. 27.

29. Every one acting under a warrant or process which is bad in law on account of some defect in substance or in form apparent on the face of it, if he in good faith and without culpable ignorance and negligence believes that the warrant or process is good in law, shall be protected from criminal responsibility to the same extent and subject to the same provisions as if the warrant or process were good in law, and ignorance of the law shall in such case be an excuse. Irregular warrant or process.

2. It shall be a question of law whether the facts of which there is evidence may or may not constitute culpable ignorance or negligence in the belief of such person that the warrant or process is good in law. 55-56 V., c. 29, s. 21. Question of law.

A peace officer executing a warrant of arrest which he believes to be good is exempt from criminal responsibility therefor by this section, although the warrant was bad on its face as following a conviction also bad on its face. Gaul v. Township of Ellice (1902), 6 Can. Cr. Cas. 15.

A resolution of a municipal council to pay the costs of enforcing an invalid conviction in a criminal matter to which it is not a party is ultra vires. Ibid.

A police officer is not the agent of the municipal corporation which appoints him to the position and, if he is negligent in performing his duty as a guardian of the public peace, the corporation is not responsible for such negligence in provinces where the English common law applies. McCleave v. City of Moncton, 6 Can. Cr. Cas. 219.

See also note to sec. 27.

Arrest by peace officer.

30. Every peace officer who, on reasonable and probable grounds, believes that an offence for which the offender may be arrested without warrant has been committed, whether it has been committed or not, and who, on reasonable and probable grounds, believes that any person has committed that offence, is justified in arresting such person without warrant, whether such person is guilty or not. 55-56 V., c. 29, s. 22.

Justification both civil and criminal.]—This section operates, not merely to protect the officer from civil or criminal proceedings, but also to authorize the arrest and make it lawful; and it applies, not only when the arrest could be made by any person without a warrant, but also to cases in which a peace officer only may so arrest. R. v. Cloutier (1898), 2 Can. Cr. Cas. 43.

Issuing warrant without sworn information.]—If a justice of the peace is not himself personally arresting the offender on view or upon suspicion, or personally acting in effecting the arrest by calling some one to his assistance in making the same, he can legally direct the arrest only by a warrant issued upon a written complaint or information upon oath. A justice of the peace who illegally issues a warrant without having received a sworn information in respect of the charge is liable in trespass for the arrest made thereunder, and he cannot justify the commanding of the constable to make the arrest by shewing that he, the justice, had a reasonable suspicion that an offence had been committed. McGuiness v. Dafoe, 3 Can. Cr. Cas. 139, 23 Ont. App. R. 704.

Neither a magistrate nor a constable is allowed to act officially in his own case, except "flagrante delicto," while there is otherwise danger of escape, or to suppress an actual disturbance and enforce the law while it is in the act of being resisted. P. hearing of a complaint against him from the constable who had the warrant, went voluntarily before the magistrate, who did not examine into the matter and bail him, but allowed him to depart, with a direction to appear at the police office in the morning; and afterwards the magistrate sent the constable to whom the warrant had before been delivered, to take him in custody to the station house, which he did that evening, it being alleged that he had assaulted the magistrate on the previous evening. It was held that this did not warrant the imprisonment, as the magistrate might at the time of the assault have ordered him into custody; but here, the act was over, and time had intervened, so there was no present disturbance. Powell v. Williamson (1843), 7 U.C.Q.B. 154.

Constable acting without warrant.]—A constable in the service of a municipality is not justified in taking a person into custody on an allegation of theft said to have been committed on the previous day and not being of the class of offences mentioned in sec. 33, without any sworn complaint having been made, and without a warrant issued by competent authority—more especially where there was no reason to suspect that he would attempt to evade arrest. But where the officer has acted in good faith, and on information which excuses him to some extent, these facts should be taken into consideration in the award of damages. Mousseau v. City of Montreal (1898), Q.R. 12 S.C. 61. As to arrest of suspects and of persons found committing offences, see secs. 32-37.

Justification apart from existing warrant.]—The mere fact that the constable had a warrant and that he told the accused that that was the cause of his arrest would not deprive him of the right to reply on the statute for his justification in a civil or criminal proceeding founded thereon. See the cases referred to in Jordan v. McDonald (1898), 31 N.S.R. 135, and the observations of Tindal, C.J., in Hoye v. Bush (1840), 1 M. & G. 785, where he said: "Where indeed it can be shewn that a felony has been actually committed the constable may throw the warrant aside. It will be sufficient in such a case for the constable to shew that he has taken the person really charged with the offence however he may have been misdescribed in the warrant."

A constable is not deprived of his protection because he does not give notice of the warrant or of the cause of the arrest as required by sec. 40. R. v. Sabeans (1903), 7 Can. Cr. Cas. 498, 37 N.S.R. 223.

And where a peace officer would be justified by virtue of this section in arresting a person without a warrant, the justification will extend to an arrest in respect of which he held a warrant which was insufficient because of the misnomer of the person intended to be charged. Ibid.

The arrest of a person, charged with obtaining goods by false pretences with intent to defraud, on a request by telegram from another province of Canada, where the offence is alleged to have been committed, may be justified by a peace officer by alleging either that the prisoner has actually committed such offence or that such officer, on reasonable and probable grounds, believes that the prisoner has committed the offence charged. R. v. Cloutier, 2 Can. Cr. Cas. 43.

Reasonable and probable grounds.]—On an indictment of an officer for manslaughter in shooting a person fleeing to avoid arrest, it was held in Manitoba that the question of reasonable and probable grounds was to be left to the jury with a direction to apply the law as stated by the trial judge. R. v. Smith (1907), 7 Western L.R. 92, 17 Man. R. 282, 13 Can. Cr. Cas.

Persons assisting peace officer.

31. Every one called upon to assist a peace officer in the arrest of a person suspected of having committed such offence is justified in assisting, if he knows that the person calling on him for assistance is a peace officer, and does not know that there is no reasonable ground for the suspicion. 55-56 V., c. 29, s. 23.

See note to sec. 30.

Arrest of persons found committing offence.

32. Every one is justified in arresting without warrant any person whom he finds committing any offence for which the offender may be arrested without warrant, or may be arrested when found committing. 55-56 V., c. 29, s. 24.

Arrest after commission of certain offences.

33. If any offence for which the offender may be arrested without warrant has been committed, any one who, on reasonable and probable grounds, believes that any person is guilty of that offence is justified in arresting him without warrant, whether such person is guilty or not. 55-56 V., c. 29, s. 25.

Arrest without warrant.]—The words "may be" in this section refer to those provisions of the Code which authorize arrest without warrant, and which include the offence of unlawfully wounding under sec 274. Jordan v. McDonald (1898), 31 N.S.R. 129.

Defendant, a police officer in and for the town of Windsor, N.S., arrested plaintiff at Halifax, on a charge of having unlawfully assaulted, beaten, wounded and illtreated P., a police officer, while in the discharge of his duty, occasioning actual bodily harm. Defendant, at the time, held a warrant for plaintiff's arrest, but it had not been indorsed for execution in another county. Apart from the warrant defendant had actual knowledge of the commission of the offence for which the arrest was made. In an action by plaintiff claiming damages for unlawful arrest and imprisonment, it was held that it was competent for defendant to contend that the arrest was made independent of the warrant, and to justify such arrest by shewing that at the time the arrest was made he was aware that plaintiff had committed the offence of unlawfully wounding. Jordan v. McDonald (1898), 3 N.S.R. 129.

Subject to the provisions of sec. 649, when a private person—that is, a person not by office a keeper of the peace, or a justice, or a constable—takes upon himself to arrest another without a warrant for a supposed offence in respect of which a warrant is not required, he must be prepared to prove that such an offence has been committed, for in that respect he acts at his own peril. Mere suspicion that such an offence has been committed by some one will not do, though if he is prepared to shew that it has really been committed by some one, then he may justify arresting a particular person, upon reasonable grounds of suspicion that he was the offender; and mistake on that point, when he acts sincerely upon strong grounds of suspicion, will not be fatal to his defence. McKenzie v. Gibson (1851), 8 U.C.Q.B. 100.

Arrest during night.

34. Every one is protected from criminal responsibility for arresting without warrant any person whom he, on reasonable and probable grounds, believes he finds committing by night any offence for which the offender may be arrested without warrant. 55-56 V., c. 29, s. 26.

Night.]—This expression is defined by sec. 2(23) to mean the interval between 9 p.m. and 6 a.m.

While committing offence.

35. Every peace officer is justified in arresting without warrant any person whom he finds committing any offence. 55-56 V., c. 29, s. 27.

See secs. 646 to 652, inclusive.

By night.

36. Every one is justified in arresting without warrant any person whom he finds by night committing any offence.

2. Every peace officer is justified in arresting without warrant any person whom he finds lying or loitering in any highway, yard or other place by night, and whom he has good cause to suspect of having committed or being about to commit any offence for which an offender may be arrested without warrant. 55-56 V., c. 29, s. 28. Loitering by night.

Finds committing.]—A person is "found committing" an offence if he is either caught in the act or is pursued immediately and continuously after he had been seen committing it; but in the latter case there must be such fresh and continuous pursuit of him from the time of his being seen that both events may be said to be part of the one occurrence. R. v. Curran (1828), 3 C. & P. 397. Pursuit begun after the lapse of three hours from the commission of the offence is insufficient to justify the apprehension under this clause. Downing v. Capel, L.R. 2 C.P. 461.

Night.]—The interval between 9 p.m. and 6 a.m. See sec. 2(23).

Arrest without warrant.]—See secs. 646 to 652, inclusive, and sec. 35 supra.

37. Every one is protected from criminal responsibility for arresting without warrant any person whom he, on reasonable and probable grounds, believes to have committed an offence and to be escaping from and to be freshly pursued by those whom he, on reasonable and probable grounds, believes to have lawful authority to arrest that person for such offence. 55-56 V., c. 29, s. 29. Arrest during flight.

Reasonable and probable grounds.]—See secs. 30 and 33.

Flight as evidence.]—The fact of the flight of the accused or his attempts to escape, is a circumstance in the chain of evidence from which guilt may be inferred, unless it appear that the act was for another reason. Lawson's Presumptive Ev., 2nd ed. 619. So a prisoner's attempt to escape implies guilt and operates against the party like a confession, but the fact that the prisoner had an opportunity or offer of assistance to escape but did not avail himself of it is not relevant. Ibid. 621. The fact that the accused fled because of a fear of violence at the hands of their pursuers overthrows the presumption. Ibid. And if the suspected person had changed his residence but it appeared that he was a peddler and accustomed to go from place to place, no presumption of guilt would arise. Best Ev., sec. 461. Evidence of the flight of persons charged as co-conspirators with the prisoner is not admissible against him. People v. Sharp, 107 N.Y. 427. And where a prisoner confined in gaol for two distinct offences attempts to escape, it has been held that the attempt is not evidence of guilt as to either charge, as it is impossible to say which offence prompted the attempt. People v. McKean, 19 N.Y. 486.

38. Nothing in this Act shall take away or diminish any authority given by any Act in force for the time being to arrest, detain or put any restraint on any person. 55-56 V., c. 29, s. 30. Statutory power of arrest.

Force in executing warrant, process or sentence.

39. Every one executing any sentence, warrant or process, or in making any arrest, and every one lawfully assisting him, is justified, or protected from criminal responsibility, as the case may be, in using such force as may be necessary to overcome any force used in resisting such execution or arrest, unless the sentence, process or warrant can be executed or the arrest effected by reasonable means in a less violent manner. 55-56 V., c. 29, s. 31.

Overcoming resistance in executing process.]—Where an officer of justice is resisted in the legal execution of his duty he may repel force by force, and if in doing so he kills the party resisting him, it is justifiable homicide. Archbold's Cr. Plead. (1900), 778; 1 Hale, 494; R. v. Porter, 12 Cox C.C. 444.

Although a police constable may not be bound in the execution of his duty to assist the occupier of a house in putting out an intruder, yet he may lawfully do so, and if he is assaulted by the intruder while so doing, the latter, though he may not be indictable for assaulting a peace officer in the execution of his duty, will be liable to a conviction for an assault, as he cannot justify resistance to the force lawfully used to eject him. R. v. Roxburgh, 12 Cox C.C. 8.

By sec. 167, every one is guilty of an indictable offence and liable to six months' imprisonment who, having reasonable notice that he is required to assist a peace officer in the execution of his duty in arresting any person or in preserving the peace, without reasonable excuse omits so to do.

Resisting peace officer.]—See secs. 168 and 169.

Duty of person arresting.

40. It is the duty of every one executing any process or warrant to have it with him, and to produce it if required.

Notice.

2. It is the duty of every one arresting another, whether with or without warrant, to give notice, where practicable, of the process or warrant under which he acts, or of the cause of the arrest.

Failure in duty.

3. A failure to fulfil either of the two duties last mentioned shall not of itself deprive the person executing the process or warrant, or his assistants, or the person arresting, of protection from criminal responsibility, but shall be relevant to the inquiry whether the process or warrant might not have been executed, or the arrest effected, by reasonable means in a less violent manner. 55-56 V., c. 29, s. 32.

Manner of arrest.]—Where a constable tells a person given into his charge that he must go with him before a magistrate, and such person, in consequence, goes quietly, and without force being used, it is an arrest. Chinn v. Morris, 2 C. & P. 361; Joyce v. Perrin, 3 U.C.O.S. 300.

And where the constable said to the plaintiff "You must go with me," on which the plaintiff said he was ready to go, and went with the constable towards a police office, without being seized or touched, this was ruled to be an imprisonment. Pocock v. Moore, Ry. & M. 321; Forsyth v. Goden, 32 C.L.J. 499.

If the party is under restraint and the officer manifests an intention to make a captive, it is not necessary that there should be an actual contact. Grainger v. Hill, 4 Bing. N.C. 212, Vaughan, J.; McIntosh v. Demeray, 5 U.C.Q.B. 343; Wilson v. Brecker, 11 U.C.C.P. 268.

Defendant was convicted of a fourth offence under the Canada Temperance Act. A warrant was placed in the hands of a constable, who after keeping it for some time went to defendant to execute it, and told him he would have to come to gaol with him. Defendant, complaining of the great inconvenience he would be put to if placed in custody at that time, induced the constable to hold off for a week or two longer by agreeing to deposit $100 with him. Later on the constable arrested the defendant on the same warrant and lodged him in gaol. It was held on an application for his discharge by habeas corpus on the ground that he had been twice arrested on the same warrant, that even if an arrest had been effected on the first occasion when the constable agreed to hold off, it was called off by defendant's own request and he was therefore estopped, and the application was refused. Ex parte Doherty (1899), 35 C.L.J. 765, 5 Can. Cr. Cas. 94 (N.B.).

Right of search on arrest.]—The right of an officer to search the person of one arrested for felony has always been assumed, as well as the right to keep the goods found on him if necessary for the purposes of the trial. See Tomlin's Law Dictionary, sub-tit. Constable, IV., "A constable must keep goods found on a felon till trial, and then return them according to the directions of the court." In the case of Dillon v. O'Brien, 16 Cox C.C., at page 245, the Irish Exchequer Division extended the rule to cases of misdemeanour. Palles, C.B., says:—"If, then, the right here claimed, does not exist, even in treason and felony, it would follow upon the arrest of a murderer caught in the act and on the moment lawfully arrested, whilst the weapon with which the crime had been committed was in his hand it would be illegal for the constable to detain that weapon for the purpose of evidence; so also would it be illegal for the officers of the law to take possession of poisons found in the possession of one who had caused death by poison, and even in treason letters from co-traitors evidencing the common treasonable design, found in the possession of a traitor, would be safe from capture upon his arrest, although from the earliest times it has been the settled and unvarying practice to seize such proofs of guilt and give them in evidence at the trial." The case of Leigh v. Cole, 6 Cox C.C. 329 (cited with approbation by the Ontario Court of Appeal in Gordon v. Denison, 22 A.R., p. 326), was a charge to the jury by Mr. Justice Vaughan Williams on the subject of the right of constables to search and handcuff persons in custody for breaches of the peace, and the learned judge made use of the following language: "With respect to searching a prisoner there is no doubt that a man when in custody may so conduct himself, by reason of violence of language or conduct, that a police officer may reasonably think it prudent and right to search him, in order to ascertain whether he has any weapon with which he might do mischief to the person or commit a breach of the peace; but at the same time it is quite wrong to suppose that any general rule can be applied to such a case. Even when a man is confined for being drunk and disorderly it is not correct to say that he must submit to the degradation of being searched, as the searching of such a person must depend on all the circumstances of the case." In the case of persons in custody not accused of an indictable offence no general rule can be applied, and it would always be for a jury to say whether the case is one in which a search should have been made. Ibid.

Where a letter-carrier violates the rules of the post office department by failing to enter a letter bearing a non-existent address in the book provided for that purpose, or to return the letter to the post office, there is reasonable and probable cause for detaining and searching him, and an action for damages against the peace officer who effected the arrest is not maintainable in the absence of evidence that the officer had made an improper and illegal use of his authority in the manner in which he effected such detention and search. Mayer v. Vaughan (No. 2), 6 Can. Cr. Cas. 68, 11, Que. K.B. 340, affirming Mayer v. Vaughan (No. 1), 5 Can. Cr. Cas. 392.

Restoration of property taken from prisoner.]—If a constable improperly deprives a prisoner of his property, an application may be made to the justice for its restoration, which on hearing all the parties concerned, he should order, if it appears just. If the property is clearly not connected with the crime to be investigated, or of any other crime, and is not such as it is unlawful for the prisoner to have upon his person, and is not of such a nature that it will be unsafe to allow him to retain it, it ought to be restored. R. v. Barnett, 3 C. & P. 600; R. v. Frost (1839), 9 C. & P. 129.

Handcuffing.]—No one should be handcuffed, unless from the nature of the offence, and the supposed character of the prisoner, or for violent resistance to arrest or attempt to escape, or for some other sufficient reason, the constable has reasonable apprehension that the prisoner would otherwise escape, or that there is danger that he might do so. Wright v. Court, 4 B. & C. 596; Griffin v. Coleman, 4 H. & N. 265; Hamilton v. Massie, 18 O.R. 585.

Temporary release of prisoner from the officer's custody.]—Where the officer executing a warrant of commitment releases the prisoner, at his request, for a temporary period, on his promise to surrender himself, such does not constitute a voluntary abandonment of the arrest, and a re-arrest is justified upon the same warrant. The King v. O'Hearon (No. 2) (1901), 5 Can. Cr. Cas. 531.

Peace officer preventing escape.

41. Every peace officer proceeding lawfully to arrest, with or without warrant, any person for any offence for which the offender may be arrested without warrant, and every one lawfully assisting in such arrest, is justified, if the person to be arrested takes to flight to avoid arrest, in using such force as may be necessary to prevent his escape by such flight, unless such escape can be prevented by reasonable means in a less violent manner. 55-56 V., c. 29, s. 33.

Re-arrest after escape.]—In criminal cases, where a prisoner escapes, if the escape be negligent merely, the goaler or officer may retake him, at any time, without warrant (Dalt. c. 169); if voluntary, he cannot afterwards be retaken by virtue of the same warrant under which he was at first arrested (2 Hawk. ch. 14, sec. 9); but he may be retaken on a fresh warrant, or without a warrant in cases where he might have been arrested without a warrant originally. Archbold's Criminal Pleading and Evidence, 22nd ed., p. 852. R. v. O'Hearon (1901), 5 Can. Cr. Cas. 531 (N.S.).

Shooting.]—Only in the last extremity should a peace officer resort to such a dangerous weapon as a revolver in order to prevent the escape of an accused person who is attempting to escape by flight. R. v. Smith (1907), 7 Western L.R. 92, 95, per Perdue, J.A.

Private person preventing escape.

42. Every private person proceeding lawfully to arrest without warrant any person for any offence for which the person to be arrested takes to flight to avoid arrest, in using such force as may be necessary to prevent his escape by flight, unless such escape can be prevented by reasonable means in a less violent manner, if such force is neither intended nor likely to cause death or grievous bodily harm. 55-56 V., c. 29, s. 34.

"It is the duty of every citizen to assist in the pursuit and capture of a criminal who is fleeing from arrest, when such citizen is called upon to do so by a peace officer." R. v. Smith (1907), 7 Western L.R. 92, 95, per Perdue, J.A.; and see Code sec. 167.

Preventing escape in other cases.

43. Every one proceeding lawfully to arrest any person for any cause other than an offence in the last section mentioned is justified, if the person to be arrested takes to flight to avoid arrest, in using such force as may be necessary to prevent his escape by flight, unless such escape can be prevented by reasonable means in a less violent manner, if such force is neither intended nor likely to cause death or grievous bodily harm. 55-56 V., c. 29, s. 35.

Preventing escape or rescue of arrested person.

44. Every one who has lawfully arrested any person for any offence for which the offender may be arrested without warrant is protected from criminal responsibility in using such force in order to prevent the rescue or escape of the person arrested as he believes, on reasonable grounds, to be necessary for that purpose. 55-56 V., c. 29, s. 36.

Idem.

45. Every one who has lawfully arrested any person for any cause other than an offence for which the offender may be arrested without warrant is protected from criminal responsibility in using such force in order to prevent his escape or rescue as he believes, on reasonable grounds, to be necessary for that purpose, if such force is neither intended nor likely to cause death or grievous bodily harm. 55-56 V., c. 29, s. 37.

Preventing breach of peace.

46. Every one who witnesses a breach of the peace is justified in interfering to prevent its continuance or renewal and may detain any person committing or about to join in or renew such breach of the peace, in order to give him into the custody of a peace officer, if the person interfering uses no more force than is reasonably necessary for preventing the continuance or renewal of such breach of the peace, or than is reasonably proportioned to the danger to be apprehended from the continuance or renewal of such breach of the peace. 55-56 V., c. 29, s. 38.

Into the custody of a peace officer.]—The term peace officer is defined by sec. 2, sub-sec. 26.

Arrest in such case.

47. Every peace officer who witnesses a breach of the peace, and every person lawfully assisting him, is justified in arresting any one whom he finds committing such breach of the peace, or whom he, on reasonable and probable grounds, believes to be about to join in or renew such breach of the peace.

Giving person in charge.

2. Every peace officer is justified in receiving into custody any person given into his charge as having been a party to a breach of the peace by one who has, or whom such peace officer, upon reasonable and probable grounds, believes to have, witnessed such breach of the peace. 55-56 V., c. 29, s. 39.

Peace officer.]—The definition of this term is found in sec. 2(26), ante.

Finds committing.]—See note to sec. 36.

Breach of the peace.]—A justice of the peace may apprehend, or cause to be apprehended by a verbal order merely, any person committing a breach of the peace in his presence. 2 Hale 86. A constable may also arrest for a breach of the peace committed in his presence. 1 Hale 587. But a private person is not justified in arresting or giving in charge of a policeman, without a warrant, a party who has been engaged in an affray, unless the affray is still continuing or there is reasonable ground for apprehending that he intends to renew it. Price v. Seeley (1843), 10 Clark & Fin. (H.L.) 28.

A private person cannot of his own authority arrest another for a bare breach of the peace after it is over. 3 Hawkins P.C. 164.

Any one who sees others fighting may lawfully part them and also stay them until the heat be over, and then deliver to the constable who may carry them before a justice of the peace in order to their finding security for the peace. Hawkins P.C., book 1, ch. 63, sec. 11. And while those are assembled together who have committed acts of violence, and the danger of their renewal continues, the affray itself may be said to continue; and during the affray the constable may, not merely on his own view, but on the information and complaint of another, arrest the offenders or either of them. Price v. Seeley, 10 Cl. & F. 28.

Affray.]—An affray is the act of fighting in any public street or highway, or fighting to the alarm of the public in any other place to which the public have access. Sec. 100.

Riot and unlawful assembly.]—See secs. 87 to 93, inclusive.

Suppression of riot by magistrate.

48. Every sheriff, deputy sheriff, mayor or other head officer or acting head officer of any county, city, town or district, and every magistrate and justice of the peace, is justified in using, and ordering to be used, and every peace officer is justified in using, such force as he, in good faith, and on reasonable and probable grounds, believes to be necessary to suppress a riot, and as is not disproportioned to the danger which he, on reasonable and probable grounds, believes to be apprehended from the continuance of the riot. 55-56 V., c. 29, s. 40.

See also secs. 87 to 95, inclusive, and sec. 167.

49. Every one, whether subject to military law or not, acting in good faith in obedience to orders given by any sheriff, deputy sheriff, mayor or other head officer or acting head officer of any county, city, town or district, or by any magistrate or justice, for the suppression of a riot, is justified in obeying the orders so given unless such orders are manifestly unlawful, and is protected from criminal responsibility in using such force as he, on reasonable and probable grounds, believes to be necessary for carrying into effect such orders. Suppression of riot by persons commanded thereto.

2. It shall be a question of law whether any particular order is manifestly unlawful or not. 55-56 V., c. 29, s. 41. Question of law.

Magistrates must keep the peace when a riot occurs and restrain the rioters, and they may call upon all subjects to render assistance, and the latter may be given firearms for that purpose. R. v. Pinney, 5 C. & P. 261.

A person who after reasonable notice omits without reasonable excuse to assist any sheriff, or peace officer, in suppressing a riot is guilty of an indictable offence. Sec. 95.

50. Every one, whether subject to military law or not, who in good faith and on reasonable and probable grounds believes that serious mischief will arise from a riot before there is time to procure the intervention of any of the authorities aforesaid, is justified in using such force as he, in good faith and on reasonable and probable grounds, believes to be necessary for the suppression of such riot, and as is not disproportioned to the danger which he, on reasonable grounds, believes to be apprehended from the continuance of the riot. 55-56 V., c. 29, s. 42. Suppression of riot by persons apprehending serious mischief.

By the common law, a private individual might lawfully endeavour, of his own authority and without any warrant or sanction from a magistrate, to suppress a riot by every means in his power; he might disperse or assist in dispersing those assembled and stay those engaged in it from executing their purpose, as well as stop and prevent others whom he saw coming up from joining the rest. Phillips v. Eyre, L.R. 6 Q.B. 15. If the occasion demanded immediate action and no opportunity occurred for procuring the advice or sanction of a magistrate, it was the duty of every subject to act for himself and upon his own responsibility in suppressing a riotous and tumultuous assembly, and the law protected him in all that he honestly did in the prosecution of that purpose. Ibid, per Willes, J., approving the charge of Tindal, C.J., to the grand jury of Bristol (1832), 5 C. & P. 261(n).

51. Every one who is bound by military law to obey the lawful command of his superior officer is justified in obeying Protection of persons subject to military law. any command given him by his superior officer for the suppression of a riot, unless such order is manifestly unlawful.

Question of law. 2. It shall be a question of law whether any particular order is manifestly unlawful or not. 55-56 V., c. 29, s. 43.

See secs. 48-50, and 91-93.

Use of force. **52.** Every one is justified in using such force as may be reasonably necessary in order,—

To prevent commission of offence. *(a)* to prevent the commission of any offence for which, if committed, the offender might be arrested without warrant, and the commission of which would be likely to cause immediate and serious injury to the person or property of any one; or,

Act amounting to offence. *(b)* to prevent any act being done which he, on reasonable grounds, believes would, if committed, amount to any such offence. 55-56 V., c. 29, s. 44.

The circumstances under which an arrest without warrant is allowed are set forth in secs. 31-39 and 646-652.

Where A., to prevent B. from fighting with his brother, laid hold of him and held him down but struck no blow, upon which B. stabbed A., it was held that if A. had done nothing more than was necessary to prevent B. from beating his brother, and if he had died of the stab, the offence of B. would have been murder; but that if A. did more than was necessary to prevent the beating of his brother, it would have been manslaughter only. R. v. Bourne, 5 C. & P. 120.

And where, under circumstances that might reasonably have induced the belief that a man was cutting his wife's throat, their son shot at and killed his father, it was held that if the son had reasonable grounds for believing and honestly believed that his act was necessary for the defence of his mother, the homicide was excusable. R. v. Rose, 15 Cox 540, Lopes, J.

53. Every one unlawfully assaulted, not having provoked such assault, is justified in repelling force by force, if the force he uses is not meant to cause death or grievous bodily harm, and is no more than is necessary for the purpose of self-defence.

Extent justified. 2. Every one so assaulted is justified, though he causes death or grievous bodily harm, if he causes it under reasonable apprehension of death or grievous bodily harm from the violence with which the assault was originally made or with which the assailant pursues his purpose, and if he believes, on reasonable grounds, that he cannot otherwise preserve himself from death or grievous bodily harm. 55-56 V., c. 29, s. 45.

Self-defence in assault, etc.]—It is a good defence in justification, even of a wounding or mayhem, to prove that the prosecutor assaulted or beat the defendant first, and that the defendant committed the alleged battery merely in his own defence. Archbold's Crim. Plead. (1900), 802. The difficulty arises in drawing the line between mere self-defence and fighting. R. v. Knock, 14 Cox C.C. 1.

If the prosecutor lifted up his cane and offered to strike him, the defendant is justified in striking the prosecutor without waiting for the blow. Buller N.P. 18.

A husband may justify a battery in defence of his wife, a wife in defence of her husband, a parent in defence of his child, a child in defence of his parent, a master in defence of his servant, and a servant in defence of his master. 1 Hawkins P.C., ch. 60, secs. 23, 24; Code sec. 16. If, however, the battery were greater than was necessary for mere defence, or if it were after all danger from the assailment was passed and by way of revenge, the prior assault will not justify. R. v. Driscoll, C. & M. 214; Anon., 2 Lewin C.C. 48.

Defendant being justified by this section if the force used by him to repel an unprovoked assault was not meant to cause death or grievous bodily harm, or was no more than was necessary for the purposes of self-defence, and there being evidence which, if believed, would have enabled the jury to find for defendant, the trial judge erred in charging the jury that there must be evidence that defendant could not otherwise preserve himself from death or grievous bodily harm. R. v. Ritter (1904), 8 Can. Cr. Cas. 31, 36 N.S.R. 417.

Ordinarily the person beset is permitted to act only in self-defence; he cannot take the law into his own hands to inflict punishment for the injury. R. v. Milton, 3 C. & P. 31; R. v. Mabel, 9 C. & P. 474; 2 Bishop Crim. Law 44.

But where there is a manifest intent or endeavour by the assailant to commit by violence or surprise an offence formerly a felony, such as murder, robbery, burglary and the like, the party assailed is not obliged to retreat, but may pursue his adversary until he has secured himself from all danger and if he kill him in so doing, it is called justifiable self-defence. 1 East P.C. 271.

If in attempting to turn a mere trespasser out of a house, the householder is assaulted by the trespasser, he may kill him if he was not able by any other means to avoid the assault or retain his lawful possession, and in such case a man need not fly as far as he can as in other cases of self-defence for he has a right to the protection of his own house. 2 Burn's Justice, 13th ed., p. 1315. In the New Brunswick case of R. v. Theriault (1894), 2 Can. Cr. Cas. 444, a new trial was ordered where the trial judge had instructed the jury that, to justify or excuse the homicide, the prisoner must be found to have had reasonable grounds for apprehending imminent peril to his life or the lives of his wife and children, and had made no mention of a reasonable apprehension of grievous bodily harm as a ground of justification although the evidence pointed to both.

Not having provoked such assault.]—The provocation may be given by blows, words or gestures. Section 54(2).

Self defence in case of aggression.

54. Every one who has without justification assaulted another, or has provoked an assault from that other, may nevertheless justify force subsequent to such assault, if he uses such force under reasonable apprehension of death or grievous bodily harm from the violence of the person first assaulted or provoked, and in the belief, on reasonable grounds, that it is necessary for his own preservation from death or grievous bodily harm, if he did not commence the assault with intent to kill or do grievous bodily harm, and did not endeavour, at any time before the necessity for preserving himself arose, to kill or do grievous bodily harm, and if before such necessity arose, he declined further conflict, and quitted or retreated from it as far as was practicable.

Provocation. 2. Provocation, within the meaning of this and the last preceding section, may be given by blows, words or gestures. 55-56 V., c. 29, s. 46.

Declining further conflict.]—Two or more persons engage in a mutual combat, without any original intent to proceed to extreme measures; or, after an assailant has been met by his adversary, he becomes weary of a conflict which is likely to be more serious than he anticipated or too much for him to withstand; here, if one of the combatants already in the wrong either as a beginner or continuer of the fight wishes to retrace his error, he must retreat. 2 Bishop Cr. Law 565. And though, contrary to his original expectation, he finds himself so hotly pressed as renders the killing of the other necessary to save his own life, he is guilty of a felonious homicide if he kills him unless he first actually puts into exercise this duty of withdrawing from the place. Foster 227; The State v. Hill, 4 Dev. & Bat. 491. If the first assailant, knowing his advantage of strength or skill or weapon, retreated to the wall merely as a design to protect himself under the shelter of the law, as in his own defence, but really intended the killing of the other man, then it is murder or manslaughter as the circumstance of the case requires. 1 Hale P.C. 479, 480.

Where, upon a quarrel, one of the parties retreated fifty yards desiring to avoid the conflict, but the other pursued him with uplifted arm and a deadly weapon, and being first struck by the retreating one with the fist, the other stabbed and killed him, the case was held to be one of murder, for the law did not require the deceased to wait till the prisoner had executed his threat but justified him in anticipating the premeditated assault. The State v. Howell, 9 Ired. 485.

Provocation in homicide cases.]—See sec. 261.

Prevention of insulting assault. **55.** Every one is justified in using force in defence of his own person, or that of any one under his protection, from an assault accompanied with insult, if he uses no more force than is necessary to prevent such assault, or the repetition of it.

Disproportionate hurt not justified. 2. This section shall not justify the wilful infliction of any hurt or mischief disproportionate to the insult which the force used was intended to prevent. 55-56 V., c. 29, s. 47.

An assault is not justified by the circumstance that the person assaulted had then and there sworn at the defendant and used insulting language towards him but without any attempt to assault the defendant, whereupon the defendant assaulted the complainant. Wentzell v. Winacht (1907), 41 N.S.R. 406.

Defence of movable property. **56.** Every one who is in peaceable possession of any movable property or thing, and every one lawfully assisting him, is justified in resisting the taking of such thing by any trespasser, or in retaking it from such trespasser, if in either case he does not strike or do bodily harm to such trespasser.

2. If, after any one, being in peaceable possession as aforesaid, has laid hands upon any such thing, such trespasser persists in attempting to keep it or to take it from the possessor, or from any one lawfully assisting him, the trespasser shall be deemed to commit an assault without justification or provocation. 55-56 V., c. 29, s. 48. **Assault by trespasser.**

Justifiable battery.]—In the case of trespass in taking goods, the owner may justify beating the trespasser in order to make him desist. 1 Hale 486; R. v. Wild, 2 Lewin C.C. 214.

A battery is justifiable by proving that it was committed to restrain another from unlawfully taking or destroying his goods. 2 Rol. Abr. 549.

57. Every one who is in peaceable possession of any movable property or thing under a claim of right, and every one acting under his authority, is protected from criminal responsibility for defending such possession, even against a person entitled by law to the possession of such property or thing, if he uses no more force than is necessary. 55-56 V., c. 29, s. 49. **Defence with claim of right.**

If one comes to beat another or to take his goods as a trespasser, though the owner may justify a battery for the purpose of making him desist, yet if he kill him it will be manslaughter. 1 Hale P.C. 485, 1 East P.C. 272, 277; R v. Bourne (1831), 5 C. & P. 120.

58. Every one who is in peaceable possession of any movable property or thing, but neither claims right thereto nor acts under the authority of a person claiming right thereto, is neither justified nor protected from criminal responsibility for defending his possession against a person entitled by law to the possession of such property or thing. 55-56 V., c. 29, s. 50. **Defence without claim of right.**

59. Every one who is in peaceable possession of a dwelling-house, and every one lawfully assisting him or acting by his authority, is justified in using such force as is necessary to prevent the forcible breaking and entering of such dwelling-house, either by night or day, by any person with the intent to commit any indictable offence therein. 55-56 V., c. 29, s. 51. **Defence of dwelling house.**

It has been held that a guest in a house is justified in defending the house. Curtis v. Hubbard, 4 Hill N.Y. 437; Cooper's Case, Cro. Car. 544; also that the neighbours of the occupant may assemble for its defence. Semayne's Case, 5 Co. 91.

Dwelling house.]—Every permanent building in which the renter or owner or his family dwells is a dwelling house. Archbold, Cr. Evid.

(1900), 593. And it will be sufficient if any one of the family habitually sleeps in that building. R. v. Westwood, R. & R. 495.

The mere temporary absence of the householder and his family will not prevent its remaining in contemplation of law a dwelling house. R. v. Murray, 2 East P.C. 496. But where the householder moved away from the house, not intending to return to live in it, but retained it as a warehouse in which some of his employees slept for the purpose of taking care of it, it was held not to be his dwelling house. R. v. Flannagan, R. & R. 187. And where the landlord of a dwelling house after the tenant had quitted it, put a servant into it to sleep there at night until he should re-let it to another tenant, but had no intention to reside in it himself, it could not be deemed the dwelling house of the landlord. R. v. Davis, 2 Leach 876; R. v. Harris, 2 Leach 701. A tenant put his furniture into a house preparatory to moving in with his family, but neither he nor any of his family had as yet slept in it; it was held not to be a "dwelling house" as regards burglary. R. v. Hallard, 2 East P.C. 498; R. v. Lyons, 1 Leach 185.

A temporary booth or tent in a fair or market is not a dwelling house although the owner lodge in it. 1 Hawk., ch. 38, sec. 35. But it is otherwise in respect of a permanent building although used only for the purposes of a fair. R. v. Smith, 1 M. & Rob. 256.

The extended meaning of the term "dwelling house" as set out in secs. 335 and 339 of the Code is in terms applicable only to Part VII.

Breaking and entering.]—The definition of the term "to break" given in sec. 335 in terms applies only to Part VII., but is in accordance with the previous decisions on the subject. Section 340 provides that an "entrance" into a building is made as soon as any part of the body of the person making the entrance, or any part of any instrument used by him is within the building. It would seem, however, that as to secs. 59 and 60 the common law definition applies and not that of sec. 340, and, at common law, if the instrument were used not for the purpose of committing the contemplated felony but only for the purpose of effecting the entry, its introduction was not such an entry as constituted burglary. R. v. Hughes, 2 East P.C. 491; R. v. Rust, 1 Moody C.C. 183.

Same at night.

60. Every one who is in peaceable possession of a dwelling-house, and every one lawfully assisting him or acting by his authority, is justified in using such force as is necessary to prevent the forcible breaking and entering of such dwelling-house by night by any person, if he believes, on reasonable and probable grounds, that such breaking and entering is attempted with the intent to commit any indictable offence therein. 55-56 V., c. 29, s. 52.

The mere threat of parties standing outside of a dwelling house that they will break in, does not justify the householder in shooting at and wounding them, unless the householder has first warned them to desist and depart or that he would fire. Spires v. Barrick, 14 U.C.Q.B. 420.

Defence of real property.

61. Every one who is in peaceable possession of any house or land, or other real property, and every one lawfully assisting him or acting by his authority, is justified in using force to prevent any person from trespassing on such property, or to remove him therefrom, if he uses no more force than is necessary.

2. If such trespasser resists such attempt to prevent his entry or to remove him such trespasser shall be deemed to commit an assault without justification or provocation. 55-56 V., c. 29, s. 53. Assault by trespasser.

Forcible ejection of trespasser.]—If A., a trespasser, enters B.'s house and refuses to leave, B. has a right to remove A. by force, but not to kick or strike him unless the force used to remove him be necessary. Wild's Case, 2 Lewin C.C. 214. But if the trespasser resists such force the householder may use any degree of force necessary to defend himself and to remove the trespasser from the house. 1 Hale P.C. 486.

In the case of a trespass in law merely, without actual force, the owner must first request the trespasser to depart before he can justify laying his hand on him for the purpose of removing him; and even if he refuse he can only justify so much force as is necessary to remove him. Weaver v. Bush, 8 T.R. 78.

Resists such attempt.]—The words are "if such trespasser resists such attempt," the word "such" applies to an attempt by force referred to in the former part of the section, and will not apply to mere words of warning or of request to leave. Packett v. Pool (1896), 11 Man. R. 275, 32 C.L.J. 523. The latter part of the section does not apply until there is an overt act on the part of the person in possession towards prevention or removal, and an overt act of resistance on the part of the trespasser. Ibid.

62. Every one is justified in peaceably entering in the daytime to take possession of any house or land to the possession of which he, or some person under whose authority he acts, is lawfully entitled. Assertion of right to house or land.

2. If any person, not having or acting under the authority of one having peaceable possession of any such house or land with a claim of right, assaults any one peaceably entering as aforesaid, for the purpose of making him desist from such entry, such assault shall be deemed to be without justification or provocation. Assault in case of lawful entry.

3. If any person having peaceable possession of such house or land with a claim of right, or any person acting by his authority, assaults any one entering as aforesaid, for the purpose of making him desist from such entry, such assault shall be deemed to be provoked by the person entering. 55-56 V., c. 29, s. 54. Trespasser provoking.

63. It is lawful for every parent, or person in the place of a parent, schoolmaster or master, to use force by way of correction towards any child, pupil or apprentice under his care, provided that such force is reasonable under the circumstances. 55-56 V., c. 29, s. 55. Correction of child by force.

Apprentices.]—Formerly a right of chastisement of servants by way of correction was recognized. R. v. Mawgridge, 16 St. Tr. 57; but as to servants who are not apprentices it is in desuetude. Archbold Crim. Evid. (1900), 762.

Child.]—The law as to correction of children has reference only to a child capable of appreciating correction and not to an infant two years and a half old. R. v. Griffin, 11 Cox C.C. 402. If the correction be inflicted with a deadly weapon and the party dies of it it will be murder; if with an instrument not likely to kill, though improper for the purpose of correction, it will be manslaughter. Foster 262; R. v. Hopley (1860), 2 F. & F. 201.

School teacher and pupil.]—A school teacher who inflicts unreasonably severe chastisement upon a pupil is criminally responsible, under Code secs. 63 and 66, for the excess of force used, although the punishment occasioned no permanent injury and was inflicted without malice. R. v. Gaul (1904), 8 Can. Cr. Cas. 178.

The following principles are laid down by Judge Chipman in the Nova Scotia case of R. v. Robinson (1899), 7 Can. Cr. Cas. 52:—

(1) The authority of a school teacher to chastise a pupil is to be regarded as a delegation of parental authority.

(2) Corporal punishment inflicted by a school teacher upon a pupil is presumed to be reasonable and for sufficient cause, until the contrary is shewn.

(3) Where there is a sufficient cause for punishing the pupil, and the chastisement produces only temporary pain and no serious injury, it will be presumed to be reasonable.

(4) Any punishment with an instrument calculated to produce danger to life or limb in unreasonable and unlawful.

(5) Any punishment protracted beyond the child's powers of endurance is excessive and unlawful.

(6) Any punishment which ordinarily may seriously endanger life, limbs, or health, or which disfigures the child, or causes any other permanent injury, is in itself unreasonable and unlawful.

(7) If there is any reasonable doubt whether the punishment was excessive, the school teacher should have the benefit of the doubt.

Master of ship.

64. It is lawful for the master or officer in command of a ship on a voyage to use force for the purpose of maintaining good order and discipline on board of his ship, provided that he believes, on reasonable grounds, that such force is necessary, and provided also that the force used is reasonable in degree. 55-56 V., c. 29, s. 56.

This right includes the right of the shipmaster to inflict reasonable corporal punishment at sea on seamen for disobeying orders. The Agincourt, 1 Hagg. 271; Lamb v. Burnett, 1 Cr. & J. 291.

Surgical operations.

65. Every one is protected from criminal responsibility for performing with reasonable care and skill any surgical operation upon any person for his benefit, provided that performing the operation was reasonable, having regard to the patient's state at the time, and to all the circumstances of the case. 55-56 V., c. 29, s. 57.

Surgical operations for patient's benefit.]—In these cases there is no difference between a licensed physician or surgeon and a person acting as physician or surgeon without license; in either case if a party having a competent degree of skill and knowledge makes an accidental mistake in his treatment of a patient, through which mistake death ensues, he is not thereby guilty of manslaughter; but if, where proper medical assistance can be had, a person totally ignorant of the science of medicine takes on himself to administer a violent and dangerous remedy to one labouring under disease, and death ensues in consequence of that dangerous remedy having been so administered, then he is guilty of manslaughter. R. v. Webb, 1 M. & Rob. 405, 2 Lewin 196, per Lord Lyndhurst; R. v. Williamson, 3 C. & P. 635.

It must appear that there was gross ignorance or inattention to human life. R. v. Long, 4 C. & P. 423. If any person, whether he be a regular or licensed medical man or not, professes to deal with the life or health of His Majesty's subjects, he is bound to have competent skill to perform the task that he holds himself out to perform, and he is bound to treat his patients with care, attention and assiduity. R. v. Spiller, 5 C. & P. 333

It is for the jury to say whether in the execution of the duty which the prisoner had undertaken to perform he is proved to have shewn such a gross want of care, or such a gross and culpable want of skill, as any person undertaking such a charge ought not to be guilty of. R. v. Ferguson, 1 Lewin C.C. 181. See also sec. 246.

66. Every one authorized by law to use force is criminally responsible for any excess, according to the nature and quality of the act which constitutes the excess. 55-56 V., c. 29, s. 58. *Excess.*

See note to secs. 63, 64 and 65.

67. No one has a right to consent to the infliction of death upon himself. *Consent to death.*

2. If such consent is given, it shall have no effect upon the criminal responsibility of any person by whom such death may be caused. 55-56 V., c. 29, s. 59. *Causing death with consent.*

If two persons enter into an agreement to commit suicide together and the means employed to produce death prove fatal to one only, the survivor is guilty of murder. R. v. Jessop, 16 Cox C.C. 204.

It is uncertain to what extent any person has a right to consent to his being put in danger of death or bodily harm by the act of another. Burbidge Cr. Law 201.

68. Every one is protected from criminal responsibility for any act done in obedience to the laws for the time being, made and enforced by those in possession *de facto* of the sovereign power in and over the place where the act is done. 55-56 V., c. 29, s. 60. *Obedience to de facto law.*

Parties to Offences.

69. Every one is a party to and guilty of an offence who,— *Who parties to offence.*

(*a*) actually commits it; or,

(*b*) does or omits an act for the purpose of aiding any person to commit the offence; or,

(*c*) abets any person in commission of the offence; or,

(*d*) counsels or procures any person to commit the offence.

Common intention by several persons.

2. If several persons form a common intention to prosecute any unlawful purpose, and to assist each other therein, each of them is a party to every offence committed by any one of them in the prosecution of such common purpose, the commission of which offence was, or ought to have been known to be a probable consequence of the prosecution of such common purpose. 55-56 V., c. 29, s. 61.

Principals in second degree and accessories before the fact.]—This section makes any person who does an act for the purpose of aiding any other person to commit an offence, or who abets any other person in commission of an offence, a party to the offence committed by such other person. To abet is to be personally or constructively present at the commission of an offence, and to assist in the criminal act; but to aid is to help, or in any way to promote, facilitate or bring about the accomplishment of any criminal purpose by another, and this may be done without being present when the offence is perpetrated. Under the old rule of law the abettor, or the person who was present inciting or helping, was a principal in the second degree, while the person who, being absent, counselled, helped or facilitated in any way the commission of an offence which was afterwards perpetrated was an accessory before the fact. R. v. Roy (1900), 3 Can. Cr. Cas. 472.

To counsel and procure a person to commit an offence constitutes the counsellor or inciter a party to the offence, when it is committed; and by this section he can be proceeded against as a principal. The Queen v. Gregory (1867), L.R. 1 C.C.R. 79; Benford v. Sims, [1898] 2 Q.B. 641.

Du Cros v. Lambourne (1907), 1 K.B. 40, was an appeal from a conviction for driving a motor car at an unlawful speed. The evidence was that the appellant owned the car and was sitting in the front seat with a lady, who was driving it, and that it was going at the rate of fifty miles an hour, which was dangerous to the public. The Divisional Court (Lord Alverstone, C.J., and Ridley and Darling, JJ.), held that the conviction was right and that the appellant was aiding and abetting the offence, and as such might properly be convicted as himself doing the unlawful act complained of, and that it was not necessary to charge him expressly with aiding and abetting.

By this and the following section accessories before the fact and aiders and abettors are declared to be guilty of the offence itself and may be charged as principals in the first degree. As to accessories after the fact see sec. 71.

Aiding or abetting.]—The words aider, abettor, accessory and accomplice as applied to crime, are often used as having the same meaning. But they are by no means synonymous. It is unlawful to aid or encourage the commission of crime. It is unlawful under certain circumstances to conceal the commission of crime. One who aids is, in ordinary language, called an aider or abettor. An accessory is one who takes an active but subordinate part. An accomplice, according to the ordinary meaning of the word, would seem to imply one who not only takes an active part, but positively aids in the accomplishment or completion of the crime. R. v. Smith (1876), 38 U.C.Q.B. 218, 227.

To make a person an "aider and abettor" he must have been present either actually or constructively.

A person is present in construction of law aiding and abetting if with the intention of giving assistance he is near enough to afford it should occasion arise; thus if he was watching at a proper distance to prevent a surprise, or to favour the escape of those who were immediately engaged, then he would be a principal in the second degree. Per MacMahon, J., in R. v. Lloyd (1890), 19 O.R. 352.

If a person sees that a crime is about to be committed in his presence and does not interfere to prevent it, that is not a participation rendering him liable, without evidence that he was there in pursuance of a common unlawful purpose with the principal offender. R. v. Curtley, 27 U.C.Q.B. 613.

Aid rendered to the principal offenders after the commission of the crime is alone insufficient to justify the conviction of the person so aiding, as a principal under this section. R. v. Graham (1898), 2 Can. Cr. Cas. 388.

Aiders and abettors are principals in the second degree and are sometimes called accomplices; but the latter term will not serve as a definition as it includes all the participes criminis, whether they are considered as principals in the first or second degree or merely as accessories before or after the fact. R. v. Smith (1876), 38 U.C.Q.B. 218, 228.

Form of charge.]—An information and warrant of arrest thereunder, charging the accused as an accessory to the violation of a statute named, without specifying the fact as to which he is alleged to be an accessory is void for uncertainty. R. v. Holley (1893), 4 Can. Cr. Cas. 510 (N.S.).

Such a warrant charges no offence, and neither it, nor a demand thereon is validated by Code sec. 669, which provides that no irregularity or defect in the substance or form of the warrant shall affect the validity of any proceeding at or subsequent to the preliminary enquiry before the justice. Ibid.

It has been held that the owner of a house who leases it to another person knowing and assenting when the lease was made to the purpose of the latter to maintain it as a common bawdy house, thereby does an act for the purpose of aiding the lessee to commit the indictable offence of keeping a disorderly house, and he may be indicted and convicted as a principal under sec. 69. R. v. Roy, 3 Can. Cr. Cas. 472 (Que.).

In cases of theft.]—On an indictment for, with three other persons, attempting to steal goods in a store, evidence was given by an accomplice that prisoner went with him to see a store, that prisoner went into the store to buy something to see how the store could be got into and that they and others planned the robbery and fixed the date; prisoner saw them off but did not go with them, the others went out and made the attempt, which was frustrated. It was held that as those actually engaged were guilty of the attempt to steal, the prisoner was properly convicted under 27 and 28 Vict. ch. 19, sec. 9, which enacted that whosoever shall aid, abet, counsel or procure the commission of any misdemeanour shall be liable to be tried, indicted and punished as a principal offender. R. v. Esmonde (1866), 26 U.C.Q.B. 152.

A person who knowingly assists a thief to conceal stolen money which he is in the actual and proximate act of carrying away, by receiving the money for the purpose of concealing it, is guilty of aiding and abetting in the theft, and may under sub-sec. (c) be convicted as a principal. R. v. Campbell (1899), 2 Can. Cr. Cas. 357.

Although the theft may be complete by the mere taking and carrying away of stolen property, the subsequent carrying of same to a place of concealment by a person who did not participate in the taking, if done with a guilty knowledge and as a continuation of and proximately at the same time as the theft, is an "aiding and abetting" of the same. Ibid.

An act done which may enter into the offence, although the crime may be complete without it, may be considered as a continuation of the criminal transaction so as to make the participator an aider and abettor, although his participation occurs only after such acts have been done as in themselves would constitute the crime. Ibid.

Abettor of theft receiving stolen goods.]—If the accused were not an aider and abettor or a principal in the second degree in the commission of the theft, the circumstance that he was an accessory before the fact by counselling and procuring the commission of the theft, and therefore liable under sec. 69 to be convicted as a principal, does not prevent his conviction for the substantive offence of afterwards receiving the stolen property knowing it to have been stolen. Such an accessory before the fact who afterwards becomes a receiver of the stolen property may be legally convicted both of the theft and of "receiving." R. v. Hodge (1898), 2 Can. Cr. Cas. 350.

Under liquor laws.]—If it be contrary to law to sell liquor or any other article in a shop a sale by any clerk or assistant in his shop would primâ facie be the act of the shopkeeper. It may be, if he could shew that the act of sale was an isolated act, wholly unauthorized by him, and not in any way in the course of his business, but a thing done wholly by the unwarranted or wilful act of the subordinate, he might escape personal responsibility. Where one H. swore that he got a bottle of brandy and paid for it $1 in K.'s shop, that a woman served him, and no one else was in the store at the time, K. was convicted and the court upheld the conviction. R. v. King (1869), 20 U.C.C.P. 247; Reg. v. Williams, 42 U.C.Q.B. 464; R. v. Conrod, 5 Can. Cr. Cas. 414.

A buyer of liquor cannot, in respect of an illegal sale thereof made to him contrary to the Canada Temperance Act, be regarded in point of law as an aider or abettor. R. v. Heath (1887), 13 O.R. 471; Ex parte Armstrong, 30 N.B.R. 425.

In gaming.]—A broker who merely acts as such for two parties, one a buyer and the other a seller, without having any pecuniary interest in the transaction beyond his fixed commission and without any guilty knowledge on his part of the intention of the contracting parties to gamble in stocks or merchandise, is not liable as an accessory. R. v. Dowd (1899), 4 Can. Cr. Cas. 170 (Que.).

A person who acts as agent for another in managing a branch office for gambling transactions in stocks within Code sec. 231, knowing that there was no intention of transferring any property or title to property, is liable to conviction as an accessory under Code sec. 69, although his sole interest in the transaction was in the commissions paid to him for effecting the same. The King v. Harkness (No. 1), 10 Can. Cr. Cas. 193.

Mere acquiescence by a director in prohibited acts of a corporation is not such a participation therein as will constitute him an aider or abettor or make him criminally liable as a party under Code sec. 69, for the illegal acts of the corporation. The King v. Hendrie, 10 Can. Cr. Cas. 298, 11 O.L.R. 202.

Where an hotel keeper was not aware that gaming was being carried on in his hotel, and the only employee who knew it was not in charge of the premises, but was employed in a menial capacity, the hotel keeper was held not to be guilty of "suffering" gaming to be carried on in his premises contrary to a Licensing Act. Somerset v. Hart, 12 Q.B.D. 360.

Joint indictment.]—If the abettor and principal are indicted together as principals, the abettor may be convicted although the principal is acquitted. R. v. Burton, 13 Cox C.C. 71.

Common design of prisoners to escape.]—Where a parcel containing revolvers was thrown into a cab conveying prisoners and the defendant and at least one of the other prisoners in the cab armed themselves with the revolvers and formed the common intention of, by the use thereof, prosecuting the unlawful purpose of escaping from lawful custody and of assisting each other therein, the shooting by one of them of the constable in charge was an offence committed by one of them in the prosecution of such common purpose, and the commission thereof was or ought to have been known to be a possible consequence of the prosecution of such common purpose; each of them was, therefore, a party to such offence, and the offence, being murder in the actual perpetrator thereof, was murder in the defendant, even if he were not the actual perpetrator thereof, and he was properly found guilty by the jury of that offence. R. v. Rice (1902), 5 Can. Cr. Cas. 509, 4 O.L.R. 223.

Trade mark offences.]—No servant of a master, resident in Canada, who bonâ fide acts in obedience to the instructions of such master, and, on demand made by or on behalf of the prosecutor, gives full information as to his master, is liable to any prosecution or punishment for any offence defined in the part of the Code relating to trade mark offences, sec. 495.

70. Every one who counsels or procures another person to be a party to an offence of which that person is afterwards guilty, is a party to that offence, although it may be committed in a way different from that which was counselled or suggested. **Person counselling offence.**

2. Every one who counsels or procures another to be a party to an offence is a party to every offence which that other commits in consequence of such counselling or procuring, and which the person counselling or procuring knew, or ought to have known, to be likely to be committed in consequence of such counselling or procuring. 55-56 V., c. 29, s. 62. **Idem.**

71. An accessory after the fact to an offence is one who receives, comforts or assists any one who has been a party to such offence in order to enable him to escape, knowing him to have been a party thereto. **Accessory after the fact.**

2. No married person whose husband or wife has been a party to an offence shall become an accessory after the fact thereto by receiving, comforting or assisting the other of them, and no married woman whose husband has been a party to an offence shall become an accessory after the fact thereto, by receiving, comforting or assisting in his presence and by his authority any other person who has been a party to such offence in order to enable her husband or such other person to escape. 55-56 V., c. 29, s. 63. **Husband or wife.**

Accessory at common law.]—At common law the term accessory after the fact only applied to felonies for in misdemeanours all were principals.

R. v. Tisdale, 20 U.C.Q.B. 273; R. v. Campbell, 18 U.C.Q.B. 417; R. v. Benjamin, 4 U.C.C.P. 189.

Who are accessories.]—Any assistance given to the person known to be the offender, in order to hinder his apprehension, trial or punishment is sufficient to make the assisting party an accessory after the fact, as for instance, that he concealed him in his house; Dalt. 530, 531; or shut the door against his pursuers until he should have a chance of escaping; 1 Hale 619; or took money from him to allow him to escape; Year Book, 9 M. 4 pl. 1; or supplied him with money, a horse or other necessaries in order to enable him to escape; Hale 218; 2 Hawk., ch. 29, sec. 26; or that the principal was in prison, and the alleged accessory after the fact bribed the gaoler to let him escape, or conveyed instruments to him to enable him to break prison and escape. 1 Hale 621.

It is necessary that the accessory have notice, direct or implied, at the time he assists or comforts the offender, that he had committed the offence. 2 Hawk., ch. 29, sec. 32; and the assisting party is an accessory after the fact to whatever offence is complete at the time the assistance is given. So if one wounds another mortally, and after the wound is given but before death ensues, a person assists or receives the delinquent, this does not make him accessory to the homicide, for until death ensues no murder or manslaughter is committed. 2 Hawk., ch. 29, sec. 35.

Who are not accessories.]—But to merely suffer the principal to escape will not make the party an accessory after the fact, for it amounts at most but to a mere omission. Year Book, 9 H. 4, pl. 1, 1 Hale 619. A physician or surgeon may professionally attend a sick or wounded man, although he knew him to be a felon. 1 Hale 332. A person does not become an accessory by advising the principal offender's friends to write to the witnesses not to appear against him at the trial although they do so write. 1 Hale 620. There must be an act to assist the felon personally to constitute an accessory after the fact. R. v. Chapple, 9 C. & R. 355. And it is not sufficient that the person knew of the felony and did not disclose it. 1 Hale 371, 618; or that he agreed for money not to give evidence against the offender. Moor 8.

Receiving stolen goods.]—The receiving of stolen goods did not at common law constitute the receiver an accessory but was a separate and distinct misdemeanour, punishable by fine and imprisonment. Hale 620; and it is treated in the Code as a distinct offence. See secs. 399 and 849.

Husband or wife.]—At common law a wife was not punishable as accessory after the fact in receiving and assisting her husband for she was presumed to act under his coercion. R. v. Manning, 2 C. & K. 903(n). But a husband receiving and assisting his wife after the felony became liable as an accessory. 1 Hale 48, 621. This is now changed by sub-sec. 2, supra.

Other relationships.]—No other relationship than that of husband and wife will excuse the wilful receiving or assisting of the offender; a father cannot legally assist his child, a child his parent, a brother his brother, a master his servant, or a servant his master. 1 Hale 48, 621.

Misprison.]—It was a misdemeanour at common law for any person, who knew that another had committed a felony, to "conceal or procure the concealment thereof." 3 Co. Inst. 140, 1 Hawkins P.C. 731, 1 Hale 373. The common law as to crimes is still in force except in so far as the Code has otherwise provided, and it would seem that technically this offence remains in respect of what was formerly a felony. Its definition is extremely vague and there have been few, if any, prosecutions for it in modern times. Burbidge Cr. Law 508.

Punishment.]—Accessories after the fact to treason are liable to two years' imprisonment under sec. 76. And by sec. 267 "every one is guilty of an indictable offence and liable to imprisonment for life who is an accessory after the fact to murder." Where no express provision is made by the Code for the punishment of an accessory after the fact to an indictable offence, for which the principal would be liable, on a first conviction, to imprisonment for fourteen years or over or to imprisonment for life, such accessory is liable to seven years' imprisonment. Section 574. And where the principal cannot be sentenced to imprisonment for so long a term as fourteen years, the accessory after the fact to any other indictable offence is liable to one half of the longest term to which a person the principal may be sentenced, except where there is an express provision of law for the punishment of such accessory. Section 575.

Assisting prisoner to escape.]—See secs. 191-195.

Indicting accessory after the fact without proceeding against principal.]—Every one charged with being an accessory after the fact to any offence, may be indicated, whether the principal offender or other party to the offence or person by whom such property was so obtained has or has not been indicted or convicted, or is or is not amenable to justice, and such accessory may be indicted either alone as for a substantive offence or jointly with such principal or other offender or person. Code sec. 849.

72. Every one who, having an intent to commit an offence, does or omits an act for the purpose of accomplishing his object is guilty of an attempt to commit the offence intended whether under the circumstances it was possible to commit such offence or not. **Attempts.**

2. The question whether an act done or omitted with intent to commit an offence is or is not only preparation for the commission of that offence, and too remote to constitute an attempt to commit it, is a question of law. 55-56 V., c. 29, s. 64. **Question of law.**

Attempts.]—Special provision is made by the Code in respect of "attempt" offences as follows: To break prison, sec. 188; to commit sodomy, sec. 203; to procure girl to have unlawful carnal connection with a third party, sec. 216; to commit murder, sec. 264; to commit suicide, sec. 270; to cause bodily injuries by explosives, sec. 280; to commit rape, sec. 300; to defile children under fourteen, sec. 301; to set fire to crops, sec. 514; to wreck, sec. 523; to injure or poison cattle, sec. 536; to commit other indictable offences punishable by imprisonment, secs. 570 and 571; to commit other statutory offences, sec. 572.

An assault with intent to commit an offence is an attempt to commit such offence, and, on an indictment for rape, a conviction for an assault with intent to commit rape is valid. R. v. John (1888), 15 Can. S.C.R. 385, Code sec. 951.

Full offence charged.]—When the complete commission of the offence charged is not proved, but the evidence establishes an attempt to commit the offence, the accused may be convicted of such attempt and punished accordingly. Code secs. 949 and 951.

Attempt charged.]—When an attempt to commit an offence is charged, but the evidence establishes the commission of the full offence, the accused shall not be entitled to be acquitted, but the jury may convict him of the attempt, unless the court before which such trial is had thinks fit, in its discretion, to discharge the jury from giving any verdict upon such trial, and to direct such person to be indicted for the complete offence. Code sec. 950.

After a conviction for such attempt the accused shall not be liable to be tried again for the offence which he was charged with attempting to commit. Code sec. 950(2).

Where a prisoner is indicted for an attempt to steal, and the proof establishes that the offence of larceny was actually committed, the jury may convict of the attempt, unless the court discharges the jury and directs that the prisoner be indicted for the complete offence. R. v. Taylor (1895), 5 Can. Cr. Cas. 89, 4 Que. Q.B. 226. This is a departure from the rule which prevailed before the Code, as to which see Leblanc v. R., 16 Montreal Legal News 187.

Full offence and attempt both charged.]—Where on an indictment for a principal offence and for an attempt to commit such an offence, the evidence is wholly directed to the proof of the principal offence, the jury's verdict of guilty of the attempt only, will not be set aside, although there were no other witnesses in respect of the attempt than those whose testimony, if wholly believed, shewed the commission of the greater offence. R. v. Hamilton (1897), 4 Can. Cr. Cas. 251 (Ont.). It is within the province of the jury, to believe, if it sees fit to do so, a part only of a witness's testimony, and to disbelieve the remainder of the same witness's testimony, and it may therefore credit the testimony in respect of a greater offence only in so far as it shews a lesser offence. Ibid.

Mens rea or intent.]—It is a general principle of the criminal law that there must be as an essential ingredient in a criminal offence some blameworthy condition of mind—something of the mind which is designated by the expression mens rea. It is also a principle of the criminal law that the condition of the mind of the servant is not to be imputed to the master. This principle applies also to statutory offences, with this difference, that it is in the power of the Legislature, if it so pleases, to enact that a man may be convicted and punished for an offence, although there was no blameworthy condition of mind about him; but it lies on those who assert that the Legislature has so enacted to make it out convincingly by the language of the statute. Per Cave, J., in Chisholm v. Doulton, 22 Q.B.D. 736; cited by Osler, J.A., in R. v. Potter (1893), 20 Ont. App. 516, 523; Somerset v. Wade, [1894] 1 Q.B. 576; R. v. Vachon (1900), 3 Can. Cr. Cas. 558.

In order to constitute a crime it is necessary that there should be not only an act, but also a criminal intent. This is embodied in the maxim "actus non facit reum, nisi mens sit rea," 3 Inst. 107; Broom's Legal Maxims 226; R. v. Prince (1875), 2 C.C.R. 154; R. v. Tolson (1889), 23 Q.B.D. 168.

Motive generally precedes intent, for a man usually has some inducement or cause for doing a thing before he makes up his mind to do it. There are some cases in which no more need be done to the criminal intent that to prove the mere doing of the act; as where the act is such as to shew within itself the guilty intent, so that there can be but one reasonable inference, which of necessity arises from the facts proved. Every sane man is presumed to contemplate the ordinary natural and probable consequences of his acts. Townsend v. Wathen, 9 East 277; R. v. Dixon, 3 M. & S. 15. The question of fraudulent intent or guilty mind (mens rea) enters into the majority of criminal offences.

In the recent case of Bank of N.S.W. v. Piper (1897), 66 L.J.P.C. 76, the law is stated as follows: "It is strongly urged that in order to the constitution of a crime whether common law or statutory, there must be a mens rea on the part of the accused, and he may avoid conviction by shewing that such mens rea did not exist. This is a proposition which their lordships do not desire to dispute; but the questions whether a particular intent is made an element of a statutory crime, and, where that is not the case, whether there is an absence of mens rea in the accused, are questions entirely different, and depend on different considerations. In cases where a statute requires a motive to be proved as an essential element of the crime, the prosecution must fail if it is not proved. On the other hand the absence of mens rea really consists in an honest and reasonable belief entertained by the accused of the existence of facts which, if true, would make the act charged against him innocent. The case of Sherras v. De Rutzen, 64 L.J. M.C. 218; [1895] 1 Q.B. 918, is an instance of its absence." See note in 12 Can. Cr. Cas. 250.

If a man knowingly does acts which are unlawful, the presumption of law is that the mens rea exists; and ignorance of the law will not excuse him. R. v. Mailloux, 3 Pugsley (N.B.) 493.

Mens rea, in the legal sense of the expression, should not be confounded with a guilty conscience or evil intention. A statute, which prohibits an act, would be violated, though the act was done without evil intention, or even under the influence of a good motive. R. v. Hicklin. L.R. 3 Q.B. 360; Starey v. Chilworth Gunpowder Co., 24 Q.B.D. 90. And see article in Can. Law Jour. (1903), p. 691.

Rebutting criminal intent.]—Drunkenness may be taken into consideration to explain the probability of a party's intention in the case of violence committed on sudden provocation. Pearson's Case (1835), 2 Lewin 144. So in cases of attempted suicide the mere fact of drunkenness is not an excuse for the crime, but it is "a material fact in order to arrive at the conclusion whether or not the prisoner really intended to destroy his life." Per Wightman, J., in Regina v. Doody (1854), 6 Cox C.C. 463.

Motive.]—When any act done by any person is either a fact in issue, or is relevant to the issue, any fact which supplies a motive for such act is relevant, and proof of it is admissible even if such fact should tend to affect and damage such person's good character. Stephen's Digest of the Law of Evidence, article 7. While the law does not allow evidence of general bad character to be adduced in the first instance as a criminative circumstance, whenever it is necessary to prove a motive on the part of the defendant to commit the offence charged, it is competent to prove particular facts which are of a nature to shew a motive, even when they may injuriously affect his reputation, and the reason is that proof of the existence of a motive is not in itself a criminative circumstance but is only a circumstance which tends to remove the improbability of the act which has been proved to have been done having been done without criminal intent. R. v. Barsalou (No. 2) (1901), 4 Can. Cr. Cas. 347. A motive may, under peculiar circumstances, become an exceedingly important element in a chain of presumptive proof, as where a man, accused of the murder of his wife, has previously formed an adulterous connection with another female. On the other hand, the absence of any apparent motive is always a fact in favour of the accused. Best on Presumptions, p. 310.

Intent should not be confounded with motive. The terms "intention" and "motive" are often used indiscriminately to denote the same thing, but motive and intention are really two different things, and a distinction ought to be made in the use of the terms. Motive is the moving cause or that which induces an act, while intent is the purpose or design with which it is done. Motive has to do with desire, and intent with will. Burrill's Circ. Evid. 283, 284.

PART II.

OFFENCES AGAINST PUBLIC ORDER, INTERNAL AND EXTERNAL.

Interpretation.

As to information illegally obtained or communicated.

73. In the sections of this Part relating to information illegally obtained or communicated, unless the context otherwise requires,—

Reference to place.

(a) any reference to a place belonging to His Majesty includes a place belonging to any department of the Government of the United Kingdom, or of the Government of Canada, or of any province, whether the place is or is not actually vested in His Majesty;

Reference to communications.

(b) expressions referring to communications include any communication, whether in whole or in part, and whether the document, sketch, plan, model or information itself or the substance or effect thereof only be communicated;

'Document.'

(c) 'document' includes part of a document;

'Model.'

(d) 'model' includes design, pattern and specimen;

'Sketch.'

(e) 'sketch' includes any photograph or other mode of expression of any place or thing;

'Office under His Majesty.'

(f) 'office under His Majesty' includes any office or employment in or under any department of the Government of the United Kingdom, or of the Government of Canada or of any province. 55-56 V., c. 29, s. 76.

Treason and other Offences against the King's Authority and Person.

Treason.

74. Treason is,—

Bodily harm to His Majesty.

(a) the act of killing His Majesty, or doing him any bodily harm tending to death or destruction, maim or wounding, and the act of imprisoning or restraining him; or,

Intention with overt act.

(b) the forming and manifesting by an overt act an intention to kill His Majesty, or to do him any bodily harm tending to death or destruction, maim or wounding, or to imprison or to restrain him; or,

(c) the act of killing the eldest son and heir apparent of His Majesty, or the Queen consort of any King of the United Kingdom of Great Britain and Ireland; or, **Killing heir apparent.**

(d) the forming and manifesting, by an overt act, an intention to kill the eldest son and heir apparent of His Majesty, or the Queen consort of any King of the United Kingdom of Great Britain and Ireland; or, **Intention with overt act.**

(e) conspiring with any person to kill His Majesty, or to do him any bodily harm tending to death or destruction, maim or wounding, or conspiring with any person to imprison or restrain him; or, **Conspiring to do His Majesty bodily harm.**

(f) levying war against His Majesty either **Levying war.**

(i) with intent to depose His Majesty from the style, honour and royal name of the Imperial Crown of the United Kingdom of Great Britain and Ireland or of any other of His Majesty's dominions or countries, or **To depose His Majesty.**

(ii) in order, by force or constraint, to compel His Majesty to change his measures or counsels, or in order to intimidate or overawe both Houses or either House of Parliament of the United Kingdom or of Canada; or, **To overawe His Majesty.**

(g) conspiring to levy war against His Majesty with any such intent or for any such purpose as aforesaid; or, **Conspiring to levy war.**

(h) instigating any foreigner with force to invade the said United Kingdom or Canada or any other of the dominions of His Majesty; or, **Instigating invasion.**

(i) assisting any public enemy at war with His Majesty in such war by any means whatsoever; or, **Assisting enemy.**

(j) violating, whether with her consent or not, a Queen consort, or the wife of the eldest son and heir apparent, for the time being, of the King or Queen regnant. **Violating person or wife of heir apparent.**

2. Every one who commits treason is guilty of an indictable offence and liable to suffer death. 55-56 V., c. 29, s. 65; 57-58 V., c. 57, s. 1. **Penalty.**

Legislative power.]—There is no reason to suppose that it was not intended that the Parliament of Canada should have power to legislate regarding the crime of treason in Canada. It seems to be given when power is given to make laws for the peace, order and good government of Canada. Even jurisdiction to declare what shall be and what shall not be acts of treason, when committed within Canada, against the person of the Sovereign herself, might safely be committed to the Parliament of Canada when the Sovereign is a part of Parliament, and has also power of disallowance of Acts, even after they have been assented to by the Governor-General. R. v. Riel, 1 Terr. L.R., at p. 58, per Killam, J.; R. v. Marais, [1902] App. Cas. 51.

Overt acts.]—The indictment must state overt acts, and no evidence is admissible of any overt act not stated, unless it is otherwise relevant as tending to prove some overt act stated. Sec. 847.

Words spoken or written and published may constitute an overt act if relating to a treasonable act or design. R. v. Wedderburne, 18 St. Tr. 425; R. v. Charnock, 12 St. Tr. 1377; but not unpublished writings. R. v. Lord Preston, 12 St. Tr. 645; R. v. Layer, 16 St. Tr. 93, 280. And by sec. 1140 (2) no person shall be prosecuted under the provisions of this section for any overt act of treason expressed or declared by open and advised speaking unless information of such overt act and of the words by which the same was expressed or declared is given upon oath to a justice within six days after the words are spoken and a warrant for the apprehension of the offender is issued within ten days after such information is given.

Levying war.]—It is not necessary to set out in the indictment the particular acts of the defendant further than to allege generally that he assembled with a multitude armed and arrayed in a warlike manner and levied war. Fost. 220. As to levying war in Canada, see sec. 77.

A mere rising or tumult is not treasonable unless for a purpose of a public or general nature. R. v. Hardie, 1 St. Tr. (N.S.) 609. It is not necessary that great numbers should assemble or that military arms or array should be displayed to constitute the levying of war. Ibid; R. v. Gallagher, 16 Cox C.C. 291. Enlisting and marching are sufficient without coming to battle. Vaughan's Case, 13 St. Tr. 485, 2 Salk. 634. But there must be an insurrection and it must be for an object of a general nature, and there must be force accompanying insurrection. R. v. Frost, 9 C. & P. 129. If an armed body of men enter a town with the object merely of making a demonstration of their strength to the magistracy in order to procure the liberation of prisoners convicted of some political offence or to have their punishment mitigated, this, although an offence of a serious nature, is not treason. Ibid.

Where the levying of war is direct, i.e., open rebellion for the purpose of deposing the Sovereign, all persons assembled and marching with the rebels are guilty of treason unless compelled to join and continue with them pro timore mortis. R. v. Earl of Essex, 1 St. Tr. 1333; R. v. Slavin, 17 U.C.C.P. 205; Fost. 216. But where it is indirect or constructive only, i.e., when levied for the purpose of effecting innovations of a public and general nature by an armed force or to obtain the redress of a public grievance, real or pretended, those only of the rabble who actually aid and assist in doing those acts of violence which form the constructive treason can be convicted of treason, and the rest are merely rioters. R. v. Messenger, 6 St. Tr. 879; R. v. Gordon, 21 St. Tr. 485.

Notwithstanding the party accused did the act complained of with a view, under the influence of insane delusion, of redressing some supposed grievances or injury, or of producing some public benefit, he is nevertheless punishable according to the nature of the crime committed, if he knew at the time of committing such crime that he was acting contrary to law. R. v. Riel (1885), 2 Man. R. 321, 1 Terr. L.R. 23, 10 App. Cas. 675.

Corroboration.]—No person accused of an offence under this section shall be convicted upon the evidence of one witness, unless such witness is corroborated in some material particular by evidence implicating the accused. Sec. 1002.

Time for prosecution.]—A prosecution for treason (except treason by killing His Majesty or where the overt act alleged is an attempt to injure the person of His Majesty) must be commenced within three years from the time of the commission of the offence. Sec. 1140.

Bail.]—See sec. 699, 700.

Special provisions regarding trial.]—See sec. 897.

The ordinary power of amending indictments (sec. 898) does not extend to authorize the court to add to the overt acts charged in an indictment for treason or other offence under secs. 76 to 86, inclusive. Code sec. 847.

Naturalization.]—A British subject commits a treasonable act by becoming naturalized in the enemy's country during hostilities and is liable in respect of subsequent treasonable acts notwithstanding such attempted naturalization. R. v. Lynch, [1903] 1 K.B. 144.

Resident alien.]—In De Jager v. Attorney-General of Natal (1907), A.C. 326, the Privy Council held that where an alien resident within British territory assists invaders during the absence of the British forces, he is guilty, and may properly be convicted of high treason; and that there is no law relieving an alien from his duty of allegiance because an enemy temporarily makes good his military occupation of the district in which the alien resides.

75. In every case in which it is treason to conspire with any person for any purpose, the act of so conspiring, and every overt act of any such conspiracy, is an overt act of treason. 55-56 V., c. 29, s. 66. **Overt act.**

Treasonable conspiracy as an overt act.]—Where a conspiracy is laid as an overt act the acts of any of the conspirators in furtherance of the common design may be given in evidence against all. R. v. Hardy, 1 East P.C. 98; R. v. Stone, 6 T.R. 527; R. v. McCafferty, 10 Cox C.C. 603.

The first thing to be proved is the conspiracy and that the defendant was connected with it, and afterwards, if it is intended to put in evidence the acts of a co-conspirator, it must be shewn that such co-conspirator was a member of the same conspiracy, and that the act done was in furtherance of the common design. R. v. Sidney, 9 St. Tr. 817; R. v. Lovat, 18 St. Tr. 529.

76. Every one is guilty of an indictable offence and liable to two years' imprisonment who,— **Penalty.**

(*a*) becomes an accessory, after the fact, to treason; or, **Accessories after the fact.**

(*b*) knowing that any person is about to commit treason does not, with all reasonable despatch, give information thereof to a justice of the peace, or use other reasonable endeavours to prevent the commission of the same. 55-56 V., c. 29, s. 67. **Omitting to prevent treason.**

Indictment.]—See sec. 847.

77. Every subject or citizen of any foreign state or country at peace with His Majesty, who,— **Levying war by subject of a state at peace with His Majesty.**

(*a*) is or continues in arms against His Majesty within Canada; or,

(*b*) commits any act of hostility therein; or,

(c) enters Canada with intent to levy war against His Majesty, or to commit any indictable offence therein for which any person would, in Canada, be liable to suffer death; and,

every subject of His Majesty who,—

Subjects assisting. (a) within Canada levies war against His Majesty in company with any of the subjects or citizens of any foreign state or country at peace with His Majesty; or,

(b) enters Canada in company with any such subjects or citizens with intent to levy war against His Majesty, or to commit any such offence therein; or,

(c) with intent to aid and assist, joins himself to any person who has entered Canada with intent to levy war against His Majesty, or to commit any such offence in Canada;

Penalty. is guilty of an indictable offence and liable to suffer death. 55-56 V., c. 29, s. 68.

This offence is triable either before a superior court of criminal jurisdiction or by a militia general court-martial. The superior court has no discretion as to the punishment to be awarded, but a court-martial has. Burbidge Cr. Law Dig. 46.

As to the jurisdiction of courts martial, see the Militia Act, R.S.C. (1906), ch. 41, secs. 102-104.

Indictment.]—See sec. 847.

Treasonable offences. **78.** Every one is guilty of an indictable offence and liable to imprisonment for life who forms,—

Intention to depose His Majesty. (a) an intention to depose His Majesty from the style, honour and royal name of the Imperial Crown of the United Kingdom of Great Britain and Ireland, or of any other of His Majesty's dominions or countries; or,

Intention to levy war. (b) an intention to levy war against His Majesty within any part of the said United Kingdom, or of Canada, in order by force or constraint to compel him to change his measures or counsels, or in order to put any force or constraint upon or in order to intimidate or overawe both Houses or either House of Parliament of the United Kingdom or of Canada; or,

Intention to induce invasion. (c) an intention to move or stir any foreigner or stranger with force to invade the said United Kingdom, or Canada, or any other of His Majesty's dominions or countries under the authority of His Majesty;

Manifestation. and manifests any such intention by conspiring with any person to carry it into effect, or by any other overt act, or by publishing any printing or writing. 55-56 V., c. 29, s. 69.

Limitations.]—A prosecution under this section cannot be commenced after the expiration of three years from the time of the commission of the offence. Section 1140. And no person shall be prosecuted under the provisions of this section for any overt act of treason expressed or declared by open and advised speaking, unless information of such overt act and of the words by which the same was expressed or declared is given upon oath to a justice within six days after the words are spoken and a warrant for the apprehension of the offender is issued within ten days after such information is given. Section 1140(2).

Indictment.]—See sec. 847.

79. Every one is guilty of an indictable offence and liable to fourteen years' imprisonment who confederates, combines or conspires with any person to do any act of violence in order to intimidate, or to put any force or constraint upon, any legislative council, legislative assembly or house of assembly. 55-56 V., c. 29, s. 70. **Conspiracy to intimidate a legislature.**

Common law offence.]—On demurrer to an indictment for conspiracy to bring about a change in the government of the Province of Ontario by bribing members of the Legislature to vote against the government, it was held that such was an indictable offence as a common law misdemeanour. R. v. Bunting, 7 Ont. R. 524. The fact that the Legislature has power by statute to punish as for a contempt does not oust the jurisdiction of the courts where the offence is of a criminal character; the same act may be in one aspect a contempt of the Legislature and in another aspect an indictable offence. Ibid.

Indictment.]—See sec. 847.

80. Every one is guilty of an indictable offence and liable to seven years' imprisonment, and to be whipped once, twice or thrice as the court directs, who,— **Assaults upon the King.**

(*a*) wilfully produces, or has, near His Majesty, any arm or destructive or dangerous thing with intent to use the same to injure the person of, or to alarm His Majesty; or, **Acts intended to alarm or injure the King.**

(*b*) wilfully and with intent to alarm or to injure His Majesty, or to break the public peace, **Other similar acts.**

(i) points, aims or presents, or attempts to point, aim or present, at or near His Majesty, any firearm, loaded or not, or any other kind of arm,

(ii) discharges or attempts to discharge at or near His Majesty any loaded arm,

(iii) discharges or attempts to discharge any explosive material near His Majesty,

(iv) strikes, or strikes at, or attempts to strike, or strike at, His Majesty in any manner whatever,

(v) throws, or attempts to throw, anything at or upon His Majesty. 55-56 V., c. 29, s. 71.

Indictment.]—See sec. 847.

Inciting to mutiny.

81. Every one is guilty of an indictable offence and liable to imprisonment for life, who for any traitorous or mutinous purpose, endeavours to seduce any person serving in His Majesty's forces by sea or land from his duty and allegiance to His Majesty, or to incite or stir up any such person to commit any traitorous or mutinous practice. 55-56 V., c. 29, s. 72.

This section is derived from the Imperial Statute 37 Geo. III., ch. 70, the Incitement to Mutiny Act of 1797.

A sailor who has been in the sick hospital for thirty days and who is, therefore, not entitled to pay nor liable to a court-martial, is still "serving" within this section. R. v. Tierney, R. & R. 74.

Indictment.]—See sec. 847.

Offence.

82. Every one is guilty of an offence punishable on indictment, or on summary conviction before two justices, who, not being an enlisted soldier in His Majesty's service, or a seaman in His Majesty's naval service,—

Persuading to desert.

(*a*) by words or with money, or by any other means whatsoever, directly or indirectly, persuades or procures, or goes about or endeavours to persuade, prevail on or procure, any such seaman or soldier to desert from or leave His Majesty's military or naval service; or,

Concealing deserter.

(*b*) conceals, receives or assists any deserter from His Majesty's military or naval service, knowing him to be such deserter;

Penalty.

and is liable, on conviction under indictment, to fine and imprisonment in the discretion of the court, and on summary conviction before two justices, to a penalty not exceeding two hundred dollars, and not less than eighty dollars and costs, and in default of payment to imprisonment for any term not exceeding six months. 55-56 V., c. 29, s. 73.

The Merchants' Shipping Act, which is in force in Canada, also makes it an offence "If a person by any means whatever persuades or attempts to persuade a seaman or apprentice to desert from his ship"; but that provision applies only to British ships. Poll v. Dambe, [1901] 2 K.B. 579.

Indictment.]—See sec. 847.

Moiety of fine to prosecutor.]—See sec. 1042.

Arrest of suspected deserters.]—See sec. 657.

83. Every one who resists the execution of any warrant authorizing the breaking open of any building to search for any deserter from His Majesty's military or naval service is guilty of an offence and liable on summary conviction before two justices to a penalty of eighty dollars. 55-56 V., c. 29, s. 74. **Resisting execution of search warrant.**

Compare sub-sec. 3 of sec. 657.

See also as to reward to prosecutor sec. 1042.

Moiety of fine to prosecutor.]—See sec. 1042.

Indictment.]—See sec. 847.

84. Every one is guilty of an offence and liable, on summary conviction, to six months' imprisonment with or without hard labour, who,— **Penalty.**

(*a*) persuades any man who has been enlisted to serve in any corps of militia, or who is a member of or has engaged to serve in the Royal Northwest Mounted Police Force, to desert, or attempts to procure or persuade any such man to desert; or, **Persuading men to desert.**

(*b*) knowing that any such man is about to desert, aids or assists him in deserting; or, **Assisting.**

(*c*) knowing that any such man is a deserter, conceals him or aids or assists in his rescue. 55-56 V., c. 29, s. 75. **Concealing.**

Indictment.]—See sec. 847.

Information Illegally Obtained or Communicated.

85. Every one is guilty of an indictable offence and liable to imprisonment for one year, or to a fine not exceeding one hundred dollars, or to both imprisonment and fine, who,— **Penalty.**

(*a*) for the purpose of wrongfully obtaining information, **For purpose of unlawfully obtaining.**

(i) enters or is in any part of a fortress, arsenal, factory, dockyard, camp, ship, office or other like place in Canada belonging to His Majesty, in which part he is not entitled to be, or **Entering fortress, etc.**

(ii) when lawfully or unlawfully in any such place as aforesaid, either obtains any document, sketch, plan, model or knowledge of anything, which he is not entitled to obtain, or takes without lawful authority any sketch or plan, or **Obtaining after entry.**

(iii) when outside any fortress, arsenal, factory, dockyard or camp in Canada, belonging to His Majesty, **Attempting to take** sketch, etc., when outside.

takes, or attempts to take, without authority given by or on behalf of His Majesty, any sketch or plan of that fortress, arsenal, factory, dockyard or camp; or,

Communication without authority.

(*b*) knowingly having possession of or control over any document, sketch, plan, model, or knowledge obtained or taken by means of any act which constitutes an offence against this and the next following section, at any time wilfully and without lawful authority communicates or attempts to communicate the same to any person to whom the same ought not, in the interests of the state, to be communicated at that time; or,

Communication in breach of confidence.

(*c*) after having been entrusted in confidence by some officer under His Majesty with any document, sketch, plan, model or information relating to any such place as aforesaid, or to the naval or military affairs of His Majesty, wilfully, and in breach of such confidence, communicates the same when, in the interests of the state, it ought not to be communicated; or,

Communication to improper persons.

(*d*) having possession of any document relating to any fortress, arsenal, factory, dockyard, camp, ship, office or other like place belonging to His Majesty, or to the naval or military affairs of His Majesty in whatever manner the same has been obtained or taken, at any time wilfully communicates the same to any person to whom he knows the same ought not, in the interests of the state, to be then communicated.

Information for foreign state.

Penalty.

2. Every one who commits any such offence intending to communicate to a foreign state any information, document, sketch, plan, model or knowledge obtained or taken by him, or entrusted to him as aforesaid, or communicates the same to any agent of a foreign state, is guilty of an indictable offence and liable to imprisonment for life. 55-56 V., c. 29, s. 77.

Origin of statute.]—This, and the following section, are an adaptation of the Imperial statute 52 & 53 Vict., ch. 52, the Official Secrets Act 1889. That Act was by its terms made applicable to British possessions not within the United Kingdom; but it is provided that if by any law made before or after the passing thereof by the Legislature of any British possessions provisions are made which appear to His Majesty the King to be of the like effect as those contained in such Act, His Majesty may by order in council, suspend the operation within such British possession of such Act or of any part thereof, so long as such law continues in force there and no longer (sec. 5). But the suspension in any British possession is limited by a proviso that it shall not extend to the holder of any office under His Majesty the King who is not appointed to that office by the government of that possession.

Interpretation.]—See sec. 73.

Limitation.]—By sec. 592 it is provided that no person shall be prosecuted for the offence of unlawfully obtaining and communicating official information, without the consent of the Attorney-General or of the Attorney-General of Canada.

Indictment.]—See sec. 847.

86. Every one who, by means of his holding or having held an office under His Majesty, has lawfully or unlawfully either obtained possession of or control over any document, sketch, plan or model, or acquired any information, and at any time corruptly, or contrary to his official duty, communicates or attempts to communicate such document, sketch, plan, model or information to any person to whom the same ought not, in the interests of the state, or otherwise in the public interest, to be then communicated, is guilty of an indictable offence and liable,— Communicating information acquired in office.

(*a*) if the communication was made, or attempted to be made, to a foreign state, to imprisonment for life; and, Penalty.

(*b*) in any other case, to imprisonment for one year, or to a fine not exceeding one hundred dollars, or to both imprisonment and fine. Idem.

2. This section shall apply to a person holding a contract with His Majesty, or with any department of the Government of the United Kingdom, or of the Government of Canada, or of any province, or with the holder of any office under His Majesty as such holder, where such contract involves an obligation of secrecy, and to any person employed by any person or body of persons holding such a contract who is under a like obligation of secrecy, as if the person holding the contract, and the person so employed were respectively holders of an office under His Majesty. 55-56 V., c. 29, s. 78. Application of section.

An indictment for inciting the commission of an offence under sub-sec. 2, in respect of the offence mentioned in sec. 85(d), was quashed for want of an averment that the person incited had obtained possession or control of the document. R. v. Stuart (1899), Central Cr. Court referred to in Archbold Cr. Plead. 965.

Limitations.]—See sec. 592.

Interpretation.]—See sec. 73.

Indictment.]—See sec. 847.

Unlawful Assemblies and Riots.

87. An unlawful assembly is an assembly of three or more persons who, with intent to carry out any common purpose, assemble in such a manner or so conduct themselves when Definition of unlawful assembly.

assembled as to cause persons in the neighbourhood of such assembly to fear, on reasonable grounds, that the persons so assembled will disturb the peace tumultuously, or will by such assembly needlessly and without any reasonable occasion provoke other persons to disturb the peace tumultuously.

Intention not necessary.

2. Persons lawfully assembled may become an unlawful assembly if they conduct themselves with a common purpose in such a manner as would have made their assembling unlawful if they had assembled in that manner for that purpose.

Exception.

3. An assembly of three or more persons for the purpose of protecting the house of any one of their number against persons threatening to break and enter such house in order to commit any indictable offence therein is not unlawful. 55-56 V., c. 29, s. 79.

Examples of unlawful assembly.]—The difference between a "riot" and an "unlawful assembly" is that the former is a tumultuous meeting of persons upon some purpose which they actually execute with violence, and the latter is a mere assembly of persons for treasonable or seditious purposes; R. v. Rankin, 7 St. Tr. (N.S.) 711; or upon a purpose which, if executed, would make them rioters, but which they do not execute nor make any motion to execute. R. v. Kelly, 6 U.C.C.P. 372; R. v. Birt, 5 C. & P. 154. The offence formerly known as "rout" was an unlawful assembly in which the parties had made some motion to execute the purpose, which, if executed, would make them rioters. R. v. Vincent, 9 C. & P. 91. But such would now be "riot" under the statutory definitions contained in sec. 80.

The march of a Salvation Army band through the streets of a town in which street music was prohibited, and which resulted in a breach of the peace, was held not to be an unlawful assembly where the bandsmen did not have any reason to believe that their acts would cause a breach of the peace. R. v. Clarkson, 17 Cox C.C. 483.

Persons assembling with intent to carry out a common purpose must not do so in such a manner as to needlessly and without any reasonable occasion provoke other persons to disturb the peace tumultuously, and if they do so, and persons in the neighbourhood are on reasonable grounds afraid that such a result will follow, the assembly will be unlawful under the definition in the section. This extends the common law offence and makes the decision in Beatty v. Gillbanks (1882), 9 Q.B.D. 308, inapplicable. In that case members of the Salvation Army assembled together in the street for a lawful object, but with a knowledge that their assembly would be opposed and resisted by other persons in such a way as would in all probability tend to the commission of a breach of the peace on the part of the opposing persons. The procession of the Salvation Army was forcibly opposed by a number of persons but no violence was used by the Salvation Army members. It was held by Field and Cave, JJ., that the assembly of the latter was not unlawful, and that a man is not to be convicted for doing a lawful act, although he knows that his doing it may cause another to do an unlawful act.

A meeting lawfully convened may become unlawful if seditious words are spoken of such a nature as to be likely to produce a breach of the peace. R. v. Burns (1886), 16 Cox C.C. 355.

Assemblies to obstruct the officers of the law are unlawful. R. v. Mc-

Naughten, 14 Cox C.C. 576; or to witness a prize fight. R. v. Billingham, 2 C. & P. 234; R. v. Perkins, 4 C. & P. 537. See sec. 95 as to the offence of promoting a prize fight.

Suppressing unlawful assembly.]—The magistrates and the police are justified in dispersing an assembling which is unlawful. O'Kelly v. Harvey, 15 Cox C.C. 435. Redford v. Birley, 1 St. Tr. (N.S.) 1071, 1239; R. v. Neale, 3 St. Tr. (N.S.) 1312. After refusal to disperse, force may be used to compel them to do so, and the persons resisting may be punished ar rioters. R. v. Jones, 6 St. Tr. (N.S.) 811; R. v. Fursey (1833), St. Tr. (N.S.) 543. 6 C. & P. 81. Nor is it necessary to first read the Riot Act or to proclaim the meeting unlawful before using force to disperse it. Ibid.

Punishment.]—See sec. 89.

88. A riot is an unlawful assembly which has begun to disturb the peace tumultuously. 55-56 V., c. 29, s. 80. **Definition of riot.**

Riot at common law.]—At common law a riot was "a tumultuous disturbance of the peace by three persons or more assembling together of their own authority, with an intent mutually to assist one another against any who shall oppose them in the execution of some enterprise of a private nature, and afterwards actually executing the same in a violent and turbulent manner to the terror of the people, whether the act intended was of itself lawful or unlawful." Hawkins P.C., ch. 28, sec. 1, p. 513; Field v. Metropolitan Police, [1907] 2 K.B. 853.

Distinguished from unlawful assembly.]—Where before the Code a person was indicted for a riot and assault, and the jury found him guilty of a riot, but not of the assault charged; it was held that the conviction for riot could not be sustained, the assault, the object of the riotous assembly, not having been executed; although the defendant might have been guilty of joining in an unlawful assembly. R. v. Kelly (1857), 6 U.C.C.P. 372. The present section makes it unnecessary that the object of the disturbance should have been actually carried out if there has been a tumultuous disturbance of the peace.

A procession having been attacked by rioters, the prisoner, one of the processionists, and in no way connected with the rioters, was proved during the course of the attack to have fired off a pistol on two occasions, first in the air and then at the rioters. So far as appeared from the evidence, the prisoner acted alone and not in connection with any one else. It was held that a conviction for riot could not be sustained. R. v. Corcoran (1876), 26 U.C.C.P. 134.

Punishment and procedure.]—See secs. 90-97, inclusive.

89. Every member of an unlawful assembly is guilty of an indictable offence and liable to one year's imprisonment. 55-56 V., c. 29, s. 81. **Punishment of unlawful assembly.**

Unlawful assembly defined.]—See sec. 87.

Evidence of other meetings.]—It has been held in New Brunswick that it is not a ground for quashing a conviction for unlawful assembly on a certain day that evidence of an unlawful assembly on another day has been improperly received, if the latter charge was abandoned by the prosecuting counsel at the close of the case, and there was ample evidence to sustain the conviction. R. v. Mailloux, 3 Pugsley (N.B.) 493. And evidence of the conduct of the accused persons on the day previous to their alleged unlawful assembly is not admissible on their behalf to explain or qualify their conduct at the time of the alleged offence. Ibid.

Punishment of riot.

90. Every rioter is guilty of an indictable offence and liable to two years' imprisonment with hard labour. 55-56 V., c. 29, s. 82.

Suppression of riot.]—See secs. 48-51, inclusive, 89-97, inclusive, and sec. 167.

If the magistrate neither reads the Riot Act nor restrains nor apprehends the rioters, nor gives any orders to fire on them, nor makes use of an available military force, such will be primâ facie evidence of criminal neglect on his part. R. v. Kennett, 5 C. & P. 282. He is justified in using such force as he on good faith and on reasonable and probable grounds believes necessary, but it must not be out of proportion to the danger to be reasonably apprehended from a continuance of the riot. Section 48. Stevenson v. Wilson, 2 L.C.J. 254; R. v. Pinney (1832), 5 C. & P. 254.

Evidence.]—To prove a person to be a rioter, it is not sufficient to merely shew that the riot took place and that the accused was present among them. It must be shewn that he did something by work or act to take part in, help or incite the riotous proceedings. R. v. Atkinson, 11 Cox 330. If, however, his assistance is demanded by officers of the law to aid in suppressing the riot, his failure to aid them is indictable under sec. 95. R. v. Sherlock, 10 Cox C.C. 170; R. v. Brown, C. & Mar. 314.

The acts of the rioters may be proved severally, as in conspiracy, before evidence is given to connect their fellow rioters. R. v. Cooper, 1 Russ. Crimes, 6th ed. 585.

Reading the Riot Act.

91. It is the duty of every sheriff, deputy sheriff, mayor or other head officer, and justice, of any county, city or town, who has notice that there are within his jurisdiction persons to the number of twelve or more unlawfully, riotously and tumultuously assembled together to the disturbance of the public peace, to resort to the place where such unlawful, riotous and tumultuous assembly is, and among the rioters, or as near to them as he can safely come, with a loud voice to command or cause to be commanded silence, and after that openly and with loud voice to make or cause to be made a proclamation in these words or to the like effect:—

Proclamation.

'Our Sovereign Lord the King charges and commands all persons being assembled immediately to disperse and peaceably to depart to their habitations or to their lawful business, upon the pain of being guilty of an offence on conviction of which they may be sentenced to imprisonment for life.

'GOD SAVE THE KING.'

55-56 V., c. 29, s. 83.

The Riot Act is not validly proclaimed if the concluding words of the proclamation, "God save the King," are omitted. R. v. Child, 4 C. & P. 442.

92. All persons are guilty of an indictable offence and liable to imprisonment for life who,— **Penalty.**

(*a*) with force and arms wilfully oppose, hinder or hurt any person who begins or is about to make the said proclamation, whereby such proclamation is not made; or, **Preventing proclamation.**

(*b*) continue together to the number of twelve for thirty minutes after such proclamation has been made, or if they know that its making was hindered as aforesaid, within thirty minutes after such hindrance. 55-56 V., c. 29, s. 83. **Not dispersing.**

A prosecution for opposing the reading of the Riot Act or for continuing together after proclamation, must be brought within one year from the commission of the offence. Section 1140 (c).

93. If the persons so unlawfully, riotously and tumultuously assembled together, or twelve or more of them, continue together, and do not disperse themselves, for the space of thirty minutes after the proclamation is made or after such hindrance as aforesaid, it is the duty of every such sheriff, justice and other officers, and of all persons required by them to assist, to cause such persons to be apprehended and carried before a justice. **Duty of officers if rioters do not disperse.**

2. If any of the persons so assembled are killed or hurt in the apprehension of such persons or in the endeavour to apprehend or disperse them, by reason of their resistance, every person ordering them to be apprehended or dispersed, and every person executing such orders, are indemnified against all proceedings of every kind in respect thereof. **Indemnification of officers.**

3. Nothing in this section contained shall, in any way, limit or affect any duties or powers imposed or given by this Act as to the suppression of riots before or after the making of the said proclamation. 55-56 V., c. 29, s. 84. **Section not restrictive.**

See secs. 48-51 and 94-95.

94. Every sheriff, deputy sheriff, mayor or other head officer, justice, or other magistrate, or other peace officer, of any county, city, town, or district, who has notice that there is a riot within his jurisdiction, who, without reasonable excuse omits to do his duty in suppressing such riot, is guilty of an indictable offence and liable to two years' imprisonment. 55-56 V., c. 29, s. 140. **Neglect of peace officer to suppress riot.**

95. Every one is guilty of an indictable offence and liable to one year's imprisonment who, having reasonable notice that **Neglect to aid peace**

officer thereat.

he is required to assist any sheriff, deputy sheriff, mayor, or other head officer, justice, magistrate, or peace officer in suppressing any riot, without reasonable excuse omits to do so. 55-56 V., c. 29, s. 141.

It was an indictable misdemeanour at common law to refuse to assist a peace officer in quelling a riot. R. v. Brown, C. & Mar. 314; R. v. Sherlock, L.R. 1 C.C.R. 20, 10 Cox C.C. 170.

The procedure governing the calling out of the militia in aid of the civil power is contained in the Militia Act, R.S.C. 1906, ch. 41, secs. 80-90, inclusive.

Riotous destruction of property.

96. All persons are guilty of an indictable offence and liable to imprisonment for life who, being riotously and tumultuously assembled together to the disturbance of the public peace, unlawfully and with force demolish or pull down, or begin to demolish or pull down, any building, or any machinery, whether fixed or movable, or any erection used in farming land, or in carrying on any trade or manufacture, or any erection or structure used in conducting the business of any mine, or any bridge, wagon-way or track for conveying minerals from any mine. 55-56 V., c. 29, s. 85.

It is not a defence that the offender believed he had a right to act as he did, unless he actually had such a right. Section 97(2). Formerly if the demolition was executed in pursuance of the bonâ fide belief that the house belonged to one of the rioters, this would be a defence although the belief was erroneous. R. v. Langford, Carr. & M. 602; R. v. Casey (1874), Irish R. 8 C.L. 408.

As to similar offences without riot, see sec. 510; secs. 482-511; and as to riotous injury or damage to buildings, see sec. 97.

Begin to demolish.]—This means not simply the demolition of a part, but of a part with intent to demolish the whole. R. v. Ashton, 1 Lewin C.C. 296. In that case the parties first broke the windows and then entered the house and set fire to the furniture, but no part of the house was burned. Park, J., thus instructed the jury:—"If you think the prisoners originally came there without intent to demolish, and that the setting fire to the furniture was an afterthought but with that intent, then you must acquit because no part of the house having been burned there was no beginning to destroy the house. If they came originally without such intent but had afterwards set fire to the house the offence is arson. If you have doubts whether they originally came with an intent to demolish, you may use the setting fire to the furniture under such circumstances and in such manner as that the necessary consequence, if not for timely interference, would have been the burning of the house, as evidence to shew that they had such intent, although they began to demolish in another manner." Ibid.

If rioters destroy a house by fire the offence is within this section, and they need not be indicted for arson. R. v. Harris, Carr. & M. 661. If some of the prisoners set fire to the house itself, and others carried furniture out of the house and burned it in a fire made outside, it will be for the jury to say whether the latter were not encouraging and taking part in a general design of destroying both the house and the furniture, and if so the jury ought to convict. Ibid.

Where rioters destroy a house by fire it is not essential to prove that the person accused was present when the house was originally set on fire, if it was shewn that he was one of the rioters present while the fire was burning. R. v. Simpson, Carr. & M. 669.

It is immaterial that the principal intent of the rioters was the capture or personal injury of an individual therein, if it was also their object to demolish the house. R. v. Batt, 6 C. & P. 329.

Where the rioters break the doors and windows and destroy furniture in the house and then go away, although there was nothing to prevent them committing further injury, the offence is not within this section, for their going away under the circumstances shews that they had completed their purpose and had done all the injury they intended to do. R. v. Thomas, 4 C. & P. 237; R. v. Adams, Carr. & M. 299.

Form of indictment.]—That on ...... at ...... A.B. and C.D. [together with divers other evil-disposed persons, to the jurors aforesaid unknown,] unlawfully, riotously and tumultuously did assemble together, to the disturbance of the public peace; and being then and there so unlawfully, riotously and tumultuously assembled together as aforesaid, did then and there, unlawfully and with force [begin to] demolish and pull down the dwelling-house of (name), there situate, against the peace, etc., and against the form of the statute in such case made and provided, Criminal Code, sec. 96.

97. All persons are guilty of an indictable offence and liable to seven years' imprisonment who, being riotously and tumultuously assembled together to the disturbance of the public peace, unlawfully and with force injure or damage any of the things mentioned in the last preceding section. **Riotous damage to property.**

2. It shall not be a defence to a charge of an offence against this or the last preceding section that the offender believed he had a right to act as he did, unless he actually had such a right. 55-56 V., c. 29, s. 86. ***Bonâ fides* no defence.**

Form of indictment.]—That on ...... at ...... A. B. and C.D. [together with divers other evil-disposed persons, to the said jurors unknown,] unlawfully, riotously, and tumultuously did assemble together to the disturbance of the public peace, and being then and there so unlawfully, riotously and tumultuously assembled together as aforesaid, did then and there unlawfully and with force injure [or damage] a certain dwelling-house of one (name) there situate, against the form, etc.

Unlawful assembly.]—See sec. 87.

Unlawful Drilling.

98. The Governor in Council is authorized from time to time to prohibit assemblies, without lawful authority, of persons for the purpose of training or drilling themselves, or of being trained or drilled to the use of arms, or for the purpose of practising military exercises, movements or evolutions, and to **Prohibition of assemblies.**

prohibit persons when assembled for any other purpose from so training or drilling themselves or being trained or drilled.

General or special.

2. Any such prohibition may be general or may apply only to a particular place or district or to assemblies of a particular character, and shall come into operation from the publication in the *Canada Gazette* of a proclamation embodying the terms of such prohibition, and shall continue in force until the like publication of a proclamation issued by the authority of the Governor in Council revoking such prohibition.

Penalty.

3. Every person is guilty of an indictable offence and liable to two years' imprisonment who, without lawful authority and in contravention of such prohibition or proclamation,—

Being present for purpose of drilling others.

(*a*) is present at or attends any such assembly for the purpose of training or drilling any other person to the use of arms or the practice of military exercises or evolutions; or,

Drilling others.

(*b*) at any assembly trains or drills any other person to the use of arms or the practice of military exercises or evolutions. 55-56 V., c. 29, s. 87.

The prosecution must be commenced within six months from the commission of the offence. Section 1140(d).

Being unlawfully drilled.

99. Every one is guilty of an indictable offence and liable to two years' imprisonment who, without lawful authority, attends, or is present at, any such assembly as in the last preceding section mentioned, for the purpose of being, or who at any such assembly is, without lawful authority and in contravention of such prohibition or proclamation, trained or drilled to the use of arms or the practice of military exercises or evolutions. 55-56 V., c. 29, s. 88.

The prosecution must be commenced within six months from the time when the offence was committed. Section 1140(d).

Affrays and Duels.

Definition of affray.

100. An affray is the act of fighting in any public street or highway, or fighting to the alarm of the public in any other place to which the public have access.

Penalty.

2. Every one who takes part in an affray is guilty of an indictable offence and liable to one year's imprisonment with hard labour. 55-56 V., c. 29, s. 90.

If the fighting be in private it is not an affray, but an assault. 4 Bl. Com. 145; R. v. Hunt, 1 Cox C.C. 177. Mere quarrelsome words will not make an affray. I Russ. Cr. 5th ed. 390. It differs from a riot in that two persons may be guilty of an affray, but it requires three or more to constitute a riot. Sections 87 and 88.

101. Every one is guilty of an indictable offence and liable to three years' imprisonment who challenges or endeavours by any means to provoke any person to fight a duel, or endeavours to provoke any person to challenge any other person so to do. 55-56 V., c. 29, s. 91. **Challenge to fight a duel.**

Sending challenge to fight.]—It was a very high offence at common law to challenge another, either bv work or letter, to fight a duel; or to be the messenger of such a challenge or even barely to provoke another to send such a challenge or to fight, e.g., by dispersing letters to that purpose containing reflections and insinuating a desire to fight. Hawk. P.C., b. 1, ch. 63, sec. 3; R. v. Phillips, 6 East 464; R. v. Rice, 3 East 581.

If the defendant's intent does not sufficiently appear from the words proved, the prosecution should give evidence of circumstances from which the jury may infer the intent. R. v. Phillips, 6 East 464; Archbold Cr. Evid. 1060.

Where a letter challenging to fight is put into the post office in one county and delivered to the party in another, the venue may be laid in the former county. R. v. Williams (1810), 2 Camp. 506. The sending of the challenge is the offence and the offence is complete if the letter be mailed, although it does not in fact reach the person to whom it is addressed. Ibid.

Forcible Entry and Detainer.

102. Forcible entry is where a person, whether entitled or not, enters in a manner likely to cause a breach of the peace, or reasonable apprehension thereof, on land then in actual and peaceable possession of another. **Definition of forcible entry.**

2. Forcible detainer is where a person in actual possession of land, without colour of right, detains it in a manner likely to cause a breach of the peace, or reasonable apprehension thereof, against a person entitled by law to the possession thereof. **Definition of forcible detainer.**

3. What amounts to actual possession or colour of right is a question of law. 55-56 V., c. 29, s. 89. **Question of law.**

Forcible entry.]—"Entering" here means not merely going upon land or trespassing upon it; there must accompany the act of going upon the land some intent to take possession of the land itself and deprive the possessor of the land. Such an interference with the possession as trespassing upon it for the purpose of taking away chattels upon the land is not an "entering" within the Code. R. v. Pike (1898), 2 Can. Cr. Cas. 314, 12 Man. R. 314.

Forcible entry of a dwelling house may consist of an entry made with such threats and shew of force as would, if resisted, cause a breach of the peace, although no actual force was used. R. v. Walker (1906), 12 Can. Cr. Cas. 197, 4 W.L.R. 288. In the same case it was said that evidence relating to the title of the occupant is not admissible as to which see R. v. Child, 2 Cox 102; R. v. Hoar, 6 M. & S. 266.

Lord Tenterden, C.J., expressed himself as follows, in Rex v. Smyth, 5 C. & P. 201: "An indictment for a forcible entry cannot be supported by evidence of a mere trespass; but there must be proof of such force, or at least of such kind of force as is calculated to prevent any resistance."

To enter upon lands with such force as to exceed a bare trespass and so as to cause a public breach of the peace was an indictable offence at common law. R. v. Wilson, 8 T.R. 357; R. v. Bake, 3 Burr. 1731.

Everyone commits the offence of forcible entry, who, in order to take possession thereof, enters upon any lands or tenements in a violent manner, whether such violence consists in actual violence applied to any other person, or in threats, or in breaking open any house, or in collecting together an unusual number of persons for the purpose of making such entry. Stephen's Digest of Crim. Law, p. 51.

Where, therefore, from thirty to forty employees of the G. W. Railway Co. went upon land then in possession of the S. & H. Railway Co., and those resisting had good reason to apprehend violence in the event of further resistance, and yielded possession in the apprehension of such violence, it was held that the entry was a forcible one. R. v. Smith (1878), 43 U.C.Q.B. 369.

The evidence which supported the allegation of forcible entry in the case of R. v. Smith, supra, was held to support the allegation of forcible detainer. Ib., p. 383.

The gist of the offence is the forcible depriving of the other's actual and peaceable possession in a manner likely to cause a breach of the peace. R. v. Cokely, 13 U.C.Q.B. 521; R. v. Studd, 14 W.R. 806; Beddall v. Maitland, 17 Ch.D. 174. Even if the defendant had a right of entry, the assertion of that right "with strong hand or with multitude of people" is equally an offence as if he had no right. Taunton v. Costar, 7 T.R. 431.

A landlord may not so eject his tenant although the term of the tenancy has expired. But it has been held that the English statute regarding forcible entry (5 Ric. 2, ch. 7) does not apply to the ejectment of a mere trespasser. Browne v. Dawson, 12 A. & E. 624; Scott v. Browne, 51 L.T. 747.

A person who forcibly enters upon lands of his own which are in the custody of his servant or bailiff, is not guilty of forcible entry. 1 Hawk., ch. 64, sec. 32.

Actual possession does not necessarily imply actual residence, either personally or by a servant or agent. 13 Am. & Eng. Encyc. of Law, 2nd ed., p. 750.

Forcible detainer.]—Everyone commits the offence called forcible detainer, who, having wrongfully entered upon any lands or tenements, detains such lands and tenements in a manner which would render an entry upon them for the purpose of taking possession forcible. Stephen's Digest of Crim. Law, p. 51.

Restitution.]—It is within the discretion of the judge who tries the cause either to grant or refuse restitution. R. v. Wightman (1869), 29 U.C.Q.B. 211; R. v. Smith (1878), 43 U.C.Q.B. 369; R. v. Jackson Draper's Rep., Upper Canada, 53.

Penalty.

103. Every one who forcibly enters or forcibly detains land is guilty of an indictable offence and liable to one year's imprisonment. 55-56 V., c. 29, s. 89.

Prize Fights.

104. Every one is guilty of an offence and liable, on summary conviction, to a penalty not exceeding one thousand dollars and not less than one hundred dollars, or to imprisonment for a term not exceeding six months, with or without hard labour, or to both, who sends or publishes, or causes to be sent or published or otherwise made known, any challenge to fight a prize fight, or accepts any such challenge, or causes the same to be accepted, or goes into training preparatory to such fight, or acts as trainer or second to any person who intends to engage in a prize fight. 55-56 V., c. 29, s. 93.

Challenging, etc.

Accepting challenge, etc.

Prize fight defined.]—See sec. 2(31).

105. Every one is guilty of an offence and liable, on summary conviction, to imprisonment for a term not exceeding twelve months and not less than three months, with or without hard labour, who engages as a principal in a prize fight, 55-56 V., c. 29, s. 94.

Engaging as principals.

Prize fight.]—A sparring match with gloves, fairly conducted, is not unlawful. R. v. Young, 10 Cox C.C. 371. If, however, the parties meet intending to fight till one gives in from exhaustion or injury received, such fighting in unlawful whether the combatants fight with gloves or not. R. v. Orton, 14 Cox C.C. 226.

A sparring match with gloves, under Queensberry or similar rules given merely as an exhibition of skill and without any intention to fight until one is incapacitated by injury or exhaustion is not a "prize fight" under Code secs. 105 and 2(31); to constitute a "prize fight" there must have been a previous arrangement for a "fight" in the ordinary sense of the term, and that involves an intention to continue the encounter until one or the other of the combatants gives in from exhaustion or from injury received. The King v. Littlejohn, 8 Can. Cr. Cas. 212.

The defendants advertised a boxing exhibition which was effectively held in a public hall, and was accompanied by all the particulars and circumstances of a prize fight. Complainant submitted that the accused came within the provision of the statute; and on behalf of the defendants it was contended that the encounter was merely a scientific boxing match, and moreover only a sham fight, not forbidden by law:—Held, that, as the proof adduced established that the encounter in question was accompanied by all the circumstances and elements which constitute a prize fight, the defendants committed an infraction of the law, for which they must be found guilty. Steele v. Maber, 6 Can. Cr. Cas. 445, 19 Que. S.C. 392.

The injuries given and received in prize fights are injurious to the public, both because it is against the public interest that the lives and the health of the combatants should be endangered by blows and because prize fights are disorderly exhibitions, mischievous on many obvious grounds. R. v. Coney, 8 Q.B.D. 534, 30 W.R. 678, per Stephen, J. The consent of the parties to the blows which they may mutually receive does not prevent those blows from being assaults. Ibid.

The fight must be for a prize or one on the result of which the handing over or transfer of money or property depends, otherwise it is not a prize fight; sec. 108; but, where that is not shewn, it may still be punished under the latter section by a fine not exceeding $50; if the fight were bonâ fide the result of a quarrel or dispute.

Preventing and suppressing prize fights.]—See secs. 627 and 628.

Recognizance not to engage in prize fight.]—Whenever any person who has been required to enter into a recognizance with sureties, to keep the peace and be of good behaviour, or not to engage in any prize fight has, on account of his default therein, remained imprisoned for two weeks, the sheriff, gaoler or warden shall give notice, in writing, of the facts, to a judge of a superior court, or to a judge of the county court of the county or district in which such gaol or prison is situate, or, in the cities of Montreal and Quebec, to a judge of the sessions of the peace for the district, or, in the North-West Territories, to a stipendiary magistrate. Such judge or magistrate may order the discharge of such person, thereupon or at a subsequent time, upon notice to the complainant or otherwise, or may make such other order as he sees fit, respecting the number of sureties, the sum in which they are to be bound and the length of time for which such person may be bound. Section 1059.

Attending or promoting.

106. Every one is guilty of an offence and liable, on summary conviction, to a penalty not exceeding five hundred dollars and not less than fifty dollars, or to imprisonment for a term not exceeding twelve months, with or without hard labour, or to both, who is present at a prize fight as an aid, second, surgeon, umpire, backer, assistant or reporter, or who advises, encourages or promotes such fight. 55-56 V., c. 29, s. 95.

Leaving Canada to engage in prize fight.

107. Every inhabitant or resident of Canada is guilty of an offence and liable, on summary conviction, to a penalty not exceeding four hundred dollars and not less than fifty dollars, or to imprisonment for a term not exceeding six months, with or without hard labour, or to both, who leaves Canada with intent to engage in a prize fight without the limits thereof. 55-56 V., c. 29, s. 96.

When fight is not a prize fight.

108. If, after hearing evidence of the circumstances connected with the origin of the fight or intended fight, the person before whom the complaint is made is satisfied that such fight or intended fight was *bona fide* the consequence or result of a quarrel or dispute between the principals engaged or intended to engage therein, and that the same was not an encounter or fight for a prize, or on the result of which the handing over or transfer of money or property depended, such person may, in his discretion, discharge the accused or impose upon him a penalty not exceeding fifty dollars. 55-56 V., c. 29, s. 97.

Discharge or fine.

Inciting Indians.

Penalty.

109. Every one is guilty of an indictable offence and liable to two years' imprisonment who induces, incites or stirs up any three or more Indians, non-treaty Indians, or half-breeds, apparently acting in concert,—

(a) to make any request or demand of any agent or servant of the Government in a riotous, routous, disorderly or threatening manner, or in a manner calculated to cause a breach of the peace; or, **Riotous request.**

(b) to do any act calculated to cause a breach of the peace. 55-56 V., c. 29, s. 98. **Breach of the peace.**

110. Every one who incites any Indian to commit any indictable offence is guilty of an indictable offence and liable to imprisonment for any term not exceeding five years. R.S., c. 43, s. 112. **Indictable offence.**

Explosive Substances.

111. Every one is guilty of an indictable offence and liable to imprisonment for life who wilfully causes, by any explosive substance, an explosion of a nature likely to endanger life or to cause serious injury to property, whether any injury to person or property is actually caused or not. 55-56 V., c. 29, s. 99. **Causing dangerous explosions.**

At common law.]—By the common law of England to manufacture or to keep in large quantities in towns or closely inhabited places gunpowder, or other explosive substances, constitutes a nuisance and indictable offence. R. v. Lister, 1 D. & B, 209, citing R. v. Taylor, 2 Strange 1167, and R. v. Williams, 1 Russell on Crimes 298, note o., and the causing of danger is the gist of the offence; but it is not necessary to allege carelessness in the indictment, or that the quantities deposited were so great that care would not produce safety. R. v. Holmes (1884), 17 N.S.R. 499.

Explosive substance.]—This expression is defined by the interpretation clause 2(14).

Property.]—This term includes every kind of real and personal property. Section 2(32).

Likely to endanger life.]—It is not necessary to prove actual injury, and it is sufficient if such exposure to risk or chance of injury be shewn as will satisfy the jury that actual danger to life was caused. R. v. McGrath, 14 Cox C.C. 598.

Causing bodily injury by explosive.]—See sec. 279.

Causing explosion with intent.]—See sec. 280.

Seizure of explosives.]—See sec. 633.

112. Every one is guilty of an indictable offence and liable to fourteen years' imprisonment who wilfully places or throws any explosive substance into or near any building or ship with **Attempt to destroy property with explosives.**

intent to destroy or damage the same or any machinery, working tools, or chattels whatever, whether or not an explosion takes place. 55-56 V., c. 29, s. 488.

See note to sec. 111.

Doing anything with intent to cause an explosion.

113. Every one who wilfully,—

(a) does any act with intent to cause by an explosive substance, or conspires to cause by an explosive substance, an explosion of a nature likely to endanger life, or to cause serious injury to property; or,

Making or possessing explosives.

(b) makes or has in his possession or under his control any explosive substance with intent by means thereof to endanger life or to cause serious injury to property, or to enable any other person by means thereof to endanger life or to cause serious injury to property;

Penalty.

is guilty of an indictable offence and liable to fourteen years' imprisonment, whether an explosion takes place or not, and whether any injury to person or property is actually caused or not. 55-56 V., c. 29, s. 100.

Evidence.]—If several persons are connected in a common design to have explosive substances made for an unlawful purpose, each of the confederacy is responsible in respect of such articles as are in the possession of others connected in the carrying out of their common design. R. v. Charles, 17 Cox C.C. 499.

The Imperial Act, 24 & 25 Vict., ch. 97, sec. 10, declared it an offence to "unlawfully and maliciously place or throw in, against or near any building any gunpowder or other explosive substance with intent to destroy or damage any building, etc., whether or not any explosion take place and whether or not any damage be caused." On a prosecution under that statute for throwing gunpowder against a house, the evidence proved that the prisoner had thrown a bottle containing gunpowder against the house, and that there was a fuse in the neck of the bottle. Kelly, C.B., ruled that, unless the fuse was lighted at the time the bottle was thrown against the house, the offence was not made out, as, "if the fuse was not lighted, it could not cause an explosion and it would be merely throwing a bottle against a house." R. v. Sheppard (1868), 11 Cox C.C. 302.

Consent of Attorney-General.]—See sec. 594.

Making or possessing explosives.

114. Every one is guilty of an indictable offence and liable to seven years' imprisonment who makes, or knowingly has in his possession or under his control, any explosive substance under such circumstances as to give rise to a reasonable suspicion that he is not making it, or has it not in his possession or under his control, for a lawful object, unless he can show that he made it or had it in his possession or under his control for a lawful object. 55-56 V., c. 29, s. 101.

Use of explosives in fishing.]—See Fisheries Regulations (1902), 5 Can. Cr. Cas. 558.

Offensive Weapons.

115. Every one is guilty of an indictable offence and liable to five years' imprisonment who has in his custody or possession, or carries any offensive weapon for any purpose dangerous to the public peace. 55-56 V., c. 29, s. 102. Possession of weapon.

A prosecution under this section shall not be commenced after the expiration of six months from the commission of the offence. Section 1140(d).

116. If two or more persons openly carry offensive weapons in a public place in such a manner and under such circumstances as are calculated to create terror and alarm, each of such persons is liable, on summary conviction before two justices, to a penalty not exceeding forty dollars and not less than ten dollars, and in default of payment to imprisonment for any term not exceeding thirty days. 55-56 V., c. 29, s. 103. Openly carrying weapons.

The prosecution must be commenced within one month from the commission of the offence. Section 1140(f).

117. Every one is guilty of an indictable offence and liable to imprisonment for ten years who, while carrying offensive weapons, is found with any goods liable to seizure or forfeiture under any law relating to inland revenue, the customs, trade or navigation, knowing such goods to be so liable. 55-56 V., c. 29, s. 104. Smuggler carrying weapons.

118. Every one is guilty of an offence and liable, on summary conviction, to a penalty not exceeding twenty-five dollars and not less than five dollars, or to imprisonment for one month who, not being a justice or a public officer, or a soldier, sailor, or volunteer in His Majesty's service, on duty, or a constable or other peace officer, and not having a certificate of exemption from the operation of this section as hereinafter provided for, and not having at the time reasonable cause to fear an assault or other injury to his person, family or property, has upon his person a pistol, or air-gun elsewhere than in his own dwelling-house, shop, warehouse, or counting-house. Carrying pistol or air-gun. Justification.

2. If sufficient cause be shown upon oath to the satisfaction of any justice, he may grant to any applicant therefor not under the age of sixteen years and as to whose discretion and good character he is satisfied by evidence upon oath, a certifi- Certificate of exemption.

cate of exemption from the operation of this section, for such period, not exceeding twelve months, as he deems fit.

Evidence.

3. Such certificate, upon the trial of any offence, shall be *prima facie* evidence of its contents and of the signature and official character of the person by whom it purports to be granted.

Operation of section suspended.

4. Whenever the Governor in Council deems it expedient in the public interest, he may by proclamation suspend the operation of the provisions of the first and second subsections of this section respecting certificates of exemption, or exempt from such operation any particular part of Canada, and in either case for such period, and with such exceptions as to the persons affected by this section as he deems fit. 55-56 V., c. 29, s. 105.

Limitation.]—The limit of time for prosecution is one month. Section 1140(f).

Soldiers, peace officers, etc.]—See also sec. 125.

Peace officer.]—See the definition of this term in sec. 2(26).

Public officer.]—See definition in 2(29).

Return as to certificates to carry weapons.]—See sec. 1135.

Selling pistol or air-gun to minor.

119. Every one is guilty of an offence and liable, on summary conviction, to a penalty not exceeding fifty dollars, who sells or gives any pistol or air-gun, or any ammunition therefor, to a minor under the age of sixteen years, unless he establishes to the satisfaction of the justice before whom he is charged that he used reasonable diligence in endeavouring to ascertain the age of the minor before making such sale or gift, and that he had good reason to believe that such minor was not under the age of sixteen.

Exception.

Record of sale.

2. Every one is guilty of an offence and liable, on summary conviction, to a penalty not exceeding twenty-five dollars, who sells any pistol or air-gun without keeping a record of such sale, the date thereof, and the name of the purchaser and of the maker's name, or other mark by which such arm may be identified. 55-56 V., c. 29, s. 106.

The limit of time for prosecution is one month. Section 1140(f).

Having pistol or air-gun on person when arrested.

120. Every one who when arrested, either on a warrant issued against him for an offence or while committing an offence, has upon his person a pistol or air-gun is guilty of an offence and liable, on summary conviction before two justices, to a penalty not exceeding fifty dollars and not less than twenty dollars, or to imprisonment for any term not exceeding three months, with or without hard labour. 55-56 V., c. 29, s. 107.

Limitation.]—The limit of time for prosecution is one month. Section 1140 (f).

Exemption.]—As to soldiers, peace officers, etc., see sec. 125.

Impounding.]—See sec. 622.

121. Every one who has upon his person a pistol or air-gun, with intent therewith unlawfully to do injury to any other person, is guilty of an offence and liable, on summary conviction before two justices, to a penalty not exceeding two hundred dollars and not less than fifty dollars, or to imprisonment for any term not exceeding six months, with or without hard labour. 55-56 V., c. 29, s. 108.

Having pistol or air-gun with intent to injure any person.

Limitation.]—The limit of time for prosecution is one month. Section 1140 (f).

Personal possession.]—A conviction for "procuring" a pistol with intent unlawfully to do injury to another person, is not to be held a sufficient conviction for "having on his person a pistol, etc.," and is bad as not disclosing an offence known to the law. R. v. Mines (1894), 1 Can. Cr. Cas. 217 (Ont.).

Impounding.]—See sec. 622.

122. Every one who, without lawful excuse, points at another person any firearm or air-gun, whether loaded or unloaded, is guilty of an offence and liable, on summary conviction before two justices, to a penalty not exceeding one hundred dollars and not less than ten dollars, or to imprisonment for any term not exceeding thirty days, with or without hard labour. 55-56 V., c. 29, s. 109.

Pointing any firearm or air-gun at any person.

Limitation.]—The limit of time for prosecution is one month. Section 1140 (f).

Impounding.]—See sec. 622.

123. Every one who carries about his person any bowie-knife, or any dagger, dirk, metal knuckles, skull cracker, slung shot, or other offensive weapon of a like character, or secretly carries about his person any instrument loaded at the end, or sells or exposes for sale, publicly or privately, any such weapon, or, being masked or disguised, carries, or has in his possession any firearm or air-gun, is guilty of an offence and liable, on summary conviction before two justices, to a penalty not ex-

Carrying offensive weapons.

ceeding fifty dollars and not less than ten dollars, and in default of payment thereof, to imprisonment for any term not exceeding thirty days, with or without hard labour. 55-56 V., c. 29, s. 110.

Limitation.]—The limit of time for prosecution is one month. Section 1140 (f).

Exemption.]—As to usual arms of soldiers, sailors, etc., see sec. 125.

Impounding.]—See sec. 622.

Carrying sheath-knife in town or city.

124. Every one, not being thereto required by his lawful trade or calling, who is found in any town or city carrying about his person any sheath-knife is liable, on summary conviction before two justices, to a penalty not exceeding forty dollars and not less than ten dollars, and in default of payment thereof, to imprisonment for any term not exceeding thirty days, with or without hard labour. 55-56 V., c. 29, s. 111.

Limitation.]—The limit of time for prosecution is one month. Section 1140 (f).

Impounding.]—See sec. 622.

Sailors, soldiers, etc.]—See sec. 125.

The terms "public officer" and "peace officer" are defined by sec. 2, sub-secs. 26 and 29.

Exception as to soldiers, etc.

125. It is not an offence for any soldier, public officer, peace officer, sailor or volunteer in His Majesty's service, or constable or other policeman, to carry loaded pistols or other usual arms or offensive weapons in the discharge of his duty. 55-56 V., c. 29, s. 112.

This section constitutes an exception from the operation of secs. 120, 123 and 124. Section 118 by its terms also excepts the same classes from its operation.

Refusing to deliver offensive weapon.

126. Every one attending any public meeting or being on his way to attend the same who, upon demand made by any justice within whose jurisdiction such public meeting is appointed to be held, declines or refuses to deliver up, peaceably and quietly, to such justice, any offensive weapon with which he is armed or which he has in his possession, is guilty of an indictable offence.

Procedure and penalty.

2. The justice may record the refusal and adjudge the offender to pay a penalty not exceeding eight dollars, or the offender may be proceeded against by indictment, as in other cases of indictable offences. R.S., c. 152, s. 1; 55-56 V., c. 29, s. 113.

Limitation.]—The prosecution must be commenced within one year from the commission of the offence. Section 1140(c).

Disarming persons attending meeting.]—See secs. 619, 620 and 621.

127. Every one, except the sheriff, deputy sheriff and justices for the district or county, or the mayor, justices or other peace officer for the city or town, respectively, in which any public meeting is held, and the constables and special constables employed by them, or any of them, for the preservation of the public peace at such meeting, is guilty of an indictable offence, and liable to a penalty not exceeding one hundred dollars, or to imprisonment for a term not exceeding three months, or to both, who, during any part of the day upon which such meeting is appointed to be held, comes within one mile of the place appointed for such meeting armed with any offensive weapon. 55-56 V., c. 29, s. 114. **Coming armed within one mile of public meeting.**

The limit of time for prosecution is one year. Section 1140(c).

128. Every one is guilty of an indictable offence and liable to a penalty not exceeding two hundred dollars, or to imprisonment for a term not exceeding six months, or to both, who lies in wait for any person returning, or expected to return from any such public meeting, with intent to commit an assault upon such person, or with intent, by abusive language, opprobrious epithets or other offensive demeanour, directed to, at or against such person, to provoke such person, or those who accompany him, to a breach of the peace. 55-56 V., c. 29, s. 115. **Lying in wait for persons returning therefrom.**

The limit of time for prosecution is one year. Section 1140(c).

Seditious Offences.

129. Every one is guilty of an indictable offence and liable to fourteen years' imprisonment who,— **Penalty.**

(*a*) administers, or is present at and consenting to the administration of, any oath or any engagement purporting to bind the person taking the same to commit any crime punishable by death or imprisonment for more than five years; or, **Administering oath to commit crime.**

(*b*) attempts to induce or compel any person to take any such oath or engagement; or, **Inducing oath.**

(*c*) takes any such oath or engagement. 55-56 V., c. 29, s. 120. **Taking oath.**

Origin.]—This and the following two sections were adopted by the Dominion Parliament from the Quebec consolidated statutes of 1860,

C.S.L.C., ch. 10, secs. 1, 2, 3 and 4. That statute was in turn modelled upon the English statutes of 1797 and 1799 respecting Unlawful Societies and Unlawful Oaths, 37 Geo. III., ch. 123 and 39 Geo. III., ch. 79, referred to in R. v. Dixon, 6 C. & P. 601.

Evidence.]—Although the oath were read from a paper at the time it was administered, it may be proved by parol evidence without giving the accused notice to produce the paper. R. v. Moors, 6 East 419(n).

Penalty.

130. Every one is guilty of an indictable offence and liable to seven years' imprisonment who,—

Administering oaths binding to.

(*a*) administers or is present at and consenting to the administration of any oath or engagement purporting to bind the person taking the same

Sedition.

(i) to engage in any mutinous or seditious purpose,

Disturbance of peace.

(ii) to disturb the public peace or commit or endeavour to commit any offence,

Not to inform.

(iii) not to inform and give evidence against any associate, confederate or other person,

Not to reveal illegal combination, etc.

(iv) not to reveal or discover any unlawful combination or confederacy, or any illegal act done or to be done, or any illegal oath or obligation or engagement which may have been administered or tendered to or taken by any person, or the import of any such oath or obligation or engagement; or,

Attempts.

(*b*) attempts to induce or compel any person to take any such oath or engagement; or,

Taking oath.

(*c*) takes any such oath or engagement. 55-56 V., c. 29, s. 121.

See note to sec. 129.

Compulsion thereto no excuse unless declaration made.

131. Any one who, under such compulsion as would otherwise excuse him, offends against either of the last two preceding sections, shall not be excused thereby unless, within the period hereinafter mentioned, he declares the same and what he knows touching the same, and the persons by whom and in whose presence, and when and where, such oath or obligation or engagement was administered or taken, by information on oath before a justice for the district or city or county in which such oath or engagement was administered or taken.

Limitation of time for declaration.

2. Such declaration may be made by such person within fourteen days after the taking of the oath, unless he is hindered from making it by actual force or sickness, in which case it may be made within eight days of the cessation of such hindrance.

At trial.

3. The declaration may be made on such person's trial if it

happens before the expiration of either of the periods aforesaid. 55-56 V., c. 29, s. 122.

See note to sec. 129.

132. Seditious words are words expressive of a seditious intention. **Seditious words.**

2. A seditious libel is a libel expressive of a seditious intention. **Seditious libel.**

3. A seditious conspiracy is an agreement between two or more persons to carry into execution a seditious intention. 55-56 V., c. 29, s. 123. **Seditious conspiracy.**

133. No one shall be deemed to have a seditious intention only because he intends in good faith,— **Intentions not seditious.**

(*a*) to show that His Majesty has been misled or mistaken in his measures; or,

(*b*) to point out errors or defects in the government or constitution of the United Kingdom, or of any part of it, or of Canada or any province thereof, or in either House of Parliament of the United Kingdom or of Canada, or in any legislature, or in the administration of justice; or to excite His Majesty's subjects to attempt to procure, by lawful means, the alteration of any matter in the state; or,

(*c*) to point out, in order to their removal, matters which are producing or have a tendency to produce feelings of hatred and ill-will between different classes of His Majesty's subjects. 55-56 V., c. 29, s. 123.

134. Every one is guilty of an indictable offence and liable to two years' imprisonment who speaks any seditious words or publishes any seditious libel or is a party to any seditious conspiracy. 55-56 V., c. 29, s. 124. **Seditious words, punishment.**

Sedition.]—Sedition whether by words spoken or written, or by conduct was a misdemeanour at common law. Stroud's Case, 3 St. Tr. 242. It embraces all those practices whether by word, deed or writing, which fall short of treason (as which see sec. 74, et seq.). but directly tend or have for their object to excite discontent or dissatisfaction, to excite ill-will between different classes of the King's subjects, to create public disturbance or to lead to civil war, to bring into hatred or contempt the sovereign or the government, the laws or constitution of the realm, and generally all endeavours to promote public disorder, or to incite people to unlawful associations or assemblies, insurrections, breaches of the peace, or forcible obstruction of the execution of the law. Archbold Cr. Ev. (1900), 942; R. v. Pigott, 11 Cox C.C. 44; R. v. Fussell, 3 Cox C.C. 291. But a bonâ fide intention to point out errors or defects in the government or in the administration of justice or to excite His Majesty's subjects to attempt to procure by lawful means the alteration of any matter in the state, is not seditious; sec. 133 (b); nor the like intention to point out, *in order to their removal*, matters which are producing or have a tendency to produce feelings of hatred and ill-will between different classes of His Majesty's subjects; sec. 133 (c); or to shew that His Majesty has been misled or mistaken in his measures; sec. 133 (a).

A writer may criticise or censure the conduct of the servants of the Crown or the acts of the government, he can do it freely and liberally, but it must be without malignity and not imputing corrupt or malicious motives; the law only interferes when plainly and deliberately the limits of frank and candid and honest discussion are passed. R. v. Sullivan, 11 Cox C.C. 44; R. v. Burns, 16 Cox C.C. 355; R. v. Lambert, 2 Camp. 398, 11 Revised Reports 748.

Seditious words.]—This expression here means words expressive of a seditious intention, sec. 132. Where the words are spoken at a meeting, those who do anything, as by expressions of approval, to help the speaker to produce upon the hearers the natural effect of the words spoken, are guilty of uttering seditious words just as if they spoke them themselves. R. v. Burns, 16 Cox C.C. 355; but a person merely standing by when they are uttered, and himself saying nothing, does not thereby make himself guilty of the uttering. Ibid.

Seditious libel.]—A seditious libel is defined by the preceding sec. 132, as being "a libel expressive of a seditious intention." A seditious libel may be evidenced by a woodcut or engraving. R. v. Sullivan, 11 Cox C.C. 44, 51. Publication must be proved, but if the manuscript of it be proved to be in the handwriting of the accused, and it be also proved to have been printed and published, such is evidence to go to the jury that the publication was *by* the accused, although there is no express evidence that he authorized the printing or publishing. R. v. Beare, 1 Ld. Raym. 414; R. v. Lovett, 9 C. & P. 462.

It is not necessary to prove the falsity of a seditious libel. R. v. Duffy, 2 Cox C.C. 45; Ex parte O'Brien, 15 Cox C.C. 180. Section 911 which allows a plea of the truth of the libel and of its publication in the public interest is limited to defamatory libels, and no such rule applies to seditious libels. But after verdict, the defendant has been allowed to prove in mitigation of sentence that he had published the libel through having himself read it in a newspaper in which it had previously appeared. R. v. Burdett, 4 B. & Ald. 95.

Seditious conspiracy.]—If several persons form a common intention to prosecute any unlawful purpose and to assist each other therein, each of them is a party to every offence committed by any one of them in the prosecution of such common purpose, the commission of which offence was or ought to have been known to be a probable consequence of the prosecution of such common purpose. Section 69 (2).

Libel on foreign sovereign.

135. Every one is guilty of an indictable offence and liable to one year's imprisonment who, without lawful justification, publishes any libel tending to degrade, revile or expose to hatred and contempt in the estimation of the people of any foreign state, any prince or person exercising sovereign authority over such state. 55-56 V., c. 29, s. 125.

Spreading false news.

136. Every one is guilty of an indictable offence and liable to one year's imprisonment who wilfully and knowingly publishes any false news or tale whereby injury or mischief is or is likely to be occasioned to any public interest. 55-56 V., c. 29, s. 126.

Offence at common law.]—The ancient statute, 3 Edw. I., ch. 34, enacted as follows:—"Forasmuch as there have been oftentimes found in the country devisers of tales whereby discord, or occasion of discord, hath many times arisen between the King and his people, or great men of the realm, for the damage that hath and may thereof ensue it is commanded, that, from henceforth, none be so hardy to tell or publish any false news or tales, whereby discord or occasion of discord or slander may grow between the King and his people, or the great men of the realm; and he that doth so shall be taken and kept in prison until he hath brought him into the court which was the first author of the tale."

This statute proceeds on the idea, that, by the common law, as well understood at the time, and enforced by the courts, the author of the tale was punishable by indictment—as undoubtedly was the propagator of it also—and the statute merely provided a means by which he should be effectually discovered and brought to justice. Bishop on Criminal Law, 5th ed. (1872), par. 473.

In 1778 Alexander Scott was indicted at the Old Bailey "for that he on the 23rd of April last, unlawfully, wickedly, and maliciously did publish false news, whereby discord, or occasion of discord, might grow between our lord the King and his people, or the great men of the realm, by publishing a certain printed paper, containing such false news, which said, printed paper is of the tenor following:—'In pursuance of His Majesty's order in council to me directed, these are to give public notice, that war with France will be proclaimed on Friday next, etc., etc.'" The defendant was a bill sticker; and it appearing on the trial that he had been imposed upon, and induced to stick up the bills containing the false matter believing it to be true whereas it was a forgery, he was acquitted. There does not seem to have been any doubt that the act with which he was charged was indictable. Scott's Case, 5 New Newgate Calendar 284.

Canadian decision.]—Hoaglin's Case is the first decision reported in Canada under this section of the Criminal Code.

It was there held by Harvey, J., that the publication of a placard stating that settlers from the United States are not wanted in Canada is an injury to the public interests and under sec. 136 of the Code the person wilfully and knowingly publishing such false statements is properly convicted of spreading false news. R. v. Hoaglin (1907), 12 Can. Cr. Cas. 226.

Piracy.

137. Every one is guilty of an indictable offence who does any act which amounts to piracy by the law of nations, and is liable,— **Piracy by the law of nations.**

(*a*) to the penalty of death, if in committing or attempting to commit such crime the offender murders, attempts to murder or wounds any person, or does any act by which the life of any person is likely to be endangered; **Punishment in case of violence to person.**

(*b*) to imprisonment for life in all other cases. 55-56 V., c. 29, s. 127. **Other cases.**

Piracy at common law.]—The offence of piracy at common law is nothing more than robbery upon the high seas; but by statutes passed at various times and still in force many artificial offences have been created which are to be deemed to amount to piracy. Roscoe Cr. Evid. 11th ed., 817.

Slave trading.]—By the Imperial statute, 5 Geo. IV., ch. 113, secs. 9 and 10, the carrying away, conveying, or removing of any person upon the high seas for the purpose of his being imported or brought into any place as a slave, or being sold or dealt with as such or the embarking or receiving on board any person for such purpose, is declared to be piracy. The provisions of that statute apply not only to acts done by British subjects in furtherance of the slave trade in England and the British colonies but to acts done by them outside of the British dominions. R. v. Zulueta, 1 C. & K. 215.

Evidence.]—The subject of a friendly foreign power may be punished for piracy committed upon British property. Roscoe Cr. Evid. 11th ed., 820.

Where several seamen on board a ship seized the captain and after putting him ashore carried away the ship and subsequently committed several piracies, it was held that the seizure of the captain and of the ship was an act of piracy. R. v. May, 2 East P.C. 796.

And where certain pilots had in collusion with the master of a vessel cut away a cable for the purpose of defrauding the underwriters for the benefit of the owners, it was held that they were rightly convicted of piratically stealing the cable. R. v. Curling, Russ. & Ry. 123.

But where the master of a vessel with goods on board ran the goods ashore and burned the ship with intent to defraud the owners and insurers, it was held that, as the accused held the goods under a special trust, he could not, before that trust was ended, be guilty of piracy by converting then to his own use. R. v. Mason, 2 East P.C. 796.

Extradition.]—Piracy is extradictable between Canada and the United States under the Ashburton treaty of 1843.

Piratical acts.

Penalty.

138. Every one is guilty of an indictable offence and liable to imprisonment for life who, within Canada, does any of the piratical acts specified in this section, or who, having done any of such piratical acts, comes or is brought within Canada without having been tried therefor, that is to say:—

British subject—hostility or robbery or adhering to King's enemies.

(*a*) Being a British subject, on the sea, or in any place within the jurisdiction of the Admiralty of England, under colour of any commission from any foreign prince or state, whether such prince or state is at war with His Majesty or not, or under pretense of authority from any person whomsoever commits any act of hostility or robbery against other British subjects, or during any war is in any way adherent to or gives aid to His Majesty's enemies;

Entering British ship and destroying goods.

(*b*) Whether a British subject or not, on the sea or in any place within the jurisdiction of the Admiralty of England, enters into any British ship, and throws overboard, or destroys any part of the goods belonging to such ship, or laden on board the same;

(*c*) Being on board any British ship on the sea or in any place within the jurisdiction of the Admiralty of England, **Certain acts done upon British ship.**

(i) turns enemy or rebel, and piratically runs away with the ship, or any boat, ordnance, ammunition or goods,

(ii) yields up voluntarily any ship, boat, ordnance, ammunition or goods to any pirate,

(iii) brings any seducing message from any pirate, enemy or rebel,

(iv) counsels or procures any persons to yield up or run away with any ship, goods or merchandise, or to turn pirate or to go over to pirates,

(v) lays violent hands on the commander of any such ship, in order to prevent him from fighting in defence of his ship and goods,

(vi) confines the master or commander of any such ship

(vii) makes or endeavours to make a revolt in the ship; or,

(*d*) Being a British subject in any part of the world, or whether a British subject or not, being in any part of His Majesty's dominions or on board a British ship, knowingly **British subject does certain acts.**

(i) furnishes any pirate with any ammunition or stores of any kind, **Pirate supplies.**

(ii) fits out any ship or vessel with a design to trade with or supply or correspond with any pirate, **Fitting out ship.**

(iii) conspires or corresponds with any pirate. 55-56 V., c. 29, s. 128. **Assisting pirate.**

Offence on the high seas.]—By sec. 591 it is enacted that proceedings for the trial and punishment of a person who is not a subject of His Majesty, and who is charged with any offence committed within the jurisdiction of the Admiralty of England shall not be instituted in any court in Canada except with the leave of the Governor-General and on his certificate that it is expedient that such proceedings should be instituted. In a recent Nova Scotia case, R. v. Heckman (1902), 5 Can. Cr. Cas. 242, it was held that a charge against a seaman on a British ship not a British subject, for inciting a revolt upon the ship while on the high seas cannot, if taken only under Code sec. 138, be made without the consent of the Governor-General, under sec. 591, obtained prior to the laying of the information. Mr. Justice Ritchie held further that if the proceedings for the offence are taken under the Merchant Shipping Act 1894 (Imp.), sec. 686, the consent of the Governor-General is not required and Code sec. 591 would not apply. But a different view was taken by Mr. Justice Weatherbe (now chief justice) who held that sec. 591 applies to the procedure in Canadian Courts in respect of offences committed within the Admiralty jurisdiction whether the proceedings are taken under the

Criminal Code or the Imperial Merchant Shipping Act or the Admiralty Offence Act, 1849 (Imp.).

Piratical act with violence.

139. Every one is guilty of an indictable offence and liable to suffer death who, in committing or attempting to commit any piratical act, assaults with intent to murder, or wounds, any person, or does any act likely to endanger the life of any person. 55-56 V., c. 29, s. 129.

Not resisting pirate.

140. Every one is guilty of an indictable offence and liable to six months' imprisonment, and to forfeit to the owner of the ship all wages then due to him, who, being a master, officer or seaman of any merchant ship which carries guns and arms, does not, when attacked by any pirate, fight and endeavour to defend himself and his vessel from being taken by such pirate, or who discourages others from defending the ship, if by reason thereof the ship falls into the hands of such pirate. 55-56 V., c. 29, s. 130.

Conveying Liquor on board His Majesty's Ships.

Penalty.

141. Every one is guilty of an offence and liable, on summary conviction before two justices, to a fine not exceeding fifty dollars for each offence, and in default of payment to imprisonment for a term not exceeding one month, with or without hard labour, who, without the previous consent of the officer commanding the ship or vessel,—

Offence.

Taking liquor on board ship.

(*a*) conveys any intoxicating liquor on board any of His Majesty's ships or vessels; or,

Attempting to take.

(*b*) approaches or hovers about any of His Majesty's ships or vessels for the purpose of conveying any such liquor on board thereof; or,

Delivering.

(*c*) gives or sells to any man in His Majesty's service, on board any such ship or vessel, any intoxicating liquor. 55-56 V., c. 29, s. 119.

Any officer in His Majesty's service, any warrant or petty officer in the navy, and any non-commissioned officer of marines may arrest without warrant any person found committing any of the offences mentioned in sec. 141. See sec. 651.

Intoxicating liquor.]—See statutory definition in sec. 2 (17).

PART III.

RESPECTING THE PRESERVATION OF PEACE IN THE VICINITY OF PUBLIC WORKS.

Interpretation.

142. In this Part, unless the context otherwise requires,— **Definitions.**

(a) 'this Part' means such section or sections thereof as are in force, by virtue of any proclamation, in the place with reference to which the Part is to be construed and applied; **'This Part.'**

(b) 'commissioner' means a commissioner under this Part; **'Commissioner.'**

(c) 'public work' includes any railway, canal, road, bridge or other work of any kind, and any mining operation constructed or carried on by the Government of Canada, or of any province of Canada, or by any municipal corporation, or by any incorporated company, or by private enterprise. R.S., c. 151, s. 1. **'Public work.'**

Commissioner.]—See sec. 2(42).

Proclamation.

143. The Governor in Council may, as often as occasion requires, declare, by proclamation, that upon and after a day therein named, this Part, or any section or sections thereof, shall be in force in any place in Canada in such proclamation designated, within the limits or in the vicinity whereof any public work is in course of construction, or in any place in the vicinity of any public work, within which he deems it necessary that this Part, or any section or sections thereof, should be in force; and this Part, or any such section or sections thereof, shall, upon and after the day named in such proclamation, take effect within the place or places designated therein. **Part may be declared in force.**

2. The Governor in Council may, in like manner, from time to time, declare this Part, or any section or sections thereof, to be no longer in force in any such place, and may again, from **Declared no longer in force.**

And again in force. time to time, declare this Part, or any section or sections thereof, to be in force therein.

No effect in city. 3. No such proclamation shall have effect within the limits of any city.

Judicial notice. 4. All courts, magistrates and justices shall take judicial notice of every such proclamation. R.S., c. 151, s. 2.

Weapons.

Delivery of arms to commissioner. **144.** On or before the day named in such proclamation, every person employed on or about the public work to which the same relates, shall bring and deliver up, to some commissioner or officer appointed for the purposes of this Part, every weapon in his possession, and shall obtain from such commissioner or officer a receipt for the same. R.S., c. 151, s. 3.

Seizure of arms not delivered. **145.** Every weapon found in the possession of any person employed, as aforesaid, after the day named in any proclamation and within the limits designated in such proclamation, may be seized by any justice, commissioner, constable or other peace officer, and shall be forfeited to the use of His Majesty. R.S., c. 151, s. 4.

Possessing weapons near public works. **146.** Every one employed upon or about any public work, within any place in which this Part is in force, who, upon or after the day named in such proclamation, keeps or has in his possession or under his care or control within any such place, any weapon, is liable on summary conviction to a penalty not exceeding four dollars and not less than two dollars for every such weapon found in his possession or under his care or control. R.S., c. 151, s. 5; 55-56 V., c. 29, s. 117.

Receiving or concealing arms with intent. **147.** Every one who, for the purpose of defeating the enforcement of this Part, receives or conceals, or aids in receiving or concealing, or procures to be received or concealed, within any place in which this Part is in force, any weapon belonging to or in the custody of any person employed on or about any public work, is liable, on summary conviction, to a penalty not exceeding one hundred dollars and not less than forty dollars; and a moiety of such penalty shall belong to the informer and the other moiety to His Majesty, for the public uses of Canada. R.S., c. 151, s. 6; 55-56 V., c. 29, s. 117.

Employees carrying weapons. **148.** Every person employed on any public work found carrying any weapon, within any place in which this Part is at the time in force, for purposes dangerous to the public peace, is guilty of an indictable offence. R.S., c. 151, s. 7.

149. Whenever this Part ceases to be in force within the place where any weapon has been delivered and detained in pursuance thereof, or whenever the owner or person lawfully entitled to any such weapon satisfies the commissioner that he is about to remove immediately from the limits within which this Part is at the time in force, the commissioner may deliver up to the owner or person authorized to receive the same, any such weapon, on production of the receipt given for it. R.S., c. 151, s. 11. **Return of weapons when Part ceases to be in force.**

Intoxicating Liquor.

150. (*As amended*, 1907.) Upon and after the day named in such proclamation and during such period as such proclamation remains in force, no person shall, at any place within the limits specified in the proclamation, sell, barter or, directly or indirectly, for any matter, thing, profit or reward, exchange, supply or dispose of, or shall give to any other person any intoxicating liquor; or shall expose, keep or have in his possession any intoxicating liquor intended to be dealt with in any such way. **Sale of liquor prohibited.**

2. The provisions of this section shall not extend to any person selling intoxicating liquor by wholesale, and not retailing it, if the said person is a licensed distiller or brewer; nor shall they apply where liquor is supplied for *bonâ fide* medicinal purposes upon the prescription of a duly qualified medical practitioner. R.S., c. 151, s. 13; 55-56 V., c. 29, s. 118; 6 & 7 E., c. 9, s. 2. **As to retail only.**

Intoxicating liquor.]—See statutory definition in sec. 2(17).

151. (*As amended*, 1907.) Every one who, by himself, his clerk, servant, agent or other person, violates any of the provisions of the last preceding section, is guilty of an offence against this Part and liable on summary conviction to a penalty of fifty dollars and costs, and, in default of payment, to imprisonment for a term not exceeding three months; and upon any subsequent conviction to a penalty of one hundred dollars and costs or to imprisonment for a term not exceeding six months, or to both, and, in default of payment of such penalty, to imprisonment, or to further imprisonment for a term not exceeding three months; and imprisonment in each case shall be either with **Penalty for contravention.**

or without hard labour. R.S., c. 151, s. 14; 55-56 V., c. 29, s. 118; 6 & 7 E., c. 9, s. 3.

Agent liable to same penalties as principal.

152. Every clerk, servant, agent or other person who, being in the employment of, or on the premises of another person, violates or assists in violating any of the said provisions for the person in whose employment or on whose premises he is, shall be equally guilty with such person, and shall be liable to the punishment mentioned in the last preceding section. R.S., c. 151, s. 15; 55-56 V., c. 29, s. 118.

Considera-tion given for purchase may be recovered.

153. Any payment or compensation, whether in money or securities for money, labour or property of any kind, for intoxicating liquor sold, bartered, exchanged, supplied or disposed of, contrary to the provisions aforesaid, shall be held to have been criminally received without consideration, and against law, equity and good conscience, and the amount or value thereof may be recovered from the receiver by the person making, paying or furnishing such payment or compensation. R.S., c. 151, s. 18.

Transfer for liquor void.

154. All sales, transfers, conveyances, liens and securities of every kind, which either in whole or in part have been made or given for or on account of intoxicating liquor sold, bartered, exchanged, supplied or disposed of contrary to such provisions, shall be void against all persons, and no right shall be acquired thereby.

No action on account of sale of liquor.

2. No action of any kind shall be maintained, either in whole or in part, for or on account of intoxicating liquor sold, bartered, exchanged, supplied or disposed of, contrary to the said provisions. R.S., c. 151, s. 18.

PART IV.

OFFENCES AGAINST THE ADMINISTRATION OF LAW AND JUSTICE.

Interpretation.

155. In this Part, unless the context otherwise requires,— Definitions.

(*a*) 'the government' includes the government of Canada, and the government of any province of Canada, as well as His Majesty in the right of Canada or of any province thereof, and the Commissioners of the Transcontinental Railway; 'The government.'

(*b*) 'official or person in the employment of the government' and 'official or employee of the government,' extend to and include the Commissioners of the Transcontinental Railway and the persons holding office as such commissioners, and the engineers, officials, officers, employees and servants of the said commissioners; 'Official or employee of the government.'

(*c*) 'office' includes every office in the gift of the Crown or of any officer appointed by the Crown, and all commissions, civil, naval and military, and all places or employments in any public department or office whatever, and all deputations to any such office and every participation in the profits of any office or deputation. 55-56 V., c. 29, ss. 133 and 137; 6 E. VII., c. 7, s. 1. 'Office.'

Corruption and Disobedience.

156. Every one is guilty of an indictable offence and liable to fourteen years' imprisonment who,— Penalty.

(*a*) holding any judicial office, or being a member of Parliament or of a legislature, corruptly accepts or obtains, or agrees to accept, or attempts to obtain for himself or any other person, any money or valuable consideration, office, place, or employment on account of anything already done or omitted, or to be afterwards done or omitted, by him in his judicial capacity, or in his capacity as such member; or, Judicial, etc., officer accepting or obtaining office for consideration.

Giving or offering bribe.

(*b*) corruptly gives or offers to any such person or to any other person, any such bribe as aforesaid on account of any such act or omission. 55-56 V., c. 29, s. 131.

No one holding any judicial office shall be prosecuted for the offence of judicial corruption, as defined in this section, without the leave of the Attorney-General of Canada. Section 593.

Penalty.

157. Every one is guilty of an indictable offence and liable to fourteen years' imprisonment who,—

Officer taking bribe.

(*a*) being a justice, peace officer, or public officer, employed in any capacity for the prosecution or detection or punishment of offenders, corruptly accepts or obtains, or agrees to accept or attempts to obtain for himself, or for any other person, any money or valuable consideration, office, place or employment, with the intent to interfere corruptly with the due administration of justice, or to procure or facilitate the commission of any crime, or to protect from detection or punishment any person having committed or intending to commit any crime; or,

Offering bribe to officer.

(*b*) corruptly gives or offers to any officer aforesaid any such bribe as aforesaid with any such intent. 55-56 V., c. 29, s. 132.

Peace officer or public officer.]—See definitions in sec. 2, sub-secs. (26) and (29).

Extortion by public officers, justices, etc.]—In R. v. Tisdale (1860), 20 U.C.Q.B. 272, two justices of the peace were tried before McLean, J., and a jury and found guilty upon an indictment for extortion in exacting from a person charged on a preliminary enquiry before them with a felony 25 shillings as fees due to them as justices and for fees for his arrest. The magistrates had held that the charge was not sustained by the evidence, but had collected the costs above mentioned from the accused as a condition of his discharge.

Robinson, C.J., in delivering the judgment of the court, said:—"They cannot set up as a defence such extraordinary ignorance of the law as it would be necessary to believe they laboured under, before it could be credited that they had fallen into a mistake as to their right to charge the defendant with costs in such a case and under such circumstances."

Extortion is the taking of money or any valuable thing by any public officer by colour of his office and otherwise than in good faith on a mistake as to the law, where none or less is due or before it is due. 5 Encyc. Laws of England (1898), p. 262; Stephen's Dig. Cr. Law, 5th ed., p. 88.

The offence is not constituted by demand only without actual receipt of the illegal fee. Ibid; Parsons v. Crabb, 31 U.C.C.P. 151.

The statute of 1275, 3 Edw. I., ch. 26, which deals with both civil and criminal process therefor is declaratory of the common law in enacting the offence of extortion by the King's officers to be indictable; the offence is a common law misdemeanour punishable, on indictment or information, by fine and imprisonment and removal from office. Ibid. The repeal of that statute as regards Ontario by Ont. Stat. 1902, 2 Edw. VII., ch. 1, is in terms as well as constitutionally limited to such portions of same as are within the provincial legislative authority. Stat. Law Revision Act (Ont.), 1902, ch. 1, sec. 2.

Justices of the peace and their clerks, and clerks of the peace are liable to indictment for extortion. Anon. (1700), 12 Modern R. 512.

The indictment should specify a sum certain as having been extorted: R. v. Burdett, 1 Ld. Raym. 149; R. v. Gilham (1795), 6 T.R. 265; and when the extortion is of an excess above the legal fee, the sum legally payable should be specified in the indictment. Lake's Case, 3 Leon. 268.

It was formerly considered necessary that the indictment should contain the words "extorsively and in colour of office." R. v. Baynes, 2 Salk. 680; R. v. Cumberland Justices, 11 Mod. R. 80.

Form of indictment.]—That W., late of, etc., on the day of , at the town of , in the county of , then being one of the of the said county, by colour of his said office unlawfully, unjustly and extorsively did exact, extort, receive and have, of and from one Y., the sum of of lawful money of Canada as and for a pretended fee of him the said W. for, etc., whereas in truth and in fact no fee whatever was then due to the said W. in that behalf, to the great damage of the said Y. and against the peace of our Lord the King, his Crown and dignity.

Oppression by public officers.]—At common law every public officer commits a misdemeanour who, in the exercise, or under colour of exercising the duties of his office, does any illegal act, or abuses any discretionary power with which he is invested by law from an improper motive, the existence of which motive may be inferred either from the nature of the act, or from the circumstances of the case. But an illegal exercise of authority, caused by a mistake as to the law, made in good faith, is not a misdemeanour within this rule. Burbidge's Digest of Crim. Law (1890), article 148.

If the illegal act consists in inflicting upon any person any bodily harm, imprisonment, or other injury, not being extortion, the offence is called "oppression."

So if A. and B., justices of the peace with licensing powers refuse licenses to the keepers of public houses, because they refuse to vote as the justices wish, A. and B. commit oppression.

And if A., a justice, acting as such, orders B. to be whipped, without any such proof or information as the law requires, A. commits oppression.

Evidence of corrupt motive must be adduced in order to obtain leave to exhibit a criminal information against a justice of the peace for malfeasance of office. The King v. Currie, 11 Can. Cr. Cas. 343.

British Columbia Crown Rules.]—The British Columbia Crown Rules 9-11 are as follows:—

(9) With the exception of ex-officio informations filed by the Attorney-General on behalf of the Crown, no criminal information or information in the nature of a quo warranto shall be exhibited or received in the Supreme Court without an express order of a judge of the Supreme Court, nor shall any process be issued upon any information until the person procuring such information to be exhibited, shall have filed in the registry of the Supreme Court a recognizance in the penalty of $100, effectually to prosecute such information, and to abide by and observe such orders as the court shall direct; such recognizance to be entered into before some justice of the peace or registrar of the Supreme Court.

(10) No application shall be made for a criminal information against a justice of the peace for misconduct in his magisterial capacity unless a notice containing a distinct statement of the grievances or acts of misconduct complained of be served personally on him or left at his residence with some member of his household six days before the time named in it for making the application.

(11) The application for a criminal information shall be made to the court by a motion for an order nisi within a reasonable time after the offence complained of, and if the application be made against a justice of the peace for misconduct in his magisterial capacity, the applicant must depose on affidavit to his belief that the defendant was actuated by corrupt motives, and further, if for an unjust conviction, that the defendant is innocent of the charge.

Frauds upon the government.

Penalty.

158. Every one is guilty of an indictable offence and liable to a fine of not less than one hundred dollars, and not exceeding one thousand dollars, and to imprisonment for a term not exceeding one year and not less than one month, and in default of payment of such fine to imprisonment for a further time not exceeding six months who,—

Making offer or gift to unduly influence officer.

(*a*) makes any offer, proposal, gift, loan or promise, or gives or offers any compensation or consideration, directly or indirectly, to any official or person in the employment of the government, or to any member of his family, or to any person under his control or for his benefit, with intent to obtain the assistance or influence of such official or person to promote either the procuring of any contract with the government for the performance of any work, the doing of any thing, or the furnishing of any goods, effects, food or materials, the execution of any such contract, or the payment of the price or consideration stipulated therein, or any part thereof, or of any aid or subsidy payable in respect thereof; or,

Accepting such offer or gift.

(*b*) being an official or person in the employment of the government, directly or indirectly, accepts or agrees to accept, or allows to be accepted by any person under his control or for his benefit, any such offer, proposal, gift, loan, promise, compensation or consideration; or,

Procuring withdrawal of tenders.

(*c*) in the case of tenders being called for by or on behalf of the government for the performance of any work, the doing of any thing, or the furnishing of any goods, effects, food or materials, directly or indirectly, by himself, or by the agency of any other person on his behalf, with intent to obtain the contract therefor, either for himself or for any other person, offers to make, or makes, any gift, loan, offer or promise, or offers or gives any consideration or compensation whatsoever to any person tendering for such work or other service, or to any member of his family or other person for his benefit, to induce such person to withdraw his tender for such work or other service, or to compensate or reward him for having withdrawn such tender; or,

(*d*) in case of tendering for the performance of any work, the doing of any thing, or the furnishing of any goods, effects, food or materials, for the government when tenders are called for by or on behalf of the government, accepts or receives, directly or indirectly, or permits, or allows to be accepted or received by any member of his family, or by any other person under his control, or for his benefit, any such gift, loan, offer, promise, consideration or compensation, as a consideration or reward for withdrawing or for having withdrawn such tender; or,

Accepting gift, etc., as consideration for withdrawing tender.

(*e*) being an official or employee of the government, receives, directly or indirectly, whether personally or by or through any member of his family or person under his control or for his benefit, any gift, loan, promise, compensation or consideration whatsoever, either in money or otherwise, from any person whomsoever, for assisting or favouring any individual in the transaction of any business whatsoever with the government, or who gives or offers any such gift, loan, promise, compensation or consideration; or,

Officer accepting or person making any gift concerning government business.

(*f*) by reason of, or under the pretense of, possessing influence with the government, or with any minister or official thereof, demands, exacts or receives from any person, any compensation, fee or reward, for procuring from the government the payment of any claim, or of any portion thereof, or for procuring or furthering the appointment of himself, or of any other person, to any office, place or employment, or for procuring or furthering the obtaining for himself or any other person, of any grant, lease or other benefit from the government; or offers, promises or pays to such person, under the circumstances and for the causes aforesaid, or any of them, any such compensation, fee or reward; or,

Compensation for procuring settlement of claim.

(*g*) having dealings of any kind with the government through any department thereof, pays to any employee or official of the government, or to any member of the family of such employee or official, or to any person under

Giving reward or commission to officer.

his control or for his benefit, any commission or reward; or within one year before or after such dealings, without the express permission in writing of the head of the department with which such dealings have been had, the proof of which permission shall lie upon him, makes any gift, loan, or promise of any money, matter or thing, to any such employee or other person aforesaid; or,

Acceptance. *(h)* being an employee or official of the government, demands, exacts or receives from such person, directly or indirectly, by himself, or by or through any other person for his benefit, or permits or allows any member of his family, or any person under his control, to accept or receive

Commission. (i) any such commission or reward, or

Gift within a year. (ii) within the said period of one year, without the express permission in writing of the head of the department with which such dealings have been had, the proof of which permission shall lie upon him, accepts or receives any such gift, loan or promise; or,

Contractor subscribing, etc., to election fund of candidate. *(i)* having any contract with the government for the performance of any work, the doing of any thing, or the furnishing of any goods, effects, food or materials, and having or expecting to have any claim or demand against the government by reason of such contract, directly or indirectly, by himself or by any person on his behalf, subscribes, furnishes or gives, or promises to subscribe, furnish or give, any money or other valuable consideration for the purpose of promoting the election of any candidate, or of any number, class or party of candidates, to a legislature or to Parliament, or with the intent in any way of influencing or affecting the result of a provincial or Dominion election.

Penalty if value exceeds $1,000. 2. If the value of the amount or thing paid, offered, given, loaned, promised, received or subscribed, as the case may be, exceeds one thousand dollars, the offender under this section is liable to any fine not exceeding such value. 55-56 V., c. 29, s. 133; 56 V., c. 32, s. 1.

Limitation.]—No prosecution for this offence shall be commenced after the expiration of two years from its commission. Section 1140 (b).

Misfeasance in government office.]—Misbehaviour in office is an indictable offence at common law and it is not essential that pecuniary damage should have resulted to the public by reason of such irregular conduct, nor that the defendant should have acted from corrupt motives. R. v.

John R. Arnoldi (1893), 23 O.R. 201. A man accepting an office of trust concerning the public, especially, if attended with profit, is answerable criminally to the King for misbehaviour in his office. R. v. Bembridge, 22 St. Tr. 1; 3 Doug. 327. And where there is a breach of trust, fraud or imposition in a matter concerning the public, though as between individuals it would only be actionable, yet as between the King and the subject it is indictable. Ibid.

On the trial of an indictment charging a misdemeanour against the Principal Registrar of Deeds of a County and his deputy jointly for misfeasance in not recording deeds in their due order, it was objected that they could not be indicted together in one indictment, and legally convicted at one and the same time; but it was held by the full court on the points reserved, that though the principal might perhaps not be indictable for the wrongful act of his deputy committed in his absence and without his knowledge or consent, it is a different thing when he is present and knowing and consenting to the act; that in such a case both are wrong doers and *particeps criminis.* It was also contended, in the same case, that the deputy registrar could not be legally convicted so long as his principal legally held the office; but it was held that the deputy was liable to be indicted not only while the principal holds office, but even after the deputy himself has been dismissed from his office. R. v. Benjamin (1853), 4 U.C.C.P. 179.

159. Every person convicted of an offence under the last preceding section shall be incapable of contracting with the Government, or of holding any contract or office with, from, or under it, or of receiving any benefit under any such contract. 55-56 V., c. 29, s. 134.

Other consequences.

160. Every public officer is guilty of an indictable offence and liable to five years' imprisonment who, in the discharge of the duties of his office, commits any fraud or breach of trust affecting the public, whether such fraud or breach of trust would have been criminal or not if committed against a private person. 55-56 V., c. 29, s. 135.

Breach of trust by public officer.

See notes to secs. 157 and 158.

161. Every one is guilty of an indictable offence and liable to a fine not exceeding one thousand dollars and not less than one hundred dollars, and to imprisonment for a term not exceeding two years and not less than one month, and in default of payment of such fine to imprisonment for a further term not exceeding six months, who directly or indirectly,—

Municipal corruption.

Penalty.

(*a*) makes any offer, proposal, gift, loan, promise or agreement to pay or give any money or other material compensation or consideration to any member of a municipal council, whether the same is to enure to his own advantage or to the advantage of any other person, for the purpose of inducing such member either to vote or to abstain from

Corruptly offering gift to municipal councillor to vote or abstain from voting.

voting at any meeting of the council of which he is a member or at any meeting of a committee of such council, in favour of or against any measure, motion, resolution or question submitted to such council or committee; or,

Corruptly offering gift to secure aid of municipal officers.

(*b*) makes any offer, proposal, gift, loan, promise or agreement to pay or give any money or other material compensation or consideration to any member or to any officer of a municipal council for the purpose of inducing him to aid in procuring or preventing the passing of any vote or the granting of any contract or advantage in favour of any person; or,

Other corrupt proposals to officers.

(*c*) makes any offer, proposal, gift, loan, promise or agreement to pay or give any money or other material compensation or consideration to any officer of a municipal council for the purpose of inducing him to perform or abstain from performing or to aid in procuring or preventing the performance of, any official act; or,

Members of council corruptly accepting gift.

(*d*) being a member or officer of a municipal council, accepts or consents to accept any such offer, proposal, gift, loan, promise, agreement, compensation or consideration in this section mentioned; or in consideration thereof votes or abstains from voting in favour of or against any measure, motion, resolution or question, or performs or abstains from performing any official act; or,

Use of threats or fraud to influence vote.

(*e*) attempts by any threat, deceit, suppression of the truth or other unlawful means to influence any member of a municipal council in giving or withholding his vote in favour of or against any measure, motion, resolution or question, or in not attending any meeting of the municipal council of which he is a member, or of any committee thereof; or,

Threats or fraud to secure or prevent vote or official act.

(*f*) attempts by any such means as in the last preceding paragraph mentioned to influence any member or any officer of a municipal council to aid in procuring or preventing the passing of any vote or the granting of any contract or advantage in favour of any person, or to perform or abstain from performing, or to aid in procuring or preventing the performance of, any official act. 55-56 V., c. 29, s. 136.

Limitation.]—No prosecution for an offence under this section shall be commenced after the expiration of two years from its commission. Section 1140(b).

162. Every one is guilty of an indictable offence who, directly or indirectly,— Offence.

(*a*) sells or agrees to sell any appointment to or resignation of any office, or any consent to any such appointment or resignation, or receives, or agrees to receive, any reward or profit from the sale thereof; or, Selling office.

(*b*) purchases or gives any reward or profit for the purchase of any such appointment, resignation or consent, or agrees or promises to do so; Purchasing office.

and in addition to any other penalty incurred, forfeits any right which he may have in the office and is disabled for life from holding the same. 55-56 V., c. 29, s. 137. Forfeiture.

Punishment.]—No specific punishment being provided for an offence under this section, it falls within sec. 1052, which provides that "every person convicted of an indictable offence for which no imprisonment is specially provided shall be liable to imprisonment for five years.

163. Every one is guilty of an indictable offence who, directly or indirectly,— Offence.

(*a*) receives or agrees to receive any reward or profit for any interest, request or negotiation about any office, or under pretense of using any such interest, making any such request or being concerned in any such negotiation; or, Receiving reward for corrupt municipal act.

(*b*) gives or procures to be given any profit or reward, or makes or procures to be made any agreement for the giving of any profit or reward, for any such interest, request or negotiation as aforesaid; or, Giving or procuring any reward.

(*c*) solicits, recommends or negotiates in any manner as to any appointment to or resignation of any office in expectation of any reward or profit; or, Being a party to negotiations.

(*d*) keeps any office or place for transacting or negotiating any business relating to vacancies in, or the sale or purchase of, or appointment to or resignation of offices. 55-56 V., c. 29, s. 137. Keeping office for the purpose.

Punishment.]—No specific punishment being provided for an offence under this section, it falls within sec. 1052, which provides that "every person convicted of an indictable offence for which no imprisonment is specially provided shall be liable to imprisonment for five years."

164. Every one is guilty of an indictable offence and liable to one year's imprisonment who, without lawful excuse, disobeys any Act of the Parliament of Canada or of any legislature in Canada by wilfully doing any act which it forbids, Disobeying a statute.

or omitting to do any act which it requires to be done, unless some penalty or other mode of punishment is expressly provided by law. 55-56 V., c. 29, s. 138.

Evidence.]—A wilful disobedience of the statute must be shewn. Re E. J. Parke (1899), 3 Can. Cr. Cas. 122, 30 Ont. R. 498.

If the magistrate holding the preliminary enquiry should be of opinion that the act was not "wilfully" committed, but under a misapprehension of the law, he would not be bound to commit. Ex parte MacMahon, 48 J.P. 70; R. v. Meehan (No. 2) (1902), 5 Can. Cr. Cas., at p. 321.

The manager of a corporation is not criminally liable as for wilful disobedience of a statute under sec. 164 in respect of the corporation's neglect not due to any active participation on his part, to perform a statutory duty imposed upon it. R. v. Hays (1907), 12 Can. Cr. Cas. 423.

A person who without lawful excuse wilfully and corruptly votes more than once at a municipal election for city aldermen under the Ontario Municipal Act is guilty of an indictable offence by virtue of this section. R. v. Meehan (No. 2), 5 Can. Cr. Cas. 312.

Wrongfully voting twice at an election would not be indictable at common law unless prohibited by statute, and, semble, every contempt of a statute is indictable at common law where no other mode of punishment is provided. Ibid.

Disobeying orders of court.

165. Every one is guilty of an indictable offence and liable to one year's imprisonment who, without lawful excuse, disobeys any lawful order, other than for the payment of money, made by any court of justice, or by any person or body of persons authorized by any statute to make or give such order, unless some penalty is imposed, or other mode of proceeding is expressly provided, by law. 55-56 V., c. 29, s. 139.

Misconduct of officers entrusted with execution of writs.

166. Every one is guilty of an indictable offence and liable to a fine and imprisonment who, being a sheriff, deputy-sheriff, coroner, elisor, bailiff, constable or other officer entrusted with the execution of any writ, warrant or process, wilfully misconducts himself in the execution of the same, or wilfully, and without the consent of the person in whose favour the writ, warrant or process was issued, makes any false return thereto. 55-56 V., c. 29, s. 143.

At common law.]—Every malfeasance or culpable nonfeasance of an officer of justice with relation to his office was a misdemeanour at common law and punishable with fine or imprisonment, or both. 1 Russ. Cr., 6th ed., 416.

Evidence.]—On a charge against a constable for negligently permitting an escape, the warrant of commitment may be proved either by its production, or, after proving the service upon the accused of a notice to produce it, by parol or other secondary evidence of its contents. It should then be proved that the warrant was delivered to the defendant and that he was one of the peace officers to whom it was addressed, and that the defendant had the person against whom the warrant was issued in actual custody under it. The escape from custody must then be proved, and the law thereupon presumes the defendant's negligence. 1 Hale 600.

But the presumption is rebuttable, and it is open to the defendant to shew that the escape was not due to his negligence, that the person under arrest rescued himself by force or was forcibly rescued by others and that the defendant made fresh pursuit after him for the purpose of recapturing him. Archbold Crim. Evid. (1900), 983.

in the discretion of the court (sec. 1029).

Punishment.]—Imprisonment may be for five years (sec. 1052) or fine

Peace Officers.

Neglect to aid peace officers in arresting offenders.

167. Every one is guilty of an indictable offence and liable to six months' imprisonment who, having reasonable notice that he is required to assist any sheriff, deputy-sheriff, mayor or other head officer, justice, magistrate, or peace officer, in the execution of his duty in arresting any person, or in preserving the peace, without reasonable excuse omits to do so. 55-56 V., c. 29, s. 142.

Obstructing public officer.

168. Every one is guilty of an indictable offence and liable to ten years' imprisonment who resists or wilfully obstructs any public officer in the execution of his duty or any person acting in aid of such officer. 55-56 V., c. 29, s. 144.

Public officer.]—See sec. 2(29) for statutory definition.

Resisting a de facto public officer.]—In Bishop on Criminal Law, sec. 464, under the head "Resisting or assaulting officers de facto," it is said:—"The difficult question is whether third persons are indictable for resisting or for the aggravated offence of assaulting a mere officer de facto. And, though the decisions on it are not harmonious, the better opinion is that they are, the law not permitting them to test in this way the claim to an office of one who exercises it under an apparent right. Other methods of testing the right are open."

Obstructing peace officer.

169. Every one who resists or wilfully obstructs,—

(a) any peace officer in the execution of his duty or any person acting in aid of such officer;

Person executing process.

(b) any person in the lawful execution of any process against any lands or goods or in making any lawful distress or seizure;

is guilty of an offence punishable on indictment or on summary conviction and liable if convicted on indictment to two years' imprisonment, and, on summary conviction before two justices, to six months' imprisonment with hard labour, or to a fine of one hundred dollars. 55-56 V., c. 29, s. 144.

Peace officer.]—See sec. 2(26) for statutory definition.

Obstruction.]—In an English case under a similar statute it was said that the obstruction need not necessarily be a physical obstruction. Bastable v. Little, 23 Times L.R. 38.

Where a bystander states to other bystanders, in the hearing of a police officer making an arrest for drunkenness, that the person being arrested is not drunk, such does not constitute the offence of obstructing a peace officer, if the statement was made bonâ fide and in the belief of its truth. If, in an unwarranted attempt of the police to arrest the bystander, the latter strikes a policeman, he is not guilty of assault upon a peace officer in the execution of his duty, for the policeman had no duty to arrest him. The King v. Cook, 11 Can. Cr. Cas. 32.

Process against goods.]—Where the process of an inferior court is void by reason of its containing a direction to a peace officer to seize certain goods at a place outside of the territorial jurisdiction of the court, such process is insufficient upon which to base a conviction for resisting the officer in its execution. R. v. Finlay (1901), 4 Can. Cr. Cas. 539 (Man.).

Where a bailiff obtained possession of goods under a writ of replevin, but at the request of the party in whose possession they were seized they were given by the bailiff into the possession of a third party, the latter giving the bailiff an undertaking or agreement to deliver him the goods on demand, it was held that in attempting to retake the goods in the possession of the third party the bailiff was not acting in the execution of any "process," but merely upon the undertaking. R. v. Carley, 18 C.L.T. 26.

Seizure under lien contract.]—The re-taking of possession by the vendor under a contract for the conditional sale of chattels is not within the term "lawful distress or seizure" as here used, and an obstruction of the vendor's bailiff in regaining possession is not an offence under this section. R. v. Shand (1904), 8 Can. Cr. Cas. 45, 7 O.L.R. 190.

A "lawful siezure" in connection with such provisions must be something ejusdem generis, a seizure made in due course of or by the authority of law. The word itself denotes a taking of that character and is not apt to describe the recaption or resumption of possession of goods by the mere act of the owner: Sweet's Law Dictionary, pp. 672, 749; Bouvier's Law Dictionary, vol. 2, pp. 831, 976.

Where goods are improperly detained by one in defiance of his agreement to yield them up to the owner with or without demand, and the owner can acquire possession peaceably, he may do so. If he attempts to take possession forcibly and in a riotous manner, he becomes himself a breaker of the law, as much so as one who attempts to take possession of real property by a forcible entry, contrary to 5 Rich. II., Stat. 1, ch. 8, even when it has been agreed that he was to re-enter. Edwick v. Hawkes (1881), 18 Ch.D. 199; and see Beddall v. Maitland (1881), 17 Ch.D. 174. If resistance is offered or possession refused he should have recourse to his action, and the Code would then have its full force in making unlawful any resistance to seizure made in due course of law. That is what is meant by a lawful seizure. It was never intended to enlarge the civil rights or powers of individuals, or to convert a breach of contract or resistance to private force into a criminal offence. Ibid.

Summary convictions or summary trials procedure.]—The offence of obstructing a peace officer is also dealt with by sec. 773(e) in Part XVI. relating to summary trials of indictable offences. Section 781 provides a maximum penalty for the offence, when dealt with under sec. 773, of 6 months' imprisonment and a fine of $100 and costs.

As the penalty on summary conviction cannot be both fine and imprisonment, the question has arisen whether a magistrate having "summary trials" powers must not be guided by them to the exclusion of the power here given of summary conviction by two justices and the general authority given by sec. 604 to police magistrates to exercise the powers of two justices. There is a conflict of opinion as will be seen by the following cases, which leaves the question still unsettled.

In R. v. Crossen (1899), 3 Can. Cr. Cas. 153 (Man.), it was held by the Court of Queen's Bench of Manitoba that this offence could only be tried by a "magistrate" having the powers of two justices as set forth in sec. 771 by following the procedure as to "summary trials," and that, where the charge was brought before an official empowered to proceed on a "summary trial" only upon the consent of the accused, the "summary convictions" clauses of the Code did not enable such official to proceed summarily as a justice of the peace.

That decision is followed in R. v. Carmichael (1902), 7 Can. Cr. Cas. 167 by Judge Weatherbe, now chief justice of Nova Scotia.

It is opposed however to the British Columbia cases of R. v. Nelson (1901), 4 Can. Cr. Cas. 461 and R. v. Jack (No. 2) (1902), 5 Can. Cr. Cas. 304, 9 B.C.R. 19.

In R. v. Nelson, Mr. Justice Drake held that the accused can be tried under the summary convictions clauses, before a police magistrate and that the provision of this clause (now sec. 169) of the Code is not limited by Code secs. 773 and 778 as to summary trials.

In R. v. Jack (No. 2) (1902), 5 Can. Cr. Cas. 304, Mr. Justice Walkem, of the Supreme Court of British Columbia, held that the offence of obstructing a peace officer in the performance of his duty, where an assault upon the officer is not also charged, may be summarily tried either by two justices of the peace or a police magistrate under the summary convictions part of the Code by virtue of sec. 169; and that the latter section is not controlled by the provisions of secs. 773 and 781 as to the summary trial of the like offence before a magistrate with the consent of the accused.

In the opinion of Walkem, J., the punishment on summary conviction is limited to that specified in sec. 169. Section 781 providing a different punishment on a trial before a magistrate with the consent of the accused would have no application where the procedure under the summary convictions clauses was followed.

Semble, if the charge were for an assault of the officer in the performance of his duty, secs. 773 and 781 would then apply and not sec. 169.

In the Province of British Columbia the magistrate has absolute jurisdiction to proceed under the summary trials part (LV.) by sec. 784 (3) without the consent of the accused, and to award both fine and imprisonment under sec. 776.

Distress for rent.]—It has always been lawful for a tenant before the goods seized under a distress warrant have been impounded to resist their seizure, or to rescue them if there is no rent due.

But it is a general rule that no rescue can be made of a distress after the goods are impounded, for then they are in the custody of the law. Am. & Eng. Encyc., 2nd ed., vol. 9, p. 656. And see Rex v. Bradshaw (1835), 7 C. & P. 233, 236; Reg. v. Brenan (1854), 6 Cox Cr. Cas. 381; Reg. v. Pigott (1851), 1 Ir. C.L. Rep. 471, 478.

It is therefore necessary for the prosecution to prove that rent was due and in arrear before a conviction can be made under this section for the offence of wilfully obstructing a lawful distress. On such a charge evidence is admissible for the defence in proof that no rent was due. R. v. Harron (1903), 7 Can. Cr. Cas. 543, 6 O.L.R. 668.

Misleading Justice.

Definition of perjury.

170. Perjury is an assertion as to a matter of fact, opinion, belief or knowledge, made by a witness in a judicial proceeding as part of his evidence, upon oath or affirmation, whether such evidence is given in open court, or by affidavit or otherwise, and whether such evidence is material or not, such assertion being known to such witness to be false, and being intended by him to mislead the court, jury or person holding the proceeding.

Subornation.

2. Subornation of perjury is counselling or procuring a person to commit any perjury which is actually committed.

Evidence.

3. Evidence in this section includes evidence given on the *voir dire* and evidence given before a grand jury. 55-56 V., c. 29, s. 145.

Judicial proceeding.]—An examination for discovery is a "judicial proceeding" as defined by this section, but the court has a discretion to refuse to hear a charge of perjury alleged in respect of civil proceedings while such proceedings are pending. R. v. Thickens (1906), 11 Can. Cr. Cas. 274.

False oath before de facto legal tribunal.]—It is perjury under the Code to give false testimony before a justice of the peace holding a judicial proceeding under a provincial law, although the justice was by the terms of that law disqualified from hearing the charge because he was not a resident of the county in which the alleged offence took place. Drew v. The King, 6 Can. Cr. Cas. 424, 33 Can. S.C.R. 228, affirming Drew v. The King, 6 Can. Cr. Cas. 241.

Materiality.]—Under the Code, the giving of false evidence constitutes perjury, whether such evidence is material or not, if the false assertion were known to such witness to be false, and intended by the witness to mislead the court, jury, or person holding the proceeding.

Statutory declaration.]—A false statement, made in a statutory declaration administered under the "Canada Evidence Act," may be the subject of a charge akin to perjury under Code sec. 175, for the object of sec. 36 of the Evidence Act, was to provide a means by which certain statements not authorized to be made on oath could be verified.

At common law.]—It has always been an offence at common law for a competent witness upon oath in a judicial proceeding, before a court of competent jurisdiction, to give evidence material to the issue, which he believes to be false. The common law, however, stopped there and took no notice of false statements, whether made upon oath or not, made under other conditions. The perjury had also to be in a judicial proceeding before a competent tribunal. R. v. Townsend, 10 Cox C.C. 356; R. v. Row (1864), 14 U.C.C.P. 307; R. v. Baker, [1895] 1 Q.B. 797. And it was therefore formerly the law that false evidence given upon an examination in the absence of the authority competent to hold such examination was not perjury. R. v. Lloyd, L.R. 19 Q.B.D. 213; R. v. Gibson, 7 Revue Legale (Que.) 573.

Known to be false.]—The false oath must be taken deliberately and intentionally, for if done from inadvertence or mistake it cannot amount to voluntary and corrupt perjury. 1 Hawk., ch. 69, sec. 2. Where perjury is assigned on an affidavit, the part on which the perjury is assigned may be explained by reference to the remainder of the affidavit. 1 Sid. 419.

The evidence of the false statement must be clear and precise and not ambiguous. R. v. Bird, 17 Cox C.C. 387.

Intended to mislead.]—Although an "intent to mislead" is an essential ingredient of the offence, a charge which does not specifically allege such intent may be sufficient if it gives to the accused notice that he is charged with having "falsely, wilfully and corruptly" sworn to, or solemnly declared a statement to the effect and in the words set forth. R. v. Skelton (1898), 4 Can. Cr. Cas. 467; 2 N.W.T. Rep. 210, 215; R. v. Dewar, 2 N.W.T. Rep. 194; Cr. Code, sec. 852(3).

Contradictory evidence.]—If the evidence adduced in proof of the crime of perjury consist of two opposing statements of the prisoner and nothing more, he cannot be convicted; for if only one was delivered under oath, it must be presumed, from the solemnity of the sanction, that that declaration was the truth, and the other an error or a falsehood, though the latter being inconsistent with what he has sworn may form important evidence, *with other circumstances*, against him. 1 Greenleaf on Evidence, 259. And if both the contradictory statements were delivered under oath, there is still nothing to shew which of them is false, where no other evidence of the falsity is given.

If a person swears one thing at one time, and another at another, he cannot be convicted where it is not possible to tell which is the true and which is the false. R. v. Jackson, 1 Lewin C.C. 270. Nor is it a necessary consequence that a person has committed perjury when he has sworn on both occasions to conflicting statements, for there are cases in which a person might very honestly and conscientiously swear to a particular fact from the best of his recollection and belief, and from other circumstances at a subsequent time be convinced that he was wrong, and swear to the reverse, without meaning to swear falsely either time. Ibid., per Holroyd, J.

Joint affidavit.]—A joint affidavit made by the defendant and one D. stated: "Each for himself maketh oath and saith that he this deponent is not aware of any adverse claim to or occupation of said lot." The defendant having been convicted of perjury on this latter allegation, it was held that there was neither ambiguity or doubt in what each defendant said, but that each in substance stated that he was not aware of any adverse claim to or occupation of said lot. R. v. Atkinson (1866), 17 U.C.C.P. 295. And it has been held that a statutory declaration made jointly by several persons that they know certain alleged facts is to be construed as a statement by each of them severally that he knows the matters alleged. R. v. Skelton (1898), 4 Can. Cr. Cas. 467 (N.W.T.).

171. Every person is a witness within the meaning of the last preceding section who actually gives his evidence, whether he was competent to be a witness or not, and whether his evidence was admissible or not. *Witness defined.*

2. Every proceeding is judicial within the meaning of the last preceding section which is held in or under the authority of any court of justice, or before a grand jury, or before either the Senate or House of Commons of Canada, or any committee *Judicial proceeding.*

of either the Senate or House of Commons, or before any legislative council, legislative assembly or house of assembly or any committee thereof, empowered by law to administer an oath, or before any justice, or any arbitrator or umpire, or any person or body of persons authorized by law or by any statute in force for the time being to make an inquiry and take evidence therein upon oath, or before any legal tribunal by which any legal right or liability can be established, or before any person acting as a court, justice or tribunal, having power to hold such judicial proceeding, whether duly constituted or not, and whether the proceeding was duly instituted or not before such court or person so as to authorize it or him to hold the proceeding, and although such proceeding was held in a wrong place or was otherwise invalid. 55-56 V., c. 29, s. 145.

Perjury.

False statement under oath within Canada.

172. Every one is guilty of perjury who,—

(a) having taken or made any oath, affirmation, solemn declaration or affidavit where, by any Act or law in force in Canada, or in any province of Canada, it is required or permitted that facts, matters or things be verified, or otherwise assured or ascertained by or upon the oath, affirmation, declaration or affidavit of any person, wilfully and corruptly, upon such oath, affirmation, declaration or affidavit, deposes, swears to or makes any false statement as to any such fact, matter or thing; or,

False oath, etc., in verification of statement.

Subscribing affirmation as affidavit.

(b) knowingly, wilfully and corruptly, upon oath, affirmation or solemn declaration, affirms, declares or deposes to the truth of any statement for so verifying, assuring or ascertaining any such fact, matter or thing, or purporting so to do, or knowingly, wilfully and corruptly takes, makes, signs or subscribes any such affirmation, declaration or affidavit as to any such fact, matter or thing, if such statement, affidavit, affirmation or declaration is untrue in whole or in part. 55-56 V., c. 29, s. 148.

Oath to voter.]—A person applying for a ballot at a Dominion election in the name of another person entitled to vote may be convicted of perjury in taking the oath of identity with that person, although the Elections Act authorizes the administration of the oath of qualification to an "elector" only, and that term must be held to include, for the purposes of administering such oath and prosecuting the personator, the person representing himself at the polls as an elector. R. v. Chamberlain, 10 Man. R. 261.

Declaration under provincial law.]—Perjury is not proved in respect of a solemn declaration that there was "no lawful hindrance" to deponent's proposed marriage by shewing that the deponent knew the girl to be under twenty-one and that her parent's consent had not been obtained as required by the provincial law, if the marriage was valid notwithstanding the absence of such consent. The King v. Moraes (1907), 12 Can. Cr. Cas. 145.

173. Every person who wilfully and corruptly makes any false affidavit, affirmation or solemn declaration, out of the province in which it is to be used but within Canada, before any person authorized to take the same, for the purpose of being used in any province of Canada, is guilty of perjury in like manner as if such false affidavit, affirmation or declaration were made before a competent authority in the province in which it is used or intended to be used. 55-56 V., c. 29, s. 149. Making false affidavit out of the province but within Canada.

174. Every one is guilty of an indictable offence and liable to fourteen years' imprisonment who commits perjury or subornation of perjury. Penalty for perjury or subornation.

2. If the crime is committed in order to procure the conviction of a person for any crime punishable by death, or imprisonment for seven years or more, the punishment may be imprisonment for life. 55-56 V., c. 29, s. 146. Increased in certain cases.

Perjury defined.]—See sec. 170.

Form of indictment.]—Code form No. 64 contains two examples of indictments for perjury, which by sec. 1152 are valid in the cases for which they respectively provide, and may be varied to suit the case.

An indictment or charge for perjury in which it is alleged that the accused committed perjury by falsely, wilfully and with intent to mislead the magistrate, swearing to a certain statement, involves a charge that the accused knew such statement to be false and will not be quashed for failure to more specifically charge such knowledge. R. v. Doyle (1906), 12 Can. Cr. Cas. 69.

Where the statutory form of indictment is not followed but the indictment contains all the averments which the statute requires, the addition of other unnecessary averments does not invalidate it. R. v. Coote (1903), 8 Can. Cr. Cas. 199, 10 B.C.R. 285.

In R. v. Cohon (1903), 6 Can. Cr. Cas. 386, the Supreme Court of Nova Scotia held that a charge of perjury is defective as not disclosing a crime, if it does not allege that the statement was sworn to knowing the same to be false, or if such is not the necessary inference from what is alleged, apart from the declaration in the charge that the accused "thereby committed wilful and corrupt perjury."

But the decision of the Cohon Case is in conflict with the Quebec decisions under the statute preceding the Code. It has been held in the latter province that an indictment following the statutory form is sufficient if it charges that the accused "committed perjury" by swearing that (specifying the false oath), without including a specific statement that it was so done knowing the same to be false. R. v. Bain (1877), Ramsay's Cases (Que.) 192; R. v. Bownes, Ramsay's Cases (Que.) 192. See sec. 862 as to statements now unnecessary in counts for perjury.

Where a prosecutor has been bound by recognizance to prosecute and give evidence against a person charged with perjury in the evidence given by him on the trial of a certain suit, and the grand jury has found an indictment against the defendant, the court will not quash the indictment because there is a variance in the specific charge of perjury contained in the information and that contained in the indictment, provided the indictment sets forth the substantial charge contained in the information. R. v. Broad (1864), 14 U.C.C.P. 168; and see secs. 852-855.

A count charging the accused with having committed perjury at an inquest before a coroner is not invalid by reason of the fact that the tribunal was a coroner and a jury. R. v. Thompson (1896), 4 Can. Cr. Cas. 265, 2 Terr. L.R. 383.

Evidence.]—D. being charged with perjury, in the assignments of perjury and in the negative averments certain facts sworn to by D. in answering to faits et articles on the contestation of a saisie ârret or attachment were distinctly negatived, in the terms in which they were made. It was held that under the general terms of the negative averments it was competent for the prosecution to prove special facts to establish the falsity of the answers given by D. in his answers on faits et articles, and the conviction could not be set aside because of the admission of such proof. Downie v. R. (1888), 15 Can. S.C.R. 358.

In a prosecution for perjury where it appears that the false oath was taken before a justice receiving the complaint of an offence committed within his jurisdiction, and acting in the matter within his jurisdiction, it is unnecessary to offer further evidence that he had authority to administer an oath. R. v. Callaghan (1860), 19 U.C.Q.B. 364.

A charge of perjury cannot be sustained against a boy under fourteen without proof of guilty knowledge of wrong doing. Code sec. 18 has not changed the common law which presumed against guilty knowledge where the accused was under the age of fourteen. The King v. Carvery, 11 Can. Cr. Cas. 331.

It is not essential to the offence of perjury that the notary or other official should have uttered the words of obligation in administering the oath; such words used by the deponent and accompanied by a request that the affidavit already signed by the deponent should be certified as sworn, will be sufficient. Re Collins (No. 2), 10 Can. Cr. Cas. 73.

A plea of aufrefois acquit to a charge of perjury in taking the oath of identity at a polling booth is not supported by a record of acquittal on a charge of personating an elector at the same time and place, although the oath of identity and the alleged personation were in regard to the same elector. A verdict for personation could not have been received under an indictment for perjury in taking the oath of identity, although the facts constituting personation must necessarily be shewn in order to prove the perjury. The King v. Quinn, 10 Can. Cr. Cas. 412.

Proof of judicial proceedings.]—Evidence of any proceeding or record whatsoever of, in, or before any British or Canadian court or before any justice of the peace or any coroner in any province of Canada, or in any court of record in the United States may be made by an exemplification or certified copy thereof, purporting to be under the seal of such court, or under the hand or seal of such justice or coroner, as the case may be, without any proof of the authenticity of such seal or of the signature of such justice or coroner, or other proof whatever; and if any such court, justice or coroner, has no seal, or so certifies, then by a copy purporting to be certified under the signature of a judge or presiding magistrate of such court or of such justice or coroner, without any proof of the authenticity of such signature or other proof whatsoever. Can. Evid. Act, sec.

23; subject however to the provision that the party intending to produce the same shall before the trial give to the party against whom it is intended to be produced reasonable notice of such intention. The reasonableness of the notice shall be determined by the court or judge, but the notice shall not in any case be less than ten days. 2 Can. Evid. Act sec. 28.

The provisions of the Canada Evidence Act are in addition to and not in derogation of any powers of proving documents given by any existing statute or existing at law. Ibid., sec. 34.

Subject to the provisions made by federal law the laws of evidence in force in the province in which such proceedings are taken, apply. Ibid., sec. 35.

On a charge of perjury committed at the trial of an indictment such trial and the indictment, verdict, and judgment therein must be proved as matters of record. Such proof may be given either by the production of the original record or of an exemplification thereof, or by a certificate under Code sec. 979 of the substance and effect of the indictment and trial. The viva voce testimony of the clerk of assize and of the official stenographer with the production of the official book of entry in which the clerk recorded his memoranda of the proceedings and of the stenographer's notes of the evidence, are insufficient as legal proof of the fact of the former trial. Where a conviction has been made without the legal proof required by law of an essential part of the crime, such defect is a "substantial wrong or miscarriage at the trial" and the conviction must be set aside. The King v. Drummond, 10 Can. Cr. Cas. 340, 10 O.L.R. 456.

A witness present at the trial when the alleged perjury was committed may be called to state from recollection the evidence given by the accused. It will be sufficient if the witness can state with certainty that what he relates was all the evidence given by the accused on the point regarding which perjury is charged and that the accused said nothing to qualify it, although he is unable to state in effect all the evidence which the accused then gave. R. v. Rowley, 1 Mood. C.C. 111; R. v. Munton, 3 C. & P. 498; R. v. Browne, 3 C. & P. 572.

Besides proving the whole of what is set out in the indictment as having been falsely sworn to, the prosecution should prove the evidence connected with and necessary for the explanation of the alleged false evidence. R. v. Jones, Peake 51; R. v. Dowlin, Peake 227. But statements made by the judge presiding when the alleged perjury was committed are not admissible. R. v. Britton, 17 Cox C.C. 627.

The judge's notes are not admissible except to refresh the memory of the judge if called as a witness. R. v. Child, 5 Cox C.C. 197; R. v. Morgan, 6 Cox C.C. 107.

The judges of superior courts ought not to be called upon to produce their notes, but the same objection is not applicable to the judges of inferior courts, especially where the judge is willing to appear. R. v. Harvey, 8 Cox 99.

A certificate containing the substance and effect only, omitting the formal part, of the indictment and trial for any offence, purporting to be signed by the clerk of the court or other officer having the custody of the records of the court whereat the indictment was tried, or among which such indictment has been filed, or by the deputy of such clerk or other officer, shall, upon the trial of an indictment for perjury or subornation of perjury, be sufficient evidence of the trial of such indictment without proof of the signature or official character of the person appearing to have signed the same. Code sec. 979.

And apart from the statutory enactment contained in sec. 979 it seems that the caption of the *same* court of oyer and terminer or gaol delivery at which the indictment for perjury is preferred, the former indictment with plea verdict and sentence indorsed together with the minutes of the trial made by the court officer constituted sufficient evidence of the former trial without a regular record or any certificate thereof. Reg. v. Newman, 2 Den. C.C. 390.

Upon a charge of perjury in respect of evidence taken by a magistrate on requiring sureties to keep the peace under sec. 748(2) the false statement may be proved by oral testimony, although not recorded in the minutes of evidence then made by the magistrate. R. v. Doyle (1906), 12 Can. Cr. Cas. 69.

The finding in the case in which the false evidence was given is not evidence on the perjury trial. R. v. Goodfellow, C. & M. 569.

Corroboration.]—Corroboration is required on a charge of perjury. See sec. 1002.

It is not, however, imperative that there should be two witnesses to disprove the fact sworn to by the accused, for if any other material circumstance be proved by other witnesses in confirmation of the witness who gives the direct testimony of perjury, it may turn the scale and warrant a conviction. R. v. Lee, 3 Russell on Crimes, 5th ed., 72. Two witnesses are not essentially necessary to contradict the oath on which the perjury is assigned, but there must be something more than the oath of one, to shew that one party is more to be believed than the other. Reg. v. Boulter (1852), 5 Cox C.C. 543; 3 Car. & Kir. 236. And it has been held that a letter written by the accused contradicting his statement upon oath would be sufficient to make it unnecessary to have a second witness. Rex v. Mayhew, 6 Carrington & Payne, 315.

Several charges on one affidavit.]—Upon a "speedy trial" upon several charges of perjury in respect of one affidavit, the trial judge is bound to regard the whole affidavit as the sworn statement in respect of each charge, and should not treat each paragraph of the affidavit as an entire statement independently of the other paragraphs. The King v. Cohon, 6 Can. Cr. Cas. 386.

Trial by police magistrate.]—A police magistrate in Ontario has jurisdiction with the consent of the accused to try the offence of perjury. R. v. Burns (No. 2) (1901), 4 Can. Cr. Cas. 330 (Ont.); and by sub-sec. (2) of sec. 777, police magistrates of cities and incorporated towns in every other part of Canada have the like jurisdiction.

Judge's order for prosecution for perjury before him.]—See sec. 870.

Perjury in capital cases.]—Procuring by false evidence the conviction and death of any person by the sentence of the law shall not be deemed to be homicide. Section 253.

Perjury in pending civil action.]—Where a charge of perjury is brought on for trial during the pendency of the civil action in which it is alleged to have been committed and where the question of fact on which the perjury is alleged is the same as that involved in the civil action, the criminal court should exercise its discretion to postpone the criminal trial until after judgment in the civil action. The King v. Cohon, 6 Can. Cr. Cas. 386; R. v. Ingham, 14 Q.B. 396; R. v. Ashburn, 8 C. & P. 50.

Proof of civil proceedings.]—The existence of a civil action as a judicial proceeding in which the false oath was taken may be proved by producing the copy of writ filed on the issue of the writ of summons under the Judicature Act and the filed copies of pleadings, if any. Reg. v. Scott, L.R. 2 Q.B.D. 415.

A person charged with perjury committed in a civil action is entitled to have put in evidence those parts of his testimony in the civil action which may explain or qualify the statements in respect of which the perjury is charged. R. v. Coote (1903), 8 Can. Cr. Cas. 199, 10 B.C.R. 285.

But the non-production by the prosecution, on a trial for perjury, of the plea which was filed in the civil suit wherein the defendant is alleged to have given false testimony, is not material when the assignment of perjury has no reference to the pleading, but the defendant may, if he wishes, in case the plea is not produced, prove its contents by secondary evidence. R. v. Ross, 1 Montreal L.R. (Q.B.) 227; 28 L.C.J. 261.

175. Every one is guilty of an indictable offence and liable to seven years' imprisonment who, being required or authorized by law to make any statement on oath, affirmation or solemn declaration, thereupon makes a statement which would amount to perjury if made in a judicial proceeding. 55-56 V., c. 29, s. 147. **False oaths in extra judicial proceedings.**

False statutory declaration under Evidence Act.]—On a charge under this section of making a false statutory declaration, it is not necessary to allege in the indictment that the false statement was made with intent to mislead. R. v. Skelton (1898), 4 Can. Cr. Cas. 467 (N.W.T.).

A statutory declaration jointly made by several persons and stating the matter declared in the following form, *i.e.*:—"*We* know that, etc., is to be construed as a statement by each of the declarants severally, that he knows the matters alleged. Ibid.

The permission granted by the Canada Evidence Act to certain officials to "receive" the solemn declarations of persons voluntarily making the same in the statutory form includes an authorization to the declarant to make the same, and constitutes him a person "authorized by law to make a solemn declaration." Ibid.

176. Every one is guilty of an indictable offence and liable to two years' imprisonment who, upon any occasion on which he is permitted by law to make any statement or declaration before any officer authorized by law to permit it to be made before him, or before any notary public to be certified by him as such notary, makes a statement which would amount to perjury if made on oath in a judicial proceeding. 55-56 V., c. 29, s. 150. **False statements in extra-judicial proceedings.**

Section 176 does not refer to solemn declarations under the Canada Evidence Act but merely to statements and declarations; the former are covered by section 175. It is only in certain cases that statements and declarations other than solemn declarations are specially authorized, and sec. 176 appears to be applicable only to such cases. R. v. Skelton (1898), 4 Can. Cr. Cas. 467, 2 N.W.T. Rep. 210.

177. Every one is guilty of an indictable offence and liable to seven years' imprisonment who, with intent to mislead any **Fabricating evidence.**

court of justice or person holding any such judicial proceeding, fabricates evidence by any means other than perjury or subornation of perjury. 55-56 V., c. 29, s. 151.

Evidence.]—The offence is complete if the evidence is fabricated with intent to mislead a judicial tribunal even if the evidence is not used. R. v. Vreones, [1891] 1 Q.B. 360; 17 Cox C.C. 267; 60 L.J.M.C. 62.

Where an act has been proved and the question is whether it was done by a given party, the fabrication or suppression of evidence is one of the circumstances of subsequent conduct admissible to connect the person procuring the same with the original transaction. Phipson Evid. (1898) 117.

Inciting to give false evidence.]—It is a common law misdemeanour to incite a witness to give particular evidence where the inciter does not know whether it be true or false. Ex parte Overton, 2 Rose 257. This offence differs from subornation in that it is not necessary to prove that the evidence was in fact given, or was false to the knowledge of the witness. Archbold Cr. Evid. (1900), 1019. And by Code sec. 70 every one who counsels or procures another to be a party to an offence is a party to every offence which that other commits in consequence of such counselling or procuring, and which the person counselling or procuring knew, or ought to have known, to be *likely* to be committed in consequence of such counselling or procuring. (Sub-sec. 2.)

In Archbold's Criminal Pleading, 22nd ed., p. 1019, it is laid down that "It is a misdemeanour to incite a witness to give particular evidence, when the inciter does not know whether it is true or false . . . The offence differs from subornation in that it is not necessary to prove that the evidence was in fact given, or was actually false to the knowledge of the witness." To the same effect is the language of Holt, C.J., in The Queen v. Darby (1702), 7 Mod. at p. 101: "It seemed to be a common law offence, to offer money to swear to a particular thing whether true or false." R. v. Cole (1901), 5 Can. Cr. Cas. 330, 335.

Bribing or corrupting witnesses.]—See sec. 180.

Conspiring to bring false accusations.

178. Every one is guilty of an indictable offence who conspires to prosecute any person for any alleged offence, knowing such person to be innocent thereof, and shall be liable,—

Penalty.

(a) to imprisonment for fourteen years if such person might, upon conviction for the alleged offence, be sentenced to death or imprisonment for life;

Penalty.

(b) to imprisonment for ten years if such person might, upon conviction for the alleged offence, be sentenced to imprisonment for any term less than life. 55-56 V., c. 29, s. 152.

Administering oaths without authority.

179. Every justice or other person who administers, or causes or allows to be administered, or receives, or causes or allows to be received, any oath or affirmation touching any matter or thing whereof such justice or other person has not jurisdiction or cognizance by some law in force at the time being, or not authorized or required by any such law, is guilty of an indictable offence and liable to a fine not exceeding fifty dollars, or to imprisonment for any term not exceeding three months. Penalty.

2. Nothing in this section contained shall be construed to extend to any oath or affirmation before any justice in any matter or thing touching the preservation of the peace, or the prosecution, trial or punishment of any offence, or to any oath or affirmation required or authorized by any law of Canada, or by any law of the province wherein such oath or affirmation is received or administered, or is to be used, or to any oath or affirmation, which is required or authorized by the laws of any foreign country to give validity to an instrument in writing or to evidence designed or intended to be used in such foreign country. 55-56 V., c. 29, s. 153. Saving.

Administering oath.]—The Canada Evidence Act, sec. 13, provides that every court and judge, and every person having, by law or consent of parties, authority to hear and receive evidence, shall have power to administer an oath to every witness who is legally called to give evidence before that court, judge or person.

180. Every one is guilty of an indictable offence and liable to two years' imprisonment who,— Penalty.

(*a*) dissuades or attempts to dissuade any person by threats, bribes, or other corrupt means from giving evidence in any cause or matter, civil or criminal; or, Corrupting witness.

(*b*) influences or attempts to influence, by threats or bribes or other corrupt means, any juryman in his conduct as such, whether such person has been sworn as a juryman or not; or, Corrupting juryman.

(*c*) accepts any bribe or other corrupt consideration to abstain from giving evidence, or on account of his conduct as a juryman; or, Accepting bribes.

(*d*) wilfully attempts in any other way to obstruct, pervert or defeat the course of justice. 55-56 V., c. 29, s. 154. Otherwise obstructing justice.

Obstructing justice.]—In The King v. Tibbits, [1902] 1 K.B. 77, 18 T.L.R. 49, the Court for Crown Cases Reserved upheld the conviction of the editor and a reporter of a newspaper upon an indictment charging them with "an unlawful attempt to obstruct and pervert the due course of law and justice," and with "a conspiracy to obstruct and pervert the course of law and justice." In the paper in question there were published sensational accounts of alleged investigations of the reporter, referred to in the articles as "Our Special Crime Investigator." These articles related to a charge then pending against a person accused of the crime, and after his conviction the Crown prosecuted the editor and reporter. Lord Alverstone, C.J., said:—"A person accused of crime in this country can properly be convicted in a court of justice only upon evidence which is legally admissible, and which is adduced at his trial in legal form and shape. Assume the accused to be really guilty of the offence charged against him. The due course of law and justice is perverted and obstructed nevertheless if those who have to try him are induced to approach the question of his guilt or innocence with minds into which prejudice has been instilled by published assertions of his guilt, or imputations against his life and character to which the laws of the land refuse admissibility as evidence."

An indictment or charge that the accused paid money to a person not to attend a court of revision in connection with an election, does not disclose a "perversion or defeat of justice" under Code sec. 180(d) where it does not shew any ground for supposing that the non-attendance would defeat justice, and where the person receiving the money was the person whose right to vote was in question and might therefore abandon his claim. The offence disclosed may properly be charged under sub-sec. (a) of Code sec. 180, as an attempt to dissuade a person by a bribe from giving evidence. The King v. Lake, 11 Can. Cr. Cas. 37.

Embracery.]—Any attempt to corrupt or influence or instruct a jury or to incline them to be more favourable to one side than the other, by money, promises, letters, threats or persuasions, except only by the strength of the evidence and the arguments of the counsel in open court at the trial of the cause constituted the common law offence of embracery, whether the jurors gave any verdict or not and whether the verdict given were true or false. R. v. Cornellier, 29 L.C.J. 69; Hawk. P.C., b. 1, ch. 85, sec. 1. And the giving of money to a juror after the verdict without any preceding contract is an offence savouring of embracery; but it is otherwise of the payment of a juror's travelling expenses. Ibid, sec. 3.

It is essential that there should be a judicial proceeding pending at the time of the alleged offence. R. v. Leblanc, 8 Montreal Legal News 114.

At one time it seems to have been considered that a mere stranger could not lawfully labour a juror to appear and act according to his conscience; Hawk. P.C., b. 1, ch. 85, sec. 2; but such appears to be no longer the law for an honest exhortation to do justice should never be construed into guilt. Bishop Crim. Law 317.

Tampering with witnesses.]—At common law interference with witnesses in courts of justice by threats or persuasion to induce them not to give evidence was an indictable misdemeanour. R. v. Steventon, 2 East 362; Stone's Justice's Manual, 28th ed., 242. It is also punishable summarily as a contempt of court. Bromilow v. Phillips (1891), W.N. 209; 1 Russ. Crim., 6th ed., 487(n).

Witnesses in liquor cases.]—It is provided by the Canada Temperance Act, R.S.C. 1906, ch. 152, sec. 150, that every one who on any prosecution under that Act or any Act in force in any province respecting the issue of licenses for the sale of fermented or spirituous liquors, or under "The Temperance Act of 1864," tampers with a witness, either before or after he is summoned or appears as such witness, or by the offer of money, or by threats, or in any other way, either directly or indirectly, induces or attempts to induce any such witness to absent himself or to swear falsely, shall incur a penalty of fifty dollars for each offence. This special provision is not affected by the Code. R. v. Gibson, 29 N.S.R. 88.

Conspiracy to pervert justice.]—By sec. 573 every one is guilty of an indictable offence and liable to seven years' imprisonment who conspires with any person to commit an indictable offence where the Code does not specially provide a different punishment.

A conspiracy whereby a witness bound over to attend a trial was to absent himself is indictable. R. v. Hamp, 6 Cox C.C. 157. And so is a conspiracy to charge a man falsely with any crime. Poulterer's Case, 9 Co. Rep. 55; R. v. Spragg, 2 Burr. 993, 1027; R. v. Macdaniel, 1 Leach C.C. 45; and see Code sec. 453.

It is immaterial whether the conspiracy proceeds so far as actually indicting the person falsely accused, and if the object of the conspiracy is extortion, the truth or falsity of the charge is immaterial. R. v. Hollingberry, 4 B. & C. 329; R. v. Gill, 2 B. & A. 204.

Where a money lender to whom a small sum of money was due conspired with a solicitor by abuse of legal process to enforce payment of a sum known not to be legally due, a conviction for the conspiracy was upheld. R. v. Taylor, 15 Cox C.C. 265.

A conviction may be made under this section of the Code for dissuading a person by corrupt means from giving evidence under the Ontario Liquor License Act. R. v. Holland, 14 C.L.T. notes 294.

181. Every one is guilty of an indictable offence and liable to a fine not exceeding the penalty compounded for who, having brought, or under colour of bringing, an action against any person under any penal statute in order to obtain from him any penalty, compounds the said action without order or consent of the court, whether any offence has in fact been committed or not. 55-56 V., c. 29, s. 155. Compounding penal actions.

Compounding penal actions.]—The compounding of an information on penal statutes is a misdemeanour against public justice, by contributing to make the laws odious to the people. Therefore in order to discourage malicious informers, and to provide that when offences are once discovered they shall be duly prosecuted, 18 Eliz., ch. 5 was passed, providing a fine upon a informer for taking money to settle the charge. But that statute did not apply to penalties which are only recoverable by information before justices, and an indictment for making a composition in such a case was held bad in arrest of judgment. R. v. Crisp, 1 B. & Ald. 282, cited by Richards, C.J., in R. v. Mason (1867), 17 U.C.C.P. 534.

Compounding criminal prosecution.]—It is not every misdemeanour the compounding of which is an offence. Fallowes v. Taylor, 7 T.R. 475; Keir v. Leeman, 9 Q.B. 371. An indictment will lie if the offence compounded is of such a public nature that its predominating feature is that the public must be protected against it as distinguished from misdemeanours essentially in the nature of private injuries. State v. Carver, 39 Atl. Rep. 973, (N.H.); 1 Bishop Cr. Law, sec. 711. And the receipt of money in consideration of the non-prosecution of a charge for the infraction of liquor laws is indictable as compounding a misdemeanour of a public nature. Re Fraser, 1 C.L.J. 326; R. v. Mabey, 37 U.C.Q.B. 248; State v. Carver, supra.

If an offence which was formerly a misdemeanour were compounded under circumstances constituting a conspiracy to obstruct or defeat the course of justice, the accused might be punished for the conspiracy. And a conspiracy with a witness bound over to attend a trial to absent himself from the trial is indictable. R. v. Hamp, 6 Cox 157. And where an assault is coupled with riot a compromise of the charge is illegal and will not bar an action for malicious prosecution, although riot is only a misdemeanour at common law. Keir v. Leeman, 6 Q.B. 308; 9 Q.B. 371.

It has been held that where the prosecutor has the choice between civil and criminal remedies, he may legally compromise as to the criminal remedy, ex gr. for a trade-mark offence. Fisher v. Appolinaris Co., L.R. 10 Ch. App. 297. So also the offence of common assault may be compromised. Keir v. Leeman, 6 Q.B. 308; 9 Q.B. 371.

Where, however, the offence was not under former law a felony, and the compounding is not an indictable conspiracy, there seems to be no precedent for holding that the compounding of an offence which was only a misdemeanour before the Code, is in itself indictable. Archbold Cr. Pleading (1900), 1035.

An agreement after conviction to pay part of the expenses of a prosecution for misdemeanour has been held legal. Beely v. Wingfield, 11 East 46. But such arrangements are seldom approved by the court. Re Parkinson, 76 L.T.N.S. 215.

Compounding a felony is a misdemeanour at common law, punishable by fine and imprisonment. It consists in an agreement for reward not to prosecute an indictment for any felony. Roscoe Crim. Ev., 11th ed., 395. The offence of compounding is complete when the agreement not to prosecute is made whether it be performed or not. R. v. Burgess, 16 Q.B.D. 141.

In Jones v. Merionethshire Permanent, [1892] 1 Ch. 173, affirming [1891] 2 Ch. 587, the facts shewn were that the secretary of a building society, who had made default in accounting for money paid to him, was threatened by the society with a prosecution for embezzlement. He thereupon applied to certain relatives for assistance and they gave a written undertaking to the society to make good the greater part of the amount due from the secretary, the expressed consideration being the forbearance of the society to sue the secretary for the sum for which the relatives made themselves responsible. In pursuance of that undertaking they gave two promissory notes and some title deeds as collateral security to the society. The relatives in giving the undertaking were actuated by a desire to prevent the prosecution, and that was known to the directors of the society, but no express promise was made that there should be no prosecution. It was held by the Court of Appeal (Lindley, Bowen, and Fry, L.JJ.,) that it was an implied term of the agreement that there should be no prosecution; that the agreement was, therefore, founded on an illegal consideration and void; and that the society could not recover on the promissory notes or enforce the securities. Bowen, L.J., there said: "Reparation is a duty which the offender owes quite independently of his fear of prosecution or otherwise, and it would be absurd to lay down as an impossible counsel of perfection, that the relative of an offender, and his friends are not justified, nay, even are not bound, in certain instances, to assist him to make reparation to those whom he has injured. . . . The law certainly is not anxious to discourage reparation; but you must come back, after reparation made, to the one dominant test in each case. It is a circumstance which may be lawfully taken into consideration that the offender has done his best himself, or with the assistance of his friends, to make good his wrong. But the test is, what is the moral duty of the person who has been injured to himself and to others? He must make no bargain about that. If reparation takes the form of a bargain then, to my mind, the bargain is one which the court will not enforce."

The mere expectation on the part of the relatives who aid the offender to make reparation that a prosecution would not take place, would not be sufficient to nullify the transaction: Ward v. Lloyd (1843), 6 Man. & G. 785. In order to amount to a defence on the ground of illegality there must be an agreement not to prosecute. Jones v. Merionethshire, [1892] 1 Ch. 173, 182, per Lindley, L.J.

There is no distinction between getting a security for a debt from the debtor himself and getting it from a third person who is under no obligation to the creditor. A threat to prosecute is not of itself illegal, and does not necessarily vitiate a subsequent agreement by the debtor to give security for a debt which he justly owes to his creditor, although the transaction out of which the debt arises possibly involves a criminal as well as a civil liability. Flower v. Sadler (1882), 10 Q.B.D. 572 (C.A.).

If the agreement be made upon the understanding that the accused shall be discharged from custody, although not so stated in express terms, it is illegal and void. Leggatt v. Brown (1898), 29 Ont. R. 530, affirmed (1899), 30 Ont. R. 225.

Where the owner of goods stolen took back the goods or received other amends on condition of not prosecuting, it constituted the offence of theft-bote at common law, and this offence is not usually described as compounding a felony. Archbold Cr. Pleading (1900), 1035; Hawk. P.C., book 1, ch. 59, sec. 7.

A prosecution for a felony is not the property of those that institute it to deal with it as they please; the public have a higher interest in having redress rendered and wrong punished to deter others from offending in like manner. R. v. Hammond, 9 Sol. Jour. 216.

Unless a nolle prosequi is entered by the Attorney-General, it is necessary to obtain the leave of the court to abandon a prosecution after the indictment is found, whether the prosecution desire to effect that purpose by offering no evidence or otherwise. R. v. Nicholson Cent. Cr. Court, 1899, per Darling, J., cited Archbold Cr. Pleading (1900), 1035.

Misprision of felony.]—This offence is now in desuetude. Archbold Cr. Pleading (1900), 1238; Williams v. Bayley, L.R. 2 H.L. 200. It consisted in concealing or procuring the concealment of a felony known to have been committed. I Hawk. ch. 59. It differed from the offence of being an accessory in that neither actual assistance to the felon nor privity to the commission of the felony had to be proved. 1 Hale 373.

182. Every one is guilty of an indictable offence and liable to seven years' imprisonment who corruptly takes any money or reward, directly or indirectly, under pretense or upon account of helping any person to recover any chattel, money, valuable security or other property which, by any indictable offence, has been stolen, taken, obtained, extorted, converted or disposed of, unless he has used all due diligence to cause the offender to be brought to trial for the same. 55-56 V., c. 29, s. 156.

Corruptly taking reward without bringing offender to trial.

Origin.]—This section is in similar terms to the Imperial Statute, 24 & 25 Vict., ch. 96, sec. 101.

Evidence.]—It is not necessary to shew that the accused had any connection with the commission of the previous offence; it is sufficient if the evidence satisfies the jury that the prisoner had some corrupt and improper design when he received the money, and did not bonâ fide intend to use such means as he could for the detection and punishment of the offender. R. v. King, 1 Cox C.C. 36.

Unless due diligence is used in prosecuting the thief it has been held to be an offence under the section to take money under pretence of helping a man to recover goods stolen from him, though the defendant had no acquaintance with the felon and did not pretend that he had, and notwithstanding that he had no power to apprehend the felon, that the goods were never restored, and that the defendant had no power to restore them. R. v. Ledbitter, 1 Mood. C.C. 76.

Where A. was charged with corruptly receiving from B. money under pretence of helping B. to recover goods theretofore stolen from B. and with not causing the thieves to be apprehended the following questions were left to the jury:—(1) Did A. mean to screen the guilty parties or to share the money with them? The answer was no. (2) Did A. know the thieves and intend to assist them in getting rid of the property by promising B. to buy it? The answer was no. (3) Did A. know the thieves and assist B. as her agent and at her request in endeavouring to purchase the stolen property from them, not meaning to bring the thieves to justice? The answer was yes. It was held that B. was properly convicted. R. v. Pascoe, 1 Den. 456, 2 C. & K. 927, 18 L.J.M.C. 186.

Form of indictment.]—The jurors for Our Lord the King upon their oath present that A.B. on (time and place), unlawfully and corruptly did take and receive from one C.D. certain money and reward to wit, the sum of five dollars of the monies of the said C.D. under pretence (and upon account) of helping the said C.D. to certain goods and chattels of him the said C.D. before then stolen, taken and carried away, to wit (describe goods), the said A.B. not having used all due diligence to cause the person by whom the said goods and chattels were so stolen, taken and carried away as aforesaid, to be brought to trial for the same; against the form of the Criminal Code, sec. 182.

Penalty.

183. Every one is liable to a penalty of two hundred and fifty dollars for each offence, recoverable with costs by any person who sues for the same in any court of competent jurisdiction, who,—

Advertising reward and immunity for offender.

(*a*) publicly advertises a reward for the return of any property which has been stolen or lost, and in such advertisement uses any words purporting that no questions will be asked; or,

Making use of words in advertisement to like effect.

(*b*) makes use of any words in any public advertisement purporting that a reward will be given or paid for any property which has been stolen or lost, without seizing or making any inquiry after the person producing such property; or,

Advertising that money advanced on property stolen will be paid.

(*c*) promises or offers in any such public advertisement to return to any pawnbroker or other person who advanced money by way of loan on, or has bought, any property stolen or lost, the money so advanced or paid, or any other sum of money for the return of such property; or,

Printing advertisement.

(*d*) prints or publishes any such advertisement. 55-56 V., c. 29, s. 157.

Limitation.]—A prosecution taken against the proprietor of a "newspaper" for publishing an advertisement offering a reward for the recovery of stolen property under paragraph (d) must be commenced within six months from the commission of the offence. Section 1140(d).

184. Every one is guilty of an indictable offence and liable to two years' imprisonment, who knowingly and wilfully signs a false certificate or declaration, when a certificate or declaration is required, with respect to the execution of judgment of death on any prisoner. 55-56 V., c. 29, s. 158. False declaration in respect to execution of judgment of death.

Escapes and Rescues.

185. Every one is guilty of an indictable offence and liable to two years' imprisonment who, having been sentenced to imprisonment, is afterwards, and before the expiration of the term for which he was sentenced, at large within Canada without some lawful cause, the proof whereof shall lie on him. 55-56 V., c. 29, s. 159. Being at large while under sentence of imprisonment.

Certificate of sentence.]—The fact of the sentence being in force when the defendant was found at large is sufficiently proved by the certificate of the conviction and sentence, if the judgment remains unreversed, and this although it appears on the face of the certificate that the sentence was one which could not legally have been inflicted on the defendant for the offence of which according to the certificate he had been convicted. R. v. Finney, 2 C. & K. 274.

Escapes.]—See secs. 189 and 190.

Ticket of leave.]—It may be proved as a defence that the prisoner is at large conditionally under a license or ticket of leave or otherwise and that the conditions have been observed. R.S.C. 1906, ch. 150. The license issued under the authority of that statute may be revoked by the Governor-General either with or without cause assigned. R. v. Johnson, 4 Can. Cr. Cas. 178 (Que.). The revocation by the Crown without cause assigned does not interrupt the running of the sentence, and the latter terminates at the same time as if no license had been granted. Ibid.

Pardon.]—A pardon is a good defence. R. v. Miller, 2 W. Bl. 797, 1 Leach C.C. 74; but the sentence revives if the terms of a conditional pardon are not observed. R. v. Madan, 1 Leach C.C. 223; Aickles' Case, 1 Leach C.C. 390.

Without lawful excuse.]—Upon a summary conviction of the defendant and the passing of sentence of four months' imprisonment, for breach of a provincial law, the magistrate of his own motion required the defendant to enter into a recognizance to appear when called upon (a procedure not authorized in such cases) and upon doing so the defendant was released. The defendant having been afterwards imprisoned under a warrant issued two months after the date of sentence, held that the term of imprisonment is to be counted from the day of passing sentence and that the defendant was not liable as upon an escape to make up the period for which he was so at liberty, as there was no mens rea and the magistrate's action was a "lawful excuse" quoad the defendant. R. v. Robinson (1907), 12 Can. Cr. Cas. 447, per Riddell, J.

The time during which a person under sentence is improperly at liberty through an erroneous order for bail, is not to be counted as part of the term of imprisonment. R. v. Taylor (1906), 12 Can. Cr. Cas. 245, per Stuart, J.

Penalty.

186. Every one is guilty of an indictable offence and liable to five years' imprisonment who knowingly and wilfully,—

Assisting prisoner of war to escape.

(*a*) assists any alien enemy of His Majesty, being a prisoner of war in Canada, to escape from any place in which he may be detained; or,

Assisting while at large on parole.

(*b*) assists any such prisoner as aforesaid, suffered to be at large on his parole in Canada or in any part thereof, to escape from the place where he is at large on his parole. 55-56 V., c. 29, s. 160.

Imperial statute.]—This offence is also covered by the Imperial Statute, 52 Geo. III., ch. 156, known as the Prisoners of War Escape Act. That statute in terms applies to His Majesty's dominions and is consequently still in force in Canada. See also Code sec. 589.

Section 1 of that Act as varied by 54 & 55 Vict. (Imp.), ch. 69, sec. 1, provides that every person who shall from and after the passing thereof knowingly or wilfully assist any alien enemy of His Majesty being a prisoner of war in His Majesty's dominions, whether such prisoner shall be confined as a prisoner of war in any prison or other place of confinement or shall be suffered to be at large in His Majesty's dominions or any part thereof on his parole, to escape from such prison or other place of confinement or from His Majesty's dominions if at large on parole, shall, upon being convicted thereof, be adjudged guilty of felony and be liable to be transported as a felon for life or for such term not less than three years and not exceeding either five years or any greater period authorized by the enactment, at the discretion of the court. The same section also provides that where under any Act now in force or under any future Act a court is empowered or required to award a sentence of penal servitude, the court may in its discretion, unless such future Act otherwise provides, award imprisonment for any term not exceeding two years with or without hard labour.

Prison-breach.

187. Every one is guilty of an indictable offence and liable to seven years' imprisonment who, by force or violence, breaks any prison with intent to set at liberty himself or any person confined therein on any criminal charge. 55-56 V., c. 29, s. 161.

Evidence.]—The proof required is:—(1) the nature of the offence for which the prisoner was imprisoned; (2) the imprisonment and the nature of the prison; and (3) the breaking of the prison. Roscoe Crim. Evid., 11th ed., 837.

Any prison.]—The expression "prison" includes any penitentiary, common gaol, public or reformatory prison, lock-up, guard room or other place in which persons charged with the commission of offences are usually kept or detained in custody. Section 2(30).

Prison breach.]—An actual breaking of the prison with force, and not merely a constructive breaking, must be proved. If a gaoler sets open the prison doors and the prisoner escapes the latter is not guilty of prison breach. 1 Hale P.C. 611; and if the prison be fired and he escapes to save his life, this is not prison breach unless the prisoner himself set fire to the prison or procured it to be done. Hale P.C. 611.

If other persons without the prisoner's privity or consent break the prison and he escapes through the breach so made he is not guilty of breaking but only of the escape. 2 Hawk., ch. 18, sec. 10.

Force essential to the offence.]—Where a prisoner made his escape over the prison walls and in doing so threw down some bricks from the top of the wall which has been placed there loose without mortar in the form of pigeon holes for the purpose of preventing escapes, it was held that he was properly convicted of prison breach. R. v. Haswell, Russ. & Ry. 458.

Retaking prisoner.]—See note to sec. 189.

Escape.]—See secs. 189-196.

188. Every one is guilty of an indictable offence and liable to two years' imprisonment who attempts to break prison, or who forcibly breaks out of his cell or makes any breach therein with intent to escape therefrom. 55-56 V., c. 29, s. 162. **Attempt to break prison.**

189. Every one is guilty of an indictable offence and liable to two years' imprisonment who,— **Penalty.**

(*a*) having been convicted of any offence, escapes from any lawful custody in which he may be under such conviction; or, **Escapes after conviction.**

(*b*) whether convicted or not, escapes from any prison in which he is lawfully confined on any criminal charge. 55-56 V., c. 29, s. 163. **Escaping from prison.**

Whether convicted or not.]—These words being inserted, it is no longer a defence as it was at common law that the accused had been subsequently indicted for the original offence and acquitted. 1 Hale 611; R. v. Waters, 12 Cox 390.

Escape without force.]—It is an offence by a prisoner to escape from lawful confinement, though no force or artifice be used on his part to effect such purpose. Thus, if a prisoner go out of his prison without any obstruction, the doors being opened by the consent or negligence of the gaoler, or if he escape in any other manner, without using any kind of force or violence, he will be guilty of a misdemeanour. R. v. Nugent, 11 Cox 64.

Force in preventing escape of prisoner.]—It is laid down by the late Mr. Justice Stephen, in his Digest of the Criminal Law, article 199, that the intentional infliction of death or bodily harm is not a crime when it is done by any person in order to retake or keep in lawful custody a traitor, felon, or pirate who has escaped or is about to escape from custody, although such traitor, felon or pirate offers no violence to any person, provided that the object for which death or harm is inflicted cannot be otherwise accomplished. See also Code secs. 40-45, inclusive.

Lord Hale (1 Hale P.C. 489) says: "If a person be indicted of felony and flies, or being arrested by warrant or process of law upon such indictment escapes and flies, and will not render himself, whereupon the officer or minister cannot take him without killing of him, this is not felony, neither shall the killer forfeit his goods, or be driven to sue forth his pardon, but upon his arraignment shall plead not guilty, and accordingly it ought to be found by the jury. But if he may be taken without severity, it is at least manslaughter in him that kills him, therefore, the jury is to inquire whether it were done of necessity or not."

Sir Michael Foster draws especial attention to the distinction between cases of bare flight and cases of resistance to arrest (Foster C.L. 270), and he says: "Where a felony is committed and the felon fleeth from justice, or a dangerous wound given, it is the duty of every man to use his best endeavours for preventing an escape; and if in the pursuit the party fleeing is killed, where he cannot otherwise be overtaken, this will be deemed justifiable homicide; for the pursuit was not barely warrantable, it is what the law requireth and will punish the wilful neglect of."

Sergeant Hawkins (1 Hawk. P.C. 81), says that, "First, if a person having actually committed a felony will not suffer himself to be arrested, but stand on his own defence or fly, so that he cannot possibly be apprehended alive by those who pursue him, whether private persons or public officers, with or without a warrant from a magistrate, he may be lawfully slain by them. Secondly, if an innocent person be indicted of a felony where in truth no felony was committed, and will not suffer himself to be arrested by the officer who has a warrant for that purpose, he may be lawfully killed by him if he cannot otherwise be taken; for there is a charge against him upon record, to which, at his peril, he is bound to answer. Thirdly, if a criminal, endeavouring to break the gaol, assault his gaoler, he may be lawfully killed by him in the affray."

And it is laid down in 1 East P.C. 330, touching the safe custody of persons arrested and in confinement, that after an arrest once legally made, if the party escape, the officer may lawfully kill him—(1) in the case of a felony actually committed; (2) or whether committed by him or not if he had been arrested upon a proper warrant; (3) or hue and cry had been raised against him by name; (4) or he had stood indicted for felony; but if in any of these cases the officer might otherwise have taken him, it will be at least manslaughter.

Escape from reformatory or industrial school.]—Every one sentenced to imprisonment or to be detained in any reformatory prison, reformatory school, industrial refuge, industrial home or industrial school, who escapes or attempts to escape therefrom, may, at any time, be apprehended without warrant and brought before any magistrate, who, upon proof of his identity, and of the escape or attempt to escape, if the escape or attempt to escape be from a reformatory prison or a reformatory school, shall remand him thereto for the remainder of his original term of imprisonment or detention. R.S.C. 1906, ch. 148, sec. 22.

If the escape or attempt to escape be from an industrial refuge, industrial home or industrial school, the magistrate may remand the offender thereto for the remainder of his original term of imprisonment or detention; or if the officer in charge of such refuge, home or school certifies in writing that the removal of the offender to a place of safer or stricter imprisonment is desirable, and if the governing body of such refuge, home or school applies for such removal, and if sufficient cause therefor is shewn to the satisfaction of such magistrate, the magistrate may order the offender to be removed to and to be kept imprisoned, for the remainder of his original term of imprisonment or detention, in any reformatory prison, or reformatory school, in which by law such offender might be imprisoned for an indictable offence, and when there is no such reformatory prison or reformatory school, the magistrate may order the offender to be removed to and to be so kept imprisoned in any other place of imprisonment to which the offender may be lawfully committed. R.S.C. 1906, ch. 148, sec. 23.

In the case of any escape or attempt to escape aforesaid, whether the term of imprisonment or detention has expired or not, the magistrate may sentence the offender to such additional term of imprisonment or detention, as the case may be, not exceeding one year, as to such magistrate seems a proper punishment for the escape or attempt to escape. R.S.C. 1906, ch. 148, sec. 24.

Escape during conveyance to prison.]—See Prisons Act, R.S.C. 1906, ch. 148, sec. 35(2).

Escape of prisoner at work outside of prison.]—See Prisons Act, R.S.C. 1906, ch. 148, sec. 21.

190. Every one is guilty of an indictable offence and liable to two years' imprisonment who being in lawful custody other than as aforesaid on any criminal charge, escapes from such custody. 55-56 V., c. 29, s. 164. **Escape from custody.**

191. Every one is guilty of an indictable offence and liable to seven years' imprisonment who,— **Penalty.**

(*a*) rescues any person or assists any person in escaping, or attempting to escape, from lawful custody, whether in prison or not, under sentence of death or imprisonment for life, or after conviction of, and before sentence for, or while in such custody upon a charge of any crime punishable with death or imprisonment for life; or, **Rescue of person sentenced to death or for life.**

(*b*) being a peace officer and having any such person in his lawful custody, or being an officer of any prison in which any such person is lawfully confined, voluntarily and intentionally permits him to escape therefrom. 55-56 V., c. 29, s. 165. **Officer permitting escape.**

Rescue.]—Rescue is the deliverance of a prisoner from lawful custody by a third person. 2 Bishop Crim. Law 893. It differs from prison breach only in this that prison breach is by the prisoner himself, while rescue is by another. Escape is the allowing, voluntarily or negligently, of a prisoner lawfully in custody to leave his confinement, and the same term is also used to denote the offence of a prisoner himself going away from the place of custody without a breaking of prison. 2 Bishop Crim. Law 893.

The rescuer, where the prisoner concurs in the rescue, is an aider at the fact, and therefore a principal in the prisoner's offence of prison breach. 1 Bishop Crim. Law 456.

The act of breaking with intent to let the prisoner escape may not be a technical rescue unless he does escape, but it is nevertheless indictable as an attempt. 2 Bishop Crim. Law 915; State v. Murray, 15 Maine 100.

Aiding escape.]—By the common law any assistance given to one known to be a felon in order to hinder his being apprehended or tried or suffering the punishment to which he was condemned, was sufficient to make the person giving such assistance an accessory after the fact to such felony. 2 Hawk., ch. 29, sec. 26. And the aiding and assisting any prisoner to escape out of prison by whatever means it may have been effected or whatever was the nature of the offence with which such prisoner was charged, was viewed as an offence indictable as an obstruction to the course of justice. I Gabbett's Cr. Law 297, 303.

Penalty.

192. Every one is guilty of an indictable offence and liable to five years' imprisonment who,—

Rescuing or assisting to escape in other cases.

(a) rescues any person, or assists any person in escaping or attempting to escape, from lawful custody, whether in prison or not, under a sentence of imprisonment for any term less than life, or after conviction of, and before sentence for, or while in such custody upon a charge of any crime punishable with imprisonment for a term less than life; or,

Officer permitting escape in other cases.

(b) being a peace officer having any such person in his lawful custody, or being an officer of any prison in which such person is lawfully confined, voluntarily and intentionally permits him to escape therefrom. 55-56 V., c. 29, s. 166.

Escape by failure to perform legal duty.

193. Every one is guilty of an indictable offence and liable to one year's imprisonment, who, by failing to perform any legal duty, permits a person in his lawful custody on a criminal charge to escape therefrom. 63-64 V., c. 46, s. 3.

Negligent or voluntary escape.]—Wherever an officer having the custody of a prisoner charged with a criminal offence, knowingly gives him his liberty with an intent to save him either from his trial or punishment he is guilty of a "voluntary escape." 2 Bishop Crim. Law 920.

This formerly involved the officer in guilt for the same crime of which the prisoner was guilty and stood charged with. 2 Hawk., ch. 19, sec. 10.

A "negligent escape" is where the party arrested or imprisoned escapes against the will of him that arrests or imprisons him and is not freshly pursued and taken again before he has been lost sight of. Dalt., ch. 159, sec. 6.

A prisoner who is charged before justices with an indictable offence and who is verbally remanded, after the examination of witnesses, until the following day in order to procure bail or, in default, be committed, is not in the custody of the officer merely for the purpose of enabling him to procure bail, but under the original warrant, and the officer is liable to conviction if he negligently permits him to escape. R. v. Shuttleworth, 22 U.C.Q.B. 372.

Presumption.]—So strongly does the law incline to presume negligence in the officer where an escape occurs, that though such prisoner should break jail yet it seems that it will be deemed a negligent escape in the jailer, because it will be attributed to a want of due vigilance in the jailer or his officers. 1 Hale 601. But the presumption of default in the jailer in cases of escape may be rebutted by satisfactory proof that all due vigilance was used and that the jail was so constructed as to have been considered by persons of competent judgment a place of perfect security. 1 Russ. Cr. 371; 2 Bishop Cr. Law 921.

De facto officer.]—Whoever de facto occupies the office of jailer is liable to answer for a negligent escape, and it is not material whether or not his title to the office be legal, for the ill consequence to the public is the same in either case. 2 Hawk., ch. 19, sec. 23.

Arrest by private person.]—Wherever any person has another lawfully in his custody, whether upon an arrest made by himself or another, he is guilty of an escape if he suffers him to go at large before he has discharged himself by delivering him over to some other who by law ought to have the custody of him. 2 Hawk., ch. 20, sec. 1; 1 Hale 595.

194. Every one is guilty of an indictable offence and liable to two years' imprisonment who with intent to facilitate the escape of any prisoner lawfully imprisoned conveys, or causes to be conveyed, any thing into any prison. 55-56 V., c. 29, s. 167.

Escape by conveying things into prison.

195. Every one is guilty of an indictable offence and liable to two years' imprisonment who knowingly and unlawfully, under colour of any pretended authority, directs or procures the discharge of any prisoner not entitled to be so discharged, and the person so discharged shall be held to have escaped. 55-56 V., c. 29, s. 168.

Causing discharge of prisoner under pretended authority.

196. Every one who escapes from custody, shall, on being retaken, serve, in the prison to which he was sentenced, a term equivalent to the remainder of his term unexpired at the time of his escape, in addition to the punishment which is awarded for such escape.

Full term to be served when retaken.

2. Any imprisonment so awarded may be to the penitentiary or prison from which the escape was made. 55-56 V., c. 29, s. 169.

Place of additional imprisonment.

PART V.

OFFENCES AGAINST RELIGION, MORALS AND PUBLIC CONVENIENCE.

Interpretation.

Definitions.

197. In this Part, unless the context otherwise requires,—

'Theatre.'

(*a*) 'theatre' includes any place open to the public, gratuitously or otherwise, where dramatic, musical, acrobatic or other entertainments or representations are presented or given;

'Guardian.'

(*b*) 'guardian' includes any person who has in law or in fact the custody or control of any girl or child referred to;

'Public place.'

(*c*) 'public place' includes any open place to which the public have or are permitted to have access and any place of public resort. 57-58 V., c. 57, s. 1; 63-64 V., c. 46, s. 3; 3 E. VII., c. 13, s. 2.

Offences Against Religion.

Blasphemous libels.

198. Every one is guilty of an indictable offence and liable to one year's imprisonment who publishes any blasphemous libel.

Question of fact. Proviso. Expression of opinion.

2. Whether any particular published matter is a blasphemous libel or not is a question of fact: Provided that no one is guilty of a blasphemous libel for expressing in good faith and in decent language, or attempting to establish by arguments used in good faith and conveyed in decent language, any opinion whatever upon any religious subject. 55-56 V., c. 29, s. 170.

Blasphemy.]—Blasphemy consists in "speaking evil of the Deity with an impious purpose to derogate from the divine majesty and to alienate the minds of others from the love and reverence of God. It is purposely using words concerning God, calculated and designed to impair and destroy the reverence, respect and confidence due to him as the intelligent creator, governor and judge of the world. It embraces the idea of detraction, when used towards the supreme being as "calumny" usually carries the same idea when applied to an individual. It is a wilful and malicious attempt to lessen men's reverence of God, by denying his existence or his attributes as an intelligent creator, governor and judge of men, and to prevent their having confidence in him as such." Commonwealth v. Kneeland, 20 Pick. 106, 213, per Shaw, C.J.; 2 Bishop Cr. Law 69.

It is to be collected from the offensive levity, scurrilous and opprobrious language, and other circumstances, whether the act of the party was malicious. 2 Bishop Cr. Law 74; Updegraph v. Commonwealth, 11 S. & R. 394, 405.

Blasphemous libel.]—Publications which in an indecent and malicious spirit assail and asperse the truth of Christianity or of the Scriptures in language calculated and intended to shock the feelings and outrage the belief of mankind are punishable as blasphemous libels. R. v. Bradlaugh, 15 Cox C.C. 217; R. v. Hetherington, 4 St. Tr. (N.S.) 563, 590; R. v. Pelletier (1900), 6 Revue Legale, N.S. 116. But if the decencies of controversy are observed even the fundamentals of religion may be attacked without the writer being guilty of blasphemous libel. R. v. Ramsay & Foote, 15 Cox C.C. 231, 238, 1 Cab. & El. 126; Odgers' Libel, 3rd ed., 466.

Defence.]—No justification of a blasphemous libel can be pleaded nor is argument as to its truth permitted. Cooke v. Hughes, Ry. & M. 112; R. v. Tunbridge, 1 St. Tr. (N.S.), 1168; R. v. Hicklin, L.R. 3, Q.B. 360. The application of secs. 910 and 911 of the Code as to pleas of justification is limited to cases of defamatory libels.

Obstructing officiating clergyman.

199. Every one is guilty of an indictable offence and liable to two years' imprisonment who, by threats or force, unlawfully obstructs or prevents, or endeavours to obstruct or prevent, any clergyman or other minister in or from celebrating divine service, or otherwise officiating in any church, chapel, meeting-house, school-house or other place for divine worship, or in or from the performance of his duty in the lawful burial of the dead in any churchyard or other burial place. 55-56 V., c. 29, s. 171.

Status of clergyman.]—The offence of unlawfully obstructing divine service under Code sec. 199 is not made out where the clergyman obstructed had no legal claim to the possession of or use of the church premises and was in point of law himself a trespasser thereon. But an indictment for obstructing a clergyman in celebrating divine service will not be quashed for failure to allege therein that the clergyman was in lawful charge of the church or place of worship. R. v. Wasyl Kapij (1905), 9 Can. Cr. Cas. 186.

Violence to officiating clergyman.

200. Every one is guilty of an indictable offence and liable to two years' imprisonment who strikes or offers any violence to, or arrests upon any civil process or under the pretense of executing any civil process, any clergyman or other minister who is engaged in or, to the knowledge of the offender, is about to engage in, any of the rites or duties in the last preceding section mentioned, or who, to the knowledge of the offender, is going to perform the same, or returning from the performance thereof. 55-56 V., c. 29, s. 172.

Disturbing meetings for religious worship or special purposes.

201. Every one is guilty of an offence and liable, on summary conviction, to a penalty not exceeding fifty dollars and costs, and in default of payment to one month's imprisonment, who wilfully disturbs, interrupts or disquiets any assemblage of persons met for religious worship, or for any moral, social or benevolent purpose, by profane discourse, by rude or indecent behaviour, or by making a noise, either within the place of such meeting or so near it as to disturb the order or solemnity of the meeting. 55-56 V., c. 29, s. 173.

Disturbing religious meetings.]—A person who enters a hall, leased by a religious association or body, while a meeting for religious worship is being held in it under the direction of officers of the association, and addressing himself to the assemblage, says he is a Catholic and a French Canadian, as most of them are, that they should not stay where they are, and calls upon them to leave, is guilty of the offence of disturbing a religious meeting under Cr. Code sec. 201. The King v. Gauthier, 11 Can. Cr. Cas. 203.

At common law.]—Any disturbance of a congregation legally assembled for divine service is an indictable offence at common law. 1 Hawk., ch. 28, sec. 23; Wilson v. Greaves, 1 Burr. 243.

Evidence.]—Where in a contest for the office of clerk of a congregation, one of the candidates pulled the other from the desk, it was held that such constituted a disturbance within a corresponding English statute. R. v. Hube, 5 T.R. 542, 2 R.R. 669.

Meeting for social purpose, etc.]—A meeting of electors called by one of the candidates during a municipal election is not included. The King v. Lavoie, 6 Can. Cr. Cas. 39, 21, Que. S.C. 128.

Offences Against Morality.

Buggery.

202. Every one is guilty of an indictable offence and liable to imprisonment for life who commits buggery, either with a human being or with any other living creature. 55-56 V., c. 29, s. 174.

Buggery.]—This offence, also called sodomy, is the carnal copulation against nature by human beings with each other or with a beast. 1 Bishop Cr. Law 380. There must be a penetration per anum. Archbold Cr. Plead. (1900), 879. A penetration of the mouth is not sodomy; Rex v. Jacobs, Russ. & Ry. 331; but is an offence under sec. 206. Unlike rape, sodomy may be committed between two persons, both of whom consent, and even by husband and wife. R. v. Jellyman, 8 C. & P. 604. Whichever is the pathic, both may be indicted. R. v. Allen, 1 Den. C.C. 364; 2 C. & K. 869.

Evidence.]—The common law presumption is, that a person under fourteen is incapable of having carnal knowledge, not merely that such a person is incapable of committing rape. It is because of the presumption, so understood, that a person under fourteen cannot be convicted of rape. The report of the case of The Queen v. Allen, 1 Dennison Cr. Cas. 364, shews that the presumption applies to cases of unnatural crime. R. v.

Hartlen (1898), 2 Can. Cr. Cas. 12 (N.S.). Penetration alone is now sufficient to constitute the offence. Section 7.

Evidence is not admissible to prove that the defendant has a general disposition to commit the offence. R. v. Cole, 3 Russ. Cr., 6th ed., 251.

Form of indictment.]—"The jurors, etc., present that J. S. on the —— day of —— at the —— with a certain —— (animal), *or*, in and upon one J.N.], unlawfully wickedly and against the order of nature had a venereal affair, and then unlawfully, wickedly and against the order of nature with the said —— did commit and perpetrate that detestable and abominable crime of buggery, not to be named among Christians, against the form of the Criminal Code, sec. 174, and against the peace, etc."

Excluding public from court room.]—See sec. 645.

Assault with intent.]—See secs. 293 and 294.

203. Every one is guilty of an indictable offence and liable to ten years' imprisonment who attempts to commit the offence mentioned in the last preceding section. 55-56 V., c. 29, s. 175. **Attempt to commit.**

Excluding public from court room.]—See sec. 645.

204. Every parent and child, every brother and sister, and every grandparent and grandchild, who cohabit or have sexual intercourse with each other, shall each of them, if aware of their consanguinity, be deemed to have committed incest, and be guilty of an indictable offence and liable to fourteen years' imprisonment, and the male person shall also be liable to be whipped: Provided that, if the court or judge is of opinion that the female accused is a party to such intercourse only by reason of the restraint, fear or duress of the other party, the court or judge shall not be bound to impose any punishment on such person under this section. 55-56 V., c. 29, s. 176. **Incest.** **Effect of compulsion.**

Incest.]—Incest was not an offence punishable at common law, but was dealt with by the English ecclesiastical courts, which had power to imprison for the offence. Stephen's Dig. Cr. Law, article 170. It included other relationships than those specified in sec. 204 of the Code and applied to unlawful intercourse between parties related to each other within the degrees of consanguinity or affinity wherein marriage was prohibited by law. 2 Bishop Cr. Law 15.

Prior to the statute, 53 Vict. (Can.), ch. 37, sec. 8, from which this section is taken, it seems that incest, unless committed under circumstances amounting to rape, was not punishable in Ontario, as the ecclesiastical law of England was not introduced into that province. Re Lord Bishop of Natal, 3 Moo. P.C.N.S. 115.

There were, however, statutes dealing with the offence in the Provinces of Nova Scotia, New Brunswick and Prince Edward Island. R.S.N.S., 3rd series, ch. 160, sec. 2; R.S.N.B., ch. 145, sec. 2; 24 Vict. (P.E.I.), ch. 27, sec. 3. Quære, whether those statutes do not still apply in those provinces as to cases of incest, for which no provision is made by sec. 176.

Evidence.]—Oral evidence is not admissible to prove relationship on a charge of incest in the Province of Quebec, and the relationship must be established by the production of extracts from the registers of civil status, as required by the provincial laws of evidence made applicable to criminal proceedings by the Canada Evidence Act, sec. 35, unless the absence of such registers is proved. R. v. Garneau (1899), 4 Can. Cr. Cas. 69 (Que.). It is not too late for the accused to object that oral evidence is insufficient proof, after the case for the prosecution has been closed. Ibid.

Excluding public from court room.]—See sec. 645.

Indecent acts.

205. Every one is guilty of an offence and liable, on summary conviction before two justices, to a fine of fifty dollars or to six months' imprisonment with or without hard labour, or to both fine and imprisonment, who wilfully,—

In public places.

(*a*) in the presence of one or more persons does any indecent act in any place to which the public have or are permitted to have access; or,

As an insult.

(*b*) does any indecent act in any place intending thereby to insult or offend any person. 53 V., c. 37, s. 6; 55-56 V., c. 29, s. 177.

At common law.]—To publicly expose the naked person was a misdemeanour at common law, R. v. Sedley, 17 St. Tr. 155(n); R. v. Rowed, 3 Q.B. 180. But an indecent exposure seen by one person only was not an offence. R. v. Farrell, 9 Cox 446; R. v. Elliott, L. & C. 103. The presence of only one other person than the accused is now sufficient under this section.

A place out of sight of the public footway, where people had no legal right to go, but did habitually go without interference, is included. R. v. Wellard, L.R. 14 Q.B.D. 63, 15 Cox C.C. 559; R. v. Levasseur, 9 Montreal L.N. 386; Ex p. Walter, Ramsay's Cases (Que.) 183.

Excluding public from court room.]—See sec. 645.

Obscene song with indecent gestures.]—A person is guilty of indecent acts within the meaning of this section, who, in a public theatre in the presence of several persons, makes indecent gestures on his person or otherwise, while singing an obscene song. The Queen v. Jourdan, 8 Can. Cr. Cas. 337.

Provincial legislative power.]—A Provincial Legislature has jurisdiction to legislate concerning matters of police regulation of public morals, but in so far as the same subject is dealt with by the Dominion Parliament, the Dominion legislation will prevail. Ex parte Ashley, 8 Can. Cr. Cas. 328.

The power of enacting such police regulations may be delegated by the Provincial Legislature to municipal councils. Ibid.

"Wilfully."]—A summary conviction for "unlawfully" committing an act does not sufficiently charge that the act was "wilfully" done to constitute an offence under a statute which makes the latter an essential element of the offence. And a person who is summarily convicted on his plea of guilty upon a charge of "unlawfully" committing an indecent act and who is sentenced to imprisonment, is entitled to be discharged on habeas corpus as the commitment and conviction disclose no offence under the criminal law. The word "wilfully" as applied to the offence declared by this section implies that the act was done with evil intent and without any justifiable excuse, while the word "unlawful" does not necessarily

refer to criminal penalty or prohibition. Ex parte O'Shaughnessy, 8 Can. Cr. Cas. 136, 13 Que. K.B. 178; R. v. Tupper, 11 Can. Cr. Cas. 199.

A summary conviction for indecency under this section is bad if it does not state the offence to have been committed wilfully, but a valid conviction correcting the omission may be substituted on a habeas corpus application. The King v. Barre, 11 Can. Cr. Cas. 1.

206. Every male person is guilty of an indictable offence and liable to five years' imprisonment and to be whipped who, in public or private, commits, or is a party to the commission of, or procures or attempts to procure the commission by any male person of, any act of gross indecency with another male person. 55-56 V., c. 29, s. 178. Acts of gross indecency.

This section is similar in its terms to the English Criminal Law Amendment Act of 1885, 48-49 Vict., ch. 69, sec. 11. Under it, it has been held that it is an offence for a male person to procure the commission with himself of an act of gross indecency by another male person. R. v. Jones, [1896] 1 Q.B. 4, 18 Cox C.C. 207.

Excluding public from court room.]—See sec. 645.

Indecent assaults on males.]—See sec. 293.

207. Every one is guilty of an indictable offence and liable to two years' imprisonment who knowingly, without lawful justification or excuse,— Penalty.

(*a*) manufactures, or sells, or exposes for sale or to public view, or distributes or circulates, or causes to be distributed or circulated, any obscene book, or other printed, typewritten or otherwise written matter, or any picture, photograph, model or other object tending to corrupt morals; or, Obscene or immoral books or pictures.

(*b*) publicly exhibits any disgusting object or any indecent show; or, Indecent show.

(*c*) offers to sell, advertises, publishes an advertisement of, or has for sale or disposal, any medicine, drug, or article intended or represented as a means of preventing conception or of causing abortion or miscarriage. Drugs for abortion.

2. No one shall be convicted of any offence in this section mentioned if he proves that the public good was served by the acts alleged to have been done, and that there was no excess in the acts alleged beyond what the public good required. Excess.

3. It shall be a question for the court or judge whether the occasion of the manufacture, sale, exposing for sale, publishing, or exhibition is such as might be for the public good, and whether there is evidence of excess beyond what the public good required in the manner, extent or circumstances in, to or under Questions for judge.

which the manufacture, sale, exposing for sale, publishing or exhibition is made; but it shall be a question for the jury whether there is or is not such excess.

And for jury.

Motives.

4. The motives of the manufacturer, seller, exposer, publisher or exhibitor shall in all cases be irrelevant. 63-64 V., c. 46, s. 3.

Form of indictment.]—That A.B., at , on , unlawfully, and knowingly, and without lawful justification or excuse, did expose for sale, an obscene book called (give name or description) tending to corrupt morals.

Knowingly.]—The offence being that a person "knowingly" without lawful justification or excuse sells or distributes the obscene publication, it is obligatory upon the prosecution to prove knowledge of the contents on the part of the accused. The King v. Beaver, 9 Can. Cr. Cas. 415, 9 O.L.R. 418.

Particulars of indictment.]—By sec. 861 it is provided that no count for (inter alia) selling or exhibiting an obscene book, pamphlet, newspaper or other printed or written matter shall be deemed insufficient on the ground that it does not set forth the words thereof. But sec. 859 empowers the court to order that a particular shall be furnished by the prosecution stating what passages in such book, pamphlet, newspaper, printing or writing are relied on in support of the charge. If the obscene words complained of are in a foreign language a translation of them should be set out in the particulars. Zenobio v. Axtell, 6 T.R. 162; R. v. Peltier, 28 St. Tr. 529.

Obscenity.]—"The test of obscenity is whether the tendency of the matter charged as obscenity is to deprave and corrupt those whose minds are open to such immoral influence, and into whose hands a publication of this sort may fall." R. v. Hicklin, L.R. 3 Q.B. 371, per Cockburn, L.C.J.; R. v. Beaver (1905), 9 Can. Cr. Cas. 415, 9 O.L.R. 418.

The indiscriminate publication of a pamphlet, half of which relates to controversial questions which are not obscene, but the other half of which is obscene, as relating to impure acts and words, is an offence, although the publisher does not sell the pamphlet for the purposes of gain or to prejudice good morals (although the indiscriminate sale of it is calculated to have that effect), but sell it as a member of a politico-religious society, to promote the objects of that society and to expose what he deems to be the errors of the Roman Catholic church and the immorality of the confessional. R. v. Hicklin, supra; Steele v. Brannan, L.R. 7 C.P. 261; note in 9 Can. Cr. Cas. 424.

Indecent show.]—A herbalist, who publicly exposed in his shop a picture of a man naked to his waist and covered with sores, was held to be properly found guilty of a nuisance, though the motive for its exhibition was innocent. R. v. Grey, 4 F. & F. 73.

A person who openly exposes or exhibits in any way, street, road, highway or public place any indecent exhibtion is liable to summary conviction as a "vagrant" under secs. 238 and 239.

Publishing advertisements for sale of obscene books.]—In The King v. De Marny, [1907] 1 K.B. 388, the defendant was indicted for selling and publishing, or causing and procuring to be sold and published obscene books, papers and photograpns. He was a publisher of a newspaper and although warned by the police that certain advertisements published in his paper were for the sale of obscene books, he nevertheless continued to publish them. The police inspector wrote to the addresses given and received in return from the advertisers obscene books. On a case reserved the defendant was held guilty of having taken part or aided and abetted in the publication of the obscene books as charged.

Separate charges on same facts.]—It would seem that separate convictions cannot be had upon substantially the same evidence upon charges for (a) delivering to a certain person an obscene advertisement and (b) aiding and abetting such person in exhibiting the obscene advertisement, for the defendant has the right to set up the defence that he had already been convicted or acquitted as the case may be on the same facts. Hamilton v. Walker, [1892] 2 Q.B. 25.

Advertising drugs for procuring miscarriage.]—Upon a charge of knowingly, and without lawful excuse or justification, advertising a drug intended or represented as a means of causing abortion, the trial judge may withdraw the case from the jury if the advertisement is incapable of such meaning, but if it be held to be capable it is then for the jury to decide whether or not it actually had such meaning having regard to the context of the objectionable words and to the circumstances of the case. The King v. Karn, 5 Can. Cr. Cas. 543, reversed; R. v. Karn, 6 Can. Cr. Cas. 479, 5 O.L.R. 704.

Immoral theatrical performance.

208. Every person who, being the lessee, agent or person in charge or manager of a theatre, presents or gives or allows to be presented or given therein any immoral, indecent or obscene play, opera, concert, acrobatic, variety, or vaudeville performance, or other entertainment or representation, is guilty of an offence punishable on indictment or on summary conviction, and liable, if convicted upon indictment, to one year's imprisonment with or without hard labour, or to a fine of five hundred dollars, or to both, and, on summary conviction, to six months' imprisonment or to a fine of fifty dollars, or to both.

Penalty for lessee or manager.

Person appearing as actor.

2. Every person who takes part or appears as an actor, performer, or assistant in any capacity, in any such immoral, indecent or obscene play, opera, concert, performance, or other entertainment or representation, is guilty of an offence and liable, on summary conviction, to three months' imprisonment, or to a fine not exceeding twenty dollars, or to both.

Penalty.

Person in an indecent costume.

3. Every person who so takes part or appears in an indecent costume is guilty of an offence and liable, on summary conviction, to six months' imprisonment, or to a fine of fifty dollars, or to both. 3 E. VII., c. 13, s. 2.

Indecent theatrical performances.]—Ordinary ballet-dancing in the customary costume does not constitute an immoral or indecent play or performance within the meaning of this section. The word "indecent" has no fixed legal meaning, and it devolves upon the prosecution in a charge of presenting an indecent theatrical performance to affirmatively prove that the performance in question was of a depraving tendency. R. v. McAuliffe (1904), 8 Can. Cr. Cas. 21.

Municipal by-laws.]—A Provincial Legislature has jurisdiction to legislate concerning matters of police regulation of public morals, and to delegate the like authority to municipal councils, but in so far as the same subject is dealt with by the Dominion Parliament, the Dominion legislation will prevail. Ex parte Ashley, 8 Can. Cr. Cas. 328.

Penalty.

209. Every one is guilty of an indictable offence and liable to two years' imprisonment who posts for transmission or delivery by or through the post,—

Posting obscene publications.

(*a*) any obscene or immoral book, pamphlet, newspaper, picture, print, engraving, lithograph, photograph or any publication, matter or thing of an indecent, immoral, or scurrilous character; or,

Letters or post cards.

(*b*) any letter upon the outside or envelope of which, or any post card or post band or wrapper upon which, there are words, devices, matters or things of the character aforesaid; or,

Letters to deceive and defraud.

(*c*) any letter or circular concerning schemes devised or intended to deceive and defraud the public, or for the purpose of obtaining money under false pretenses. 63-64 V., c. 46, s. 3.

Burden of proof.

210. The burden of proof of previous unchastity on the part of the girl or woman under the three next succeeding sections shall be upon the accused. 63-64 V., c. 46, s. 3.

Seduction of girls between fourteen and sixteen.

211. Every one is guilty of an indictable offence and liable to two years' imprisonment who seduces or has illicit connection with any girl of previously chaste character, of or above the age of fourteen years and under the age of sixteen years. 55-56 V., c. 29, s. 181; 56 V., c. 32, s. 1.

Limitation.]—A prosecution under this section must be commenced within one year from the commission of the offence. Sec. 1140(c).

Previously chaste character.]—A similar statute of New York State declares the offence of seduction under promise of marriage, upon an unmarried woman of "previous chaste character." "Chaste character," as thus used in the statute, does not mean reputation for chastity, but actual personal virtue. Kenyon v. People, 26 N.Y. 203, 207. The girl must be actually chaste and pure in conduct and principle, up to the time of the commission of the offence. Carpenter v. People, 8 Barb. 603, 608.

The term "previously chaste character" is not equivalent to previously chaste reputation, but refers to the actual moral status of the woman. Semble, under certain circumstances a woman who has been guilty of unchaste conduct may subsequently become chaste in legal contemplation and be seduced a second time. The King v. Lougheed, 8 Can. Cr. Cas. 184.

The burden of proof of previous unchastity on the part of the girl is upon the accused. Section 210.

Corroboration.]—Section 1002 of the Code enacts that no person accused of an offence under this section shall be convicted upon the evidence of one witness, unless such witness is corroborated in some material particular by evidence implicating the accused.

Evidence of the girl's pregnancy, and of her having been employed in domestic service at the defendant's residence and of facts shewing merely a strong probability of there having been no opportunity at which any other man could have been responsible for her condition, does not constitute the corroborative evidence "implicating the accused" required by sec. 1002, in order to sustain a conviction. R. v. Vahey (Ont.), 2 Can. Cr. Cas. 258.

The prisoner's admission made after the girl reached the age of sixteen that he had had connection with her may be taken into consideration with the other facts, as corroboration of the charge of having had connection with her before she became of that age. R. v. Wyse (1895), 1 Can. Cr. Cas. 6. And a statement made by the accused, before he was charged with the offence, that he had been advised that if he could get the girl to marry him he would escape punishment is corroborative evidence implicating the accused. Ibid.

Evidence that the accused charged with seduction of a girl between 14 and 16 had previously told a witness other than the girl of his desire to have sexual intercourse with her, and of subsequent admissions of the accused from which it might be inferred that he had afterwards taken advantage of an opportunity when he was left in charge of the house where the girl lived, is corroborative evidence to go to the jury under sec. 1002 of the Code, although no medical evidence is adduced in support of the girl's story.

A conviction is good under this section although the evidence was sufficient, if wholly credited, to support a conviction for rape for which charge another indictment had been previously submitted to the grand jury who found no bill. R. v. Doty, 25 O.R. 362.

The corroboration need not be as to every fact in issue and it is sufficient if it confirms the belief that the prosecutrix is speaking the truth. The defendant having been convicted and no question having been reserved or appeal taken except as to the sufficiency of the corroboration, the appellate court cannot review the whole evidence but must proceed on the assumption that the charge as laid was fully proved by the complainant's testimony if the corroborative evidence satisfies the statutory requirements. The King v. Daun, 11 Can. Cr. Cas. 244, 12 O.L.R. 227.

Proving age.]—A certificate of registration of birth, coupled with evidence of identity, is legal evidence of the age of the person mentioned in it. R. v. Cox, [1899] 1 Q.B. 179, 18 Cox C.C. 672; R. v. Weaver, L.R. 2 C.C.R. 85. And see as to records of certain charitable institutions, sec. 984.

Proof of the date of birth may be given by some one who was present at the birth. R. v. Nicholls, 10 Cox 476.

The evidence of the girl as to her own age would not be admissible. R. v. Rishworth, 2 Q.B. 476; but quære, whether she might not identify the certificate of registration of her own birth if she were the custodian of it. Re Bulley (1886), W.N. 80.

Inferring age from appearance.]—See sec. 984.

Excluding public from court room.]—See sec. 645.

Seduction under promise of marriage.

212. Every one, above the age of twenty-one years, is guilty of an indictable offence and liable to two years' imprisonment who, under promise of marriage, seduces and has illicit connection with any unmarried female of previously chaste character and under twenty-one years of age. 55-56 V., c. 29, s. 182.

Limitation.]—The prosecution must take place within one year from the commission of the offence. Section 1140(c).

Where a seduction under promise of marriage has taken place and the illicit intercourse between the parties is continued, upon renewals of promise, for more than a year before the commencement of the prosecution, a prosecution for the original seduction is barred by Code sec. 1140(c), and a conviction is not warranted as for a subsequent seduction within the year as the woman is not then of "previously chaste character." R. v. Lougheed (1903), 8 Can. Cr. Cas. 184; R. v. Howard, 8 Can. Cr. Cas. 188(n).

Amending charge.]—A county judge holding a speedy trial upon a charge of seduction may substitute a new charge to conform to the evidence of the prosecution by stating it as of a prior date upon which a different occurrence is sought to be proved, but such substitution is subject to the right of the accused to re-elect the mode of trial. As regards the offence of seduction the change of the date of the alleged offence by an amendment of the indictment or charge is in substance the laying of a new charge to which a different defence might be applicable. Code sections 889 and 890 apply to authorize an amendment as to time or place in a speedy trial charge without re-election, only where the act or transaction which forms the foundation of the charge is the same, and a mistake was made in the evidence or charge as to the true date of the occurrence. The King v. Lacelle, 10 Can. Cr. Cas. 229, 11 O.L.R. 74.

Corroboration.]—A conviction is not to be made upon the evidence of one witness, unless such witness is corroborated in some material particular by evidence implicating the accused. Section 1002(c); and see note to sec. 211.

Under promise of marriage.]—A subsisting promise of marriage between the seducer and the seduced is necessary. If the man is married, living with his wife, and the woman knows it, his act of seduction is not within the section; if she were ignorant of his subsisting marriage the consequence would be otherwise, because the promise then would be binding on him to the extent of enabling her to maintain against him her civil suit for its breach. Wild v. Harris, 7 C.B. 999; Millward v. Littlewood, 5 Exch. 775; People v. Alger, 7 Parker 333.

A promise of marriage conditional upon her becoming pregnant as a result of the intercourse has been held not to be sufficient to support a charge under a similar New York law. People v. Van Alstyne, 39 N.E. Rep. 343.

It will be observed that while under sec. 211 the offence consists of either seducing *or* having illicit connection, the offence under this section is for seducing *and* having illicit connection. It is therefore necessary to prove that the intercourse was the result of the man's solicitation based upon the promise of marriage as a reason for her acquiescence.

In the North-West provinces it has been held that to constitute the offence of seduction "under promise of marriage" it must be shewn that the seduction was accomplished by means of the promise. A finding by the jury that the accused had previously become engaged to marry the girl and that he renewed the promise of marriage at the time of the seduction was held insufficient to sustain a conviction for seduction under promise of marriage. R. v. Walker (1893), 5 Can. Cr. Cas. 465, 1 Terr. L.R. 482.

The decision in R. v. Walker has been disapproved in Nova Scotia in the recent case of R. v. Romans (1908), 13 Can. Cr. Cas. 68, in which it was held that seduction and illicit connection with a girl under twenty-one and of previously chaste character is "under promise of marriage" and punishable under Cr. Code sec. 212 whether it follows immediately after the promise of marriage or afterwards during the engagement if it can be inferred that the subsistence of the promise induced the girl's consent to carnal intercourse.

Previously chaste character.]—See note to sec. 211. The burden of proof of previous unchastity is upon the accused. Section 210.

Under twenty-one.]—As to proof of age, see note to sec. 211.

Excluding public from court room.]—See sec. 645.

Subsequent marriage of parties.]—The subsequent intermarriage of the seducer and the seduced is a good plea in defence of the charge. Section 214(2).

A refusal by the prosecutrix to accept an offer from the seducer to marry her is no defence; for she may have good reasons for refusing to accept his offer. His conduct may be such after he has accomplished his purpose as to make him unworthy of an alliance, even with the woman he has seduced. His offer of marriage is not a bar to the indictment. Nothing less than an actual marriage is a bar to the prosecution. State v. Mackey, 48 N.W. 918; State v. Wise, 50 Pac. 800.

213. Every one is guilty of an indictable offence and liable to two years' imprisonment,— **Penalty.**

(*a*) who, being a guardian, seduces or has illicit connection with his ward; or, **Seducing ward.**

(*b*) who seduces or has illicit connection with any woman or girl previously chaste and under the age of twenty-one years who is in his employment in a factory, mill, workshop, shop or store, or who, being in a common, but not necessarily similar, employment with him in such factory, mill, workshop, shop or store, is, in respect of her employment or work in such factory, mill, workshop, shop or store, under or in any way subject to his control or direction, or receives her wages or salary directly or indirectly from him. 63-64 V., c. 46, s. 3. **Seducing female employee.**

In the case of the seduction of a ward by her guardian their subsequent intermarriage is not a defence. Section 214. The word "guardian" here includes any person who has in law or in fact the custody or control of the girl. Section 197(b).

Limitation.]—The prosecution must be brought within one year from the time of the offence. Section 1140(c).

Corroboration.]—See sec. 1002.

Excluding public from court room.]—See sec. 645.

Previously chaste.]—The burden of proof of previous unchastity is upon the accused. Section 210.

Seducing female passengers on vessels.

214. Every one is guilty of an indictable offence and liable to a fine of four hundred dollars or to one year's imprisonment, who, being the master or other officer or a seaman or other person employed on board of any vessel, while such vessel is in any water within the jurisdiction of the Parliament of Canada, under promise of marriage, or by threats, or by the exercise of his authority, or by solicitation, or the making of gifts or presents, seduces and has illicit connection with any female passenger.

Marriage a defence.

2. The subsequent intermarriage of the seducer and the seduced is, if pleaded, a good defence to any indictment for any offence against this or either of the two last preceding sections, except in the case of a guardian seducing his ward. 55-56 V., c. 29, s. 184.

Excluding public from court room.]—See sec. 645.

Parent or guardian procuring or party to defilement of girl or woman.

215. Every one who, being the parent or guardian of any girl or woman,—

(*a*) procures such girl or woman to have carnal connection with any man other than the procurer; or,

(*b*) orders, is party to, permits or knowingly receives the avails of, the defilement, seduction or prostitution of such girl or woman;

Penalty.

is guilty of an indictable offence, and liable to fourteen years' imprisonment, if such girl or woman is under the age of fourteen years, and if such girl or woman is of or above the age of fourteen years, to five years' imprisonment. 55-56 V., c. 29, s. 186.

Limitation.]—A prosecution under this section must be commenced within one year from the commission of the offence. Section 1140(c).

Excluding public from court room.]—See sec. 645.

Penalty.

216. Every one is guilty of an indictable offence and liable to two years' imprisonment with hard labour, who,—

Procuring girl for defilement.

(*a*) procures, or attempts to procure, any girl or woman under twenty-one years of age, not being a common prostitute or of known immoral character, to have unlawful carnal connection, either within or without Canada, with any other person or persons; or, (*b*) inveigles or entices any such woman or girl to a house of ill-fame or assignation for the purpose of illicit intercourse or prostitution, or knowingly conceals in such house any such woman or girl so inveigled or enticed; or, Enticing girl to house of ill-fame.

(*c*) procures, or attempts to procure, any woman or girl to become, either within or without Canada, a common prostitute; or, Procuring girl for prostitution.

(*d*) procures, or attempts to procure, any woman or girl to leave Canada with intent that she may become an inmate of a brothel elsewhere; or, To leave Canada for the purpose.

(*e*) procures any woman or girl to come to Canada from abroad with intent that she may become an inmate of a brothel in Canada; or, To come into Canada for the purpose.

(*f*) procures, or attempts to procure, any woman or girl to leave her usual place of abode in Canada, such place not being a brothel, with intent that she may become an inmate of a brothel, within or without Canada; or, To leave her abode for the purpose.

(*g*) by threats or intimidation procures, or attempts to procure, any woman or girl to have any unlawful carnal connection, either within or without Canada; or, Carnal connection by threats.

(*h*) by false pretenses or false representations procures any woman or girl, not being a common prostitute or of known immoral character, to have any unlawful carnal connection, either within or without Canada; or, By false pretenses.

(*i*) applies, administers to, or causes to be taken by any woman or girl any drug, intoxicating liquor, matter, or thing with intent to stupefy or overpower so as thereby to enable any person to have unlawful carnal connection with such woman or girl. 55-56 V., c. 29, s. 185. Administering drugs for the purpose.

Form of indictment under sub-sec. (*a*).]—That C.D. on the day of , in the year by falsely pretending and representing unto one A.B., that here set out the false pretences or representations) did procure the said A.B., to have illicit carnal connection with a certain man named (or to the jurors aforesaid unknown) she, the said A.B., at the time of such procurement, being then a woman (or girl) under the age of twenty-one years, to wit, of the age of whereas the truth and in fact (negative the pretences or representations).

A conviction for "unlawfully procuring or attempting to procure" a girl to become a prostitute, is void for duplicitly and for uncertainty. R. v. Gibson (1898), 2 Can. Cr. Cas. 302.

Limitation.]—Prosecutions for offences under this section must be brought within one year from the commission of the offence. Section 1140(c).

Corroboration.]—No person accused of an offence under this section shall be convicted upon the evidence of one witness unless such witness is corroborated in some material particular by evidence implicating the accused. Section 1002.

In R. v. McNamara (1891), 20 O.R. 489, it was held that on an indictment for attempting to procure a woman to become a prostitute, it is admissible to prove in corroboration of the woman's evidence, that the house to which the prisoner had taken her had the general reputation of being a bawdy house; (Galt, C.J., Rose and MacMahon, JJ.,). Mr. Justice Rose there adopts the opinion of O'Neall, J., in State v. McDowell, Dudley's South Carolina Law & Eq. Reports 346, in which that judge propounds a much more extensive rule and says:—

"Every corrupting fact which can be supplied by general proof should be excluded. The general proof here is just as satisfactory as the most direct proof can be. . . . And in a case in which character is its very gist I am willing to make that which everybody says, the evidence on which a jury may, if they choose, convict defendants for keeping a bawdy house." Dudley S.C.L. & Eq. R. 346.

With reference to the opinion just quoted, Osler, J.A., said in The Queen v. St. Clair, 3 Can. Cr. Cas. 551, that he was not prepared to concur with it unreservedly.

Search for women in house of ill-fame.]—See sec. 640.

Excluding public from court room.]—See sec. 645.

By false pretences.]—Sub-section (h) declares it to be an offence by false pretences or false representations to procure any unlawful carnal connection with the exception therein stated. It will be observed that the words "with any *other* person or persons" which are used in sub-sec. (a) are not used in sub-sec. (h). Under a similar English statute a conviction was upheld under the false pretence clause for procuring the unlawful connection between the prosecutrix and the accused himself upon the false representation of the accused that he was not a married man. R. v. Williams (1898), 33 Eng. L.J. 253; R. v. Jones, [1898] 1 Q.B. 4.

Inducing to come from abroad.]—Upon a charge of procuring a girl to come to Canada from abroad with intent that she may become an inmate of a brothel in Canada, the acts of inducement must be shewn to have been committed in Canada to give jurisdiction to a Canadian court, unless the accused is a British subject. Re Gertie Johnson, 8 Can. Cr. Cas. 243.

Householder permitting defilement.

217. Every one who, being the owner or occupier of any premises, or having, or acting or assisting in, the management or control thereof, induces or knowingly suffers any girl under the age of eighteen years to resort to or be in or upon such premises for the purpose of being unlawfully and carnally known by any man, whether such carnal knowledge is intended to be with any particular man, or generally, is guilty of an indictable offence, and is liable,—

Penalty. Age.

(a) to ten years' imprisonment if such girl is under the age of fourteen years;

Penalty. Age.

(b) to two years' imprisonment if such girl is of or above the age of fourteen years. 63-64 V., c. 46, s. 3.

Evidence.]—On a charge of allowing a girl under 18 to be upon premises for immoral purposes, the evidence of the girl proving that she shared with the proprietor the money she obtained by prostitution there carried on, is sufficiently corroborated under Code sec. 1002, by the evidence of another witness tending to shew that the place was a bawdy house. The King v. Brindley (1903), 6 Can. Cr. Cas. 196.

A father was convicted under a similar section of the English Criminal Law Amendment Act, 1885, of knowingly suffering his daughter under sixteen to be on the premises for the purpose mentioned, although occupied by the father and daughter as their home. R. v. Webster, 16 Q.B.D. 134, 15 Cox C.C. 775; but a mother was held not to be guilty under it where, for the purpose of obtaining conclusive evidence against a man who had seduced her daughter, she permitted him to come to her house to repeat his unlawful intercourse. R. v. Merthyr Tydfil Justices, 10 Times L.R. 375.

Corroboration required.]—See sec. 1002.

Limitation.]—The prosecution must be commenced within one year from the commission of the offence. Section 1140(*c*).

Excluding public from court room.]—See sec. 645.

218. Every one is guilty of an indictable offence and liable to two years' imprisonment who conspires with any other person by false pretenses, or false representations or other fraudulent means to induce any woman to commit adultery or fornication. 55-56 V., c. 29, s. 188. Conspiracy to defile.

Corroboration.]—See sec. 1002.

Excluding public from court room.]—See sec. 645.

219. Every one is guilty of an indictable offence and liable to four years' imprisonment who unlawfully and carnally knows, or attempts to have unlawful carnal knowledge of, any female idiot or imbecile, insane or deaf and dumb woman or girl, under circumstances which do not amount to rape but where the offender knew or had good reason to believe, at the time of the offence, that the woman or girl was an idiot, or imbecile, or insane or deaf and dumb. 63-64 V., c. 46, s. 3. Carnally knowing idiots.

It has been held that, in the case of alleged rape on an idiot or lunatic the mere proof of connection will not warrant the case being left to the jury; that there must be some evidence that it was without her consent, e.g., that she was incapable, from imbecility, of expressing assent or dissent; and that if she consent from mere animal passion it is not rape. R. v. Connolly (1867), 26 U.C.Q.B. 317.

Corroboration.]—See sec. 1002.

Excluding public from court room.]—See sec. 645.

220. Every one is guilty of an indictable offence and liable to a penalty not exceeding one hundred dollars and not less than ten dollars, or six months' imprisonment,— Penalty.

Keeping habitation for prostitution of Indian women.

(*a*) who, being the keeper of any house, tent or wigwam, allows or suffers any unenfranchised Indian woman to be or remain in such house, tent or wigwam, knowing or having probable cause for believing that such Indian woman is in or remains in such house, tent or wigwam with the intention of prostituting herself therein; or,

Prostitution therein.

(*b*) who, being an Indian woman, prostitutes herself therein; or,

Frequenting the same.

(*c*) who, being an unenfranchised Indian woman, keeps, frequents or is found in a disorderly house, tent or wigwam used for any such purpose.

Who deemed keeper.

2. Every person who appears, acts or behaves as master or mistress, or as the person who has the care or management, of any house, tent or wigwam in which any such Indian woman is or remains for the purpose of prostituting herself therein, is deemed to be the keeper thereof, notwithstanding he or she is not in fact the real keeper thereof. 55-56 V., c. 29, s. 190.

Corroboration.]—See sec. 1002.

Excluding public from court room.]—See sec. 645.

Nuisances.

Common nuisance defined.

221. A common nuisance is an unlawful act or omission to discharge a legal duty, which act or omission endangers the lives, safety, health, property or comfort of the public, or by which the public are obstructed in the exercise or enjoyment of any right common to all His Majesty's subjects. 55-56 V., c. 29, s. 191.

Common law.]—This section is a statement of the common law in regard to indictable nuisances.

The injury or annoyance must be to the whole community in general to constitute a common (*i.e.*, a public) nuisance, and whether or not the number of persons affected is sufficient to make it a common nuisance is a question for the jury. R. v. White, 1 Burr. 337.

The omission of an electric railway company operating their cars upon a highway to use reasonable precautions so as to avoid endangering the lives of the public using the highway in common with the company, is a breach of legal duty constituting a common nuisance for which an indictment will lie. R. v. Toronto Ry. Co. (1900), 4 Can. Cr. Cas. 4, 10 Can. Cr. Cas. 106.

The carrying on of an offensive tradé is indictable where it is destructive of the health of the neighbourhood or renders the houses untenantable. R. v. Davey, 5 Esp. 217; R. v. Neil, 2 C. & P. 485. But if a noxious trade is already established in a place remote from habitations and public roads, and persons afterwards come and build houses within the reach of its noxious effects; or if a public road be made so near to it that the carrying on of the trade becomes a nuisance to the persons using the road, in those cases the party is entitled to continue his trade because it was legal before the erecting of the houses in the one case and the making of the road in the other. R. v. Cross, 2 C. & P. 483, per Abbott, C.J.; R. v. Nevill, Peake R. 93. If, however, the annoyance is much increased by the extension of the trade carried on, a conviction is proper. R. v. Watt, Moo. & Mal. N.P. 281.

Manufacturing or keeping large quantities of gunpowder in towns or closely inhabited places is an indictable offence at common law. R. v. Williams, 1 Russ. Cr. 5th ed. 421; R. v. Taylor, 2 Str. 1167; Crowder v. Tinkler, 19 Ves. 617; and the same rule applies to the keeping and storing of large quantities of naphtha and rectified spirits of wine, the same being proved to be more inflammable than either spirits or gunpowder and there being no efficient means of putting out a fire if communicated to the premises. R. v. Lister, Dears. & B. 209, 26 L.J.M.C. 196. As to the illegal possession of explosives for an unlawful object, see sec. 114, ante.

Nuisance by noise if sufficiently great is indictable. Walker v. Brewster, L.R. 5 Eq. 25; Bellamy v. Wells, 39 W.R. 158; Christie v. Davey, [1893] 1 Ch. 316; excepting, however, noise made in the exercise of statutory powers and without negligence. Harrison v. Southwark W.W. Co., [1891] 2 Ch. 409.

Omission to discharge a legal duty.]—If the legal duty does not exist at common law, and a particular penalty is imposed by the statute creating the duty, the remedy by indictment for common nuisance is probably excluded. Bulbrook v. Goodere, 3 Burr. 1768; Saunders v. Holborn Board, [1895] 1 Q.B. 64, 61 L.J.Q.B. 101.

The object with which the omission is made is immaterial if the probable result is to affect the public or any appreciable part of the public injuriously in any of the ways stated in the section. R. v. Moore, 3 B. & Ad. 184; R. v. Carlisle, 6 C. & P. 636; R. v. Lloyd, 4 Esp. 200; Barber v. Penley, [1893] 3 Ch. 447.

Master's liability.]—Where works are so carried on as to be a nuisance, and the proprietor is indicted therefor, it has been held not to be a defence that he did not personally superintend the works and that he had given express orders to his employees that the works should be carried on in a manner which, had it been followed, would not have caused a nuisance. R. v. Stephens, L.R. 1 Q.B. 702.

Time.]—The public have a right to demand the suppression of a common nuisance though of long standing. Weld v. Hornby, 7 East 199; Anonymous, 3 Camp. 227; Fowler v. Sanders, Cro. Jac. 446. But where the alleged nuisance relates to the carrying on of a trade, the fact that it has been of long standing militates against a finding of nuisance. 1 Russ. Cr. 5th ed. 442; R. v. Nevill, Peake R. 93; R. v. Smith, 4 Esp. 111.

Abatement.]—See sec. 223.

Highway repairs.]—Alterations authorized by statute to be made upon highways must be made with reasonable care and so as to cause no unnecessary danger to the travelling public or the parties doing the work may be indicted under this section. R. v. Burt, 11 Cox 339.

222. Every one is guilty of an indictable offence and liable to one year's imprisonment or a fine who commits any common nuisance which endangers the lives, safety or health of the public, or which occasions injury to the person of any individual. 55-56 V., c. 29, s. 192. **Criminal common nuisances.**

Common law indictment.]—An indictment for a nuisance in obstructing a public highway is insufficient to charge a criminal offence under this section if it does not allege danger to the public or injury to the person of some one; and personal injury is not to be inferred from a count which states "actual" injury to a person named. Obstruction of a highway is indictable at common law although injury to the person has not resulted, if it constitutes a common nuisance to His Majesty's subjects passing along the same; but since the Criminal Code the procedure by indictment where there has been no personal injury, remains only for the purpose of abatement or remedy of the nuisance.

An indictment at common law for a nuisance in obstructing a highway must contain the words "to the common nuisance of all His Majesty's subjects passing, etc., along such highway," and must particularize the highway and the nature of the obstruction. The King v. Reynolds (1906), 11 Can. Cr. Cas. 312.

See also sec. 284 as to negligently causing bodily injury.

Non-criminal common nuisances.

223. Any one convicted upon any indictment or information for any common nuisance other than those mentioned in the last preceding section, shall not be deemed to have committed a criminal offence; but all such proceedings or judgments may be taken and had as heretofore to abate or remedy the mischief done by such nuisance to the public right. 55-56 V., c. 29, s. 193.

Other common nuisances not criminal.]—Quære whether the intention of Parliament was simply to declare by this section that the remedy by abatement should apply to the exclusion of other and more rigorous modes of punishment incident to "criminal offences."

A strict construction of the words declaring that persons convicted of other common nuisances shall not be deemed to have committed "criminal offences" seems to place the excluded class of cases wholly outside of the criminal law and to relegate that class to provincial jurisdiction. So long as the nuisance is dealt with as a criminal offence, the Parliament of Canada would have undoubted jurisdiction to deal with the remedy by abatement or otherwise. But viewed as a non-criminal offence, the provincial law prior to admission into Confederation would become applicable subject to the legislation of the Provincial Legislature since Confederation. The latter portion of the section as to proceedings being, taken as heretofore for abatement may, in this view, be considered as a saving clause (probably unnecessary) to preserve the common law remedy of indictment in such cases, subject to provincial legislation.

In a recent Nova Scotia case, Judge Graham said:—

"After the Parliament of Canada has divided nuisances into those which constitute criminal offences and those which do not, one cannot probably look in the Statutes of Canada for further provisions on the subject of those nuisances which are not criminal offences. We have to look to the proceedings which, before the existence of the Criminal Code, might be taken to abate or remedy the mischief, that is, to the common law." R. v. Reynolds (1906), 11 Can. Cr. Cas. 312.

As to the power of a local Legislature to declare an offence a "nuisance" and to provide the punishment when it would not per se be indictable at common law, see Pillow v. City of Montreal (1885), Mont. L.R. 1 Q.B. 401.

Abatement of nuisance.]—If the nuisance is alleged in the indictment to be still continuing the judgment may direct that the defendant shall remove it at has own cost. 1 Hawk., ch. 75, sec. 14.

A railroad company was found guilty on an indictment for a nuisance by obstructing a public highway, by lowering the same at a point of intersection and thereby making the highway dangerous. Time having elapsed, and nothing having been done to abate the nuisance, a motion was made for judgment on the verdict, and it was held that the proper sentence was that defendants should pay a fine, and that the nuisance complained of be abated. R. v. The Grand Trunk Railway Co. (1858), 17 U.C.Q.B. 165.

It is the duty of a municipality, in whom a highway is vested, to see that obstructions on the highway are removed. R. v. Cooper (1876), 40 U.C.Q.B. 294.

It is a nuisance also to obstruct the navigation of a public river, but it is a question for the jury in each case to determine whether or not the erection of a bridge or wall partly in the river constitutes an actual obstruction. R. v. Betts, 16 Q.B. 1022.

A permanent obstruction erected upon a highway without lawful authority and which renders the way less commodious than before to the public is a common nuisance, although the safety of the public is not endangered. R. v. United Kingdom Telegraph Co., 31 L.J.M.C. 166. And this notwithstanding the fact that sufficient space was left for traffic and that the telegraph poles which constituted the obstruction were not placed on the travelled portion of the road. Ibid.

Where a county council is liable to repair a bridge, the proper remedy is inductment, not mandamus. Re Jamieson and County of Lanark (1876), 38 U.C.Q.B. 647.

Where land, which was part of the lands reserved to the Hudson's Bay Company was sold in a state of nature to a purchaser, who obtained a certificate of ownership therefor under the Territories Real Property Act, and cultivated and enclosed it, thus preventing the use of an old trail, which, subsequently, was surveyed and transferred to the Lieutenant-Governor for the use of the Territories. Held, that the purchaser was rightly convicted of obstructing a public highway. The Queen v. Nimmons (1892), 1 Terr. L.R. 415.

Costs.]—If a municipality found guilty of maintaining a nuisance by not repairing a highway, makes default under the judgment ordering abatement thereof, but repairs the highway pending a motion for a writ of de nocumento, the court may in its discretion order the costs of the motion to be paid by the defendant. The King v. Portage la Prairie, 10 Can. Cr. Cas. 125.

Where an indictment for obstructing a highway had been removed by certiorari, at the instance of the private prosecutor into the Court of Queen's Bench and defendant was acquitted, it was held that the court had no power to impose payment of costs on such prosecutor, except as a condition of any indulgence granted in such a case, such as a postponement of the trial, or a new trial. R. v. Hart (1880), 45 U.C.Q.B. 1.

224. Every one is guilty of an indictable offence and liable to one year's imprisonment who knowingly and wilfully exposes for sale, or has in his possession with intent to sell, for human food articles which he knows to be unfit for human food. **Knowingly selling unfit food.**

Penalty for subsequent offence.

2. Every one who is convicted of this offence after a previous conviction for the same crime shall be liable to two years' imprisonment. 55-56 V., c. 29, s. 194.

At common law.]—The selling of food which is dangerous or unfit for human food with knowledge of the fact is an offence at common law. R. v. Dixon (1814), 3 M. & Sel. 11; 15 R.R. 381; Shillito v. Thompson (1875), 1 Q.B.D. 12. If death ensues from eating such food, the seller knowing that it is dangerous is indictable for manslaughter. R. v. Stevenson (1861), 3 F. & F. 106; R. v. Kempson (1893), 28 L.J. (Eng.) 477.

Procedure.]—It is not competent for magistrates where an information charges an offence under this section which they have no jurisdiction to try summarily, to convert the charge into one under a municipal by-law which they have jurisdiction to try summarily, and to so try it on the original information. R. v. Dungey (1901), 5 Can. Cr. Cas. 38.

Adulterated foods and drugs.]—Other provisions regarding the adulteration of foods and drugs and the sale or exposure for sale of the adulterated article are contained in the Adulteration Act (Canada).

Common bawdy-house defined.

225. (*As amended*, 1907). A common bawdy-house is a house, room, set of rooms or place of any kind kept for purposes of prostitution, or occupied or resorted to by one or more persons for such purposes. 55-56 V., c. 29, s. 195; 6 & 7 Edw. VII., c. 8.

Bawdy house with only one occupant.]—Since the amendment of 1907 the numerous decisions under the old section, holding that the use of the house by more than one prostitute was essential to the offence, are no longer applicable. See R. v. Young (1902), 6 Can. Cr. Cas. 42; R. v. Osberg, 9 Can. Cr. Cas. 180, 15 Man. R. 147; R. v. Mannix, 10 Can. Cr. Cas. 150, 10 O.L.R. 303.

At common law.]—The keeping of a bawdy house is a nuisance at common law, on the ground both of its corrupting public morals and its endangering the public peace by reason of dissolute persons resorting thereto. 1 Russell on Crimes, 5th ed., 427; Hawkins Pleas of the Crown, b. 1, ch. 47, sec. 1.

It is immaterial whether indecent or disorderly conduct is or is not perceptible from the outside. Steph. Crim. Law, 122; R. v. Rice (1866), L.R. 1 C.C.R. 21.

The term "house of ill-fame" is synonymous with "bawdy house," Century Dict., *verb*, "house."

The common law punishment was by fine or imprisonment, but without hard labour.

A feme covert may be guilty of the offence as well as if she were a feme sole, for the *keeping* the house does not necessarily import property but may signify that share of government which the wife has in a family as well as the husband. R. v. Williams (1712), 1 Salk. 383.

Bawdy house defined.]—The statutory definition of a "common bawdy house" contained in this section of the Code is intended merely to define the nature of the premises within which a bawdy house may be kept, and not as stating what acts constitute such keeping. R. v. Osberg, 9 Can. Cr. Cas. 180; R. v. Mannix, 10 Can. Cr. Cas. 150, 10 O.L.R. 303.

In The King v. Shepherd (1902), 6 Can. Cr. Cas. 463, Townshend, J., of the Supreme Court of Nova Scotia, held that a conviction by a magistrate on a summary trial for keeping a common bawdy house need not specify the location of the house further than to shew that it was at a place within the jurisdiction of the court, and that a conviction for keeping a common bawdy house is sufficient without the addition of particulars shewing what part of the statutory definition here given is the basis for the adjudication. But in the same case, upon another writ of habeas corpus, Weatherbe, J., held that this section enlarges the meaning of the term "common bawdy house," and that it is necessary that a conviction for keeping "a disorderly house, that is to say a bawdy house," should shew further particulars of the offence by specifying what was the subject of the keeping for purposes of prostitution, *i.e.*, whether a "house," "room," "set of rooms," or other "place," so as to come within the definition.

A tent, shed or camp, or other place, may be brought within the Act, provided it be used for the purpose as defined by the Act. 9 Am. & Eng. Ency. of Law, 2nd ed., p. 512; R. v. Shepherd (1902), 6 Can. Cr. Cas. 463.

226. A common gaming-house is,— **Common gaming-house defined.**

(a) a house, room or place kept by any person for gain, to which persons resort for the purpose of playing at any game of chance, or at any mixed game of chance and skill; or,

(b) a house, room or place kept or used for playing therein at any game of chance, or any mixed game of chance and skill, in which

(i) a bank is kept by one or more of the players exclusively of the others; or,

(ii) any game is played the chances of which are not alike favourable to all the players, including among the players the banker or other person by whom the game is managed, or against whom the game is managed, or against whom the other players stake, play or bet.

2. Any such house, room or place shall be a common gaming-house, although part only of such game is played there and any other part thereof is played at some other place, either in Canada or elsewhere, and although the stake played for, or any money, valuables, or property depending on such game, is in some other place, either in Canada or elsewhere. 55-56 V., c. 29, s. 196; 58-59 V., c. 40, s. 1. **Effect of part of game only being played there or stake elsewhere.**

At common law.]—The maintenance of common gaming houses was punishable as a nuisance at common law on the ground that they are detrimental to the public, as they promote cheating and other corrupt practices; and incite to idleness and avaricious ways of gaming property, great numbers whose time might otherwise be employed for the good of the community. Jenks v. Turpin (1884), 13 Q.B.D. 505, 514; Russell on Crimes, 1896, 6th ed. 1, 741.

Evidence.]—It makes no difference that the use of the house and the gaming therein was limited to the subscribers and members of a club, and that it was not open to all persons who might be desirous of using the same; a common gaming house is that which is forbidden—that is, a house in which a large number of persons are invited habitually to congregate for the purposes of gaming. Per Hawkins, J., in Jenks v. Turpin (1884), 13 Q.B.D. 505, 516.

Proof that a game with cards, dice and "chips" was being played by several people seated at tables, each player procuring the "chips" from the accused, the proprietor of the place, and handing over to him the money therefor and that the accused said that the game was "fan tan" and that he was "doing well out of it," is evidence that the game was a game of chance and that the place was being kept by the accused "for gain" under Code secs. 196 and 198. R. v. Mah Kee (1905), 9 Can. Cr. Cas. 47 (N.W.T.).

Proof that persons other than those resident at or belonging to the house, room or place at which the proprietor operates for gain a game of chance or a mixed game of chance and skill, were in attendance there and participated in such game is evidence that such persons "resorted" to such place for the purpose of playing such game, and of the place being a common gaming house under secs. 226 and 228. Ibid.

The keeping of a house, room or place for playing a game of chance or mixed game of chance and skill in which the chances of the game are in favour of the player who is the dealer or banker therein for the time being, is an indictable offence under secs. 226 and 228, if the position of dealer or banker passes from one player to another by the chances of the game and not by rotation. R. v. Petrie (1900), 3 Can. Cr. Cas. 439 (B.C.).

A magistrate might reasonably decide that a room was a common gaming house if it is commonly used or adopted for gaming, frequented by many people promiscuously, especially if by many various persons, by a fortuitous concourse, or without the necessity of any direct or personal invitation from the occupier or other person legally entitled to the sole enjoyment of the room or place, and if thereby a general opportunity of gaming was afforded though without any fixed intention or invitation to do so. Per Begbie, C.J., in R. v. Ah Pow (1880), B.C.R., pt. 1, p. 152.

Such an establishment will be a common gaming house though a large part of the general public are excluded by keys or watch-words, or in any other manner. Ibid; R. v. Laird (1894), 3 Rev. de Jur. (Que.) 389.

Euchre is a game of chance, and not a game of mere skill. R. v. Laird (1903), 7 Can. Cr. Cas. 318 (Ont.).

The proprietor of a place in which the game known as "darts" is carried on under conditions which make the chances of the proprietor much more favourable than that of the customers is properly convicted of keeping a gaming house. R. v. Cashen (1906), 11 Can. Cr. Cas. 183 (N.S.).

It is a question of fact and not of law whether the use of a slot machine for selling cigars, whereby customers obtained for the one price a number of cigars varying according to the working of the machine, is or is not a game of chance, a mixed game of chance and skill, or a game of skill only. The King v. Fortier (1903), 7 Can. Cr. Cas. 417 (Que.).

The proprietor of a place in which a cane and ring game is carried on under conditions which make the chances of the proprietor much more favourable than that of the customer is properly convicted of keeping a gaming house. The King v. Russell, 11 Can. Cr. Cas. 180.

In R. v. James (1903), 6 O.L.R. 35, 7 Can. Cr. Cas. 196, the defendant was indicted for keeping a common gaming house. The evidence shewed that the defendant was the manager of a cigar shop, in the rear of which was a room to which persons, chiefly customers, commonly resorted for the purpose of playing "poker." Out of the stakes on most of the hands a sum of five cents was withdrawn to cover the expenses of refreshments consumed by the players. No charge was made for the use of the room. The "rake-off" did not more than cover a fair price for the refreshments. The proprietor or manager derived an indirect advantage from the sale of cigars to the players, from 50 to 100 being sold to them in the course of a night's play. Held, that "gain" may be derived indirectly as well as directly; that by what the defendant allowed to be done in the room mentioned, the profits of his usual business were increased more or less owing to the sale of the goods in which he dealt, and so he might be found to have kept the room for gain, though the gain was confined to the profits on the cigars which he sold to the players. The question of what is a keeping for gain ought not to be embarrassed by the consideration of whether the amount the defendant receives is an actual substantial profit to him over the price of the cigars which he sells and the refreshments which he furnishes to the players. R. v. James (1903), 6 O.L.R. 35, 7 Can. Cr. Cas. 196. And see R. v. Brady (1896), 10 Que. S.C. 539.

The decision in R. v. Saunders (1900), 3 Can. Cr. Cas. 495, must now be considered as overruled by the decision in R. v. James, supra.

In The Queen v. Humphrey, [1898] 1 Q.B. 875, an archway which was a private thoroughfare leading from a public street into a yard containing dwelling houses, stables and workshops, which the prisoner was accustomed to resort to for the purpose of betting with persons who came to him there, was held to be a "place" within the meaning of the Betting Act, 1853, (16 & 17 Vict. (Imp.), ch. 119) secs. 1, 3. And see Brown v. Patch, [1899] 1 Q.B. 892; Belton v. Busby, [1899] 2 Q.B. 380; Powell v. Kempton Park, [1899] App. Cas. 143.

Even if the Provincial Legislature of Ontario has authority to authorize municipalities to pass by-laws "for suppressing gambling houses," a municipal by-law assuming to prohibit a person from allowing a game of cards to be played for money in his house is invalid as being in excess of the power delegated. R. v. Spegelman (1904), 9 Can. Cr. Cas. 169. The older provinces may still have special laws passed before Confederation and not repealed which as to them are portions of the criminal law.

In Manitoba it has been held that the offence of keeping a common gaming house is an offence against the general criminal law, and that consequently it can be dealt with only by the Parliament of Canada, and cannot be made an offence by a provincial statute or by a municipal by-law passed under the authority of such a statute. Reg. v. Shaw, 7 Man. R. 518.

A game of whist played on licensed premises for prizes given by third persons does not constitute "gaming" within the meaning of the English Licensing Act. Lockwood v. Cooper, [1903] 2 K.B. 428.

Search in gaming house.]—See secs. 641 and 642.

Statutory presumptions of unlawful gaming.]—See secs. 985 and 986.

Property in Canada or elsewhere.]—The decision in R. v. Wettman (1894), 1 Can. Cr. Cas. 287, is no longer applicable since the enactment of the second sub-section in 1895. Compare sec. 227, sub-sec. (d).

Gaming in stocks.]—See secs. 231-233.

Looking on in gaming house.]—See sec. 229.

Obstructing police officer from entering gaming house.]—See sec. 230.

Common betting-house defined.

227. A common betting-house is a house, office, room or other place,—

(*a*) opened, kept or used for the purpose of betting between persons resorting thereto and

(i) the owner, occupier or keeper thereof,

(ii) any person using the same,

(iii) any person procured or employed by, or acting for or on behalf of any such person,

(iv) any person having the care or management, or in any manner conducting the business thereof; or,

(*b*) opened, kept or used for the purpose of any money or valuable thing being received by or on behalf of any such person as aforesaid, as or for the consideration

(i) for any assurance or undertaking, express or implied, to pay or give thereafter any money or valuable thing on any event or contingency of or relating to any horse race or other race, fight, game or sport, or

(ii) for securing the paying or giving by some other person of any money or valuable thing on any such event or contingency; or,

(*c*) opened, or kept for the purpose of recording or registering bets upon any contingency or event, horse race or other race, fight, game or sport, or for the purpose of receiving money or other things of value to be transmitted for the purpose of being wagered upon any such contingency or event, horse race or other race, fight, game or sport, whether any such bet is recorded or registered there, or any money or other thing of value is there received to be so transmitted or not; or,

(*d*) opened, kept or used for the purpose of facilitating or encouraging or assisting in the making of bets upon any contingency or event, horse race or other race, fight, game or sport, by announcing the betting upon, or announcing or displaying the results of, horse races or other races, fights, games or sports, or in any other manner, whether such contingency or event, horse race or other race, fight, game or sport occurs or takes place in Canada or elsewhere. 55-56 V., c. 29, s. 197; 58-59 V., c. 40, s. 1.

Race course of incorporated association.]—A moveable booth used on the race course of an incorporated racing association for the purpose of making bets is an "office" or "place" used for betting between persons resorting thereto as defined in sec. 227, and the bookmaker using it is properly convicted of keeping a common betting house. Sub-section 2 of sec. 235, which exempts from the provisions of the main section (dealing with the recording or registering in bets, etc.), bets made on the race course of an incorporated association does not apply to the offence of keeping a common betting house. The King v. Saunders, 12 Can. Cr. Cas. 33, affirmed by Supreme Court of Canada, 12 Can. Cr. Cas. 174, sub-nom. Saunders v. The King. See also note to sec. 235.

It is an offence under the Criminal Code to keep a common betting house whether or not it is kept on the race course of an incorporated association, and is operated only during the actual progress of a race meeting. R. v. Hanrahan (1902), 5 Can. Cr. Cas. 430, 3 O.L.R. 659; Walsh v. Trebilcock, 23 Can. S.C.R. 695.

In order to constitute a "place" within the meaning of section 227 of the Criminal Code, there must be a measure of fixity, localization and exclusive right of user. The defendants were two of a number of bookmakers who, on payment of the usual entrance fee, were admitted, along with the general public, to a fenced enclosure owned and controlled by the Ontario Jockey Club, an incorporated racing association. These bookmakers laid bets from day to day, through their assistants, with members of the general public attending the races. They did not use any desk, stool, umbrella, tent or booth, or erection of any kind to mark any place where bets were made, and no part of the general enclosure was especially allocated to them, nor did they occupy a fixed position, but during each race stood as much as possible about the same spot within a radius of from five to ten feet. The betting operations were carried on in the same method as in the case of Rex v. Saunders, except that in that case the bookmakers used a wooden box or booth, moved about on castors from one part of the grounds to another during the progress of the race meeting.

Held, that the defendants did not occupy a "house, office, room or other place" within the meaning of section 227 of the Criminal Code, and were, therefore, not guilty of the offence of keeping a "common betting house" under section 228 of the Code. (Powell v. Kempton Park Racecourse Co. (1899), A.C. 143, followed, and Rex v. Saunders (1907) (No. 2), 12 Can. Cr. Cas. 174, 38 S.C.R. 382, distinguished.) R. v. Moylett (1907), 15 O.L.R. 348.

Incorporated jockey club.]—Mere acquiescence by a director in prohibited acts of a corporation is not such a participation therein as will constitute him an aider or abettor or make him criminally liable as a party under Code sec. 69 for the illegal acts of the corporation. And the lease by an incorporated jockey club of the betting privileges at the race tracks of the club with the knowledge and acquiescence of the club's president in the making of the lease and in the use of the covered betting inclosure by bookmakers exercising its privileges but without his taking part otherwise in the betting or in the management of the enclosure, does not involve the club's president in criminal liability as the keeper of a common betting house under Code secs. 227 and 228. The King v. Hendrie, 10 Can. Cr. Cas. 298, 11 O.L.R. 202.

Betting—Deposit of post-dated cheques.]—Where two parties enter into a voidable betting or gaming contract, each putting up his own cheque post-dated the day on which the result of the bet would be ascertained, the fact that the loser's cheque was dishonoured because he had no account at the bank will not support a charge that he obtained the execution of the winner's cheque delivered to the stakeholder for a like amount by false pretences with intent to defraud. The giving of a post-dated cheque implies no more than a promise to have sufficient funds in the bank on the date thereof and is not, in itself, a false representation of a fact past or present. Intent to defraud could not be found because the complainant was legally entitled to withdraw from the voidable contract even after the event upon which the bet was placed. The King v. Richard, 11 Can. Cr. Cas. 279.

Facilitating betting by announcing results.]—The publication in a newspaper of an advertisement soliciting bets to be placed upon horse races and also of the results from day to day of said races is illegal; and the newspaper proprietor is liable under sec. 227 (d) for the indictable offence of using the newspaper office for the purpose of facilitating the making of bets upon a horse race, and keeping a common betting house within the statutory definition of that offence. The King v. Smallpiece, 7 Can. Cr. Cas. 556; McKenzie v. Hawk, [1902] K.B. 215; Hawk v. McKenzie, 2 K.B. 225.

"In Canada or elsewhere."]—Betting in Canada upon a horse race run in the United States is prohibited by this section. R. v. Giles, 26 O.R. 586.

A bank, a telegraph office, and another office were simultaneously opened in a town. Moneys were deposited in the bank by various persons, who were given receipts therefor in the name of a person in the United States, which receipts were taken to the telegraph office, where information as to horse races being run in the United States was furnished to the holders of the receipts, who telegraphed instructions to the person there for whom the receipts were given to place, and who placed bets equivalent to the amounts deposited on horses running in the races, and on their winning the amounts won were paid to the holders of the receipts at the third office by telegraphic instructions from the persons making the bets in the United States. Held, on the evidence and admission to the above effect, that the defendant, who kept the telegraph office, was properly convicted of keeping a common betting house. R. v. Osborne (1896), 27 O.R. 185.

In Stoddart v. Hawke, 18 T.L.R. 22, an unsuccessful attempt was made to evade the prohibition of the Betting Act, 1853, against keeping a place for the purpose of receiving money on wagering contracts. The modus operandi was to issue coupons in connection with sporting competitions at an office in London, and these coupons with the money staked were sent by the persons betting to an office in Holland. It was held that the use of the office in London was a necessary part of the system for the receipt of money, and that the office was therefore kept for that purpose, and a conviction of the keeper was upheld.

Other place.]—In construing the words "other place" the doctrine of "ejusdem generis" is applicable, and the meaning of the word "place" must be controlled by the specific words, "house, office, or room." Powell v. Kempton Park, [1897] 2 Q.B. 242, [1899] A.C. 143; R. v. Moylett, 10 O.W.R. 803.

In The Queen v. Humphrey, [1898] 1 Q.B. 875, an archway which was a private thoroughfare leading from a public street into a yard containing dwelling houses, stables and workshops, which the prisoner was accustomed to resort to for the purpose of betting with persons who came to him there, was held to be a "place" within the meaning of the Betting Act 1853, (16 & 17 Vict. (Imp.), ch. 119) secs. 1, 3. And see Brown v. Patch, [1899] 1 Q.B. 892; Belton v. Busby, [1899] 2 Q.B. 380.

Disorderly house.

228. Every one is guilty of an indictable offence and liable to one year's imprisonment who keeps any disorderly house, that is to say, any common bawdy-house, common gaming-house or common betting-house, as hereinbefore defined.

2. Any one who appears, acts or behaves as master or mistress, or as the person having the care, government or management, of any disorderly house, shall be deemed to be the keeper thereof, and shall be liable to be prosecuted and punished as such, although in fact he or she is not the real owner or keeper thereof. 55-56 V., c. 29, s. 198. Who deemed keeper.

Bawdy house.]—The offence of keeping a common bawdy house may be proceeded with by indictment under sec. 228, which authorizes one year's imprisonment therefor; or proceedings may be taken under the "summary trials" clauses, secs. 773 and 774, the latter section giving to the magistrate under Part XVI. an absolute jurisdiction in respect of that offence, independently of the consent of the accused. Such magistrate proceeding under sec. 774 may impose imprisonment with or without hard labour for any term not exceeding six months or may impose a fine not exceeding with the costs in the case, $100, or to both fine and imprisonment not exceeding such sum and term; and such fine may be levied by warrant of distress or the person convicted may be condemned, in addition to any other imprisonment on the same conviction, to be committed for a further term not exceeding six months unless such fine is sooner paid. Section 781. These provisions are in addition to the special powers given by sec. 777 to police and stipendiary magistrates of cities and incorporated towns, and to recorders exercising judicial functions, authorizing them to try any offence for which in Ontario the accused might be tried by a Court of General Sessions and to impose the same punishment as might be imposed by that court, but where the magistrate has jurisdiction only by virtue of sec. 777 no person shall be summarily tried thereunder without his consent. Section 777(2). The result appears to be that the magistrate having authority under both secs. 773 and 777 may, without the consent of the accused, try the offence of keeping a bawdy house but is then restricted to the penalty provided by sec. 781; but if the trial be with the consent of the accused, the latter preferring to consent rather than defend a like charge by indictment before a court and jury, sec. 781 will not then apply, sec. 777(3) and the punishment may be as onerous as could be imposed on indictment under sec. 228. In the Province of Ontario the powers conferred by sec. 777 may also be exercised by a police or stipendiary magistrate "in any county district or provisional county in such province." Section 777(1).

This jurisdiction of summary trial relates to the keeping of common bawdy houses mentioned in Code sec. 225 which is a criminal and indictable offence. R. v. Bougie, 3 Can. Cr. Cas. 491.

By the vagrancy clauses secs. 238 and 239 a summary conviction is authorized with a fine not exceeding $50 or imprisonment with or without hard labour for any term not exceeding six months, or both fine and imprisonment, for the offence of keeping a bawdy house (sub-sec. j of sec. 238) or house for the resort of prostitutes.

Where there is nothing upon the face of a conviction for keeping a house of ill-fame to shew whether the police magistrate who tried the case acted under the "summary trials" clauses of the Code, by virtue of which he has an absolute jurisdiction in respect of that offence, or simply as a justice of the peace under the "summary convictions" clauses and of Code secs. 238 and 239, and the conviction is defective in form but is amendable if within the "summary conviction" clauses and not amendable if under the "summary trials" clauses, the court will treat it as a "summary conviction" and correct the same under Code sec. 1124, by reducing the term of imprisonment where the sentence is in excess of that authorized by law. R. v. Spooner (1900), 4 Can. Cr. Cas. 209 (Ont.).

A prosecution against the keeper of a common bawdy house may be brought either by indictment or under the summary trials procedure, or the keeper may be charged as a vagrant under the summary convictions procedure, and neither the provision for summary trial nor that for summary conviction abrogates the right of the Crown to bring an indictment. The different methods of procedure with the varying penalties dependent upon the class of tribunal selected are not inconsistent but are alternative. The King v. Sarah Smith, 9 Can. Cr. Cas. 338 (N.S.).

A charge of "keeping a bawdy house for the resort of prostitutes" charges one offence only, although keeping a bawdy house is in itself an offence, and so also under Code sec. 238(j), is the keeping of a house for the resort of prostitutes. R. v. McKenzie, 2 Man. R. 168.

Evidence in bawdy house cases.]—A conviction should not be made upon a charge of keeping a bawdy house upon evidence of general reputation only, and the prosecution should be required to produce proof of acts or conduct from which the character of the house may be inferred. R. v. St. Clair (1900), 3 Can. Cr. Cas. 551 (Ont. C.A.).

Though the charge is a general one, yet at the trial evidence may be given of particular facts and the particular time of doing them. Witnesses who speak simply to a general reputation without being able to point to anything particular, may easily attribute the character of a common bawdy house or a house of ill-fame to a house to which the law does not affix that character, however irregular may be the life of its inmates. R. v. St. Clair, supra.

The owner of a house who leases it to another person knowing and assenting when the lease was made to the purpose of the later to maintain it as a common bawdy house, thereby does an act for the purpose of aiding the lessee to commit the indictable offence of keeping a disorderly house, and he may be indicted and convicted as a principal under sec. 69. R. v. Roy (1900), 3 Can. Cr. Cas. 472.

In R. v. Barrett (1862), 32 L.J.M.C. 36, the accused let a house to a weekly tenant who used it as a brothel, but it was not proved that the accused received any additional rent by reason of the nature of the occupation or in any way participated in the direct profits of the immorality carried on there; but he had notice that the house was used for immoral purposes, and he did not give the tenant notice to quit. It was held that he could not be convicted of keeping the house as a disorderly house.

In R. v. Stannard (1863), 33 L.J.M.C. 61, the owner of a house let it in separate apartments on weekly tenancies to several women, who with his knowledge and consent used them for purposes of prostitution. He did not himself live in the house, and received no direct share in the immoral gains of the women, nor had he any control over them except such as might arise indirectly from his power as landlord to terminate any tenancy at the end of a week. It was held that he could not be convicted of keeping the house.

Cumulative offence.]—Keeping a house of ill-fame or disorderly house is a cumulative offence, and although the charge is in general terms, evidence may be given of particular facts and of the particular time of such facts. Clark v. Periam (1742), 2 Atk. 339; Roscoe's Crim. Evid., 11th ed., 773. It is no necessary to prove who frequents the house, which in many cases it might be impossible to do, but if unknown persons are proved to have been there, conducting themselves in a disorderly manner, it will maintain an indictment. I'Anson v. Stuart (1787), 1 T.R. 754. It is immaterial whether indecent or disorderly conduct is or is not perceptible from the outside. Steph. Crim. Law 122. R. v. Rice (1866), L.R. 1 C.C.R. 21.

Appearing as the keeper.]—The sub-section as to acting or appearing as the mistress of the house, originated in the English "Disorderly Houses Act, 1751," 25 Geo. 2, ch. 36. By sec. 8 of that statute it was enacted that any person who shall appear, act or behave himself or herself as master or mistress, or as the person having the care, government, or management of any bawdy house, gaming house, or other disorderly house, shall be deemed and taken to be the keeper thereof, and shall be liable to be prosecuted and punished as such, notwithstanding he or she shall not be in fact the real owner or keeper thereof.

In R. v. Spooner (1900), 4 Can. Crim. Cas. 209, a plea of guilty to the charge of "*appearing* the keeper of a house of ill-fame" was held equivalent to an admission that the accused kept a house of ill-fame. It is submitted however that those words used in a charge do not charge an offence known to the law and while one who appears to have the management of the house is deemed to be the keeper, the offence is the keeping and not appearing to keep.

Appeal from summary trial of bawdy house case.]—When the offence of keeping a disorderly house, house of ill-fame or bawdy house is tried in any of the provinces under the summary trials Part, an appeal shall lie from a conviction for the offence in the same manner as from summary convictions under Part XV., and all provisions of that Part relating to appeals shall apply to every such appeal: Provided that in the Province of Saskatchewan or Alberta there shall be no appeal if the conviction is made by a judge of a superior court. Code sec. 797.

229. Every one who plays or looks on while any other person is playing in a common gaming-house is guilty of an offence and liable, on summary conviction before two justices, to a penalty not exceeding one hundred dollars and not less than twenty dollars, and in default of payment to two months' imprisonment. 55-56 V., c. 29, s. 199. **Playing or looking on in gaming-house.**

Looking on in common gaming house.]—A notice of appeal purporting to be from a summary conviction for "looking on" while another person was playing in a common gaming house is not a good notice of appeal from a conviction for "playing" in a common gaming house. The King v. Ah Yin (No. 1), 6 Can. Cr. Cas. 63, 9 B.C.R. 319.

A summary conviction based upon the uncorroborated evidence of an accomplice who is shewn to have received money to testify against the accused is properly set aside on appeal. The King v. Ah Jim, 10 Can. Cr. Cas. 126.

Betting house raid.]—The statute 33 Hen. VIII., ch. 9, empowered magistrates themselves to enter gaming houses, and then and there to arrest and bind over persons found there. The duty of entering and arresting is now performed by the police acting upon the magistrate's order (see sec. 641). When the persons so arrested were brought before the magistrate he had the same powers, sitting as a court of summary jurisdiction, to bind them over in recognizances with or without sureties not to game or frequent gaming houses as he would have had if he himself entered the premises under the statute of Hen. VIII. Murphy v. Arrow (1897), 32 Eng. L.J. 544; Code secs. 10-12.

Arrest of persons found in gaming house.]—See secs. 641 and 642.

Penalty.

230. Every one is guilty of an offence and liable, on summary conviction before two justices, to a penalty not exceeding one hundred dollars, and to six months' imprisonment with or without hard labour who,—

Preventing officer entering.

(a) wilfully prevents any constable or other officer duly authorized to enter any disorderly house, from entering the same or any part thereof; or,

Obstructing.

(b) obstructs or delays any such constable or officer in so entering; or,

Securing door.

(c) by any bolt, chain or other contrivance secures any external or internal door of, or means of access to, any common gaming-house so authorized to be entered; or,

Means to prevent.

(d) uses any means or contrivance whatsoever for the purpose of preventing, obstructing or delaying the entry of any constable or officer, authorized as aforesaid, into any such disorderly house or any part thereof. 55-56 V., c. 29, s. 200.

Order to search gaming house.]—See secs. 641 and 642.

Gaming in stocks or merchandise.

231. Every one is guilty of an indictable offence and liable to five years' imprisonment, and to a fine of five hundred dollars, who, with the intent to make gain or profit by the rise or fall in price of any stock of any incorporated or unincorporated company or undertaking, either in Canada or elsewhere, or of any goods, wares or merchandise,—

Making contract without intention of acquiring or selling.

(a) without the *bonâ fide* intention of acquiring any such shares, goods, wares or merchandise, or of selling the same, as the case may be, makes or signs, or authorizes to be made or signed, any contract or agreement, oral or written, purporting to be for the sale or purchase of any shares of stock, goods, wares or merchandise; or,

Contract without delivery or intention of receiving delivery.

(b) makes or signs, or authorizes to be made or signed, any contract or agreement, oral or written, purporting to be for the sale or purchase of any such shares of stock, goods, wares or merchandise in respect of which no delivery of the thing sold or purchased is made or received, and without the *bonâ fide* intention to make or receive such delivery.

Saving.

2. It is not an offence under this section if the broker of the purchaser receives delivery, on his behalf, of the articles sold, notwithstanding that such broker retains or pledges the same as security for the advance of the purchase money or any part thereof. 55-56 V., c. 29, s. 201.

In Ontario.]—Until the passing of the original statute, 51 Vict., ch. 42(D.), "An Act respecting gaming in stocks and merchandise," such transactions were perfectly valid, whether they were simple wagers or not, because they did not come within the Statute of Anne, not being in connection with games or pastimes. They were thus legal in Ontario, wager or no wager. This was decided in Bank of Toronto v. McDougall, 28 U.C.C.P. 345, an action on a bill of exchange in respect of what was really gambling in differences.

Evidence.]—Three essential elements must co-exist in order to constitute an offence under the provisions of this section: (1) having an intent to make gain or profit; (2) making or signing contracts purporting to be for the sale or purchase of certain commodities; (3) absence of a bonâ fide intention to make or receive delivery of such commodities. R. v. Dowd, 4 Can. Cr. Cas. 170.

In British Columbia Stock Exchange v. Irving, 8 B.C.R. 186, an action by brokers against a customer, claiming payment for stock transactions, it was held that as no stock was ever delivered or intended to be delivered, and as the intent was to make a profit from the fluctuations of the stock market, the transactions were illegal as being a breach of this section Code, and that the plaintiffs could not recover.

A person who acts as agent for another in managing a branch office for gambling transactions in stocks within sec. 231, knowing that there was no intention of transferring any property or title to property, is liable to conviction as an accessory under Code sec. 69, although his sole interest in the transactions was in the commissions paid to him for effecting the same. Such agent is also liable under Code sec. 231 as the keeper of a common gaming house, and upon a "speedy trial" is liable to imprisonment for five years under Code sec. 1052. Upon a trial under this section for unlawfully making gaming contracts by conducting bucket shop transactions in stocks, it is open for the jury (or the judge trying the case without a jury), to find, notwithstanding the form of the papers which passed between the parties, that there was a secret understanding between them that there should be no delivery of the stocks or property, but payment of differences only. But the reception of opinion testimony as to the illegality of the transactions is improper. The King v. Harkness (No. 2), 10 Can. Cr. Cas. 199.

Pearson v. Carpenter (1904), 35 Can. S.C.R. 380, was a civil action in which this section was considered. Pearson speculated on margin in stocks, grain, etc., through C. & Son, brokers in Toronto, and in March, 1901, directed them to buy 30,000 bushels of May wheat at stated prices. The order was placed with a firm in Buffalo and the price going down C. & Son forwarded money to the latter to cover the margins. P. having written the brokers to know how he stood in the transaction received an answer stating that "no doubt the wheat was bought and has been carried, and whether it has or not our good money has gone to protect the deal for you" on which he gave them his note for $1,500 which they represented to be the amount so advanced. Shortly after the Buffalo firm failed and Pearson became satisfied that they had only conducted a bucket shop and the transaction had no real substance. He accordingly repudiated his liability on the note and C. & Son sued him for the amount of the same. Held, (Davies and Killam, JJ., dissenting), that the evidence shewed that the transaction was not one in which the wheat was actually purchased; that C. & Son were acting therein as agents for the Buffalo firm; that the transaction was not completed until the acceptance by the firm in Buffalo was notified to Pearson in Toronto; and being consummated in Toronto it was within the terms of sec. 201 now 231 of the Code and plaintiff could not recover.

The test is whether there was an intention on the defendant's part to actually deliver the stock or whether it was a mere bargain for differences. Forget v. Ostigny, [1895] A.C. 318; Philp v. Bennett, 18 Times L.R. 129; Re Cronmire, [1898] 2 Q.B. 383; Re Gieve, [1899] 1 Q.B. 794.

Onus of proof.]—By sec. 987, whenever, on the trial of a person charged with making an agreement for the sale or purchase of shares, goods, wares or merchandise in the manner set forth in section two hundred and one, it is established that the person so charged has made or signed any such contract or agreement of sale or purchase, or has acted, aided or abetted in the making or signing thereof, the burden of proof of the bonâ fide intention to acquire or to sell such goods, wares or merchandise, or to deliver or to receive delivery thereof, as the case may be, shall rest upon the person so charged.

Place of such business is common gaming-house.

232. Every office or place of business wherein is carried on the business of making or signing, or procuring to be made or signed, or negotiating or bargaining for the making or signing of contracts of sale or purchase prohibited by the last preceding section is a common gaming-house, and every one who as principal or agent occupies, uses, manages or maintains the same is the keeper of a common gaming-house. 55-56 V., c. 29, s. 201.

Frequenting places where gaming in stocks carried on.

233. Every one is guilty of an indictable offence and liable to one year's imprisonment who habitually frequents any office or place wherein the making or signing or procuring to be made or signed, or the negotiating or bargaining for the making or signing, of such prohibited contracts of sale or purchase is carried on. 55-56 V., c. 29, s. 202.

Penalty.

234. Every one is guilty of an indictable offence and liable to one year's imprisonment who,—

Obtaining money, etc., by gambling in public conveyances.

(*a*) in any railway car or steamboat, used as a public conveyance for passengers, by means of any game of cards, dice or other instrument of gambling, or by any device of like character, obtains from any other person any money, chattel, valuable security or property; or,

Attempting.

(*b*) attempts to commit such offence by actually engaging any person in any such game with intent to obtain money or other valuable thing from him.

Arrest of offender.

2. Every conductor, master or superior officer in charge of, and every clerk or employee when authorized by the conductor, master or superior officer in charge of, any railway train or steamboat, station or landing place in or at which any such offence, as aforesaid, is committed or attempted, shall, with or without warrant, arrest any person whom he has good reason to believe to have committed or attempted to commit any such

offence, and take him before a justice, and make complaint of such offence on oath, in writing.

3. Every conductor, master or superior officer in charge of any such railway car or steamboat, who makes default in the discharge of any such duty is liable, on summary conviction, to a penalty not exceeding one hundred dollars and not less than twenty dollars. **Penalty for omitting.**

4. It shall be the duty of every person who owns or works any such railway car or steamboat to keep a copy of this section posted up in some conspicuous part of such railway car or steamboat. **Posting up section.**

5. Every person who makes default in the discharge of such duty is liable to a penalty not exceeding one hundred dollars and not less than twenty dollars. 55-56 V., c. 29, s. 203. **Penalty.**

235. Every one is guilty of an indictable offence and liable to one year's imprisonment, and to a fine not exceeding one thousand dollars, who,— **Betting and pool-selling. Penalty.**

(*a*) uses or knowingly allows any part of any premises under his control to be used for the purpose of recording or registering any bet or wager, or selling any pool; or,

(*b*) keeps, exhibits, or employs, or knowingly allows to be kept, exhibited or employed, in any part of any premises under his control, any device or apparatus for the purpose of recording any bet or wager or selling any pool; or,

(*c*) becomes the custodian or depositary of any money, property or valuable thing staked, wagered or pledged; or,

(*d*) records or registers any bet or wager, or sells any pool, upon the result

(i) of any political or municipal election,

(ii) of any race,

(iii) of any contest or trial of skill or endurance of man or beast.

2. The provisions of this section shall not extend to any person by reason of his becoming the custodian or depositary of any money, property or valuable thing staked, to be paid to the winner of any lawful race, sport, game or exercise, or to the owner of any horse engaged in any lawful race, or to bets between individuals or made on the race course of an incorporated association during the actual progress of a race meeting. 55-56 V., c. 29, s. 204. **Saving.**

Betting and pool selling.]—The general provisions of sec. 235 are directed against the use, whether continuous or casual, of premises either for registering bets or pool selling upon horse races, elections and trials of skill, and they also, with certain qualifications, prohibit the holding of stakes or recording of wagers upon the like events.

Sub-sections (a) and (b) apply only to the person having the premises or a part of any premises under his control. That person must not himself use his premises for the purpose of registering bets of the nature specified nor knowingly allow any other person to so use the premises (sub-sec. a). The next sub-sec. (b) contemplates a condition of affairs which might or might not, according to circumstances, constitute a user of the premises for the purpose of recording bets. It makes it an offence for the person in charge of premises to keep, exhibit or employ a bet-recording apparatus thereon if the betting be upon the result of an election or a race or contest of skill or endurance. This sub-section would make the proprietor of the premises liable if he allows another person to place a bet-recording apparatus on the premises for public use although the person in charge of the premises had nothing to do with its operation and received no rental or share of profits.

Sub-sections (c) and (d) are not restricted to the proprietors of premises as are sub-secs. (a) and (b) but have a general application to stake-holders, pool-sellers and bet-recorders where the result upon which the wager turns is within the scope of the section.

While the typographical arrangement of sec. 235 and of the former sec. 204 of the Criminal Code of 1892 is not of the best to shew the association of words "upon the result of any political or municipal election, of any race, of any contest or trial of skill or endurance of man or beast," a reference to the Lotteries and Betting Act, R.S.C. 1886, ch. 159, from which these Code sections were taken, seems to make it plain that the words last quoted apply not to sub-sec. (d) alone but to all the sub-secs. (a), (b), (c) and (d), which precede the quoted words. If such be the case then the Code offence of being the custodian of money staked applies only where the staking is upon the result of an election, race or contest as before set forth.

The exceptions to these general provisions are stated in paragraph (2). The first applies particularly to paragraph (c) as to custodians. The custodian of money to be paid to the winner shall be exempt from its penalties if the race, sport, game or exercise which was the subject of the bet is a lawful one but not otherwise. The custodian of money to be paid to the owner of a horse engaged in a race shall be exempt if the race was a lawful one and not otherwise. The separate mention of the winner and the owner would indicate that as to horse races, the owner, who did not ride or drive his own horse, would not be a "winner" of a lawful race, and consequently required special mention to avoid the penalties of the section. Neither should the section apply to "bets between individuals." The latter phrase seems to have been intended to include only what may be termed casual bets—the bets of persons not engaged in betting as a pursuit and not tendering bets to the general public. In such cases the recording of the bet, the becoming depository thereof, and allowing the use of premises for the purpose of recording the bet, are all permissible.

A trotting match for fifty pounds between two horses driven in harness in sleighs on the ice was held to be a legal race within previous statutes. Fulton v. James, 5 U.C.C.P. 182.

And where two persons stake money on a bet between themselves on the result of a boat race, the custodian is not criminally liable because of the exemption above stated.

Race track betting.]—The provisions of the section shall not extend to "bets made on the race course of any incorporated association during the actual progress of a race meeting." It was held that an agreement for the sale of betting and gaming privileges at a race meeting by an incorporated association who were the lessees of an incorporated association owning the race course, was legal. Stratford Turf Association v. Fitch (1897), 28 O.R. 579. If the sale of the betting privileges be taken as a contract to permit the keeping of a common gaming house by operating bookmakers' booths in violation of the law as declared by the Supreme Court of Canada, the decision in Stratford Turf Association v. Fitch must now be considered as overruled by Saunders v. The King, 12 Can. Cr. Cas. 174.

It yet remains to be authoritatively decided whether the betting operations known as "bookmaking" can legally be carried on by professional gamblers at a race track during the races gambled upon, if the "booth" is dispensed with and the "bookmaker" keeps moving in the crowd displaying a card containing the odds he offers and recording his bets in a memorandum book, and consequently has not the exclusive use of any part of the enclosure. See R. v. Moylett, 10 O.W.R. 803; Powell v. Kempton Park, [1899] A.C. 143; and see notes to secs. 226 and 227.

Lawful race or game.]—In New Brunswick it has been decided that betting on a foot race is not illegal there being no legislation either federal or provincial to make it so and it being lawful at common law. Seely v. Dalton (1904), 36 N.B.R. 442.

The question of whether a game is lawful or not is one for the judge. Reg. v. Davies, [1897] 2 Q.B. 199.

236. Every one is guilty of an indictable offence and liable to two years' imprisonment and to a fine not exceeding two thousand dollars who,— **Penalty.**

(*a*) makes, prints, advertises or publishes, or causes or procures to be made, printed, advertised or published, any proposal, scheme or plan for advancing, lending, giving, selling or in any way disposing of any property, by lots, cards, tickets, or any mode of chance whatsoever; or, **Printing lottery scheme.**

(*b*) sells, barters, exchanges or otherwise disposes of, or causes or procures, or aids or assists in, the sale, barter, exchange or other disposal of, or offers for sale, barter or exchange, any lot, card, ticket or other means or device for advancing, lending, giving, selling or otherwise disposing of any property, by lots, tickets or any mode of chance whatsoever; or, **Selling lottery tickets, etc.**

(*c*) conducts or manages any scheme, contrivance or operation of any kind for the purpose of determining who, or the holders of what lots, tickets, numbers or chances, are the winners of any property so proposed to be advanced, loaned, given, sold or disposed of. **Conducting lottery scheme.**

2. Every one is guilty of an offence and liable on summary conviction to a penalty of twenty dollars, who buys, takes or receives any such lot, ticket or other device as aforesaid. **Buying lottery tickets, etc.**

Lottery sale void.

3. Every sale, loan, gift, barter or exchange of any property, by any lottery, ticket, card or other mode of chance depending upon or to be determined by chance or lot, is void, and all property so sold, lent, given, bartered or exchanged, is liable to be forfeited to any person who sues for the same by action or information in any court of competent jurisdiction.

Boná fide purchases.

4. No such forfeiture shall affect any right or title to such property acquired by any *boná fide* purchaser for valuable consideration without notice.

Foreign lottery included.

5. This section includes the printing or publishing, or causing to be printed or published, of any advertisement, scheme, proposal or plan of any foreign lottery, and the sale or offer for sale of any ticket, chance or share, in any such lottery, or the advertisement for sale of such ticket, chance or share, and the conducting or managing of any such scheme, contrivance or operation for determining the winners in any such lottery.

Saving.

6. This section does not apply to,—

Dividing real estate by lot.

(*a*) the division by lot or chance of any property by joint tenants or tenants in common, or persons having joint interests (*droits indivis*) in any such property; or,

Raffles at church bazaar.

(*b*) raffles for prizes of small value at any bazaar held for any charitable or religious object, if permission to hold the same has been obtained from the city or other municipal council, or from the mayor, reeve or other chief officer of the city, town or other municipality, wherein such bazaar is held, and the articles raffled for thereat have first been offered for sale and none of them are of a value exceeding fifty dollars;

London Art Union, etc.

(*c*) the Art Union of London, Great Britain, or the Art Union of Ireland. 55-56 V., c. 29, s. 205; 58-59 V., c. 40, s. 1; 1 E. VII., c. 42, s. 2; 6 E. VII., c. 6, s. 1.

Lottery defined.]—A lottery is a distribution of prizes by lot or chance without the use of any skill. Archibold Crim. Plead. (1900), 1141; R. v. Harris (1866), 10 Cox C.C. 352; Barclay v. Pearson, [1893] 2 Ch. 154; Stoddard v. Sagar, [1895] 2 Q.B. 474; Hall v. Cox, [1899] 1 Q.B. 198.

Province cannot authorize.]—Provincial Legislatures have no power to authorize the running of lotteries; and no action can be maintained for the recovery of money under a contract for the operation of a lottery scheme which would contravene the criminal law. Brault v. St. Jean Baptiste Association (1900), 4 Can. Cr. Cas. 284 (S.C. Can.).

In an Ontario case the complainant went to the defendant's place of business, and having been told by defendant that in certain spaces on two shelves there were in cans of tea, a gold watch, a diamond ring, or $20 in money, he paid $1 and received a can of tea, which, containing an article of small value, he handed the can back, paid an additional 50 cents and received another can, which also contained an article of small value; he handed this can back also, paid another 50 cents and received another can which also contained an article of small value. It was held that the object really sought for, and for the chance of obtaining which the money was paid was one of the three prizes named; and that the transaction constituted an offence. R. v. Freeman (1889), 18 Ont. R. 524.

But the offer of prizes to the nearest guesser of the number of beans contained in a jar exhibited to view is not a lottery, as it is a matter of judgment or skill and not of chance. R. v. Dodds (1884), 4 O.R. 390.

And where a shopkeeper placed in his shop window a jar containing a number of buttons of different sizes, and advertised a prize of a pony and cart, which he exhibited in his window to the person who should guess the number nearest to the number of buttons in the jar; stipulating that the successful one should buy a certain amount of his goods; this was held not to be a "mode of chance" for the disposal of property within the meaning of the Lottery Act, as the approximation of the number of buttons depended upon the exercise of judgment, observation and mental effort. R. v. Jamieson (1884), 7 O.R. 149.

The advertising by a firm of shopkeepers in a newspaper of a prize to be awarded to the one of their customers who could make the nearest guess to the number of their cash sales on a given day, is not a violation of this section. The King v. Fish, 11 Can. Cr. Cas. 201.

Defendant company, as a means of advertising their soap at an exhibition held at St. John, offered a piano as a prize for the person guessing the correct weight or the nearest to the correct weight of a large cake or block of soap exhibited at the said exhibition. The guessing was free and all persons who desired to guess were provided with coupon tickets upon which to mark their guesses. The tickets were deposited, or were supposed to be deposited, in a box, and the corresponding coupons retained by the respective guessers. The plaintiff guessed within a shade of the correct weight, and after the soap had been weighed presented her coupon with her guess marked thereon, but the judges could not find her ticket in the box and awarded the prize to another person who guess was not so near the correct weight as the plaintiff's. Plaintiff afterwards brought an action for breach of contract. It was held by the Supreme Court of New Brunswick on demurrer to plaintiff's declaration, that the competition was not a lottery within the meaning of the Criminal Code, and that the exercise of judgment required in the guessing was a sufficient consideration to support the contract. Dunham v. St. Croix Soap Co. (1897), 33 Can. Law Jour. 444.

The sale of lottery tickets is an offence, whether made for profit or not. R. v. Parker, 9 Man. R. 203.

Newspaper prize competition.]—In the case of a newspaper sold with coupons to be filled up by purchasers with the names of the winning horses in a horse race and the reward of a money prize for the correct guesses, it is a question of fact to be decided whether the money received was paid in consideration of a promise to pay a prize on the event of the race or was only the ordinary price of the newspaper. R. v. Stoddart, 70 L.J.Q.B. 189. And the sale of extra coupons at a fixed price is a fact to be taken into consideration. Ibid. Stoddart v. Sagar, [1895] 2 Q.B. 474, 18 Cox C.C. 165; Caminada v. Hulton, 17 Cox C.C. 307.

An offer of a money prize by a newspaper coupon scheme under which the readers were asked to predict the number of registered births and deaths in a certain district during a certain period, was held not to constitute a lottery. Hall v. Cox, [1899] 1 Q.B. 198.

A competition for a prize offered for the nearest estimates of the number of votes to be cast at a coming election and the sale of certificates of admission thereto in consideration of money paid or services performed, does not constitute a lottery offence under Code sec. 236. The King v. Johnston (1902), 7 Can. Cr. Cas. 525.

The proprietors of a weekly newspaper distributed to the public promiscuously a number of medals each bearing a different number and the words "Keep this, it may be worth £100. See the Weekly Telegraph today." Numbers were arbitrarily selected for prizes by them and the winning numbers were published weekly in their paper. The object of the scheme was to induce the public to buy the paper. Information as to the winners could be obtained without any payment, or sending in any coupon. The newspaper proprietors were found guilty of holding and carrying on a lottery within the Gaming Act, 1802. Wills v. Young, [1907] 1 K.B. 448.

Lottery—Proceedings against corporation.]—In the Province of Alberta which has no grand jury system, a corporation may be compelled to answer to an indictable offence (ex gr. conducting a lottery scheme) by a formal written charge in lieu of an indictment, such charge being laid by the Attorney-General or by his direction or with the consent or order of a judge and notice thereof being served on the corporation under section 918 of the Revised Code. R. v. Standard Soap Co. (1907), 12 Can. Cr. Cas. 290.

Prize dependent upon chance without skill—Illusory condition.]—Where tickets for a drawing by lot are sold as part of a scheme for the disposal of goods, and the holder of the winning ticket is required by the conditions of the drawing to shoot a turkey at fifty yards in five shots in order to win the prize, such circumstance does not necessarily take the case outside of the lottery sections of the Criminal Code. It is a question for the jury whether such condition was imposed as a contest of skill, or as a mere pretence in evasion of the lottery law. Where the evidence shews that any person could easily comply with the condition and the jury found the advertiser of the scheme guilty of advertising a lottery, the verdict will be supported as, in effect, finding that there was no real element of skill involved in the condition. The King v. Johnson, 6 Can. Cr. Cas. 48, 14 Man. R. 27.

Sweepstake on horse race.]—In Hardwick v. Lane, [1904] 1 K.B. 204, the Divisional Court (Lord Alverstone, C.J., and Lawrance and Kennedy, JJ.), held that a sweepstake on a horse race is an illegal lottery within the Gaming Act, 1802.

Search for gambling paraphernalia.]—The finding of lottery tickets and other paraphernalia of a lottery on the premises entered under a search order for instruments of gaming does not in itself constitute a primâ facie case nor shift the onus of proof to the defence. Section 985 which declares that the finding of instruments of gaming upon an order of search under Code sec. 641, shall constitute primâ facie evidence that the place is used as a common gaming house and that play was going on, has no application to a charge under section 236 for selling lottery tickets. R. v. Hong Guey (1907), 12 Can. Cr. Cas. 366 (B.C.).

Search order for lottery devices.]—See sec. 641.

Examination of person arrested on search order.]—See sec. 642.

Penalty. **237.** Every one is guilty of an indictable offence and liable to five years' imprisonment who,—

(*a*) without lawful excuse, neglects to perform any duty either imposed upon him by law or undertaken by him with reference to the burial of any dead human body or human remains; or, Not burying the dead.

(*b*) improperly or indecently interferes with or offers any indignity to any dead human body or human remains, whether buried or not. 55-56 V., c. 29, s. 206. Indignity to dead body.

At common law.]—Exposing the naked dead body of a child in or near the highway and within view therefrom is a common law nuisance. R. v. Clark, 15 Cox C.C. 171.

And to leave unburied the corpse of a person for whom the accused was bound to provide Christian burial, was an indictable misdemeanour, if the accused were shewn to have been of ability to provide such burial. R. v. Vann (1851), 2 Den. 325; R. v. Stewart, 12 A. & E. 773; Jenkins v. Tucker (1788), 1 H. Bl. 90.

It is also a common law misdemeanour to remove without authority a corpse from a grave in a church burial ground; R. v. Sharpe, Dears. & B. 160; 7 Cox 214; or to sell a dead body without lawful authority for the purpose of dissection. R. v. Lynn, 1 Leach 479, 1 R.R. 607; R. v. Gilles, R. & R. 366(n); R. v. Cundick, Dowl. & Ry. 13; R. v. Duffin, R. & R. 365.

Stranger undertaking to bury.]—The neglect to decently bury a dead human body by a person who has undertaken to do so and has removed the body with that expressed intent is an indictable offence under this section, although such person was, apart from such undertaking, under no legal obligation in respect of the burial. R. v. Newcomb (1898), 2 Can. Cr. Cas. 255.

Coroner's right.]—A coroner has a legal right to direct a disinterment for the purposes of holding an inquest. R. v. Clerk (1702), Holt 167; R. v. Bond (1716), 1 Str. 22; Jervis on Coroners, 6th ed. 37. Any disposition of a corpse to obstruct or prevent a coroner's inquest when one ought to be held is a common law misdemeanour. R. v. Stephenson, 13 Q.B.D. 331; R. v. Price, 12 Q.B.D. 247.

Vagrancy.

238. Every one is a loose, idle or disorderly person or vagrant who,— Vagrant.

(*a*) not having any visible means of subsistence, is found wandering abroad or lodging in any barn or outhouse, or in any deserted or unoccupied building, or in any cart or wagon, or in any railway carriage or freight car, or in any railway building, and not giving a good account of himself, or who, not having any visible means of maintaining himself, lives without employment; No visible means of support.

(*b*) being able to work and thereby or by other means to maintain himself and family, wilfully refuses or neglects to do so; Not maintaining family.

(*c*) openly exposes or exhibits in any street, road, highway or public place, any indecent exhibition; Indecent exhibitions.

Begging. (*d*) without a certificate signed, within six months, by a priest, clergyman or minister of the Gospel, or two justices, residing in the municipality where the alms are being asked, that he or she is a deserving object of charity, wanders about and begs, or goes about from door to door, or places himself or herself in any street, highway, passage or public place to beg or receive alms;

Loitering on highway. (*e*) loiters on any street, road, highway or public place, and obstructs passengers by standing across the footpath, or by using insulting language, or in any other way;

Disorderly conduct. (*f*) causes a disturbance in or near any street, road, highway or public place, by screaming, swearing or singing, or by being drunk, or by impeding or incommoding peaceable passengers;

Wanton disturbances. (*g*) by discharging firearms, or by riotous or disorderly conduct in any street or highway, wantonly disturbs the peace and quiet of the inmates of any dwelling-house near such street or highway;

Destroying property. (*h*) tears down or defaces signs, breaks windows, or doors or door plates, or the walls of houses, roads or gardens, or destroys fences;

Night walker. (*i*) being a common prostitute or night walker, wanders in the fields, public streets or highways, lanes or places of public meeting or gathering of people, and does not give a satisfactory account of herself;

Keeping house of ill-fame. (*j*) is a keeper or inmate of a disorderly house, bawdy-house or house of ill-fame, or house for the resort of prostitutes;

Frequenting. (*k*) is in the habit of frequenting such houses and does not give a satisfactory account of himself or herself; or,

Supported by prostitution. (*l*) having no peaceable profession or calling to maintain himself by, for the most part supports himself by gaming or crime, or by the avails of prostitution. 55-56 V., c. 29, s. 207; 63-64 V., c. 46, s. 3.

Describing the offence.]—A summary conviction for being "a loose, idle person or vagrant" without specifying in what the vagrancy consisted under Code sec. 207, is void for uncertainty. R. v. McCormack (1903), 7 Can. Cr. Cas. 135, 9 B.C.R. 497.

In Quebec it has been held that a conviction under the vagrancy clauses of the Criminal Code must find that the accused is a loose, idle or disorderly person or vagrant and a conviction which merely declares that the accused was guilty of being drunk and causing a disturbance is invalid. R. v. Harkness (1906), 12 Can. Cr. Cas. 54, per Hutchinson, J.

The correctness of the decision in the Harkness Case is doubted. Section 238 gives an enlarged statutory meaning to the word vagrant and includes with the definition many offences of varied description enumerated in its items (a) to (l) inclusive. It would seem more in harmony with the procedure of the Code and with the fundamental principles of criminal law that the accused should be charged in the information with the precise offence of the particular item of the statutory definition relied upon. The better way would no doubt be to charge that the accused is a vagrant in that he was found wandering abroad not having any visible means of subsistence and not giving a good account of himself, or (as the case may be) in that he caused a disturbance in a public place by being drunk, or other specific offence set out in sec. 238. Section 723(3) declares that the description of any offence in the words of the Act creating the offence shall be sufficient, but this does not deprive the accused of his right to be informed of the nature, time and place of the offence to which he is called upon to plead.

(*a*)—*No visible means of support.*]—By a proviso in sec. 239 no aged or infirm person shall be convicted as a loose, idle or disorderly person or vagrant, for any reason coming within paragraph (a) of this section, in the county of which he has for the two years immediately preceding been a resident.

A person suspected of being a confidence man had registered at a hotel and on the same day was arrested at a railway station as a suspicious character. On his person were found two cheques one for $700 and another for $900 which were sworn to be such as are used by confidence men, also a mileage ticket nearly used up issued in the name of another person and $8 in cash. He offered no explanation of the cheques or ticket and gave no information about himself. It was held that he could not be properly convicted as a vagrant on the evidence. R. v. Bassett, 10 Ont. Prac. R. 386, per Osler, J. Before a person can be convicted under subsec. (a), he must have acquired in some degree a character which brings him within it as an idle person, who has no visible means of maintaining himself, for example, not "paying his way" or being apparently able to earn a livelihood but without means yet lives without employment. Ibid.

If the accused resides for a portion of the year with his parents at their request, they being able and willing to provide for his support, a conviction for vagrancy under Cr. Code sec. 238(a) because "not having had any visible means of maintaining himself he had lived without employment" should be quashed. Semble, although it may appear that part of the money by which the accused is supported with his parents had been acquired by him by his gaming, etc., prior to the time of the offence charged, and that the accused while so resident with his parents idled away his time in places of public resort, such does not justify a conviction for vagrancy. R. v. Riley, 2 Can. Cr. Cas. 128.

(*b*)—*Failure to maintain the family.*]—In order to constitute a wilful refusal or neglect on the part of a husband to maintain his family, under Cr. Code sec. 238(b), it is necessary that he should be under a legal obligation to do so, and his failure to maintain his wife, who had left him without valid cause and refused to return, is not an offence under that section. R. v. Leclair (1898), 2 Can. Cr. Cas. 297; Flannagan v. Overseers (1857), 3 Jurist N.S. 1103; Morris v. Edmonds, 18 Cox C.C. 627.

To constitute a wilful refusal or neglect by a husband to maintain his wife, there must be an absence of any reasonable ground for believing the refusal or neglect to be lawful. A husband who has been ordered by a civil court in an action brought by his wife for separation to pay to his wife an interim alimentary allowance is relieved from that liability in the Province of Quebec on proof that the wife is supporting herself by immorality, and a criminal prosecution against him for non-support will be dismissed on the like proof. Anonymous case H—— v. H—— (1902), 6 Can. Cr. Cas. 163.

(*c*)—*Indecent exhibition in public place.*]—Semble—The term "public place" includes a place to which the public have access only upon payment for admission, ex gr., a theatre. Ex parte Ashley, 8 Can. Cr. Cas. 328. See also Code sec. 208.

(*d*)—***Begging.***]—It must be shewn that the wandering about and begging is a mode of life with the accused, and the section does not apply where persons with regular occupations temporarily out of employment through a "strike" go about seeking public contributions in aid of a general fund to sustain the strikers and their families. Pointon v. Hill, 12 Q.B.D. 306.

(*e*)—*Loitering, etc.*]—A licensed cabman who contrary to a city ordinance loitered on the street near the entrance of a hotel and solicited passengers to hire his cab was held not within this provision where no obstruction of passengers was shewn. Smith v. The Queen, 4 Montreal L.R. 325.

As to religious gatherings on streets and highways and their regulation by local laws and by-laws. See R. v. Watson (1896), 6 Can. Cr. Cas. 331, and note ibid., page 338.

(*f*)—*Causing disturbance.*]—It is not sufficient to charge merely that the accused was drunk on a public street without alleging further that he caused a disturbance in such street by being drunk. Ex parte Despatie, 9 Legal News (Montreal) 387; R. v. Daly, 24 C.L.J. 157, 12 Ont. Prac. 411.

"Disturbing the inhabitants" of a town was held by Wilson, C.J., to mean annoying them, as by making a noise which interferes with the thoughts or proceedings of others. R. v. Martin (1886), 12 O.R. 800. It is distinguishable from the term "creating a disturbance," which applies either to raising a clamour, commotion, quarreling or fighting, and refers to conduct of the nature of a breach of the peace. Ibid. The disturbance should be of the nature of a nuisance. Thomson v. Mayor of Croydon, 16 Q.B. 708.

It may also be observed that the mere fact of drunkenness in a street is not sufficient to create an offence under sec. 238(f), nor would the drunkenness and the making of a disturbance combined necessarily bring the case under the vagrancy clauses. Sub-section (f) declares a person a vagrant who causes a disturbance in a street, etc., by screaming, swearing or singing, or by being drunk, or by impeding or incommoding peaceable passengers. It is obvious that singing in a street road or public place is not necessarily a cause of disturbance and is not prohibited unless that result follows, and, in the same way, the state of drunkenness must cause a disturbance or it will not bring the drunken person within these sections of the Code. The offence of being drunk on a public street is a municipal one, regulated in many provinces by their municipal Acts and municipal by-laws passed thereunder.

Slandering a person in a restaurant open to the public is not an offence under sec. 238, either as an obstruction to passenger by using insulting language, or as a disturbance incommoding passengers. R. v. Mercier (1901), 6 Can. Cr. Cas. 44, 20 Que. S.C. 28.

(*f*)—*Disorderly conduct in public place.*]—A licensed saloon and billiard hall is a "public place" under Rev. Cr. Code, secs. 197 and 238, and a person causing a disturbance therein by being drunk is liable as a vagrant. The King v. Kearney (1907), 12 Can. Cr. Cas. 349.

But in Quebec Province it has been held that a restaurant open to the public is not a "public place" within the meaning of this section. R. v. Mercier (1901), 6 Can. Cr. Cas. 44, 20 Que. S.C. 28.

A municipal by-law prohibiting profane swearing, etc., in any "street or public place" was held not to include a private office in a custom house. R. v. Bell, 25 O.R. 272.

(*f*)—*Assembly in public street.*]—The mere fact of holding a meeting in a street does not necessarily imply the impeding or incommoding of peaceable passengers, and proof of actual impeding or incommoding is essential to justify a conviction. Criminal Code, sec. 238 does not apply to persons of general good character, but is intended to apply to loose, idle and disorderly persons only. The King v. Kneeland, 11 Que. K.B. 85, 6 Can. Cr. Cas. 81.

(*i*)—*Prostitutes.*]—Sub-section (i) taken from the Vagrant Act, 32 & 33 Vict. (Can.) ch. 28, does not, on its true construction, declare that being a prostitute, etc., makes such persons liable to punishment as such, but only those who when found at the places mentioned, under circumstances suggesting impropriety of purpose, on request or demand are unable to give a satisfactory account of themselves. R. v. Arscott (1885), 9 O.R. 541, per Rose, J.; but see Arscott v. Lilley, 11 O.R. 153.

"A common prostitute wandering in the public streets should not be apprehended and taken to a lock-up without knowing what it is for. In the nature of things she should know, if she is taken up, what it is for. She is not to be taken at all, until she has failed to give a satisfactory account of herself. If she is not asked what business she, a common prostitute, has wandering in the streets, or why it is she is there, she may not know whether she is taken up for murder or for robbery, or for what other offence, or whether she is taken up for any offence at all; and she cannot suppose she is taken up for wandering in the streets, though she is a common prostitute, so long as she is conducting herself harmlessly and decently, and just as other people are conducting themselves. The conviction should allege that the woman was asked before she was taken, or at the time of her being taken, to give an account of herself—that is of her wandering in the public streets, she being a common prostitute or night-walker—and that she did not give a satisfactory account of herself." R. v. Levecque (1870), 30 U.C.Q.B. 509.

(*j*)—*Houses of ill-fame.*]—Keeping the house does not necessarily import property, but may signify that share of government which the wife has in a family as well as the husband. R. v. Williams, 10 Mod. 63; R. v. Dixon, 10 Mod. 335; R. v. Warren (188), 16 O.R. 590.

Though the charge is general, yet at the trial evidence may be given of particular facts, and the particular time of doing them. Witnesses who speak simply to a general reputation without being able to point to anything particular, may easily attribute the character of a common bawdy house or a house of ill-fame to a house to which, however irregular may be the life of its inmates, the law does not affix that character. R. v. St. Clair (1900), 3 Can. Cr. Cas. 551 (Ont.).

A conviction for that the accused was on April 21 "and on divers other days and times during the month of April" the keeper of a disorderly house, based upon an information in like terms laid on April 29, is bad, because it may be read as inclusive of an offence committed subsequently to the laying of the information, and including the date of the conviction, as to which the prisoner was not charged on her trial before the convicting magistrate. R. v. Keeping (1901), 4 Can. Cr. Cas. 494 (N.S.).

It was held in R. v. Keeping (1901), 4 Can. Cr. Cas. 494, per Weatherbe, J. (N.S.), that to give jurisdiction to a justice to punish on summary conviction the keeper of a disorderly house under the vagrancy clauses of the Code, the information must charge that the accused is a loose, idle or disorderly person or vagrant, and that it is not sufficient to charge simply that the person is a keeper of a disorderly house, although that fact constitutes the person a loose, idle or disorderly person or vagrant, by virtue of sec. 238. It may be doubted whether that view is correct, as by sec. 654(2) an information may be either in the Code form 3, or to the like effect.

A conviction should not be made upon a charge of keeping, or being an inmate of, a bawdy house upon evidence of general reputation only, and the prosecution should be required to produce proof of acts or conduct from which the character of the house may be inferred. R. v. St. Clair (1900), 3 Can. Cr. Cas. 551 (Ont. C.A.).

The conduct and statements of the inmates of an alleged bawdy house at the time of their arrest therein may properly be proved in support of the charge. Ibid.

Where the "keeper" is charged, the punishment may be, (a) on summary conviction before a justice, fine of $50 or six months' imprisonment, or both; (b) on summary trial under sec. 773, fine (including costs) $100 or six months' imprisonment, or both (Code sec. 781); (c) on trial under indictment, one year's imprisonment (Code sec. 228) or a fine in discretion, or both (Code sec. 1035).

A charge of "keeping a bawdy house for the resort of prostitutes" charges one offence only although keeping a bawdy house is itself an offence and so by virtue of sub-sec. (j) is the keeping of a house for the resort of prostitutes. R. v. McKenzie, 2 Man. R. 168.

In Alberta it has been held that a conviction by a police magistrate for being an inmate of a bawdy house and imposing a fine of over $50 but which with costs is less than $100 will be considered as a conviction upon summary trial under Part XVI. of the Code if the record of proceedings shews that the charge was reduced to writing and pleaded to by the accused although the conviction itself omits the words "being charged before me" provided in Form 55. R. v. Ames (1903), 10 Can. Cr. Cas. 52.

In Nova Scotia where a conviction made by a city police or stipendiary magistrate for being an inmate of a disorderly house follows the Code form 32 and does not recite that the accused was "charged" before him in the words of form 55, the inference was held to be that the prosecution is brought under the vagrancy clauses and not under the summary trials procedure. (Per Townshend, J.) R. v. Carter (1902), 5 Can. Cr. Cas. 401.

Where the proceedings are taken under the "summary convictions" procedure, a conviction inflicting a punishment in excess of that authorized on summary conviction cannot be supported in habeas corpus proceedings as a conviction on "summary trial" under which the punishment inflicted is authorized, notwithstanding that the magistrate was one authorized to hold a summary trial, and that the offence was of the class for which the consent to such trial is dispensed with by statute. (Per Townshend, J.) Ibid.

A conviction by a city stipendiary magistrate for the offence of being an inmate of a bawdy house need not expressly state on its face that the accused is a vagrant. R. v. Young (1906), 12 Can. Cr. Cas. 109 (N.S.).

(*j*)—*Right of appeal.*]—A special right of appeal is given (subject to an exception in Saskatchewan and Alberta) by sec. 797 on a summary trial under Part XVI. in like manner as from a summary conviction under Part XV., where the charge is keeping or being an inmate or habitual frequenter of any disorderly house, house of ill-fame or bawdy house.

(*k*)—*Frequenters of houses of ill-fame.*]—Persons may be able to give the most satisfactory account of themselves although they may be in the habit of frequenting such houses. Arscott v. Lilley (1886), 11 O.R. 153, 181, 14 A.R. 283; R. v. Remon, 16 O.R. 560; R. v. Levecque, 30 U.C.Q.B. 509. As said by Wilson, C.J., in the Arscott case:—"They may go to preach to, or to admonish the inmates, to visit them in sickness, to acquire statistical information, or for police purposes, or for the discovery of crime or criminals or their apprehension, or the recovery of stolen goods, or for the collection of rent or debts." 11 O.R. p. 181.

A conviction for being an *unlawful* frequenter is not good, it should be for being an *habitual* frequenter. R. v. Clark (1883), 2 O.R. 523.

(*k*)—*Right of appeal on charge of frequenting.*]—As to the right of appeal on a "summary trial" under secs. 773 and 774 for this offence, see sec. 797.

(*l*)—*Supported by prostitution.*]—A woman who is kept by a married man and who surrenders herself to sexual intercourse with him alone, does not come under the purview of sub-section (1). R. v. Rehe (1897), 1 Can. Cr. Cas. 63 (Que.).

In Gareau's case, Que. (cited 1 Can. Cr. Cas. 66) a woman had been convicted as a vagrant for having kept for more than three months a disorderly house, for the purposes of prostitution with a man who was not her husband and who paid her; and on a writ of habeas corpus the Court of Queen's Bench at Montreal unanimously held that the resorting to her room by only one man did not constitute it a disorderly house, and that her illicit intercourse with one man alone did not constitute prostitution within the meaning of the paragraph, and the conviction was consequently quashed.

(*l*)—*Supported by gaming or crime.*]—The evidence on a charge of vagrancy under Cr. Code 238 on the ground that the accused had for the most part supported himself by gaming and crime must shew that the gaming or crime took place during the time within or for which he is charged in the information with having been a vagrant. R. v. Riley (1898), 2 Can. Cr. Cas. 128.

Semble, although it may appear that part of the money by which the accused is supported with his parents had been acquired by him by his gaming, etc., prior to the time of the offence charged, and that the accused while so resident with his parents idled away his time in places of public resort, such does not justify a conviction for vagrancy. Ibid.

An accused person was summarily convicted under 32-33 Vict. (Can.), ch. 28, sec. 1, of being "a person, who, having no peaceable profession or calling to maintain himself by, but who does for the most part support himself by crime and then was a vagrant," etc. The evidence shewed that the defendant did not support himself by any peaceable profession or calling and that he consorted with thieves and reputed thieves, but the witnesses did not positively say that he supported himself by crime. It was held that it was not to be inferred that the defendant supported himself by crime; that to sustain the conviction there should have been statements that witnesses believed he got his living by thieving or by aiding and acting with thieves or by such other acts and means as shewed he was pursuing crime. R. v. Organ, 11 Ont. Prac. 497, per Adam Wilson, C.J.

It is not to be assumed that because the accused has no visible occupation and is greatly addicted to gambling that the gambling contributes mainly to his support. R. v. Davidson, 8 Man. R. 325.

A conviction for vagrancy under Code sec. 207(1) is not warranted where the accused had at the time of his arrest sufficient money for his immediate needs and had been regularly employed in another city until two months prior thereto, although he was shewn to have been an associate of pickpockets in the city from which he came. The King v. Collette, 10 Can. Cr. Cas. 286.

Penalty for vagrancy.

239. Every loose, idle or disorderly person or vagrant is liable, on summary conviction, to a fine not exceeding fifty dollars or to imprisonment, with or without hard labour, for any term not exceeding six months, or to both: Provided that no aged or infirm person shall be convicted for any reason within paragraph *(a)* of the last preceding section, as a loose, idle or disorderly person or vagrant in the county of which he has for the two years immediately preceding been a resident. 55-56 V., c. 29, s. 208; 57-58 V., c. 57, s. 1; 63-64 V., c. 46, s. 3.

Proviso.

Vagrancy.]—Vagrancy is not an indictable offence, but loose and idle persons were liable at common law to be apprehended and bound over for their good behaviour, and were liable to summary proceedings before justices of the peace under various early statutes in England. Then under the Code, and under the Revised Act respecting Public Morals, R.S.C. 1886, ch. 157 (sec. 8), from which the vagrancy clauses are derived, "inmates" as well as "keepers" of bawdy houses were made subject to summary prosecution as vagrants, and likewise any person who is an habitual frequenter of a bawdy house and who, on being asked by a peace officer to give an account of himself or herself when found there, fails to give a satisfactory account. R. v. Levecque, 30 U.C.Q.B. 509; R. v. Clark, 2 Ont. R. 523; R. v. Arscott, 9 Ont. R. 541; Arscott v. Lilley, 11 Ont. R. 153.

Inmates and frequenters of bawdy house.]—Although secs. 771 and 773 appear under the general heading given to Part XVI., *i.e.*, "Summary trial of indictable offences," the inclusion therein of the offences of being an inmate of a bawdy house or being an habitual frequenter of same, must be taken as referring to the vagrancy clauses, secs. 238 and 239, and as providing an alternative procedure for the enforcement of those sections as well under the "summary trials" procedure, Part XVI., as under the procedure by "summary convictions by justices" (Part XV.), as there are no other sections of the Code dealing with "inmates" and "frequenters."

It is submitted that the judicial officers empowered by sec. 771 to hold summary trials are given absolute jurisdiction to summarily try the offences of being an inmate or habitual frequenter of a bawdy house (sec. 774), whether or not such officers are constituted justices of the peace under their provincial laws, and that the penalty for such offenders is limited to that imposed by sec. 239. The contrary has, however, been held by Ritchie, J., of the Supreme Court of Nova Scotia, in The King v. Roberts (1901), 4 Can. Cr. Cas. 253.

In that case it was held that the extended jurisdiction by which magistrates and certain other functionaries are empowered to summarily try that and other offences under Part XVI. of the Criminal Code, and to impose imprisonment up to six months and a fine not exceeding, with costs, $100, is not restricted as to the offence of being an inmate of a house of ill-fame by the fact that, if the accused had been prosecuted before such magistrate in his capacity of justice of the peace, under the "summary convictions" clauses for the similar offence of being a "vagrant" by reason of being such inmate, the fine could not have exceeded $50 in addition to six months' imprisonment. R. v. Roberts (1901), 4 Can. Cr. Cas. 253 (N.S.).

Keeping bawdy house.]—See note to sec. 228.

Information and particulars.]—The accused is entitled to know under which sub-section of sec. 238 he is charged, that is, what the facts are on which the prosecution relies, and it is not enough to charge simply that the accused is a loose, idle person or vagrant. R. v. McCormack (1903), 7 Can. Cr. Cas. 135, 9 B.C.R. 497.

Six months' imprisonment.]—This section only applies to authorize six months' imprisonment when imposed as the substantive punishment on summary conviction for keeping a bawdy house, and not as a means of enforcing payment of a fine. R. v. Stafford, 1 Can. Cr. Cas. 239 (N.S.).

If a fine imposed for an offence under this section either as the sole punishment or with the addition of imprisonment for a term not exceeding six months, the justice may by his conviction after adjudging payment of the fine order and adjudge that in default of payment thereof the defendant be imprisoned for any period not exceeding three months unless the fine and the expenses of conveying the defendant to gaol under the commitment for such default are sooner paid. Section 739(b).

Instead of directing imprisonment on default of payment of the fine forthwith or within a limited time, the justice may, by his conviction, order and adjudge that on such default, the penalty shall be levied by distress and, if sufficient distress cannot be found, that the defendant be imprisoned for any period not exceeding three months unless the penalty *and* the expenses of the distress *and* of conveying the defendant to gaol are sooner paid. Section 739(a).

If the justice making a summary conviction adjudges a pecuniary penalty and a distress to realize same, and in default of sufficient distress that the defendant be imprisoned, the costs of the distress and of conveying the defendant to gaol are not in the discretion of the justice, but must be included in the formal conviction. R. v. Vantassel No. 1 (1894), 5 Can. Cr. Cas. 128. The formal conviction may provide under sec. 739(a) for the payment of the costs both of the distress and of conveying to gaol, although the minute of conviction does not include the costs of distress but merely directs imprisonment unless the penalty and costs and the costs of conveying to gaol are sooner paid. Ibid. And the omission of a provision for the costs of distress and conveying to gaol from the formal conviction will invalidate the conviction. R. v. Vantassel (No. 2) (1894), 5 Can. Cr. Cas. 133.

Excluding public from court room.]—At the trial of any person charged with an offence under paragraphs (l), (j) and (k), of sec. 238, the court or judge may order that the public be excluded from the room or place in which the court is held during such trial. Section 645.

Search warrants for vagrants.]—See sec. 643.

Commitment to house of industry, etc.]—Section 30 of the Prisons Act R.S.C. 1906, ch. 148, provides as follows:—"If provision is made therefor by the laws of the province in which the conviction takes place, any such loose, idle or disorderly person may, instead of being committed to the common gaol or other public prison, be committed to any house of industry or correction, alms house, workhouse or reformatory prison."

Imprisonment in default of fine.]—A recorder has no right in condemning the accused to pay a fine and costs for vagrancy and to imprisonment in case of non-payment, to impose as a condition of the discharge of the accused at the expiry of the fixed term of imprisonment the payment of such costs and of the expenses of conveyance to gaol, and such conviction will be quashed on certiorari.

Semble, a conviction containing an adjudication so far in excess of that which might lawfully have been imposed will not be amended upon certiorari. Leonard v. Pelletier, 9 Can. Cr. Cas. 19 (Que.).

PART VI.

OFFENCES AGAINST THE PERSON AND REPUTATION.

Interpretation.

240. In this Part, unless the context otherwise requires,— **Definitions.**

(*a*) 'form of marriage' includes any form either recognized as a valid form by the law of the place where it is gone through, or which, though not so recognized, is such that a marriage celebrated there in that form is recognized as binding by the law of the place where the offender is tried; **'Form of marriage.'**

(*b*) 'guardian' includes any person who has in law or in fact the custody or control of any child referred to; **'Guardian.'**

(*c*) 'abandon' or 'expose' includes a wilful omission to take charge of any child referred to on the part of a person legally bound to take charge of such child, as well as any mode of dealing with it calculated to leave it exposed to risk without protection. 55-56 V., c. 29, ss. 216 and 275; 63-64 V., c. 46, s. 3. **'Abandon.' 'Expose.'**

Duties Tending to the Preservation of Life.

241. Every one who has charge of any other person unable by reason either of detention, age, sickness, insanity or any other cause, to withdraw himself from such charge, and unable to provide himself with the necessaries of life, is, whether such charge is undertaken by him under any contract, or is imposed upon him by law, or by reason of his unlawful act, under a legal duty to supply that person with the necessaries of life, and is criminally responsible for omitting, without lawful excuse, to perform such duty if the death of such person is caused, or if his life is endangered, or his health has been or is likely to be permanently injured, by such omission. 55-56 V., c. 29, s. 209. **Duty of person in charge to provide necessaries of life.** **Criminal responsibility.**

Preservation of life.]—Sections 241 and 242 appear in the Code under the heading of "Duties Tending to the Preservation of Life." As such headings have the same effect as preambles to statutes, the terms "necessaries of life," and "necessaries" which occur in the respective sections, mean, when read in connection with the heading mentioned, such necessaries as tend to preserve life, and not necessaries in their ordinary legal sense. R. v. Brooks (1902), 5 Can. Cr. Cas. 372, 9 B.C.R. 13.

Parents' neglect to supply medical aid to child.]—The leading English case on this subject is R. v. Senior, [1899] 1 Q.B. 283, 68 L.J.Q.B. 175, referred to in the above judgment. It was there held that a person who has the necessary means to procure medical aid for a child in his care or charge, who is, to the knowledge of such person, in a dangerous state of health, and for whom medical aid and medicine are such essential things that reasonably careful persons would have provided them for children in their care, is bound to do so. It is no excuse that the accused believed that to call in medical aid would be wrong as being contrary to the teachings of the Bible or as shewing want of faith in the Deity. If the death of the child was caused or accelerated by the neglect, the accused is guilty of manslaughter. R. v. Senior, [1899], 1 Q.B. 283; R. v. Instan, [1893] 1 Q.B. 450, 17 Cox C.C. 602; Code section 256. There must, however, be positive evidence that the death was caused or accelerated by the neglect to provide medical aid. R. v. Morby (1881), 8 Q.B.D. 571. In the last mentioned case the prisoner had been convicted of the manslaughter of his son, a child of tender years. The child died of smallpox, and the prisoner though able to do so did not supply medical aid, owing to his being one of the Peculiar People, a sect which holds religious objections to so doing, the members believing that diseases are to be cured by prayer and anointing with oil. It was proved that proper medical aid might possibly have saved or prolonged the child's life, and would have increased its chance of recovery, but that it might have been of no avail, and there was no positive evidence that the death was caused or accelerated by the neglect to provide medical aid. It was held that under the circumstances the conviction could not be sustained. R. v. Morby (1881), 8 Q.B.D. 571, 51 L.J.M.C. 85.

A presumption that the prisoner was, at the time of the neglect which caused or accelerated the death, possessed of sufficient means to have provided food and medicine is raised by proof of possession by her of such means at a certain date prior to the date of the neglect as, having regard to the circumstances, would presumably not be exhausted at the date of the neglect, and affords evidence to go to the jury of actual possession of means at the date of such neglect. Rex v. Ellen Jones (1901), 19 Cox C.C. 678, per Kennedy, J., at Worcestershire Assizes.

Medical attendance and remedies are necessaries within the meaning of Code sections 209 and 210 and also at common law, and that anyone legally liable to provide such is criminally responsible for neglect to do so. R. v. Brooks (1902), 5 Can. Cr. Cas. 372, 9 B.C.R. 13; R. v. Lewis (1903), 7 Can. Cr. Cas. 261, 6 O.L.R. 132. Conscientious belief that it is against the teachings of the Bible and therefore wrong to have recourse to medical attendance and remedies is no excuse. Ibid.

At common law.]—If a person having the care and custody of another who is helpless, neglects to supply him with the necessaries of life and thereby causes or accelerates his death, he was guilty of a criminal offence even before the statute. R. v. Nasmith (1877), 42 U.C.Q.B. 242. But if a person over the age of sixteen (see section 243) and having the exercise of free will, chooses to stay in a service where bad food and lodging are provided and death is thereby caused, the master is not criminally liable. R. v. Charlotte Smith, 10 Cox 94.

If the neglect was premeditated and there has been a deliberate omission to supply food to the helpless person in the custody or charge of the accused and death results from the omission, it is murder. R. v. Condé, 10 Cox C.C. 547; R. v. Bubb, 4 Cox C.C. 457; R. v. Self, 1 Leach 137.

If a grown-up person chooses to undertake the charge of a human creature, helpless either from infancy, simplicity, lunacy or other infirmity, he is bound to execute that charge without wicked negligence; and if a person who has chosen to take charge of a helpless creature lets it die by wicked negligence that person is guilty of manslaughter. R. v. Nicholls, 13 Cox C.C. 75. In such a case mere negligence will not establish the offence of manslaughter; there must be a wicked negligence, that is, negligence so great as to satisfy a jury that the prisoner had a wicked mind in the sense that he was reckless and careless whether the creature died or not. Ibid., per Brett, J.

If the death of an apprentice labouring under disease is caused by want of care of and harsh treatment by the master who has charge of him the master is guilty of murder. R. v. Squire, 3 Russ. Cr. 6th ed. 13.

The master is not bound to provide medicine and attendance on his servant while such servant remains under his roof as part of the family. Winnall v. Adney, 3 B. & P. 247; unless in the case of an apprentice. R. v. Stokes, 8 C. & P. 153.

A young unmarried woman being about to be confined returned to the house of her mother and stepfather. There she was taken in labour during her stepfather's absence, and the mother did not take ordinary care to procure the assistance of a midwife though she could have got one had she wished to do so. In consequence of such want of assistance the daughter died in her confinement. There was no evidence that the mother had any means of paying for the midwife's services. It was held under these circumstances that there was no legal duty on the part of the mother to call in a midwife and consequently there was no such breach of duty as to render her liable to be convicted of manslaughter. R. v. Shepherd, L. & C. 147, 31 L.J.M.C. 102.

Quebec law.]—The Civil Code of Quebec, article 166, enacts that: "Children are bound to maintain their father, mother, and other ascendants, who are in want."

Necessaries for wife or child.]—See sec. 242.

Servants or apprentices under sixteen years.]—See sec. 243.

Permanently injured.]—See note to sec. 242.

Punishment.]—For murder, see sec. 263; manslaughter, sec. 268; other cases of neglect under sec. 241, three years' imprisonment, sec. 244.

242. Every one who as parent, guardian or head of a family is under a legal duty to provide necessaries for any child under the age of sixteen years is criminally responsible for omitting, without lawful excuse, to do so while such child remains a member of his or her household, whether such child is helpless or not, if the death of such child is caused, or if his life is endangered, or his health is or is likely to be permanently injured, by such omission. **Duty of head of family to provide necessaries.**

2. Every one who is under a legal duty to provide necessaries for his wife, is criminally responsible for omitting, without lawful excuse so to do, if the death of his wife is caused, or if her life is endangered, or her health is or is likely to be permanently injured, by such omission. 55-56 V., c. 29, s. 210. **Criminal responsibility.**

Head of a family.]—A person who engages the services of a child under sixteen years, placed out with him by his legal guardian under a contract for the child's services for a fixed period, whereby the party with whom he is placed engages to furnish the child with board, lodging, clothing, and necessaries, is not as to such child a "guardian or head of a family" so as to become criminally responsible as such, under section 242, for omitting to provide "necessaries" to such child while a member of his household. The relationship in such case is that of master and servant, and comes within the provisions of section 243, under which the master is criminally responsible only in respect of a failure to provide "necessary food, clothing, or lodging." R. v. Coventry, 3 Can. Cr. Cas. 541. Section 243 of the Code does not impose a criminal responsibility upon the master to provide the servant with medical attendance or medicine.

Without lawful excuse.]—It must be shewn that the parent or guardian was in the actual possession of means to provide for the child. R. v. Saunders, 7 C. & P. 277; R. v. Edwards, 8 C. & P. 611; R. v. Chandler, Dears. 453; and see R. v. Robinson (1897), 1 Can. Cr. Cas. 28. The mere fact that he might have obtained such means by application to a relief officer is not sufficient. R. v. Chandler, Dears. 453; R. v. Rugg, 12 Cox C.C. 16.

It must also be shewn that the child was unable to provide for himself. R. v. Friend, R. & R. 20.

Permanently injured.]—It is purely a question of fact whether the acts proved are such that the health of the person is likely to be permanently injured by reason thereof; and the words "permanently injured," as here used, have no technical meaning. R. v. Bowman (1898), 3 Can. Cr. Cas. 410 (N.S.).

On a case reserved upon a conviction for failing to supply necessaries to a wife whereby her health is likely to be permanently injured, the conviction should be affirmed, if there is some evidence from which an inference may be drawn that such injury was likely to result from the non-supplying of necessaries. R. v. McIntyre (1898), 3 Can. Cr. Cas. 413 (N.S.).

Where a child's toes were so badly frozen, through the neglect of the person in whose charge the child was, that they had to be amputated, it was held in the Territories that the court should not without expert evidence upon the effect of the loss of the toes infer that the child's health had thereby been or was likely to be "permanently injured," or that his life had thereby been endangered. R. v. Coventry, 3 Can. Cr. Cas. 541 (N.W.T.). The correctness of the decision is doubted.

Non-support of wife.]—It is necessary to prove that the defendant is the husband of the prosecutrix, that the wife was in need of food, clothing or lodging, and that the husband omitted to provide the same. R. v. Nasmith (1877), 42 U.C.Q.B. 242. Under the former law it was necessary to shew that the accused wilfully and without lawful excuse refused or neglected to provide (32-33 Vict., ch. 20, sec. 25), and under it an ability to perform was necessary to constitute a neglect. R. v. Ryland, L.R. 1 C.C.R. 99. And it seems to be still necessary for the prosecution to give evidence of his ability in order to shew that the omission was without lawful excuse.

Evidence is admissible, as tending to shew a lawful excuse, of an agreement between husband and wife at time of marriage that she should be supported as before the marriage and not by him until he could earn sufficient means for the maintenance of both. Such evidence is admissible although the contract alone may not furnish an answer to the charge. The prisoner may have become possessed of ample means since his marriage, and the offence being a public one cannot be met by a mere agreement between the husband and wife. A present inability to support his wife may be proved by the accused by way of defence. R. v. Robinson (1897), 1 Can. Cr. Cas. 28.

Where the husband's failure to support his wife caused no injury to the wife's health, she having been maintained by the charity of friends on the husband's default, such default does not give rise to criminal responsibility under Code sections 242 and 244. R. v. Wilkes (1906), 11 Can. Cr. Cas. 226.

The defendant may be convicted notwithstanding that his wife has in consequence of the neglect to supply her with necessaries left him, taking with her a small sum of money belonging to him. R. v. Pennock (1898), 18 C.L.T. 79.

Where the complainant in a charge of non-support of wife had been previously married, but had always lived apart from her first husband, and swore to having heard two years before the second marriage that her husband was dying in a foreign country, and that about a year after her second marriage she again heard that her husband was dead, such was held to be evidence to go to the jury to prove that her first husband had died before her marriage to the defendant. R. v. Holmes (1898), 2 Can. Cr. Cas. 131.

Wife a compellable witness.]—Neglect under sec. 242 is punishable under section 244; and the Canada Evidence Act, sec. 4(2), specifies the latter section as one under which the wife of the accused is a competent and compellable witness for the prosecution.

What are necessaries.]—See note to sec. 241.

Guardian.]—The word "guardian" includes any person who has in law or in fact the custody or control of any child referred to. Section 240.

Proving age of juvenile.]—See sec. 984.

Proof of marriage.]—The fact that it is a foreign marriage does not affect the question of the proof, as the lex fori governs upon all questions of proof. Taylor on Evidence, p. 49; Daye v. McNeill (1904), 6 Terr. L.R. 44.

Form of indictment for non-support.]—That A.B., at , on , and on several days and times before then, being the husband of C.D., his wife, and as such husband being under a legal duty to provide necessaries for her, did then and there unlawfully omit, without lawful excuse, to provide necessaries for her, whereby the life of the said C.D. was endangered, or the health of the said C.D. is now or is likely to be permanently injured.

Duty of masters.

243. Every one who, as master or mistress, has contracted to provide necessary food, clothing or lodging for any servant or apprentice under the age of sixteen years is under a legal duty to provide the same, and is criminally responsible for omitting, without lawful excuse, to perform such duty, if the death of such servant or apprentice is caused, or if his life is endangered, or his health has been or is likely to be permanently injured, by such omission. 55-56 V., c. 29, s. 211.

Criminal responsibility.

Master and servant.]—This and the preceding section originated in 32-33 Vict. (Can.), ch. 20, sec. 25, adapted from the Imperial Statute 24 & 25 Vict., ch. 100, sec. 26. Under 32-33 Vict., the gist of the offence was the wilfully and without lawful excuse refusing or neglecting to provide. R. v.

Nasmith (1877), 42 U.C.Q.B. 242. The words of the Code constitute the mere omission an offence, if without lawful excuse.

This section does not impose a criminal responsibility upon the master to provide the servant with medical attendance or medicine. R. v. Coventry (1898), 3 Can. Cr. Cas. 541. It was held in the same case that the court should not, without expert evidence upon the effect of the loss of a child's toes resulting from exposure to cold, and their consequent amputation, infer that the child's health had thereby been or was likely to be "permanently injured," or that his life has thereby been endangered. The correctness of this decision is to be doubted.

An indictment did not lie against a master at common law for not providing sufficient food and sustenance for a servant, whereby the servant became sick and emaciated, unless it alleged that the servant was of tender years and under the dominion and control of the master. R. v. Friend, Russ. & Ry. 20; R. v. Ridley, 2 Camp. 650. The reason of the restriction is, that if the servant be not of tender years, he may if not provided with proper nourishment remonstrate, and, if necessary, leave the service. R. v. Nasmith (1877), 42 U.C.Q.B. 242, 245. The present section does not appear to have changed the law in that respect except in fixing the age limit at sixteen.

In a case before the Code where a young farm hand fifteen years of age died from gangrene resulting from frost-bites through exposure and neglect which the master could have obviated it was held that, in view of the age of the deceased, the circumstances of the country, the fact of their being no provision for maintaining poor people, it was the duty of the prisoner, as a master towards the deceased as his servant, to have taken care of him, and that by his omission to do so he was guilty of gross negligence, to which the lad's death was attributable, and that, therefore, the prisoner was guilty of manslaughter. R. v. Brown (1893), 1 Terr. L.R. 475.

Without lawful excuse.]—On a charge against a master for neglecting to supply food to his apprentice it must be shewn that the master was in the actual possession of means to provide for him. R. v. Saunders, 7 C. & P. 277; R. v. Edwards, 8 C. & P. 611; R. v. Chandler, Dears. 452, 6 Cox C.C. 519. The mere fact that he might have obtained such means by application to a relief officer is not sufficient. R. v. Chandler, Dears. 453; R. v. Rugg, 12 Cox C.C. 16.

Proof of age.]—See sec. 984.

Form of indictment against master.]—The jurors, etc., present—That B., on then being the master of M., his servant, and having contracted and then being legally liable to provide for the said M., as his servant as aforesaid, necessary food (clothing or lodging), unlawfully, wilfully and without lawful excuse did refuse and neglect to provide the same, so that the life of the said M. was thereby endangered (or the health of the said M. has been or is likely to be permanently injured) against the form of the statute, the Criminal Code secs. 243 and 244.

Omission of duty.

244. Every one is guilty of an indictable offence and liable to three years' imprisonment who, being bound to perform any duty specified in the three last preceding sections, without lawful excuse neglects or refuses to do so, unless the offence amounts to culpable homicide. 55-56 V., c. 29, s. 215; 56 V., c. 32, s. 1.

Penalty.

See notes to secs. 241 to 243 inclusive.

Wife or husband as a compellable witness.]—See Canada Evidence Act, sec. 4(2).

245. Every one is guilty of an indictable offence and liable to three years' imprisonment who unlawfully abandons or exposes any child under the age of two years, whereby its life is endangered or its health is permanently injured. 55-56 V., c. 29, s. 216.

Abandoning children under two years.

Evidence.]—A woman who was living apart from her husband, and who had the actual custody of their child under two years of age brought the child to the door of the father's house telling him she had done so. He knowingly allowed it to remain lying outside his door for four hours in the night time and it was then removed by a constable. It was held that, although the father had not the actual custody and possession of the child, yet as he was bound by law to provide for it, his allowing it to remain where he did was an abandonment and exposure of the child by him whereby its life was endangered. R. v. White (1871), L.R. 1 C.C.R. 311, 40 L.J.M.C. 134.

And where the mother of a bastard child five weeks old put the child in a hamper and shipped the hamper as a goods parcel by railway a distance of four miles to the child's putative father who had told her, prior to the child's birth, that if she sent it to him he would keep it, and the hamper was addressed for immediate delivery and was in fact delivered within an hour and a quarter from the time the mother left it, and the child died three weeks afterwards from causes not attributable to such conduct of the mother, yet it was held that she was properly convicted of abandoning and exposing the child whereby its life was endangered. R. v. Falkingham (1870), L.R. 1 C.C.R. 222, 39 L.J.M.C. 47.

Proof of age of juvenile.]—See sec. 984.

Abandon or expose.]—See sec. 240.

Form of indictment.]—That A. unlawfully did abandon and expose a certain child called M., then being under the age of two years, whereby the life of the said child was endangered (or whereby the health of such child was likely to be permanently injured) against the form of the statute made and provided and of the Criminal Code sec. 245.

246. Every one who undertakes, except in cases of necessity, to administer surgical or medical treatment, or to do any other lawful act the doing of which is or may be dangerous to life, is under a legal duty to have and to use reasonable knowledge, skill and care in doing any such act, and is criminally responsible for omitting, without lawful excuse, to discharge that duty if death is caused by such omission. 55-56 V., c. 29, s. 212.

Duty of persons undertaking acts dangerous to life.

Surgical or medical treatment.]—A medical man must, at his peril, use proper skill and caution in administering a poisonous drug. R. v. Macleod, 12 Cox C.C. 534.

If a party having a competent degree of skill and knowledge, whether a licensed physician or not, makes an accidental mistake in his treatment of a patient and the patient's death results from the mistake, such party is not thereby guilty of manslaughter; but if, where proper medical assistance can be had, a person totally ignorant of the science of medicine takes on himself to administer a violent and dangerous remedy to one labouring under disease, and death ensues in consequence of that dangerous remedy having been so administered, then he is guilty of manslaughter. R. v. Webb, 2 Lewin 196, 1 M. & Rob. 405.

It may be left to the jury to say first, whether death was occasioned or accelerated by the medicines administered, and if they find that it was, then the jury may be instructed that the prisoner is guilty of manslaughter if they think that in so administering the medicine he acted with a criminal intention or from very gross negligence. Ibid.; R. v. Chamberlain, 10 Cox C.C. 486.

Evidence cannot be gone into, on either side, of former cases treated by the prisoner, but the opinion of experts may be given as to the treatment which the evidence shews was administered in the case in question. R. v. Whitehead, 3 C. & K. 202; Archbold Cr. Plead. (1900), 755.

On an indictment against a medical man for manslaughter by administering poison by mistake for some other drug, it is not sufficient for the prosecution to shew merely that the prisoner, who dispensed his own drugs, supplied a mixture which contained a large quantity of poison; the prosecution must also shew that this happened through the gross negligence of the prisoner. R. v. Spencer, 10 Cox C.C. 525.

A woman practising "Christian science" and not called in as a medical attendant was held not guilty of manslaughter where the only treatment by her was to sit silently by the patient, a child ill of diphtheria, although the child's health might have been saved or prolonged had proper medical aid been called in. R. v. Beer, 32 C.L.J. 416. But the aiding and abetting the person charged with the duty of providing necessaries is punishable in like manner as the principal offence. Sec. 69. R. v. Brooks (1902), 5 Can. Cr. Cas. 372, 9 B.C.R. 13; R. v. Lewis (1903), 7 Can. Cr. Cas. 261, 6 O.L.R. 132.

Duty of persons in charge of dangerous things.

247. Every one who has in his charge or under his control anything whatever, whether animate or inanimate, or who erects, makes or maintains anything whatever which, in the absence of precaution or care, may endanger human life, is under a legal duty to take reasonable precautions against, and use reasonable care to avoid, such danger, and is criminally responsible for the consequences of omitting, without lawful excuse, to perform such duty. 55-56 V., c. 29, s. 213.

Criminal liability of corporation.]—A corporation is not subject to indictment upon a charge of any crime the essence of which is either personal criminal intent or such a degree of negligence as amounts to a wilful incurring of the risk of causing injury to others. R. v. Great West Laundry Co. (1900), 3 Can. Cr. Cas. 514 (Man.). Sections 247 and 252, as to want of care in the maintenance of dangerous things, do not extend the criminal responsibility of corporations beyond what it was at common law. Ibid.

Although a corporation cannot be guilty of manslaughter, it may be indicted, under Code sec. 222 and possibly also under sec. 284, for having caused grievous bodily injury by omitting to maintain in a safe condition a bridge or structure which it was its duty to so maintain, and this notwithstanding that death ensued at once to the person sustaining the grievous bodily injury. R. v. Union Colliery Co. (1900), 3 Can. Cr. Cas. 523 (B.C.) affirmed, 4 Can. Cr. Cas. 400, 31 Can. S.C.R. 81.

Under sec. 247 a corporation may be indicted for omitting, without lawful excuse, to perform the duty of avoiding danger to human life from anything in its charge or under its control. The fact that the consequence of the omission to perform such duty might have justified an indictment for manslaughter in the case of an individual is not a ground for quashing the indictment. Union Colliery Co. v. R. (1900), 4 Can. Cr. Cas. 400, 31 Can. S.C.R. 81.

As the Criminal Code provides no punishment for the offence as against a corporation, the common law punishment of a fine may be imposed on a corporation indicted under it. Ibid.

Where deceased was run over by a railroad car and died from his injuries a few hours afterwards, the statement of the deceased, made immediately after he was run over in answer to a question as to how it happened, was held admissible. Armstrong v. Canada Atlantic (1901), 2 O.L.R. 219; Thompson v. Trevanion (1693), Skin. 402; Aveson v. Kinnaird (1805), 6 East 188, at p. 193; Rex v. Foster (1834), 6 C. & P. 325.

In Mill v. Hawker, L.R. 9 Exch. 317, Cleasby, B., said: "When the acts are such as the corporate body is not by law qualified to do, and the corporate body, if they pretend to do them, are acting ultra vires, then the mere fact of giving a corporate form to the act does not prevent it from being the act of those who caused it to be done. It seems plain that in such a case the individuals and not the corporation do the act, and no authority is needed for that conclusion."

The latter opinion was concurred in by the Supreme Court of New Brunswick in Ex p. Baird (1897), 3 Can. Cr. Cas. 65.

The manager of a corporation is not criminally liable as for wilful disobedience of a statute under Code sec. 164 in respect of the corporation's neglect not due to any active participation on his part, to perform a statutory duty imposed upon it. R. v. Hays (1907), 12 Can. Cr. Cas. 423.

There are offences, such as assaults, which it is physically impossible for a corporation to commit, but for such offences as they can commit, whether of misfeasance or malfeasance, and for which the prescribed punishment is one which they can be made to endure, they are as amenable to the criminal law as are natural persons. R. v. Central Supply Association (1907), 12 Can. Cr. Cas. 371; The Queen v. The Great North of England R.W. Co. (1846), 9 Q.B. 315; The Queen v. Tyler and International Commercial Co., [1891] 2 Q.B. 588-594; Pharmaceutical Soc'y. v. London and Provincial Supply Association (1880), 5 App. Cas. 857.

Some one or more officers of the corporation may also be liable upon a criminal charge arising out of the same occurrence in respect of the officer's personal misfeasance or malfeasance. In a recent Ontario case, Rex v. Michigan Central Ry. (1907), in which the railway company had been indicted for a nuisance under the Revised Cr. Code sec. 221, in carrying dynamite without proper precautions whereby fatalities resulted and for criminal neglect under sec. 247 whereby human life was endangered, Mr. Justice Riddell said in delivering judgment after a plea of guilty: "If it were the fact that the board of directors or the general manager of the defendants' company, or anyone responsible, directly or indirectly, for the system carried on in the transportation of explosives, resided within the jurisdiction of this court, I should have recommended their being indicted as well as the company. It is right and just that employees of whatever grade shall be placed upon trial when any negligence of theirs caused wounds or death, and the higher officers through whom a defective system is put on or kept in operation should not escape."

In Ex parte Brydges (1874), 18 Lower Canada Jurist 141, the application was upon the return of rules nisi to quash a coroner's inquisition (which then had an effect similar to an indictment) and for the discharge of Mr. Brydges' recognizance, under the following circumstances:—A man named Cauchon had been killed by a G.T.R. train at a level crossing. Mr. Brydges was the managing director of the railway and on complaints made that the crossing was particularly dangerous, had admitted the fact and promised the Attorney-General that he would have a watchman placed there. He did not place a watchman as promised and the fatality to Cauchon resulted. The finding of the coroner's jury was quashed because it was insufficient in form and did not sufficiently charge a criminal offence. Mr. Justice Ramsay said in that case:—

"I do not wish, however, to be understood to say that I think a servant of a railway company cannot be held liable for an error of omission as well as for an error of commission. It will not be questioned that an engine driver may be indicted for manslaughter if he causes the death of any one by omitting to take any of the usual precautions in driving his engine. A case of this kind actually occurred in 1868. It went to the petty jury and the prisoner was acquitted on the facts. His legal responsibility was not doubted. If an engine driver can thus become liable for an omission, I cannot see why a managing director should not become liable also if he omits to do what the law imposes and what he undertakes to see done. Of course the scope of his functions is a matter of fact to be considered; but names have a meaning, and 'managing director' may signify a good deal."

Evidence.]—See note to secs. 221 and 222.

Duty to avoid omissions dangerous to life.

248. Every one who undertakes to do any act, the omission to do which is or may be dangerous to life, is under a legal duty to do that act, and is criminally responsible for the consequences of omitting, without lawful excuse, to perform that duty. 55-56 V., c. 29, s. 214.

Negligent omission by medical practitioner.]—A person acting as a medical man is not criminally responsible for the death of a patient occasioned by his treatment, unless his conduct is characterized either by gross ignorance of his art, or by gross inattention to his patient's safety. R. v. St. John Long, 4 C. & P. 398; Hunter v. Ogden, 31 Q.B. 132.

Dangerous medical treatment.]—See sec. 246.

Bodily injury.]—By sec. 284 every one is guilty of an indictable offence and liable to two years' imprisonment who, by any unlawful act, or by doing negligently or omitting to do any act which it is his duty to do, causes grievous bodily injury to any other person.

Causing bodily harm to apprentices or servants.

249. Every one is guilty of an indictable offence and liable to three years' imprisonment who, being legally liable as master or mistress to provide for any apprentice or servant, unlawfully does, or causes to be done, any bodily harm to any such apprentice or servant so that the life of such apprentice or servant is endangered or the health of such apprentice or servant has been, or is likely to be, permanently injured. 55-56 V., c. 29, s. 217.

A verdict for common assault is maintainable upon an indictment under this section. R. v. Bissonnette (1879), Ramsay's Cases (Que.) 190.

Neglect to supply necessary food, etc.]—See sec. 243.

Permanently injured.]—It is purely a question of fact whether the acts proved shew that the health is likely to be permanently injured; and the words "permanently injured" have no technical meaning as here used. R. v. Bowman (1898), 3 Can. Cr. Cas. 410.

Homicide.

250. Homicide is the killing of a human being by another, directly or indirectly, by any means whatsoever. 55-56 V., c. 29, s. 218. Definition.

Classes of homicide.]—Homicide, when not amounting to murder or manslaughter, is divided by Russell into two classes:—(1) Excusable; (2) Justifiable. 3 Russell Cr., 6th ed., 205.

Section 252, infra, divides the subject of homicide into: (1) culpable homicide, which is sub-divided into two classes: (a) murder, (b) manslaughter; (2) homicide not culpable. The same section defines what is "culpable" homicide, and declares that homicide which is not culpable is not an offence. Excusable homicide is said to be of two sorts: Either per infortunium, by misadventure: or se et sua defendendo, upon a principle of self-defence.

Excusable homicide.]—The term excusable homicide imports some fault in the party by whom it has been committed; but of a nature so trivial that the law excuses such homicide from the guilt of felony, though in strictness it deems it to be deserving of some degree of punishment. 3 Russell Cr., 6th ed., 205, 4 Bl. Com. 188.

Matters of justification or excuse.]—Not only are the rules and principles of the common law preserved as regards any circumstances which either justify or excuse the act or constitute a defence to a charge (Code sec. 16), but various rules are laid down in Part I. of the Code, secs. 17 to 68 inclusive upon the subject.

Homicide by misadventure.]—Homicide by misadventure is where one doing a lawful act, without any intention of bodily harm, and using proper precaution to prevent danger, unfortunately happens to kill another person. 1 East P.C. 5. p. 221, and sec. 36, pp. 260, 261, Fost. 258, 1 Hawk. P.C., ch. 29, sec. 1. The act must be lawful; for if it be unlawful, the homicide will amount to murder or manslaughter, and it must not be done with intention of great bodily harm, for then the legality of the act, considered abstractedly, would be no more than a mere cloak or pretence, and consequently would avail nothing. The act must also be done in a proper manner and with due caution to prevent danger. 1 East P.C., ch. 5, sec. 36, p. 261; 3 Russell 206.

This, if people following their common occupations, use due caution to prevent danger, and nevertheless happen, unfortunately to kill any one, such killing will be homicide by misadventure. 1 Hale 472, 475, 1 Hawk. P.C. ch. 629, secs. 2 and 4. Thus, where a person, driving a cart or other carriage happens to drive over another and kill him, if the accident happened in such a manner that no want of due care could be imputed to the driver, it will be accidental death, and the driver will be excused. Fost. 263, 1 Hale 476. In a case where a person was riding a horse, and the horse, being whipped by some other person sprang out of the road, and ran over a child and killed it, this was held to be misadventure only in the rider, though manslaughter in the person who whipped the horse. 1 Hawk. P.C., ch. 29, sec. 3.

Where parents, masters, and other persons having authority in foro domestico, give correction to those under their care, and such correction exceeds the bounds of due moderation, so that death ensues, the offence will be either murder or manslaughter, according to the circumstances; but if the correction be reasonable and moderate, and by the struggling of the party corrected, or by some other misfortune, death ensue, the killing will be only misadventure. 1 Hale 454, 473, 474, 4 Blac. Com. 182.

Insanity as a defence.]—See sec. 19.

Homicide in self-defence.]—See secs. 85-62.

Homicide by surgical operation.]—See sec. 65.

When a child becomes a human being.

251. A child becomes a human being within the meaning of this Act when it has completely proceeded, in a living state, from the body of its mother, whether it has breathed or not, whether it has an independent circulation or not, and whether the navel string is severed or not.

Killing child.

2. The killing of such child is homicide when it dies in consequence of injuries received before, during or after birth. 55-56 V., c. 29, s. 219.

Killing unborn child.]—A living child in its mother's womb or a child in the act of birth, even though such child may have breathed, is not a "human being," and the killing of such a child before it is born is not homicide. R. v. Enoch, 5 C. & P. 539; R. v. Wright, 9 C. & P. 754; R. v. Sellis, 7 C. & P. 850; Burb. Cr. Dig. 209.

But by sec. 306 every one is guilty of an indictable offence and liable to imprisonment for life who causes the death of any child which has not become a human being, in such a manner that he would have been guilty of murder if such child had been born. And by sub-sec. (2) of the same section no one is guilty of any offence who by means which he in good faith considers necessary for the preservation of the life of the mother of the child causes the death of any such child before or during its birth.

Homicide when culpable.

252. Homicide may be either culpable or not culpable.

2. Homicide is culpable when it consists in the killing of any person, either by an unlawful act or by an omission, without lawful excuse, to perform or observe any legal duty, or by both combined, or by causing a person, by threats or fear of violence, or by deception, to do an act which causes that person's death, or by wilfully frightening a child or sick person.

Offence.

3. Culpable homicide is either murder or manslaughter.

No offence.

4. Homicide which is not culpable is not an offence. 55-56 V., c. 29, s. 220.

Code secs. 247 and 252 do not extend the criminal responsibility of corporations beyond what it was at common law. R. v. Great West Laundry Co. (1900), 3 Can. Cr. Cas. 514 (Man.). See note to sec. 247.

Murder.]—Circumstances under which culpable homicide is murder are set out in secs. 259 and 260.

Manslaughter.]—Culpable homicide not amounting to murder is manslaughter, (sec. 262), and the circumstances which reduce to manslaughter or homicide which otherwise would be murder are stated in sec. 261.

253. Procuring by false evidence the conviction and death of any person by the sentence of the law shall not be deemed to be homicide. 55-56 V., c. 29, s. 221. **Procuring death by false evidence.**

Perjury or subornation of perjury committed in order to procure the conviction of a person for any crime punishable by death is a crime punishable with imprisonment for life. Section 174(2).

254. No one is criminally responsible for the killing of another unless the death takes place within a year and a day of the cause of death. **Death within a year and a day.**

2. The period of a year and a day shall be reckoned inclusive of the day on which the last unlawful act contributing to the cause of death took place. **How reckoned.**

3. Where the cause of death is an omission to fulfil a legal duty the period shall be reckoned inclusive of the day on which such omission ceased. **Idem.**

4. When death is in part caused by an unlawful act and in part by an omission, the period shall be reckoned inclusive of the day on which the last unlawful act took place or the omission ceased, whichever happened last. 55-56 V., c. 29, s. 222. **Idem.**

At common law.]—If the death takes place after the expiration of a year and a day from the time the deceased was wounded, the law presumes that his death had proceeded from some other cause. I Hawk., ch. 23, sec. 90; 1 East P.C. 343.

The prisoner was convicted of manslaughter in killing his wife, who died on November 10, 1881. The immediate cause of her death was acute inflammation of the liver, which the medical testimony proved might be occasioned by a blow or a fall against a hard substance. About three weeks before her death the prisoner had knocked his wife down with a bottle; she fell against a door and remained on the floor insensible for some time; she was confined to her bed soon afterwards and never recovered. Evidence was given of frequent acts of violence committed by the prisoner upon his wife within a year of her death, by knocking her down and kicking her in the side. On questions reserved, whether the evidence was properly received of assaults and violence committed by the prisoner upon the deceased prior to the date of death or prior to the occasion on which he had knocked her down with the bottle, and whether there was any evidence to leave to the jury to sustain the charge, it was held by the Supreme Court of Canada, affirming the judgment of the Supreme Court of New Brunswick, that the evidence was properly received and that there was evidence to submit to the jury that the disease which caused her death was produced by the injuries inflicted by the prisoner. Theal v. The Queen, 7 Can. S.C.R. 397.

Killing by influence on the mind.

255. No one is criminally responsible for the killing of another by any influence on the mind alone, nor for the killing of another by any disorder or disease arising from such influence, save in either case by wilfully frightening a child or sick person. 55-56 V., c. 29, s. 223.

To wilfully frighten a child or sick person as a result of which such child or sick person dies is culpable homicide. Section 252.

Acceleration of death.

256. Every one who, by any act or omission, causes the death of another, kills that person, although the effect of the bodily injury caused to such other person be merely to accelerate his death while labouring under some disorder or disease arising from some other cause. 55-56 V., c. 29, s. 224.

A., a practising physician who kept a hospital for the sick, on three successive days forced the person of B. a patient then under his control in such hospital, she being in a condition of health that rendered sexual intercourse dangerous even with her consent. B. died on the sixth day after the last occasion on which she had been ravished and her death was hastened if not caused thereby. It was held that there was sufficient evidence to justify A.'s surrender under the Ashburton treaty for extradition on a charge of murder. Re Weir, 14 Ont. R. 389.

A. inflicts bodily injury on B. who at the time is so ill that she could not possibly have lived more than six weeks if she had not been struck. In consequence B. dies earlier than she otherwise would. A. is guilty of culpable homicide. R. v. Fletcher, 1 Russ. Cr. 703.

Death which might have been prevented.

257. Every one who, by any act or omission, causes the death of another, kills that person, although death from that cause might have been prevented by resorting to proper means. 55-56 V., c. 29, s. 225.

Causing injury the treatment of which brings death.

258. Every one who causes a bodily injury, which is of itself of a dangerous nature to any person, from which death results, kills that person, although the immediate cause of death be treatment proper or improper applied in good faith. 55-56 V., c. 29, s. 226.

Bodily injury resulting in death.]—In R. v. Holland, 2 Moo. and Rob. 351, A. had assaulted B. and injured B.'s finger. B. was advised by a surgeon to allow it to be amputated but refused to do so, and lockjaw resulted causing B.'s death. It was held that these facts constituted culpable homicide. But quære whether this would be so under this section, as it could hardly be said that an injury to the finger was "of itself of a dangerous nature," i.e., dangerous to life. Cf. R. v. Coventry (1898), 3 Can. Cr. Cas. 541.

Where in a duel a wound is given which in the judgment of competent medical advisers is dangerous, and the treatment which they bonâ fide adopt is the immediate cause of death, the party who inflicted the wound is guilty of culpable homicide. R. v. Pym, 1 Cox C.C. 339.

But if a man were wounded, and another applied to his wound sulphuric acid or something else which was of a dangerous character, and ought not to be applied, and which led to fatal results, then the person who applied this remedy would be answerable, and not the person who inflicted the wound, because a new cause had supervened. Reg. v. Markuss, 4 F. & F. 356.

Murder and Manslaughter.

259. Culpable homicide is murder,— Intention.

(a) if the offender means to cause the death of the person killed;

(b) if the offender means to cause to the person killed any bodily injury which is known to the offender to be likely to cause death, and is reckless whether death ensues or not;

(c) if the offender means to cause death, or, being so reckless as aforesaid, means to cause such bodily injury as aforesaid to one person, and by accident or mistake kills another person, though he does not mean to hurt the person killed;

(d) if the offender, for any unlawful object, does an act which he knows or ought to have known to be likely to cause death, and thereby kills any person, though he may have desired that his object should be effected without hurting any one. 55-56 V., c. 29, s. 227.

Murder at common law.]—The common law definition of murder is—the killing any person under the King's peace, with malice prepense or aforethought, either express or implied by law. 3 Inst. 47, 51; 1 Hawk. P.C. ch. 31, sec. 3; Fost. 256.

Malice may be either (1) express, or (2) implied by law. Express malice is when one person kills another with a sedate deliberate mind and formed design; such formed design being evidenced by external circumstances discovering the inward intention, as lying in wait, antecedent menaces, former grudges, and concerted schemes to do the party some bodily harm. 1 Hale 451.

Malice is implied by law from any deliberate cruel act committed by one person against another, however sudden. 1 East P.C. 215; 3 Russell Crim. (1896), 2. And it is a general rule that all homicide is presumed to be malicious until the contrary appears from circumstances of alleviation, excuse or justification. R. v. Greenacre (1837), 8 C. & P. 35.

Provocation reducing offence to manslaughter.]—See sec. 261 and note to same.

Corpus delicti.]—Corpus delicti in murder, is defined, as having two components, death as the result and the criminal agency of another as the means, and it is only where there is direct proof of one that the other can be established by circumstantial evidence. This ruling is an affirmance of the holding of Lord Hale (2 P.C. 290) that a conviction of murder or manslaughter cannot be had unless the fact be proved to be done or at least the body found dead. Where one is proven by direct evidence the other may be by circumstances, and in determining a question of fact upon a criminal trial from circumstantial evidence, the facts proved must not only be consistent with and point to the guilt of the prisoner, but must be inconsistent with his innocence. And see note 9 Can. Cr. Cas. 446.

On a trial for murder, if the fact of the death of a human being is established by direct proof and the remains of the dead man have been so destroyed by fire that direct identification is impossible, circumstantial evidence is admissible to prove the identity of the remains and also the identity of the person who caused the death. While the fact of death must always be established by direct proof, the fact of the killing by the defendant as alleged may be proved by circumstantial evidence supporting the charge beyond a reasonable doubt. R. v. Charles King, 9 Can. Cr. Cas. 426.

It has been considered a rule that no person should be convicted of murder unless the body of the deceased has been found, and a very great judge says, "I would never convict any person of murder or manslaughter unless the fact were proved to be done, or at least the body be found dead." 2 Hale 290. Lord Hale only laid this down as a caution, not as a rule in every case. Per Maule, J., in R. v. Burton (1854), Dears. C.C. 282. But this rule, it seems, must be taken with some qualifications; and circumstances may be sufficiently strong to shew the fact of the murder, though the body has never been found. 3 Russell Cr., 6th ed., 158. Thus, where the prisoner, a mariner, was indicted for the murder of his captain at sea, and a witness stated that the prisoner had proposed to kill the captain, and that the witness being afterwards alarmed in the night by a violent noise, went upon deck, and there observed the prisoner take the captain up and throw him overboard into the sea, and that he was not seen or heard of afterwards, and that near the place on the deck where the captain was seen a billet of wood was found, and that the deck and part of the prisoner's dress were stained with blood, the court, though they admitted the general rule of law, left it to the jury to say, upon the evidence, whether the deceased was not killed before his body was cast into the sea; and the jury being of that opinion, the prisoner was convicted, and the conviction being unanimously approved of by the judges, was afterwards executed. R. v. Hindmarsh (1792), 2 Leach 569.

And where the mate of a ship was seen to seize the captain from behind and throw him into the sea, and the captain fell, striking a boat, and leaving marks of blood upon it, but was never seen again, Archibald, J., allowed the case to go to the jury, and the prisoner was convicted of manslaughter. R. v. Armstrong (1875), 13 Cox C.C. 184.

But where upon an indictment against the prisoner for the murder of her bastard child, it appears that she was seen with the child in her arms on the road from the place where she had been at service to the place where her father lived about six in the evening, and between eight and nine she arrived at her father's without the child, and the body of a child was found in a tide-river, near which she must have passed in her road to her father's, but the body could not be identified as that of the child of the prisoner, and the evidence rather tended to shew that it was not the body of such child, it was held that she was entitled to be acquitted. The evidence rendered it probable that the child found was not the child of the prisoner, and with respect to the child, which was really her child, the prisoner could not by law be called upon either to account for it, or to say where it was, unless there were evidence to shew that her child was actually dead. R. v. Hopkins (1838), 8 C. & P. 591, Lord Abinger, C.B.; R. v. Cheverton (1862), 2 F. & F. 833, Erle, C.J.

Post-mortem examination.]—The medical practitioner should examine all the important organs for marks of natural disease and note down any unusual pathological appearances or abnormal deviations although they may at the time appear to have no bearing on the cause of death.

Mr. Clark Bell, in his 12th Amer. edition of Taylor's Medical Jurisprudence, 1897, page 23, says: "In medico-legal cases involving questions of life and death, the examination of the body cannot be too thorough and exhaustive; the omission of any one organ is a radical and sometimes a fatal defect. This was well illustrated in 1872 by two leading cases in the United States—that of Mrs. E. G. Wharton, charged with poisoning General Ketchum, and that of Dr. Paul Schoeppe, charged with poisoning Miss Steinnecke. In neither case was the post mortem sufficiently complete."

The body is inspected not merely to shew that a person has died as a result of the criminal act, but to prove that he has *not* died from any natural cause. Medical practitioners commonly give their attention exclusively to the first point, while lawyers, defending accused parties, very properly direct a most searching examination to the last mentioned point, i.e., the healthy or unhealthy state of those organs which are essential to life. If the cause of death is obscure after the general examination of the body, there is good reason for inspecting the condition of the spinal marrow. In certain obscure cases it may become necessary to institute a microscopic examination, especially of the brain and heart. Taylor's Medical Jurisprudence, 1897, 12th Am. Ed. 23.

In a trial for murder by committing an abortion resulting in the woman's death, it appeared that the post mortem examination was insufficient, and that, so far as the medical evidence was concerned, it was possible that death might have been occasioned by some undiscovered disease which a post mortem examination of other organs than those examined might have disclosed, and none of the medical men would swear positively to the cause of death; but there was other evidence tending to shew that death was caused by a criminal operation, and connecting the prisoners therewith. It was held, that such last mentioned evidence was properly submitted to the jury. R. v. Garrow (1896), 1 Can. Cr. Cas. 246 (B.C.).

Proving cause of death.]—A question has sometimes been raised whether a prisoner can be convicted of murder where it is impossible for any evidence to be given of the cause of death, in consequence of the state in which the body was found, but it would seem that it is a question for the jury, taking all the circumstances into consideration, whether the death was caused by violence or not, and whether that violence was the act of the prisoner. Per Kennedy, J. R. v. Macrae, Northampton Winter Assizes, 1892, cited 3 Russ. Cr., 6th ed., 160.

On a trial for murder, in order to prove the state of the health of the deceased prior to the day of his death, a witness was asked in what state of health the deceased seemed to be when he last saw him, and he began to state a conversation which had then taken place between the deceased and himself on this subject; and Alderson, B., held that what the deceased said to the witness was reasonable evidence to prove his state of health at the time. R. v. Johnson (1847), 2 C. & K. 354.

Dying declaration as evidence.]—The principle upon which dying declarations are admitted as evidence is stated by Eyre, C.B., in the case of R. v. Woodcock, 1 Leach, C.C., 502, as follows:

"The general principle on which this species of evidence is admitted is that they are declarations made in extremity, when the party is at the point of death, and when every hope of this world is gone, when every motive to falsehood is silenced, and the mind is induced by the most powerful consideration to speak the truth; a situation so solemn and so awful is considered by the law as creating an obligation equal to that which is imposed by a positive oath administered in a court of justice."

A dying declaration is only admissible in criminal cases, and then only in cases of murder or manslaughter, and only where the death is the subject of the charge, and the circumstances of the death the subject of the declaration. R. v. Mead, 2 B. & C. 605. But the dying declaration of a person was admitted in a case in which the prisoner was being tried, not for murdering the declarant, but another person, by the administration of poison, but in the perpetration of that act he had also inadvertently poisoned the declarant. In that case the court held that the same act caused the death of one as the other, and that, it being all one transaction, the evidence was admissible. R. v. Baker, 2 M. & Rob. 53.

The fact of a person having received extreme unction according to the rites of the Roman Catholic Church is some evidence that she thought herself to be in a dying state. Carver v. U.S., 1897, 17 S.C.R. (U.S.), 228; Minton's case, cited in R. v. Howell, 1 Denison Crown Cases 1; and so also is the rejection by a dying man belonging to the Roman Catholic faith, of an offer to bring him a priest, some evidence to shew that he did not think himself in articulo mortis. R. v. Howell, supra.

Such declarations being necessarily ex parte, the prisoner is entitled to the benefit of any advantage he may have lost by the want of an opportunity for cross-examination. R. v. Ashton, 2 Lewin Crown Cas. 147. So it has recently been held by the Supreme Court of the United States that it is error to refuse to permit the defendant to prove by witnesses that the deceased made statements to them in apparent contradiction of her dying declaration, and tending to shew that defendant did not shoot her intentionally. Whether these statements were admissible as dying declarations or not is immaterial, since they were admissible as tending to impeach the declaration of the deceased, which had already been admitted. Carver v. U.S. (1897), 17 Sup. Ct. Rep. (U.S.) 228. A dying declaration by no means imports absolute verity. The history of criminal trials is replete with instances where witnesses, even in the agonies of death, have, through malice, misapprehension, or weakness of mind, made declarations that were inconsistent with the actual facts; and it would be a great hardship to the defendant, who is deprived of the benefit of a cross-examination, to hold that he could not explain them. Dying declarations are a marked exception to the general rule that hearsay testimony is not admissible, and are received from the necessities of the case, and to prevent an entire failure of justice, as it frequently happens that no other witnesses to the homicide are present. They may, however, be inadmissible by reason of the extreme youth of the declarant (R. v. Pike, 3 Car. & P. 598), or by reason of any other fact which would make him incompetent as an ordinary witness. They are only received when the court is satisfied that the witness was fully aware of the fact that his recovery was impossible, and in this particular the requirement of the law is very stringent. They may be contradicted in the same manner as other testimony, and may be discredited by proof that the character of the deceased was bad, or that he did not believe in a future state of reward or punishment. Carver v. U.S. (1897), 17 Sup. Ct. Rep. (U.S.) 228.

A dying declaration is not admissible if there existed in the mind of the party making it a hope of recovery or a hope of escape from almost immediate death; but if there is a firm, settled expectation by deceased of impending death and no hope of recovery remaining in his mind, the declaration is admissible, although such belief was the result of panic and not well founded. The fact, that a person making a dying declaration subsequently entertains a hope of recovery, is irrelevant, except in so far as it may be evidence of his state of mind at the time of the declaration. R. v. Davidson (1898), 1 Can. Cr. Cas. 351 (N.S.); R. v. Hubbard, 14 Cox 565; R. v. Laurin (No. 1), 5 Can. Cr. Cas. 324; R. v. Laurin (No. 4), 6 Can. Cr. Cas. 104.

The rule as to the admissibility of dying declarations in evidence is thus stated in Taylor on Evidence, 6th ed., vol. 1, p. 643: "It is not, however, necessary that the declarant should have *stated* that he was *speaking under a sense of impending death,* providing it satisfactorily appears, in any mode, that the declarations were really made under that sanction; as, for instance, if the fact can be reasonably inferred from the evident danger of the declarant, or from the opinions of the medical or other attendants stated to him, or from his conduct, such as settling his affairs, taking leave of his relations and friends, giving directions respecting his funeral, receiving extreme unction or the like. In short, all the circumstances of the case may be resorted to, in order to ascertain the state of the declarant's mind. . . . On the other hand, a firm belief that death is impending—by which is meant, not as was once thought, that it will almost immediately follow, but that it will happen shortly in consequence of the injury sustained—will suffice to render the statement evidence, though the sufferer may chance to linger on for some days, or even for two or three weeks. . . . In general, it is no objection to their admissibility that they "(the answers) were made in answer to leading questions, or obtained by earnest solicitations." R. v. Smith (1873), 23 U.C.C.P. 312.

It is essential to the *admissibility* of these declarations, and it is a preliminary fact to be proved by the party offering them in evidence, that they were *made under a sense of impending death;* but it is not necessary that they should be stated at the time to be so made; it is enough if it satisfactorily appears, in any mode, that they were made under that sanction, whether it be expressly proved by the express language of the declarant, or be inferred from his evident danger, or the opinion of the medical or other attendants, stated to him, or from his conduct, or other circumstances of the case; all of which are resorted to in order to ascertain the state of the declarant's mind. Greenleaf on Evidence, 12th ed., vol. 1, p. 183, sec. 158; R. v. Smith (1873), 23 U.C.C.P. 312; R. v. McMahon (1889), 18 O.R. 502; R. v. Jenkins, L.R. 1 C.C.R. 187.

The court must be satisfied that whatever statement is admitted in evidence must be shewn by credible testimony to have been made in full belief of approaching death, with an abandonment of all hope of life. R. v. Sparham (1875), 25 U.C.C.P. 143, 154; R. v. Osborne, 15 Cox C.C. 169.

The mere use of the words, "If I die" would not alone defeat an emphatic declaration of abandonment of all hope on the same occasion; and that the second declaration was receivable in order to explain the first. R. v. Sparham (1875), 25 U.C.C.P. 143.

An objection that part of the statement was made in answer to a leading question is not sustainable. R. v. Smith (1873), 23 U.C.C.P. 312.

The essential element of a dying declaration is the abandonment of hope of recovery, and evidence tending to shew a belief that death was impending is not displaced by a statement of deceased to his physician and members of the family that he did not think he could recover, but he knew they would do all they could for him. R. v. Magyar, 12 Can. Cr. Cas. 114.

It makes no difference that the words incriminating the prisoner preceded the words shewing the expectation of death. R. v. Sunfield, Dec. 7, 1907, Ont. C.A.

The jury should not be excluded during the preliminary enquiry as to whether a certain statement is admissible as a dying declaration. Rex v. Aho, 11 B.C.R. 114, 8 Can. Cr. Cas. 453.

The deceased must be proved to the satisfaction of the judge to have been, at the time of making the declaration, (a) in actual danger of death and (b) to have abandoned all hope of recovery. If these conditions concur, it is immaterial that he lingered for several days or even weeks. R. v. Bernadotti, 11 Cox C.C. 316; Craven's Case, 1 Lew. 77; or that he subsequently entertained hope. R. v. Hubbard, 14 Cox C.C. 565; R. v. Davidson, 1 Can. Cr. Cas. 351 (N.S.). The question as to whether there was a settled hopeless expectation of death is for the presiding judge. R. v.

Woods, 2 Can. Cr. Cas. 159 (B.C.). The whole of the surrounding circumstances including the nature and extent of the wound and its immediate result are to be considered. R. v. Davidson, 1 Can. Cr. Cas. 351 (N.S.). In a shooting case the declaration of the deceased that he was shot in the body and was "going fast" was held a sufficient indication of the settled and hopeless consciousness of the declarant that he was in a dying state. Ibid.

The settled hopeless expectation of death must not be qualified by any prospect of recovery, however slight. R. v. Jenkins, L.R. 1 C.C.R. 187; R. v. Peel, 2 F. & F. 21; R. v. Gloster (1888), 16 Cox C.C. 471, 32 Sol. J. 765.

The expectation of the declarant must be of impending and almost immediate death as distinguished from a deferred one. R. v. Forester, 10 Cox C.C. 368; R. v. Cleary, 2 F. & F. 850; R. v. Gloster, 16 Cox C.C. 471; R. v. Neill (1892), Cent. Cr. Ct., sess, papers 1417; and it has been held in some cases that the belief must be in an immediate death. R. v. Osman, 15 Cox C.C. 1; R. v. Mitchell, 17 Cox C.C. 503.

The declaration is admissible only to prove the cause and circumstances of death and not to prove previous or subsequent transactions, although such transactions may be relevant. R. v. Mead, 2 B. & C. 605; R. v. Hind, 8 Cox C.C. 300, 29 L.J.M.C. 147.

Declarations of opinion exculpatory of the prisoner have been admitted. R. v. Scaife, 1 Mo. & Rob. 551.

The declaration may be oral or written, and a deposition read over to and signed by the deponent may be admissible in evidence as a dying declaration, although irregular as a deposition under sec. 999 of the Code because taken in the absence of the accused. R. v. Woods, 2 Can. Cr. Cas. 159 B.C.; but, semble, its weight as evidence is impaired by that fact. R. v. Woodcock, 1 East P.C. 356.

If made in response to leading questions or only upon earnest solicitation these facts will be taken into consideration in giving weight to the declaration as evidence. R. v. Smith, 10 Cox C.C. 82; R. v. Fagent, 7 C. & P. 238. If given in answer to questions, both the questions and the answers should ordinarily be proved so that it may be seen how much was suggested by the questions and how much spontaneously given by the declarant. R. v. Mitchell, 17 Cox C.C. 503, per Cave, J.; R. v. Smith (1900), 17 Times L.R. 522, 65 J.P. 426.

A written statement signed and sworn to by the deceased before a justice of the peace after being read over to him was admitted as a dying declaration in a homicide case, although in narrative form not embodying the exact words of the declarant. R. v. Magyar (1906), 12 Can. Cr. Cas. 114 (N.W.T.).

But the answers given to an interpreter and translated by him in narrative form to the person writing them down in the presence of the declarant may be admitted in evidence as a dying declaration, although the exact form of the questions was not proved. A dying declaration made by a person who cannot speak the language of the country, and proved only through an interpreter, is admissible if shewn to contain the actual purport of the statement without proof of the exact language of the declarant. R. v. Louie (1903), 7 Can. Cr. Cas. 347, 10 B.C.R. 1.

Mode of taking a dying declaration.]—It is usual, when time allows, to request a magistrate to attend and take the declaration, and he having satisfied himself that the party is conscious he is in a dying state, and, if an infant, that he sufficiently understands that he is under the moral obligation of speaking the truth, takes the statement in writing of the person. The approved course is to write down the person's statement in his own words, read it over and have it signed by him; this declaration is not taken on oath. Stone's Justice (1902), p. 269.

When statements admissible as res gestæ.]—On a trial for murder by shooting, evidence of statements made by the person shot immediately after the shooting and while under apprehension of further danger from the accused and requesting assistance and protection therefrom, is admissible as part of the res gestæ, even though the person accused of the offence was absent at the time when such statements were made. Gilbert v. The King (1907), 12 Can. Cr. Cas. 125.

Statements not coincident, in point of time, with the occurrence of the shooting, but uttered in the presence and hearing of the accused and under such circumstances that he might reasonably have been expected to have made some explanatory reply to remarks in reference to them, are admissible as evidence. Ibid.

On the indictment of a prisoner for murder, a witness swore that he heard shots fired, that half an hour afterwards deceased came to his house and asked witness to take him in for he was shot, that witness did so, and deceased died some hours afterwards; it was held that evidence of statements made by deceased after being taken into the house (not provable as dying declarations) were inadmissible, as not forming part of the res gestæ, being made after all action on the part of the wrong-doer had ceased through the completion of the principal act, and after all pursuit or danger had ceased. R. v. McMahon (1889), 18 Ont. R. 502, following R. v. Bedingfield, 14 Cox 341, and R. v. Goddard, 15 Cox 7.

Inference from conduct of accused.]—Where the accused charged with murder goes into the witness box on his own behalf, and then and there for the first time makes known his claim that he was a mere eye-witness of the murder, and that the principal witness for the prosecution had committed the deed, the trial judge may properly direct the jury that they may draw inferences from the prisoner's previous silence on the matter of such claim, and consider whether the facts in evidence shewed the motive for such silence to be founded on a consciousness of innocence, eg. gr., that he would thereby the better establish his innocence, or to be a design founded on a knowledge of guilt to advance a false defence at the last moment, and to take the prosecution by surprise. R. v. Higgins (1902), 7 Can. Cr. Cas. 68, 36 N.B.R. 18.

Circumstantial evidence.]—On a trial for murder, the Crown having made out a primâ facie case by circumstantial evidence, the prisoner's daughter, a girl of fourteen, was called on his behalf, and swore that she herself killed the deceased, without the prisoner's knowledge, and under circumstances detailed, which would probably reduce her guilt to manslaughter. Held, that the judge was not bound to tell the jury that they must believe this witness in the absence of testimony to shew her unworthy of credit, but that he was right in leaving the credibility of her story to them; and, if from her manner he derived the impression that she was under some undue influence, it was not improper to call their attention to it in his charge. R. v. Jones (1868), U.C.Q.B. 416.

On a trial for murder the death of the deceased was shewn to have been caused by his being stabbed by a sharp instrument. It was proved that the prisoner struck the deceased, but neither a knife nor other instrument was seen in his hand. For the prisoner evidence was offered that on the day preceding the homicide the prisoner had a knife which could not have inflicted the wound of which deceased died; and that on that day the prisoner parted with it to a person who held it until after the crime was committed. This evidence was rejected as being too remote, and because it would not shew that it was impossible for the prisoner to have had a weapon that might have caused the wounds of which deceased died. R. v. Herod (1878), 29 U.C.C.P. 428.

Prisoner being indicted for the murder of H., the principal witness for the Crown stated that the crime was committed on a day stated, and that prisoner and one S. (who had been previously tried and acquitted) threw H. over the parapet of the bridge into the river Don. Counsel for the prisoner then proposed to prove by one D. that S. was at his place, fifty miles off, on that evening, but the judge rejected the evidence, saying that S. might be called, and if contradicted might be confirmed by other testimony. S. was called, and swore that he was not present at the time, but he not being contradicted, D. was not examined. Draper, J., who tried the case, reserved the point for the consideration of the court whether the evidence of D. might not be found to have been legally admissible. The court held that the presence of S. was a fact material to the enquiry, and that D. should have been admitted when tendered, and a new trial was ordered. Robinson, C.J., observing, "It appears to me that any fact so closely connected with the alleged offence as to be in fact part of what was transacted or said to be transacted at the very moment, cannot be treated as irrelevant in investigating the truth of the charge." . . . "It is sufficient, I think, to make the evidence that was offered admissible, that it applied to the very fact to be determined, namely, by whom and how the deceased person came to his death. R. v. Brown (1861), 21 U.C.Q.B. 338.

Where the charge depends upon circumstantial evidence, the latter must not only be consistent with the prisoner's guilt but inconsistent with any other rational conclusion. R. v. Hodge (1838), 2 Lewin 227.

Character evidence.]—See note to sec. 971.

Constructive murder.]—Where a package of revolvers was thrown into a carriage in which three prisoners conjointly charged with a crime were being conveyed under lawful arrest and the prisoners all struggled to obtain revolvers, two of them succeeding in doing so, whereupon all of them attempted to effect a forcible escape during which one of the peace officers was shot dead by one of the prisoners but by which of them is unknown, proof that the defendant had one of the revolvers in the melee and had ordered another of the peace officers present to "give up" immediately after another of the prisoners had told the defendant to "give it to him" is, with such facts, sufficient evidence of a conspiracy by the three prisoners for an unlawful purpose, to wit, the escape, and of a common design to use for its accomplishment any amount of violence and force; and a conviction of the defendant for murder is, therefore, proper without proof that he fired the fatal shot. It was proper for the trial judge to instruct the jury that "where all the parties proceed with the intention to commit an unlawful act and with the resolution or determination to overcome all opposition by force, that if by reason of such resolution one of the party is guilty of homicide, his companions would be liable to the penalty which he has incurred." The shooting of the constable by one of the conspirators, in the prosecution of such common purpose was an act which was or ought to have been known to be a probable consequence of prosecuting such purpose, and each of the conspirators become under Cr. Code sec. 69(2) a party to the homicide. R. v. Rice (1902), 5 Can. Cr. Cas. 509.

Constructive murder, as it is called, is a phrase which has no legal meaning, but is a common and convenient way of describing a homicide committed under circumstances which in law constitute the offence of murder, though the particular act which occasioned it may not have been actually done or directly authorized by the accused. R. v. Rice (1902), 5 Can. Cr. Cas. 509, per Osler, J.A.

Act likely to cause death.]—If a man does an illegal act although its immediate purpose may not be to take life, yet if it be such that life is necessarily endangered by it and the doer knows or believes that life is likely to be sacrificed by it, it is murder. London Times, April 28, 1868, per Cockburn, C.J., cited Burbidge Cr. Dig. 218, and see 11 Cox C.C. 146; R. v. Allen, 17 L.T.N.S. 223, Burb. Cr. Dig. 522-529; Code sec. 259, sub-sec. (d) supra.

In Regina v. Serné (1887), 16 Cox C.C. 311, the two prisoners were indicted for murder, it being alleged that they wilfully set on fire a house, by which act the death of a boy, the son of the prisoner Serné, had been caused. In his charge to the jury Sir J. Stephen said: "I think that instead of saying that any act done with intent to commit a felony and which causes death amounts to murder, it would be reasonable to say that any act known to be dangerous to life, and likely in itself to cause death, done for the purpose of committing a felony, which caused death, should be murder."

Proof of motive.]—To prove the alleged motive of securing life insurance moneys, in a trial for murder, evidence is properly admissible, as a part of the res gestæ of all applications for insurance made practically at the same time and forming parts of one transaction, although some of the applications were refused and no insurance effected thereupon. R. v. Hammond (1898), 1 Can. Cr. Cas. 373 (Ont.). But evidence of an attempt made some time previously by the accused to insure another person for the benefit of the accused is not admissible. R. v. Hendershott (1895), 26 Ont. R. 678.

All questions as to motive, intent, heat of blood, etc., must be left to the jury, and should not be dealt with as propositions of law. R. v. McDowell (1865), 25 U.C.Q.B. 108; R. v. Eagle, 2 F. & F. 827.

A trial would not appear to be fair if the prisoner, when defending himself for murder, is also called on for a contingent defence against charges for several alleged assaults in the course of several weeks, some of which may be open to contradiction, others to justification and others to mitigation. Per Erle, J., in R. v. Bird (1851), 5 Cox 1, 2 Den. Cr. Cas. 94; R. v. Ganes (1872), 22 U.C.C.P. 185-189.

In the case of a sudden quarrel, where the parties immediately fight, there may be circumstances indicating malice in the party killing, which killing will then be murder. R. v. McDowell (1865), 25 U.C.Q.B. 108.

Flight as evidence.]—The flight of the accused is competent evidence against him as having a tendency to establish his guilt. Wharton on Homicide, sec. 710; Hickory v. United States, 160 U.S. 408.

Relevancy of other criminal acts.]—In the case of Makin v. New South Wales, [1894] A.C. 57, the prisoners had been convicted of the wilful murder of an infant child received from its mother by the prisoners for adoption and whose body had been found buried in the garden of a house occupied by him, and it was held by the Judicial Committee of the Privy Council that evidence that several other infants had been received from their mothers by the prisoners on like representations and on like terms, and that bodies of infants had been found buried in a similar manner in the gardens of several houses occupied by the prisoners, was relevant to the issue which had been tried by the jury, and was therefore admissible.

The Geering Case (18 L.J.N.S.M.C. 215) which was there approved by the Judicial Committee, was one of arsenical poisoning, and Pollock, C.B., admitted evidence to shew that two sons of the prisoner, who had formed part of the same family, and for whom, as well as for her husband, the prisoner had cooked their food, had died of poison, the symptoms with all of them being the same. It is noteworthy, however, that in the latter case the administration to all of the parties appears to have been contemporaneous and with preparations of food made in quantities for all of the four persons and distributed to them on their leaving the house to go to their work.

In R. v. Heeson (1878), 14 Cox C.C. 40, Lush, J., approved of and followed the decision in the Geering Case and admitted evidence of both previous and subsequent deaths occurring under like circumstances and from similar symptoms, and held that where it was proved that a motive for the murder charged might exist from the fact of the prisoner having insured the life of the deceased, evidence might also be given upon the same indictment to shew an equal motive for the deaths of the others because of their having been similarly insured at the instance of the prisoner.

In an Ontario case, evidence was held admissible on a charge of murder by poisoning to shew the administration of the same kind of poison by the prisoner to another person, as proving intent. Evidence of similar symptoms of arsenical poisoning attending the death of prisoner's former husband following administration to him of food prepared by the prisoner is evidence to shew intent as regards a charge of arsenical poisoning of a second husband on evidence of arsenical poison of the latter and of similar preparation of food by the prisoner and her attendance on her husband during his illness. R. v. Sternaman (1898), 1 Can. Cr. Cas. 1 (Ont.).

Evidence of other facts are admissible where those facts tend to prove the point in issue, as where the intent of the prisoner forms part of the matter in issue, and such other facts tend to establish the intent of the prisoner in committing the act in question; so the deliberate menaces or threats of a prisoner made at a former time are admissible, where they tend to prove the intent of the party and the prisoner's malice against the deceased. It is quite proper on the count for murder to give evidence of the prisoner's previous assaults upon and threats against the deceased to shew the animus of the prisoner. Theal v. R. (1882), 7 Can. S.C. 397, 406.

Evidence of one crime may be given to shew a motive for committing another; and where several felonies are part of the same transaction evidence of all is admissible upon the trial of an indictment for any of them; but where a prisoner indicted for murder, committed while resisting constables about to arrest him, had, with others, been guilty of riotous acts several days before, it is doubtful if evidence of such riotous conduct is admissible, even for the purpose of shewing the prisoner's knowledge that he was liable to be arrested, and, therefore, had a motive to resist the officers. The Queen v. Chasson, 3 Pugs. (N.B.) 546.

Evidence of the prisoner's past offences must generally be excluded and consequently evidence of other offences (even though precisely similar) of which he has been guilty cannot be given in order to corroborate the proof of his having committed the one with which he is charged; but for the purpose of shewing the motive of the offence with which he is charged some other crime may be disclosed. Whilst the fact of a prisoner having committed other similar offences is not relevant to the question whether he committed the act of which he is accused, yet, so soon as the act has been fully established, evidence of previous offences may be relevant to his state of mind in committing the act; it is admissible to shew guilty knowledge and to prove the intention to commit a wrong. Kenny, Outlines of Criminal Law, 352-355; The Queen v. Francis (1874), L.R. 2 C.C.R. 131; Blake v. Albion Life Assurance Society (1878), 14 Cox C.C. 249.

Aiders, abettors and accessories.]—See secs. 69-71.

Two persons jointly indicted.]—Where two persons are jointly indicted for murder and one pleads guilty and the other not guilty, and the trial upon the latter plea results in an acquittal, leave should be granted the other defendant to change his plea of guilty to one of not guilty, if the circumstances of the case are such that the verdict of acquittal already given in respect of the one would be absolutely inconsistent with the guilt of the other who had pleaded guilty. The King v. Herbert, 6 Can. Cr. Cas. 214.

Medical expert evidence.]—By sec. 7 of the Canada Evidence Act, where, in any trial or other proceeding, criminal or civil, it is intended by the prosecution or the defence, or by any party, to examine as witnesses professional or other experts entitled according to the law or practice to give opinion evidence, not more than five of such witnesses may be called upon either side without the leave of the court or judge or person presiding. Such leave shall be applied for before the examination of any of the experts who may be examined without such leave.

In the course of a trial for murder by shooting a witness was called at the trial to give evidence as a medical expert, and in answer to the Crown prosecutor, he said "there are indicia in medical science from which it can be said at what distance small shot were fired at the body. I have studied this—not personal experience, but from books." He was not cross-examined as to the grounds of this statement, and no medical witnesses were called by the prisoner to confute it. The witness then stated the distance from the murdered man at which the shot must have been fired in the case before the court, and on what he based his opinion as to it, giving the result of his examination of the body. It was held by the Supreme Court of Canada, that by his preliminary statement the witness had established his capacity to speak as a medical expert, and it not having been shewn by cross-examination, or other testimony, that there were no such indicia as stated, his evidence as to the distance at which the shot was fired was properly received. R. v. Preeper (1888), 15 Can. S.C.R. 401.

The prisoner's witness having stated that death was caused by two blows from a stick of certain dimensions, it was held that a medical witness previously examined by the Crown was properly recalled to state that in his opinion the injuries found on the body could not have been so occasioned. R. v. Jones, 28 U.C.Q.B. 416.

The theory of the defence in an indictment for murder, was that the death was caused by the communication of smallpox virus by Dr. M., who attended the deceased, and one of the witnesses for the defence explained how the contagion could be guarded against. Dr. M. had not in his examination in chief or cross-examination been asked anything on this subject; it was held that he was properly allowed to be called in reply, to state that precautions had been taken by him to guard against the infection. R. v. Sparham and Greaves, 25 U.C.C.P. 143.

No bail on murder charge.]—Where a person has been committed upon a charge of wilful murder, found by a coroner's jury, upon evidence sufficient to support the finding, a superior court will not admit him to bail, especially where the accused has made a statement admitting his participation in the affair out of which the charge of murder arises. Ex parte Baronnet (1852), 1 El. & Bl. 1.

A party is committed for trial because there is a probability that he would otherwise not appear, and not because he is presumed to be guilty of the offence charged against him. The quality and circumstances of the charge must be some element in deciding whether it is to be fairly presumed that the party accused will appear to take his trial. Accordingly, the seriousness of the offence, the strength of the evidence, and the weight of the punishment, are those generally taken into consideration in deciding whether there is such a presumption or not. Where the charge is wilful murder, and there is a confession of the prisoners, the presumption has always been that no amount of bail will secure the due course of justice; and, except under very special circumstances, the court do not admit to bail. Ex parte Baronnet (1852), 1 El. & Bl. 1, per Coleridge, J.

And in Ontario it has been held that where a true bill has been found on an indictment for murder, bail will be refused. R. v. Keeler, 7 P.R. (Ont.) 117.

The fact that one assize has been passed over since the committal of the prisoner is not a ground for admitting to bail, unless on the first day of such assize he applied under 31 Car. 2, ch. 2, sec. 7, to be brought to trial. R. v. Mullady, 4 P.R. (Ont.) 314.

Prisoners held on a coroner's warrant on a charge of murder, where the circumstances raise such a presumption of guilt against them as would warrant a grand jury in finding a true bill, should not be bailed. R. v. Mullady, 4 P.R. (Ont.) 314; Ex parte Corrivean, 6 Lower Can. R. 249.

The strictness of the practice as to bail in murder cases does not extend to the case of an accessory after the fact, guilty merely of harbouring the murderer. R. v. Murphy, 1 James (Nova Scotia) 158.

But where a prisoner committed for trial on a charge of manslaughter would ordinarily be admitted to bail, bail will not be refused because the Crown prosecutor swears to a belief that he can prove the offence to have been murder. R. v. Spicer (1901), 5 Can. Cr. Cas. 229.

Benefit of doubt.]—Where the judge in a trial for murder concludes his charge thus: "The verdict of the jury is generally resumed in a few words, in the solemn words of guilty or not guilty," it is not to be inferred that such is a direction to bring in but one of the two verdicts of guilty or not guilty of murder, if in the other parts of the charge, he has sufficiently pointed out the distinction between murder and manslaughter, and instructed them as to their duty to find whether the prisoner acted with or without intent to kill.

(2) Where the judge considers that no doubt exists, he is not obliged to instruct the jury that the prisoner is entitled to the benefit of any doubt they may entertain, such a course being more likely to impede than to assist them in the discharge of their duty. The King v. Fouquet, 10 Can. Cr. Cas. 255.

Death penalty.]—See sec. 263.

Culpable homicide murder in certain cases.

260. In case of treason and the other offences against the King's authority and person mentioned in Part II., piracy and offences deemed to be piracy, escape or rescue from prison or lawful custody, resisting lawful apprehension, murder, rape, forcible abduction, robbery, burglary or arson, culpable homicide is also murder, whether the offender means or not death to ensue, or knows or not that death is likely to ensue,—

If grievous bodily harm intended.

(*a*) if he means to inflict grievous bodily injury for the purpose of facilitating the commission of any of the offences in this section mentioned, or the flight of the offender upon the commission or attempted commission thereof, and death ensues from such injury; or,

Narcotic administered.

(*b*) if he administers any stupefying or overpowering thing for either of the purposes aforesaid, and death ensues from the effects thereof; or, (*c*) if he by any means wilfully stops the breath of any person for either of the purposes aforesaid, and death ensues from such stopping of the breath. 55-56 V., c. 29, s. 228. Wilfully stopping the breath.

261. Culpable homicide, which would otherwise be murder, may be reduced to manslaughter if the person who causes death does so in the heat of passion caused by sudden provocation. Homicide reduced to manslaughter.

2. Any wrongful act or insult, of such a nature as to be sufficient to deprive an ordinary person of the power of self-control, may be provocation if the offender acts upon it on the sudden, and before there has been time for his passion to cool. Provocation defined.

3. Whether or not any particular wrongful act or insult amounts to provocation, and whether or not the person provoked was actually deprived of the power of self-control by the provocation which he received, shall be questions of fact: Question of fact. Provided that no one shall be held to give provocation to another by doing that which he had a legal right to do, or by doing anything which the offender incited him to do in order to provide the offender with an excuse for killing or doing bodily harm to any person. Proviso.

4. The illegality of an arrest shall not necessarily reduce an offence of culpable homicide from murder to manslaughter, but if the illegality was known to the offender it may be evidence of provocation. 55-56 V., c. 29, s. 229. Exception. Illegal arrest.

Provocation.]—Manslaughter is principally distinguishable from murder in this, that though the act which occasions the death is unlawful, or likely to be attended with bodily mischief, yet the malice either express or implied, which is the very essence of murder, is presumed to be wanting in manslaughter, the act being rather imputed to the infirmity of human nature. 1 East's Pleas of the Crown, 218; Roscoe's Criminal Evidence, 12th ed., 620. Murder is unlawful homicide with malice aforethought; manslaughter is unlawful homicide without malice aforethought. R. v. Doherty (1887), 16 Cox C.C. 306.

Whenever death ensues from sudden transport of passion or heat of blood, if upon reasonable provocation and without malice, or upon sudden combat, it will be manslaughter; if there be no such provocation, or if the blood has had reasonable time to cool, or if there be evidence of express malice, it will be murder. 2 East's Pleas of the Crown, 232: Foster, 313; Roscoe's Cr. Evid. 620. Where the provocation is sought by the prisoner it cannot furnish any defence against the charge of murder. 1 East P.C. 239. The provocation which is allowed to extenuate in the case of homicide must be something which a man is conscious of, which he feels and resents at the instant the fact which he would extenuate is committed. Russell on Crimes III., 38; Foster, 315. As a general rule, no provocation of words will reduce the crime of murder to that of manslaughter. Foster's Crown Law, 290; R. v. McDowell (1865), 25 U.C.Q.B. 108. But under special circumstances there may be such a provocation of words as will have that effect. Russell on Crimes (1896) III. 38. And Blackburn, J., in summing up to the jury in R. v. Rothwell (1871), 12 Cox C.C. 145, said that what they would have to consider was, whether the words which were spoken just previous to the blows amounted to such a provocation as would, in an ordinary man, not in a man of violent or passionate disposition, provoke him in such a way as to justify the prisoner in striking as he did the person who used the words.

Where, however, there are no blows there must be a provocation at least as great as blows; for instance, a man who discovers his wife in the act oi adultery and thereupon kills the adulterer is only guilty of manslaughter. Blackburn, J., in R. v. Rothwell (1871), 12 Cox C.C. 145, 147. All the circumstances of the case must lead to the conclusion that the act done, though intentional of death or great bodily harm, was not the result of a cool, deliberate judgment and previous malignity of heart, but solely imputable to human infirmity. 1 East P.C. 23(e); Russell on Crimes III. 38.

If there be a provocation by blows which would not of itself render the killing manslaughter, but it be accompanied by such provocation by means of words and gestures as would be calculated to produce a degree of exasperation equal to that which would be produced by a violent blow, it may be regarded as reducing the crime to that of manslaughter. R. v. Sherwood (1844), 1 C. & K. 556; R. v. Smith (1865), 3 F. & F. 1066.

If on any sudden provocation of a slight nature, one person beat another in a cruel and unusual manner so that he dies, it is murder by express malice, though the person so beating the other did not intend to kill him. 4 Black. Com. 199, Halloway's Case, Cro. Car. 131. Slight provocations have been considered in some cases as extenuating the guilt of homicide, upon the ground that the conduct of the party killing upon such provocations might fairly be attributed to an intention to chastise, rather than to a cruel and implacable malice; but in such cases it must appear that the punishment was not administered with brutal violence, nor greatly disproportionate to the offence, and the instrument must not be such as, from its nature, was likely to endanger life. Foster's Crown Law, 291; Russell on Crimes III. 47.

All questions as to motive, intent, heat of blood, etc., must be left to the jury and should not be dealt with as propositions of law. R. v. McDowell (1865), 25 U.C.Q.B. 108, 115.

If the circumstances of the case shew that the blow causing the death was given in the heat of passion arising on a sudden provocation and before the passion had time to cool, the inference of malice is rebutted. R. v. Eagle (1862), 2 F. & F. 827. As it may be matter of law that a blow is not sufficient to excuse homicide, so it may be matter of law that a blow is not sufficient to reduce the defence to manslaughter; or it may be matter of law that it may be so, supposing the jury find as a matter of fact that it did produce a passion which, as a matter of law, it was legally sufficient to provoke. 2 F. & F. note (b), pp. 831, 832.

Although, by sub-section (3), no one shall be held to give provocation to another by doing that which he had a legal right to do, it is for the jury, and not for the judge, to determine any preliminary question of fact upon which the alleged legal right depends. R. v. Brennan (1896), 4 Can. Cr. Cas. 41, 27 Ont. R. 659.

Where the facts shewn were that the prisoner had called at the house of the deceased and, on being forcibly ejected by the latter, drew a revolver and shot him, the jury have to consider whether the deceased before laying hands on the prisoner ordered him to leave the house, and gave him time to leave, and whether, if such were done, the violence used by the deceased in ejecting the prisoner was greater than was necessary for that purpose. It is misdirection for the trial judge in such a case to charge that the deceased had a legal right to eject the prisoner as he did, and that there-

slaughter, and such a direction is the withdrawal from the jury of the questions of fact involved in the determination of the question of legal right, and entitled the prisoner to a new trial. Ibid.

A previous conviction or acquittal on an indictment for murder is a bar to a second indictment for the same homicide charging it as manslaughter. Sec. 909 (2).

262. Culpable homicide, not amounting to murder, is manslaughter. 55-56 V., c. 29, s. 230. **Manslaughter.**

Evidence of manslaughter.]—In a criminal prosecution for manslaughter, more must be shewn than a mere error of judgment (supposing one to have been committed here). Gross neglect must be shewn. Such recklessness must appear as will amount to a wilful attempt upon the lives of people, when the latter are put to danger in consequence of the acts of the accused (Harris, pp. 180, 181, 183, 187). Absence of all unlawful or malicious intent or state of mind excludes criminal responsibility in cases of accident. Rex v. Allen and Rex v. Green, 7 Carrington & Payne, 153 and 156.

Murder is unlawful homicide with malice aforethought; manslaughter is unlawful homicide without malice aforethought. R. v. Doherty (1887), 16 Cox C.C. 306.

On a charge of manslaughter against the master of a ship in respect of a collision resulting in loss of life, such recklessness must appear as will amount to a wilful attempt upon the lives of people in putting them to danger, and not merely an error of judgment. R. v. Delisle (1896), 5 Can. Cr. Cas. 210 (Que.).

One who recklessly points a gun at another person, without previously examining whether it be loaded or not, will, if the weapon should accidently go off and kill him towards whom it is pointed, be guilty of manslaughter. R. v. Jones, 12 Cox 628; R. v. Weston, 14 Cox 346. And see sec. 122 as to the offence of pointing fire-arms.

Homicide under a mistaken Indian belief or superstition that the object shot at was not a human being but an evil spirit which had assumed human form and would attack human beings, is manslaughter. R. v. Machekequonabe (1897), 2 Can. Cr. Cas. 138.

A corporation cannot be guilty of manslaughter. R. v. Union Colliery Co. (1900), 3 Can. Cr. Cas. 523 (B.C.), affirmed 4 Can. Cr. Cas. 400 (S.C. Can.). Code secs. 247 and 252, as to want of care in the maintenance of dangerous things, do not extend the criminal responsibility of corporations beyond what it was at common law. R. v. Great West Laundry Co. (1900), 3 Can. Cr. Cas. 514 (Man.).

The managing director of a railway company is not liable to indictment for manslaughter by reason of the omission to do something which the company was not bound to do by its charter, though he had personally promised to do it. Ex p. Brydges (1874), 18 L.C. Jur. 141.

Manslaughter by neglect of dangerous excavation.]—See Code sec. 287.

Pleading previous conviction for assault, etc.]—The rule at common law is that where a person has been convicted for an offence by a court of competent jurisdiction, the conviction is a bar to all further criminal proceedings for the same offence; the principle is that no man shall be placed in peril of legal penalties more than once on the same accusation. R. v. Miels (1890), 17 Cox C.C. 9.

It is a well-established principle that a series of charges shall not be preferred, and, whether a party accused of a minor offence is acquitted or convicted, he shall not be charged again on the same facts in a more aggravated form. R. v. Elrington (1861), 1 Best & Smith 688, 696 (Cockburn, C.J., and Blackburn, J.).

It was held by the Court for Crown Cases Reserved in R. v. Morris (1867), L.R. 1 C.C.R. 90, that a conviction for assault and the imprisonment consequent thereon are not either at common law or under 24-25 Vict., ch. 100, sec. 45 (Code sec. 834), a bar to an indictment for manslaughter of the person assaulted, should be subsequently die from the effects of the assault.

In an English case at the Durham Assizes, it appeared that the defendant Hilton was indicted for the manslaughter of one Robert Jackson. The alleged assault which caused the death of Jackson occurred on the 12th of October. On the 21st of October cross-summonses for assault were heard by the justices and both cases were dismissed. At that time the deceased man's injuries were not considered serious, but on the 2nd of November he died from the effects of a clot of blood on the brain. Hilton was thereupon charged with manslaughter. Counsel for the prisoner produced a certificate of dismissal of the charge of assault by the justices under 24 & 25 Vict., ch. 100, sec. 45, and raised the plea that the prisoner had already been acquitted of the charge of assault and could not be tried again. Grantham, J., accepted this view, and the prisoner was discharged. R. v. Hilton (1895), 59 J.P. 778.

Verdict for assault not permissible.]—On an indictment for murder or manslaughter if the prisoner is guilty of an assault which has conduced to the death, he cannot in respect of that assault be convicted of assault merely; and if the assault proved did not conduce to the death, it is distinct from and independent thereof and is therefore not included in the crime charged, and is dehors the indictment; and therefore no verdict of assault can be rendered upon an indictment for homicide in respect of such an assault. R. v. Ganes (1872), 22 U.C.C.P. 185, following R. v. Bird (1851), 5 Cox 1, and R. v. Dingman (1863), 22 U.C.Q.B. 283.

Previous murder charge.]—A previous conviction or acquittal on an indictment for murder shall be a bar to a second indictment for the same homicide charging it as manslaughter; and a previous conviction or acquittal on an indictment for manslaughter shall be a bar to a second indictment for the same homicide charging it as a murder. Sec. 909 (2).

Verdict of manslaughter on murder charge.]—On an indictment charging murder, if the evidence proves manslaughter but does not prove murder the jury may find the accused not guilty of murder but guilty of manslaughter, but shall not on that count find the accused guilty of any other offence. Sec. 951 (2).

Consent to homicide.]—See sec. 67.

Provocation.]—See sec. 261.

Justification and excuse.]—See secs. 16-68, and note to sec. 250.

Degrees of homicide.]—See secs. 250-258.

Defence of insanity.]—See secs. 11, 966, 967.

Punishment for murder.

263. Every one who commits murder is guilty of an indictable offence and shall, on conviction thereof, be sentenced to death. 55-56 V., c. 29, s. 231.

Form of charge.]—Code form 64 provides the following form for stating the offence: "A. murdered B. at on ."

Joint indictment.]—Where two persons are jointly indicted for murder and one pleads guilty and the other not guilty, and the trial upon the latter plea results in an acquittal, leave should be granted the other defendant to change his plea of guilty to one of not guilty, if the circumstances of the case are such that the verdict of acquittal already given in respect of the one would be absolutely inconsistent with the guilt of the other who had pleaded guilty. R. v. Herbert (1903), 6 Can. Cr. Cas. 214.

Instruction to jury.]—On a trial for murder, if the trial judge directs the jury that imminent peril of the prisoner's own life or of the lives of his family is a ground of justification for killing, in defence of his household, one of a party committing an unprovoked assault upon him, but does not direct them that a reasonable apprehension of immediate danger of grievous bodily harm to the prisoner or to his wife and family is an equal justification, such omission constitutes a substantial wrong or miscarriage occasioned on the trial (Cr. Code 1019) and a new trial should be ordered, where the circumstances shewn in evidence are such as to point much more to the latter ground of justification than to the former. R. v. Theriault (1894), 2 Can. Cr. Cas. 444 (N.B.); Code secs. 53 and 55.

In The King v. Greenacre (1837), 8 C. & P. 35, the question was whether the offence was murder or manslaughter. Tindal, C.J., told the jury that where it appears that one person's death has been occasioned by the hand of another, "it behooves that other to shew from evidence or by inference from the circumstances of the case, that the offence is of a mitigated character and does not amount to the crime of murder."

On a trial for murder where the evidence is circumstantial, it is for the jury alone to pronounce on the question of the truth of the alleged circumstances deposed to, and also as to what inferences which the facts would warrant shall be drawn from the circumstantial evidence. It is error and ground for a new trial for the trial judge to instruct the jury that they cannot doubt that certain inferences are to be drawn on points material to the issue. R. v. Collins, 12 Can. Cr. Cas. 402.

Confessions and admissions as evidence.]—See note to sec. 685.

Prohibited comment on failure of accused to testify.]—See note to sec. 4 of Canada Evidence Act.

Evidence and defences.]—See notes to secs. 259 and 261.

Classes of homicide.]—See secs. 250-262.

Procedure on sentence of death.]—See secs. 1062-1075.

Extradition.]—Murder is an extraditable offence between Canada and the United States under the Ashburton Treaty of 1842, article 10.

264. Every one is guilty of an indictable offence and liable to imprisonment for life, who, with intent to commit murder,— **Attempts.**

(a) administers any poison or other destructive thing to any person, or causes any poison or destructive thing to be so administered or taken, or attempts to administer it, or attempts to cause it to be so administered or taken; or, **Administering poison.**

(b) by any means whatever wounds or causes any grievous bodily harm to any person; or, **Wounding.**

(c) shoots at any person, or, by drawing a trigger or in any other manner, attempts to discharge at any person any kind of loaded arms; or, **Shooting.**

Drowning. (*d*) attempts to drown, suffocate, or strangle any person; or,

Destroying building. (*e*) destroys or damages any building by the explosion of any explosive substance; or,

Burning ships. (*f*) sets fire to any ship or vessel or any part thereof, or any part of the tackle, apparel or furniture thereof, or to any goods or chattels being therein; or,

Casting away vessel. (*g*) casts away or destroys any vessel; or,

By other means. (*h*) by any other means attempts to commit murder. 55-56 V., c. 29, s. 232.

Indictment.]—An indictment that "A.B. attempted to kill and murder C.D." sufficient discloses an indictable offence, and the court has the power to allow it to be amended so as to read that "A.B. with intent to commit murder, shot at C.D." The King v. Mooney, 11 Can. Cr. Cas. 333.

An indictment multifarious in that it combines a charge of a failure to provide necessaries for a child under sixteen under secs. 242 and 244 with a charge of an attempt to murder the child and to which indictment the prisoners pleaded, is sufficient upon which to base a conviction thereon for the latter offence without a formal amendment of the indictment, where the presiding judge has withdrawn from the jury that portion of the charge based upon secs. 242 and 244. R. v. Lapierre (1897), 1 Can. Cr. Cas. 413 (Que.).

Bail.]—The court will not bail a prisoner accused under this section if evidence be positive and strong against the prisoner. Ex parte Cheevers (1880), Ramsay's Cases 180.

With intent to commit murder.]—Where the charge is in respect of the administering of poison, evidence of administering at different times may be given to shew the intent. R. v. Mogg (1830), 4 C. & P. 364; and see note to sec. 259. The prosecution must prove the intent as well as the assault. Re Kelly (1902), 5 Can. Cr. Cas. 541.

(*a.*)—"*Administers" any poison, etc.*]—Where a servant in preparing breakfast for her mistress put arsenic into the coffee, and afterwards told her mistress that she had prepared the coffee for her, and the mistress drank the coffee, it was held that this was an "administering" within the corresponding English statute, 7 Wm. IV. and 1 Vict., ch. 85, sec. 2, re-enacted 24-25 Vict., ch. 100, sec. 11. R. v. Harley (1830), 4 C. & P. 369. And it has been held that a poisonous berry given with intent to kill is "administered" although by reason of being given entire in the pod which will not dissolve in the stomach no injurious effects followed. R. v. Cluderay (1849), 1 Den. C.C. 514, 4 Cox C.C. 84.

Where the accused with intent to murder gave poison to A. to administer as a medicine to B., but A. neglecting to give it to B., it was by chance given to B. by a child, this was held an administering by the accused. R. v. Michael (1840), 2 Mood. C.C. 120, 9 C. & P. 356. But it is doubtful whether a conviction can be supported under this section, if the poison be delivered by mistake to and taken by another person than that for whom it was intended. R. v. Ryan (1839), 2 M. & Rob. 213; but see R. v. Lewis (1833), 6 C. & P. 161.

If, however, the poison was intended to reach a certain individual but through a mistake in identity on the part of the accused himself, that individual was not in fact the person against whom his animus existed, it would appear that a conviction would be supported. R. v. Hunt (1825), 1

Mood. C.C. 93; R. v. Stopford (1870), 11 Cox C.C. 643; R. v. Smith (1856), Dears. 559.

Wounds.]—To constitute a wound the continuity of the skin must be broken. R. v. Woods (1830), 1 Mood. C.C. 278. There must be a division not merely of the cuticle or upper skin, but of the whole skin. R. v. McLaughlin (1838), 8 C. & P. 635; R. v. Becket (1836), 1 M. & Rob. 526; or of the internal skin, ex. gr., of the lip or cheek. R. v. Smith (1837), 8 C. & P. 173; R. v. Warman (1846), 1 Den. 183.

A wound from a kick with a shoe is within the statute. R. v. Briggs (1831), 1 Mood. C.C. 318. If in self-defence the prosecutor force a part of his body against an instrument in the defendant's hands and so cut or wound himself, the wounding is not within this section. R. v. Becket (1836), 1 M. & Rob. 526.

(*b.*)—*Grievous bodily harm.*]—If the bodily injury be such as seriously to interfere with health or comfort that is sufficient, and it is not necessary that it should be either permanent or dangerous. R. v. Cox (1818), R. & R. 362; R. v. Ashman (1858), 1 F. & F. 88; see also sec. 284.

Upon a charge of causing grievous bodily harm to a child under defendant's care with intent to bring about the child's death, evidence of acts of cruelty by defendants to another child also in defendant's care are irrelevant to the case and inadmissible. R. v. Lapierre (1897), 1 Can. Cr. Cas. 413 (Que.).

(*c.*)—*Shooting with intent.*]—If a wound was caused, it seems that a count for wounding with intent to do grievous bodily harm must be added to enable the jury to convict of unlawful wounding should they find the accused not guilty of the more serious crime but are convinced that the lesser offence has been comitted. Archbold Cr. Plead. (1900), 785.

Where the accused was charged with wounding T. with intent to murder him, and it appeared in evidence that the defendant intended to murder M. and that he shot at and wounded T., supposing him to be M., and the jury found that he intended to murder the man at whom he shot, supposing him to be M., the conviction was upheld. R. v. Smith (1856), Dears. 559, 25 L.J.M.C. 29; R. v. Stopford (1870), 11 Cox C.C. 643.

(*c.*)—*Attempts to discharge loaded arms.*]—If a person intending to shoot another puts his finger on the trigger of a loaded firearm, but is prevented from pulling the trigger, it is nevertheless an attempt to discharge loaded arms under this section. R. v. Duckworth, [1892] 2 Q.B. 83, 17 Cox C.C. 495; R. v. Brown (1883), 10 Q.B.D. 381; R. v. St. George (1840), 9 C. & P. 483, overruled.

The expression "loaded arms" includes any gun, pistol or other arm loaded with gunpowder, or other explosive substance, and ball, shot, slug or other destructive material, or charged with compressed air and ball, shot, slug or other destructive material. Sec. 2 (19).

A man cannot be convicted of attempting to discharge a revolver with intent to murder, if it is proved that the man knew that the revolver, though apparently loaded, was loaded with cartridges not intended for it, which could not be discharged by it, the intent being in truth to frighten. R. v. Jones, 18 Times L.R. 156.

(*d.*)—*Form of indictment for attempting to drown.*]—That A. at unlawfully did take one J. N., into both the hands of him the said A., and unlawfully did cast, throw, and push the said J. N. into a certain pond, wherein there was a great quantity of water, and did thereby then feloniously and unlawfully attempt the said J. N. to drown and suffocate, with intent thereby then unlawfully, wilfully and of his malice aforethought, the said J. N. to kill and murder, against the peace, etc., and against the form of the statute, the Criminal Code sec. 264.

(*e.*)—*Form of indictment for damage by explosion.*]—That A. unlawfully and maliciously did at , by the explosion of a certain explosive substance, that is to say, gunpowder, destroy (or damage) a certain building situate with intent thereby then unlawfully, wilfully and of his malice aforethought, one J. N. to kill and murder, against the peace, etc., and of the statute, the Criminal Code sec. 264.

(*h.*)—*By any other means attempts to commit murder.*]—Where a woman jumped out of a window to avoid the violence of her husband, it was held that to constitute this offence it must be proved that he intended by his conduct to make her jump out. R. v. Donovan (1850), 4 Cox C.C. 401.

The sending or placing of infernal machines with intent to murder is within this sub-section. R. v. Mountford (1835), Mood. C.C. 441, 3 Russ. Cr., 6th ed., 280(n). Attempts to commit suicide are, however, not included. R. v. Burgess (1862), 9 Cox C.C. 302, L. & C. 258, 32 L.J.M.C. 55; but come under sec. 270 of the Code.

Circumstances disclosing intent.]—On the trial of a person accused of attempt to murder by shooting, evidence that he had burglar's tools in his possession at the time is admissible, as tending to prove criminal intent. It is proper for the judge, in charging the jury in a trial for an attempt to murder, to instruct them that they may draw an inference as to the prisoner's intent to kill from the circumstances of his being a stranger loitering in a street or park, between four and five o'clock in the morning, with a loaded revolver and burglar's tools in his possession. The King v. Mooney, 11 Can. Cr. Cas. 333.

Letters threatening murder.

265. Every one is guilty of an indictable offence and liable to ten years' imprisonment who sends, delivers or utters, or directly or indirectly causes to be received, knowing the contents thereof, any letter or writing threatening to kill or murder any person. 55-56 V., c. 29, s. 233.

Threats verbally made to burn the complainant's buildings are not indictable under the Criminal Code, and give rise only to proceedings to force the offender to give security to keep the peace. Ex parte Welsh (1898), 2 Can. Cr. Cas. 35. But a threat in writing to burn a building is punishable under sec. 516. As to extortion by threats see secs. 453 and 454.

Penalty.

266. Every one is guilty of an indictable offence and liable to fourteen years' imprisonment, who,—

Conspiring to murder.

(*a*) conspires or agrees with any person to murder or to cause to be murdered any other person, whether the person intended to be murdered is a subject of His Majesty or not, or is within His Majesty's dominions or not; or,

Counselling murder.

(*b*) counsels or attempts to procure any person to murder such other person anywhere, although such person is not murdered in consequence of such counselling or attempted procurement. 55-56 V., c. 29, s. 234.

Counselling murder.]—The offence of counselling murder may be committed by the publication of a newspaper article exulting in the assassination of a foreign monarch and commending it as an example to revolutionists throughout the world; and the counselling need not be directed to any particular person. R. v. Most (1881), 7 Q.B.D. 244; 14 Cox C.C. 583.

To solicit and incite a person to commit a felony was a misdemeanour at common law. Arch. Crim. Plead. (1900), 1224.

Where the indictment is for soliciting another to commit murder it is unnecessary to negative the commission of the murder which, if committed, would render the accused guilty of the principal offence as an accessory before the fact (sec. 69), for it cannot be intended that the principal offence has been committed where it is not charged. 1 Stark. Cr. Plead., 2nd ed., 148; R. v. Higgins (1801), 2 East 5.

Form of indictment.]—That A., B. and C. on at unlawfully and wickedly did conspire, confederate and agree together one J. N. unlawfully, wilfully, and of their malice aforethought to kill and murder, against the form of the statute, the Criminal Code sec. 266.

Accessory after the fact.

267. Every one is guilty of an indictable offence and liable to imprisonment for life, who is an accessory after the fact to murder. 55-56 V., c. 29, s. 235.

The accused must be proved to have done some act to assist the murderer personally: R. v. Chapple (1840), 9 C. & P. 355; or by employing another person to harbour or relieve him. R. v. Greenacre (1837), 8 C. & P. 35; R. v. Butterfield (1843), 1 Cox C.C. 39; R. v. Lee (1834), 6 C. & P. 536; R. v. Jarvis (1837), 2 M. & Rob. 40. See also note to sec. 71.

The accessory may be indicted without proceeding against the principal or jointly with the principal. Sec. 849.

Punishment for manslaughter.

268. Every one who commits manslaughter is guilty of an indictable offence and liable to imprisonment for life. 55-56 V., c. 29, s. 236.

Not applicable to corporation.]—There is no power under Code sec. 920 or otherwise to impose a fine or any other punishment, in lieu of imprisonment, for the offence of manslaughter, and there is consequently no judgment or sentence applicable to a conviction of a corporation for that offence even if a corporation can be guilty of manslaughter. R. v. Great West Laundry Co. (1900), 3 Can. Cr. Cas. 514 (Man.).

A corporation from its artificial nature cannot be guilty of any crime the essence of which is either personal criminal intent or such a degree of negligence as amounts to a wilful incurring of the risk of causing injury to others. Ibid.

Under sec. 247 of the Code a corporation may be indicted for omitting, without lawful excuse, to perform the duty of avoiding danger to human life from anything in its charge or under its control. And the fact that the consequence of the omission to perform such duty might have justified an indictment for manslaughter in the case of an individual is not a ground for quashing the indictment. As the Criminal Code provides no punishment for the offence, the common law punishment of a fine may be imposed on a corporation indicted under it. Union Colliery Co. v. R., 4 Can. Cr. Cas. 400, 31 Can. S.C.R. 81.

Extradition.]—"Manslaughter, when voluntary," is extraditable by the first article of the Convention of 12 July, 1889, between Great Britain and the United States of America.

Previous indictment for murder.]—A previous conviction or acquittal on an indictment for murder shall be a bar to a second indictment for the same homicide charging it as manslaughter; and a previous conviction or acquittal on an indictment for manslaughter shall be a bar to a second indictment for the same homicide charging it as murder. Sec. 909(2).

Previous conviction for assault.]—In Reg. v. Friel (1891), 17 Cox C.C. 325, it was held that when there had been a summary conviction for assault, and the person assaulted dies of the injuries, a plea of autrefois convict is no answer to an indictment for manslaughter, because the death, is a new fact, not a mere matter of aggravation, or a mere consequence, because in cases of manslaughter based on death resulting from culpable negligence there is no criminal offence unless death ensues and gives rise to a charge of manslaughter.

See also secs. 733, 734 and 909.

Suicide.

Aiding or counselling.

269. Every one is guilty of an indictable offence and liable to imprisonment for life who counsels or procures any person to commit suicide, actually committed in consequence of such counselling or procurement, or who aids or abets any person in the commission of suicide. 55-56 V., c. 29, s. 237.

Aiding suicide.]—If two persons mutually agree to commit suicide together, and accordingly take poison or attempt to drown themselves together, but only one of them dies, the survivor is guilty of murder. R. v. Dyson (1823), R. & R. 523; R. v. Alison (1838), 8 C. & P. 418; R. v. Jessop (1877), 16 Cox C.C. 204; R. v. Stornouth (1897), 61 J.P. 729; Com. v. Bowen, 13 Mass. 356; Com. Mink, 123 Mass. 429; Blackburn v. State, 23 Ohio State R. 146; Burnett v. State (1903), 204 Ill. 208.

Attempt.

270. Every one who attempts to commit suicide is guilty of an indictable offence and liable to two years' imprisonment. 55-56 V., c. 29, s. 238.

Attempted suicide.]—This offence was a misdemeanour at common law. R. v. Burgess (1862), L. & C. 258; 9 Cox C.C. 302, 32 L.J.M.C. 55.

Mere intention to commit the offence does not constitute an attempt; same act immediately connected with the principal offence must be proved to have been done by the accused. R. v. Eagleton (1855), Dears. 515, 538, 24 L.J.M.C. 158; R. v. Roberts (1855), Dears. 539, 25 L.J.M.C. 17; R. v. Cheeseman (1862), L. & C. 140, 9 Cox C.C. 100.

In cases of attempted suicide the mere fact of drunkenness is not an excuse for the crime, but it is "a material fact in order to arrive at the conclusion whether or no the prisoner really intended to destroy his life." Per Wightman, J., in Regina v. Doody (1854), 6 Cox C.C. 463.

Neglect in Childbirth and Concealing Dead Body.

Neglecting to obtain assistance

271. Every woman is guilty of an indictable offence who, with either of the intents in this section mentioned, being with child and being about to be delivered, neglects to provide reasonable assistance in her delivery, if the child is permanently injured thereby, or dies, either just before, or during, or shortly after birth, unless she proves that such death or permanent injury was not caused by such neglect, or by any wrongful act to which she was a party, and is liable,— in child-birth.

(a) if the intent of such neglect be that the child shall not live, to imprisonment for life; Penalty.

(b) if the intent of such neglect be to conceal the fact of her having had a child, to imprisonment for seven years. 55-56 V., c. 29, s. 239. Penalty.

It has been held that a woman cannot be convicted of manslaughter on evidence that, knowing she was near the time of delivery, she wilfully abstained from taking the necessary precautions to preserve the life of her child after its birth, in consequence of which neglect it died. R. v. Knights (1860), 2 F. & F. 46; but see R. v. Handley (1874), 13 Cox C.C. 79, where Brett, J., held that if the woman, without intending the death of the child, determines to be alone at the birth for the purpose of temporary concealment, and the child afterwards dies by reason of her wicked negligence, she is guilty of manslaughter. Cf. R. v. Middleship (1851), 5 Cox C.C. 275.

272. Every one is guilty of an indictable offence and liable to two years' imprisonment, who disposes of the dead body of any child in any manner, with intent to conceal the fact that its mother was delivered of it, whether the child died before, or during, or after birth. 55-56 V., c. 29, s. 240. **Concealing dead body of child.**

Form of indictment.]—The jurors, etc., present that A. on at was delivered of a child; and that the A., being so delivered of the said child as aforesaid, did then unlawfully endeavour to conceal the birth of the said child by secretly burying the dead body of the said child, against the form of the statute, the Criminal Code sec. 272. (State the means of concealment specially, when it is otherwise than by secret burying.)

Evidence.]—Leaving the dead body of a child in two boxes, closed but not locked or fastened, one being placed inside the other in a bedroom, but in such a position as to attract the attention of those who daily resorted to the room, is not a secret disposition of the body, within the meaning of the statute. R. v. George, 11 Cox C.C. 41.

Concealment of birth was dealt with by sec. 61 of 32-33 Vict., ch. 20. Although the mere denial of the birth will not support a conviction; R. v. Turner (1839), 8 C. & P. 755, it is a factor in proof of the offence. R. v. Piché (1879), 30 U.C.C.P. 409. What is a secret disposition must depend on the circumstances of each particular case. The most complete exposure of the body might be a concealment, ex gr., if placed in a secluded place where the body would not be likely to be found. R. v. Brown (1870), L.R. 1 C.C. 244.

The former statutes, R.S.C. 1886, ch. 162, sec. 49, and 24-25 Vict., ch. 100, sec. 60, required that there should be a "secret disposition" of the dead body. A disposal in any manner with the intent here specified is sufficient under the Code.

A final disposition of the body of the child is not essential, and it is an offence if it be hid in a place from which a further removal was contemplated. R. v. Goldthorpe (1841), 2 Moo. C.C. 244; R. v. Perry (1855), Dears. 471.

Where the only evidence was that the woman had been delivered of a child the body of which was taken away by two other persons, but the prisoner did not know where it was put, it was held insufficient. R. v. Bate (1871), 11 Cox C.C. 686.

There must be an identification of the body found as being that of the child of which she is alleged to have been delivered. R. v. Williams (1871), 11 Cox C.C. 684.

It must also be proved that the body concealed was that of a child dead at the time of the disposal or concealment. R. v. Bell (1874), Irish R. 8 C.L. 541; R. v. May (1867), 16 L.T. Rep. 362, 10 Cox C.C. 448.

The mere denial of the birth is not sufficient proof of intent to conceal. R. v. Turner (1839), 8 C. & P. 755. It must be shewn that the accused did some act of disposal of the body after the child was dead. Ibid.

The fact that the mother had previously allowed the birth to be known to some persons is not conclusive evidence negativing concealment. R. v. Douglas (1836), 1 Mood. C.C. 480; R. v. Cornwall (1817), R. & R. 336.

Confession as evidence.]—A. being questioned by a police constable about the concealment of a birth gave an answer which caused the officer to say to her: "It might be better for you to tell the truth and not a lie"; and it was held that a further statement made by her to the officer was inadmissible in evidence, as not being free and voluntary. She was taken into custody on the same day, placed with two accomplices, and charged with concealment of birth. All three then made statements. It was held that those made by the accomplices could not be deemed to be affected by the previous inducement to A. and were therefore admissible against themselves, although that made by A. was inadmissible. When before the magistrate for the preliminary enquiry the three prisoners received the formal caution (sec. 684) from the magistrate as to anything they wished to say in regard to the charge, and A. then made a statement which was taken down in writing and attached to the deposition, and this latter statement was admissible in evidence against her. R. v. Bate (1871), 11 Cox C.C. 686.

And see as to confessions and admissions as evidence, sec. 685 and note to same.

"Child."]—A foetus which has not reached the period at which it might have been born alive is not a "child." R. v. Berriman (1854), 6 Cox C.C. 388; but see R. v. Colmer (1864), 9 Cox C.C. 506.

Verdict of concealment of birth on charge of child murder.]—If any person tried for the murder of any child is acquitted thereof the jury by whose verdict such person is acquitted may find, in case it so appears in evidence, that the child had recently been born, and that such person did, by some secret disposition of such child or of the dead body of such child, endeavour to conceal the birth thereof, and thereupon the court may pass such sentence as if such person had been convicted upon an indictment for the concealment of birth. Sec. 952.

Bodily Injuries and Acts and Omissions Causing Danger to the Person.

Wounding with intent.

273. Every one is guilty of an indictable offence and liable to imprisonment for life who, with intent to maim, disfigure or disable any person, or to do some other grievous bodily harm to any person, or with intent to resist or prevent the lawful apprehension or detainer of any person, unlawfully by any means wounds or causes any grievous bodily harm to any person, or shoots at any person, or by drawing a trigger, or in any other manner, attempts to discharge any kind of loaded arms at any person. 55-56 V., c. 29, s. 241.

Indictment.]—If the indictment charges that the accused did "inflict" grievous bodily harm, it sufficiently charges the "causing" of grievous bodily harm. R. v. Bray (1883), 15 Cox C.C. 197.

The instrument or means by which the injury was inflicted need not be stated in the indictment, and if stated need not be proved as laid. R. v. Briggs (1831), 1 Moo. C.C. 318.

Proof of intent.]—It was held in Rex v. Linneker, [1906] 2 K.B. 99, 22 Times L.R. 495, that the accused was rightly convicted of "feloniously attempting to discharge a revolver with intent to do grievous bodily harm, when he had drawn a loaded revolver from his pocket, with an expression of intention to use it, but was seized before he could take any further step towards discharging it.

The intent may be inferred from the act committed. R. v. Le Dante, 2 Geldert & Oxley (N.S.), 401.

A person who fires a loaded pistol into a group of persons, not aiming at any one in particular, but intending generally to do grievous bodily harm, and who hits one of them, may be convicted on an indictment charging him with shooting at the person he has hit with intent to do grievous bodily harm to that person. R. v. Fretwell (1864), L. & C. 443, 9 Cox C.C. 471.

Intent against one person; wounding another.]—The statutory form 64, sub-sec. (f), shews that this section includes as an offence the causing of actual bodily harm to a person although done with intent to cause such harm to another; and also that where the intent is to prevent a lawful apprehension the person about to be apprehended is not necessarily the person charged with the wounding or other offence under this section.

Not only will an indictment charging the accused with wounding A. with intent to do him grievous bodily injury be supported by evidence that he intended to go grievous bodily harm to the man he wounded, and who, in fact was A., although the accused did not think that he was A., but somebody else, R. v. Stopford (1870), 11 Cox C.C. 643; but it will be sufficient under this section that the defendant wounded, etc., any person with intent to maim, etc., a third person. R. v. Latimer (1886), 17 Q.B.D. 359, 16 Cox 707: Archbold Cr. Plead. (1900), 806. It will be observed that there is a possible distinction in this respect between secs. 264 and 273, for in the former the words "any person" do not follow the words "with intent to commit murder," and it may consequently be inferred that the intent to murder must be directed against the very person wounded, etc. See note to sec. 264.

Maim, disfigure or disable.]—To maim is to injure any part of a man's body which may render him, in fighting, less able to defend himself or to annoy his enemy. 1 Hawk., ch. 44, sec. 1; R. v. Sullivan (1841), C. & Mar. 209. To disfigure is to do some external injury which may detract from his personal appearance. To disable is to do something which creates a permanent disability and not merely a temporary injury. Archbold Cr. Plead. (1900), 807; R. v. Boyce (1824), 1 Mood. C.C. 29.

Grievous bodily harm.]—An injury seriously interfering with health or comfort, although neither permanent or endangering life, is sufficient. R. v. Ashman (1858), 1 F. & F. 88; R. v. Cox (1818), R. & R. 362.

Intent to prevent lawful apprehension.]—It must be shewn that the arrest would have been lawful. As to when an arrest is justified, see sec. 30 et seq. and secs. 646 to 652.

Wounds.]—A wounding may be "either with or without any weapon or instrument;" sec. 242; but the skin must be broken. R. v. Wood (1830), 1 Mood. C.C. 278; R. v. Briggs (1831), 1 Mood. C.C. 318; R. v. Withers (1831), 1 Mood. C.C. 294; R. v. Sheard (1837), 7 C. & P. 846.

Verdict for lesser offence.]—A charge of wounding or causing grievous bodily harm with intent is inclusive of the offence of common assault and a verdict for the latter offence may be returned by virtue of sec. 951. R. v. Laskey, 1 P. & B. (N.B.) 194; R. v. Taylor (1869), L.R. 1 C.C.R. 194. And likewise, if the jury are not convinced as to the intent, they may find the accused guilty of unlawfully wounding if wounding be charged, or of unlawfully inflicting grievous bodily harm if that be charged, in which case the punishment is under sec. 274. R. v. Waudby, [1895] 2 Q.B. 482.

Upon an indictment charging a shooting at a person with intent, a verdict for common assault may be rendered. Re Cronan (1874), 24 U.C.C.P. 106.

Verdict of "guilty without malicious intent."]—Upon the trial of an indictment for wounding with intent to disable, a verdict of "guilt without malicious intent" is equivalent to a verdict of acquittal, although the jury were instructed that if intent to disable were negatived they might still convict of the simple offence of wounding. Such verdict is to be construed as a finding that the act of the accused which resulted in wounding the complainant was done without malice. (The King v. Slaughenwhite (No. 1), 9 Can. Cr. Cas. 53, 37 N.S.R. 382, reversed.) Slaughenwhite v. The King; The King v. Slaughenwhite (No. 2), 9 Can. Cr. Cas. 173, 35 Can. S.C.R. 607.

Self-defence.]—Upon a charge of shooting with intent to do grievous bodily harm in which the plea is self-defence, it is a question for the jury, whether the assault upon the accused, which had provoked the shooting, had ended or was still being pursued. It is mis-direction to charge the jury that, to support the plea of self-defence to the infliction of grievous bodily harm, they must find that the accused could not otherwise have preserved himself from death or grievous bodily harm, it being a sufficient justification if the accused had a reasonable apprehension of grievous bodily harm to himself from the violence of the assault upon him, and if he believed on reasonable grounds that he could not preserve himself from grievous bodily harm otherwise than by inflicting grievous bodily harm upon his assailant. The King v. Ritter, 8 Can. Cr. Cas. 31; Cr. Code secs. 53 and 54.

Attempt to commit murder.]—See sec. 264.

Pointing fire-arm loaded or unloaded.]—See sec. 122.

Wounding. Bodily harm.

274. Every one is guilty of an indictable offence and liable to three years' imprisonment who unlawfully wounds or inflicts any grievous bodily harm upon any other person, either with or without any weapon or instrument. 55-56 V., c. 29, s. 242.

Indictment for unlawfully wounding.]—That A. at one W. unlawfully and maliciously did wound against the form of the Criminal Code sec. 274 (add a count charging that the defendant "did inflict grievous bodily harm upon W.").

Grievous bodily harm.]—In Reg. v. Ashman (1858), 1 F. & F. 88, Wills, J., said that in order to constitute grievous bodily harm "it is not necessary that the injury should be either permanent or dangerous, if it be such as seriously to interfere with the comfort or health it is sufficient." In Reg. v. Clarence (1888), 22 Q.B.D. 23, the effect of a similar enactment, sec. 20 of 24-25 Vict., ch. 100 (Imp.), was considered. It provided that "whosoever shall unlawfully and maliciously wound or inflict any grievous bodily harm upon any other person, either with or without any weapon, or instrument, shall be guilty of a misdemeanour." Mr. Justice Wills expressed the opinion that "the section points to the infliction of direct and intentional violence, whether with a weapon or the fist or the foot, or any other part of the person or in any other way not involving the use of a weapon, as for instance by creating a panic at a theatre whereby people trampled on one another." (Reg. v. Martin, 8 Q.B.D. 54.) And Mr. Justice Stephen, in the Clarence Case, said: "The words appear to my mind to mean the direct causing of some grievous bodily harm to the body itself with a weapon, as by a cut with a knife, or without a weapon, as by a blow with the fist, or by pushing the person down."

A conviction for inflicting grievous bodily harm under sec. 274 which provides a punishment for the person "who unlawfully wounds or inflicts any grievous bodily harm upon any other person" need not state that the act was done "unlawfully," that term in the section being referable only to the offence of wounding. R. v. Treadwell (1902), 5 Can. Cr. Cas. 461.

The words "actual bodily harm" in sec. 295 would be fully covered by the least bodily harm, whilst the offence provided in sec. 274 has added to it an aggravating element which makes the bodily harm grievous. R. v. Hostetter (1902), 7 Can. Cr. Cas. 221.

Powers of justices.]—Justices of the peace have no power on a preliminary investigation before them of a charge of unlawfully wounding, to reduce the charge to one of common assault, over which they would have summary jurisdiction. R. v. Lee (1897), 2 Can. Cr. Cas. 233; Miller v. Lea (1898), 2 Can. Cr. Cas. 282. A conviction recorded by justices in such a case upon a plea of guilty to the charge as reduced, is not a bar to an indictment for unlawfully wounding, based upon the same state of facts, and does not support a plea of autrefois convict. Ibid.

Verdict.]—Upon an indictment for assaulting, beating, wounding and inflicting grievous bodily harm, the prisoner may be convicted of a common assault. Sec. 951. R. v. Oliver (1860), Bell C.C. 287, 30 L.J.M.C. 12; R. v. Yeadon (1862), L. & C. 81; and a verdict for common assault was held good where the indictment charged only the infliction of grievous bodily harm. R. v. Canwell, 20 L.T. 402, 11 Cox C.C. 263, and see R. v. Taylor, 11 Cox C.C. 261, L.R. 1 C.C.R. 194.

275. Every one is guilty of an indictable offence and liable to fourteen years' imprisonment who wilfully,— **Penalty.**

(*a*) shoots at any vessel belonging to His Majesty or in the service of Canada; or, **Shooting at the King's vessels.**

(*b*) maims or wounds any public officer engaged in the execution of his duty or any person acting in aid of such officer. 55-56 V., c. 29, s. 243. **Wounding public officer.**

Public officer.]—This term is inclusive of any inland revenue or customs officer, officer of the army, navy, marine, militia, North-West Mounted Police, or other officer engaged in enforcing the laws relating to the revenue, customs, trade or navigation of Canada. Sec. 2 (29).

Describing the offence.]—To justify a sentence of more than three years' imprisonment for assault and wounding a public officer, the charge must allege that the offence was committed while the officer was engaged in the execution of his duty. R. v. Dupont (1900), 3 Can. Cr. Cas. 566 (Que.). A mere description of the assaulted party in the information as an acting detective does not justify a sentence of seven years on a plea of guilty, nor does it imply that the assault took place while the officer was engaged in the execution of his duty. Ibid.

Penalty. Offence.

276. Every one is guilty of an indictable offence and liable to imprisonment for life and to be whipped, who with intent thereby to enable himself or any other person to commit, or with intent thereby to assist any other person in committing, any indictable offence,—

By strangling.

(a) by any means whatsoever, attempts to choke, suffocate or strangle any other person, or by any means calculated to choke, suffocate or strangle, attempts to render any other person insensible, unconscious or incapable of resistance; or,

By narcotic.

(b) unlawfully applies or administers to, or causes to be taken by, or attempts to apply or administer to, or attempts or causes to be administered to or taken by, any person, any chloroform, laudanum or other stupefying or overpowering drug, matter or thing. 55-56 V., c. 29, s. 244.

Form of indictment.]—That A. on at unlawfully did attempt to choke, suffocate and strangle one J. N., with intent thereby then to enable him, the said A., the monies, goods and chattels of the said J. N., from the person of the said J. N., unlawfully to steal, take and carry away, against the peace, etc., and against the form of the Criminal Code sec. 276.

Attempt to murder.]—See sec. 264.

Administering poison to endanger life.

277. Every one is guilty of an indictable offence and liable to fourteen years' imprisonment who unlawfully administers to, or causes to be administered to or taken by any other person, any poison or other destructive or noxious thing, so as thereby to endanger the life of such person, or so as thereby to inflict upon such person any grievous bodily harm. 55-56 V., c. 29, s. 245.

Form of indictment.]—That A. on at unlawfully and maliciously did administer to one J. N. a large quantity, to wit, two drachms of a certain deadly poison called white arsenic, and thereby then did endanger the life of the said J. N. (or inflict on the said J. N. grievous bodily harm) against the form of the statute, the Criminal Code sec. 277.

"Administering."]—See note to sec. 264.

Any poison or other destructive or noxious thing.]—Some drugs are noxious only when taken in large quantities; and it is doubtful whether the administering of a drug in so small a quantity as to be incapable of doing harm although a larger quantity of the drug would be a poisonous dose, is administering a "poison." R. v. Hennah (1877), 13 Cox C.C. 547; R. v. Cramp (1880), 5 Q.B.D. 307. In the latter case it is suggested that where the drug administered is a recognized "poison" it may be that the offence is complete although the quantity administered is too small to be noxious.

But if grievous bodily harm in fact results although the intent was merely to annoy (as to which see sec. 278), the offence is complete under sec. 277. Tulley v. Corrie, 10 Cox C.C. 640.

278. Every one is guilty of an indictable offence and liable to three years' imprisonment who unlawfully administers to, or causes to be administered to or taken by, any other person any poison or other destructive or noxious thing, with intent to injure, aggrieve or annoy such person. 55-56 V., c. 29, s. 246.

Administering poison with intent to injure.

If any grievous bodily harm is in fact inflicted, the offence comes under sec. 277. Tulley v. Corrie (1867), 10 Cox C.C. 640.

Any poison or other destructive or noxious thing.]—See note to sec. 277.

Intent to injure, aggrieve or annoy.]—Where the defendant administered cantharides to a woman and the jury found that it was administered with the intent to excite her sexual passion and desire, in order that the defendant might have connection with her, this was held to be an administering with intent to "injure, aggrieve and annoy" her. R. v. Wilkins (1861), L. & C. 89, 9 Cox C.C. 20, 31 L.J.M.C. 72.

279. Every one is guilty of an indictable offence and liable to imprisonment for life who unlawfully and by the explosion of an explosive substance burns, maims, disfigures, disables or does any grievous bodily harm to any person. 55-56 V., c. 29, s. 247.

Causing bodily injuries by explosives.

Explosive substance.]—This expression includes any materials for making an explosive substance; also any apparatus, machine, implement or materials used, or intended to be used or adapted for causing, or aiding in causing, any explosion in or with any explosive substance, and also any part of any such apparatus, machine or implement. Sec. 2 (14).

Dangerous storing of explosives.]—Keeping naphtha in a populous place in such quantities as to cause terror or danger is a common law nuisance as being an act injurious to public safety. R. v. Lister (1857), D. & B. 209. And so is keeping gunpowder or other explosives in dangerous proximity to streets or houses. R. v. Taylor (1742), 2 Str. 1167; 1 Russ. Cr. 6th ed., 734(n). And where defendants were charged with having unlawfully knowing and willingly deposited in a room in a lodging or boarding house in the City of Halifax near to certain streets or thoroughfares and in close proximity to divers dwelling houses excessive quantities of dynamite by reason whereof the inhabitants were in great danger, it was held that the indictment was not bad for failure to allege either carelessness or that the quantities were so great that care would not produce safety. R. v. Holmes, 5 R. & G. (N.S.) 498.

Intent to harm.

280. Every one who unlawfully,—

(a) with intent to burn, maim, disfigure or disable any person, or to do some grievous bodily harm to any person, whether any bodily harm is effected or not,

Explosives.

(i) causes any explosive substance to explode,

Sending explosives.

(ii) sends or delivers to, or causes to be taken or received by, any person any explosive substance, or any other dangerous or noxious thing,

Applying to person explosives.

(iii) puts or lays at any place, or casts or throws at or upon, or otherwise applies to, any person any corrosive fluid, or any destructive or explosive substance; or,

Throwing explosives against vessel.

(b) places or throws in, into, upon, against or near any building, ship or vessel an explosive substance, with intent to do any bodily injury to any person, whether or not any explosion takes place and whether or not any bodily injury is effected;

Penalty.

is guilty of an indictable offence and liable, in cases within paragraph *(a)* of this section, to imprisonment for life, and in cases within paragraph *(b)* of this section to fourteen years' imprisonment. 55-56 V., c. 29, s. 248.

Form of indictment.]—That A. on at unlawfully and maliciously did cast and throw upon one J. N. a certain corrosive fluid, to wit, one pint of oil of vitriol, with intent in so doing him the said J. N. thereby then to burn (or disfigure) against the peace, etc., and against the form of the Criminal Code sec. 280.

Throwing corrosive fluid.]—Unless the contrary be proved the intention will be evidenced by the act; R. v. Rhenwick Williams (1790), 1 Leach 533; and the question of intent is for the jury. R. v. Saunders, 14 Cox C.C. 180.

Throwing oil of vitriol in a person's face has been held not to be a "wounding," R. v. Murrow (1835), Mood. C.C. 456.

Destructive matter.]—Under a similar English statute 7 Wm. IV. and 1 Vict., ch. 85, sec. 5, boiling water was held to be "destructive matter." R. v. Crawford (1845), 1 Den. 100, 2 C. & K. 129. In that case the prisoner was indicted for maliciously throwing boiling water upon her husband. Under the influence of jealousy she had boiled a quart of water and while he was asleep she poured it over his face and into one of his ears and ran away boasting that she had boiled him in his sleep. The injury deprived the man of sight for some time and affected his hearing. A conviction was affirmed on a case reserved.

Negligent blasting of stone in a quarry and thereby projecting large pieces of stone so as to endanger the safety of persons in houses and on the highways adjoining the quarry was indictable at common law as a misdemeanour. R. v. Mutters (1864), L. & C. 491.

281. Every one is guilty of an indictable offence and liable to five years' imprisonment who sets or places, or causes to be set or placed, any spring-gun, man-trap, or other engine calculated to destroy human life or inflict grievous bodily harm, with the intent that the same or whereby the same may destroy, or inflict grievous bodily harm upon, any trespasser or other person coming in contact therewith. **Setting spring guns and man-traps.**

2. Every one who knowingly and wilfully permits any such spring-gun, man-trap or other engine which has been set or placed by some other person, in any place which is in, or afterwards comes into, his possession or occupation, to continue so set or placed shall be deemed to have set or placed such gun, trap or engine with such intent as aforesaid. **Permitting the same to be set.**

3. This section does not extend to any gin or trap usually set or placed with the intent of destroying vermin or noxious animals. 55-56 V., c. 29, s. 249. **Exception.**

Form of indictment.]—That A. on at unlawfully did set and place, and caused to be set and placed, in a certain garden situate a certain spring-gun which was then loaded and charged with gunpowder and divers leaden shot, with intent that the said spring-gun, so loaded and charged as aforesaid, should inflict grievous bodily harm upon any trespasser who might come in contact therewith, against the form of the Criminal Code sec. 281.

Evidence.]—A similar provision in the English statute 7 and 8 Geo. IV., ch. 18, was held not to be applicable to the setting of dog-spears on a man's own land with no intention to harm human beings and without having brought about such a result. Jordin v. Crump (1841), 8 M. & W. 782.

282. Every one is guilty of an indictable offence and liable to imprisonment for life who unlawfully,— **Penalty.**

(a) with intent to injure or to endanger the safety of any person travelling or being upon any railway, **Intent to injure traveller.**

(i) puts or throws upon or across such railway any wood, stone, or other matter or thing, **Stone on railway.**

(ii) takes up, removes or displaces any rail, railway switch, sleeper or other matter or thing belonging to such railway, or injures or destroys any track, bridge or fence of such railway, or any portion thereof, **Removing sleeper or rail.**

(iii) turns, moves or diverts any point or other machinery belonging to such railway, **Diverting points, etc.**

(iv) makes or shows, hides or removes any signal or light upon or near to such railway, **Removing signal.**

(v) does or causes to be done any other matter or thing with such intent; or, **Otherwise.**

Throwing anything at car, etc.

(*b*) throws, or causes to fall or strike at, against, into or upon any engine, tender, carriage or truck used and in motion upon any railway, any wood, stone or other matter or thing, with intent to injure or endanger the safety of any person being in or upon such engine, tender, carriage or truck, or in or upon any other engine, tender, carriage or truck of any train of which such first mentioned engine, tender, carriage or truck forms part. 55-56 V., c. 29, s. 250.

If death is caused by unlawfully setting a spring-gun the person setting it is guilty of manslaughter. R. v. Heaton (1896), 60 J.P. 508.

Form of indictment.]—An example of stating one of the offences mentioned in this section is given as follows in Code Form 64 as follows: "A., with intent to injure or endanger the safety of persons on the Canadian Pacific Railway, did an act calculated to interfere with an engine, a tender, and certain carriages on the said railway on at by (describe with so much detail as is sufficient to give the accused reasonable information as to the acts or omissions relied on against him, and to identify the transaction).

Private railway.]—The corresponding English Act, 24-25 Vict., ch. 97, secs. 35-57, has been held to apply to both public and private railways: O'Gorman v. Sweet (1890), 54 J.P. 663; and to railways not yet opened for regular traffic, but in use for the conveyance of workmen and materials. R. v. Bradford (1860), Bell C.C. 268.

Acquittal.]—An acquittal under this section will not bar an indictment under sec. 283. R. v. Gilmore (1882), 15 Cox C.C. 85.

Extradition.]—By the Extradition Convention of 1901 with the U.S.A. "wilful and unlawful destruction or obstruction of railroads which endangers human life," was added to the list of extraditable crimes between the British Empire and the United States.

Wantonly endangering safety of persons on railways.

283. Every one is guilty of an indictable offence and liable to two years' imprisonment who, by any unlawful act, or by any wilful omission or neglect of duty, endangers or causes to be endangered the safety of any person conveyed or being in or upon a railway, or aids or assists therein. 55-56 V., c. 29, s. 251.

Where the Code specifies an offence and provides for the punishment by imprisonment only, it does not necessarily follow that a corporation may not be indicted and fined for the offence so described. Union Colliery Co. v. The Queen, 4 Can. Cr. Cas. 400, 408, per Sedgwick, J. And see note to sec. 284.

Other offences relating to the operation of railways are contained in the Railway Act, and in Code secs. 499, 510, 517, 518, 519.

Omission or neglect of duty.]—There must be a duty to do the thing omitted to be done; a promise, not constituting a contract, made by a railway manager to do something which the company was under no legal obligation to do does not constitute a "duty" under this section. Ex parte Brydges, 18 L.C. Jur. 141.

Extradition.]—By the Extradition Convention of 1900, with the U.S.A. wilful and unlawful destruction or obstruction of railroads which endangers human life, is made an extraditable offence.

284. Every one is guilty of an indictable offence and liable to two years' imprisonment who, by any unlawful act, or by doing negligently or omitting to do any act which it is his duty to do, causes grievous bodily injury to any other person. 55-56 V., c. 29, s. 252. Causing bodily injury.

Corporations.]—Although a corporation cannot be guilty of manslaughter, it may be indicted under sec. 222 and possibly also under this section for having caused grievous bodily injury by omitting to maintain in a safe condition a bridge or structure which it was its duty to so maintain, and this notwithstanding that death ensued at once to the person sustaining the grievous bodily injury. A fine is the punishment which must be substituted under Cr. Code, sec. 920 in the case of a corporation, in lieu of the imprisonment mentioned in Cr. Code sec. 284, and the amount is in the discretion of the court (Cr. Code sec. 1029). The expression "grievous bodily injury" includes injuries immediately resulting in death, and as a corporation is not amenable to a charge of manslaughter, the death is as to it a circumstance in aggravation of the crime, and does not enlarge the nature of the offence. R. v. Union Colliery Co. (1900), 3 Can. Cr. Cas. 523 (B.C.); affirmed by the Supreme Court of Canada sub-nom., Union Colliery v. The Queen (1900), 4 Can. Cr. Cas. 400, 31 Can. S.C.R. 81.

285. Every one is guilty of an indictable offence and liable to two years' imprisonment who, having the charge of any carriage or vehicle, by wanton or furious driving, or racing or other wilful misconduct, or by wilful neglect, does or causes to be done any bodily harm to any person. 55-56 V., c. 29, s. 253. Injuring persons by furious driving.

Any carriage or vehicle.]—The same expression appears in the Offences against the Person Act, 1861, 24-25 Vict. (Imp.), ch. 100, sec. 35, and under it it has been decided that bicycles are included. R. v. Parker (1895), 59 J.P. 793, per Hawkins, J.

Wilful misconduct.]—An act is "wilfully" done if the defendant intentionally did it knowing that bodily harm to some person is likely to result. R. v. Holroyd (1841), 2 M. & Rob. 339; or with a reckless disregard of the natural consequences of the act. R. v. Monaghan (1870), 11 Cox C.C. 608. Compare sec. 509, defining the term "wilful" as used in Part VIII.

Wilful neglect.]—As to the meaning of the term "wilful neglect," e.g., wilfully refusing or neglecting to maintain a wife, see Anonymous Case (1902), 6 Can. Cr. Cas. 163 (Que.). A "wilful" refusal to allow a person to vote means a refusal which is perverse or malicious. Johnson v. Allen, 26 O.R. 550.

Form of indictment.]—That A. on at and then having charge of a certain carriage and vehicle called an omnibus, unlawfully did, by the wanton and furious driving of the said carriage and vehicle by him the said A., cause certain bodily harm, to wit, breaking his leg, to be done to one J. N. against the form of the Criminal Code sec. 285.

Penalty.

286. Every one is guilty of an indictable offence and liable to seven years' imprisonment,—

Impeding shipwrecked person.

(*a*) who prevents or impedes, or endeavours to prevent or impede, any shipwrecked person in his endeavour to save his life; or,

Impeding person assisting.

(*b*) who without reasonable cause prevents or impedes, or endeavours to prevent or impede, any person in his endeavour to save the life of any shipwrecked person. 55-56 V., c. 29, s. 254; 56 V., c. 32, s. 1.

Shipwrecked person.]—This term includes any person belonging to, on board of or having quitted any vessel wrecked, stranded or in distress at any place in Canada. See sec. 2 (33).

Penalty.

287. Every one is guilty of an offence and liable, on summary conviction, to a fine or imprisonment with or without hard labour, or both, who,—

Hole in ice unguarded.

(*a*) cuts or makes, or causes to be cut or made, any hole, opening, aperture or place, of sufficient size or area to endanger human life, through the ice on any navigable or other water open to or frequented by the public, and leaves such hole, opening, aperture or place, while it is in a state dangerous to human life, whether the same is frozen over or not, uninclosed by bushes or trees or unguarded by a guard or fence, of sufficient height and strength to prevent any person from accidentally riding, driving, walking, skating or falling therein; or,

Unused mine unguarded.

(*b*) being the owner, manager or superintendent of any abandoned or unused mine or quarry or property upon or in which there is any excavation of a sufficient area and depth to endanger human life, leaves the same unguarded and uninclosed by a guard or fence of sufficient height and strength to prevent any person from accidentally riding, driving, walking or falling therein; or,

Neglect to make inclosure.

(*c*) omits within five days after conviction of any such offence to so guard or inclose the same or to construct around or over such exposed opening or excavation a guard or fence of such height and strength.

Neglect to guard hole.

2. Every one whose duty it is to guard such hole, opening, aperture or place is guilty of manslaughter if any person loses his life by accidentally falling therein while the same is so unguarded or uninclosed. 55-56 V., c. 29, s. 255.

288. Every one is guilty of an indictable offence and liable to five years' imprisonment who sends, or attempts to send, or is a party to sending, a ship registered in Canada to sea, or on a voyage on any of the inland waters of Canada, or on a voyage from any port or place on the inland waters of Canada to any port or place on the inland waters of the United States, or on a voyage from any port or place on the inland waters of the United States to any port or place on the inland waters of Canada in such an unseaworthy state, by reason of overloading or underloading or improper loading, or by reason of being insufficiently manned, or from any other cause, that the life of any person is likely to be endangered thereby, unless he proves that he used all reasonable means to ensure her being sent to sea or on such voyage in a seaworthy state, or that her going to sea or on such voyage in such unseaworthy state was, under the circumstances, reasonable and justifiable. 55-56 V., c. 29, s. 256; 56 V., c. 32, s. 1.

Sending unseaworthy ships to sea.

Consent to prosecution.]—No person shall be prosecuted for any offence under this section without the consent of the Minister of Marine and Fisheries. Sec. 595.

Imperial Act.]—Section 457 of the Merchant Shipping Act, 1894 (Imp.), 57-58 Vict., ch. 60, which is applicable to British possessions as well as to the United Kingdom, also provides as follows: "If any person sends or attempts to send, or is party to sending or attempting to send a British ship to sea in such unseaworthy state that the life of any person is likely to be thereby endangered, he shall in respect of each offence be guilty of a misdemeanour unless he proves that he used all reasonable means to insure her being sent to sea in a seaworthy state, or that her going to sea in such unseaworthy state was, under the circumstances, reasonable and justifiable, and for the purpose of givng such proof he may give evidence in the same manner as any other witness." But a prosecution under that section of the Merchant Shipping Act in a British possession can only be brought by or with the consent of the governor thereof, i.e., in Canada, the Governor-General. Ibid., sec. 457 (3). See also Code sec. 289.

289. Every one is guilty of an indictable offence and liable to five years' imprisonment who, being the master of a ship registered in Canada, knowingly takes such ship to sea, or on a voyage on any of the inland waters of Canada, or on a voyage from any port or place on the inland waters of Canada to any port or place on the inland waters of the United States, or on a voyage from any port or place in the United States to any port or place on the inland waters of Canada, in such an unseaworthy state, by reason of overloading or underloading or improper loading, or by reason of being insufficiently manned, or from any other cause, that the life of any person is likely to be

Taking same to sea.

endangered thereby, unless he proves that her going to sea or on such voyage in such unseaworthy state was, under the circumstances, reasonable and justifiable. 55-56 V., c. 29, s. 257.

Consent to prosecution.]—No person shall be prosecuted for any offence under this or the preceding section without the consent of the Minister of Marine and Fisheries. Sec. 595.

Imperial Act.]—The Merchant Shipping Act, 1894 (Imp.), 57-58 Vict., ch. 60, sec. 457, which is applicable to British possessions, makes the following additional provision: "If the master of a British ship knowingly takes the same to sea in such unseaworthy state that the life of any person is likely to be thereby endangered, he shall in respect of each offence be guilty of a misdemeanour unless he proves that her going to sea in such unseaworthy state was, under the circumstances, reasonable and justifiable, and for the purpose of giving such proof he may give evidence in the same manner as any other witness." A prosecution under that section cannot, however, be brought in Canada without the consent of the Governor-General. Ibid., sec. 457 (3). And see Code sec. 288 and note to same.

Assaults.

Definition.

290. An assault is the act of intentionally applying force to the person of another, directly or indirectly, or attempting or threatening, by any act or gesture, to apply force to the person of another, if the person making the threat has, or causes the other to believe, upon reasonable grounds, that he has present ability to effect his purpose, and in either case, without the consent of the other or with such consent, if it is obtained by fraud. 55-56 V., c. 29, s. 258.

Common assault.]—To discharge a pistol loaded with powder and wadding at a person within such a short distance that the party might have been hit, is an assault. R. v. Cronan (1874), 24 U.C.C.P. 106. And see, as to pointing fire-arms, Code sec. 122.

A conviction for unlawfully assaulting V. by standing in front of the horses and carriage driven by the said V. in a hostile manner, and thereby forcibly detaining him, the said V. in the public highway against his will, was held bad, in stating the detention as a conclusion and not as part of the charge. R. v. McElligott (1883), 3 O.R. 535. It will not be inferred as a matter of law that standing in front of the horses was a forcible intention, there being no statement that the detention was by any other means than mere passive resistance. Ibid.

An indictment for rape includes the lesser charge of assault, and a verdict thereon of guilty of common assault is properly followed by a conviction although the information was laid more than six months after the offence was committed. R. v. Edwards (1898), 2 Can. Cr. Cas. 96.

A blow struck in anger or which is intended or is likely to do corporal hurt is a criminal assault, notwithstanding the consent to fight of the person struck. R. v. Buchanan (1898), 1 Can. Cr. Cas. 442 (Man.).

When one person is indicted for inflicting personal injury upon another, the consent of the person who sustains the injury is no defence to the person who inflicts the injury, if the injury is of such a nature or is inflicted under such circumstances that its infliction is injurious to the public as well as to the person injured. Reg. v. Coney (1882), 8 Q.B.D. 534.

If, whilst playing a game, a player deliberately infringes the rules, and in so doing hurts another, he is guilty of an assault, for the consent of the person injured only extends to acts committed within the rules. East, in his Pleas of the Crown, says: "If two were engaged to play at cudgels, and the one made a blow at the other likely to hurt before he was upon his guard, and without warning, and death ensued, the want of due and friendly warning would make such act amount to manslaughter, but not to murder, because the intent was not malicious." (Sol. Jour.)

And no rules or practice of any game can make that lawful which is unlawful by the law of the land; and the law of the land says you shall not do that which is likely to cause the death of another. R. v. Bradshaw (1878), 14 Cox C.C. 83.

A charge of common assault may in certain cases be completely answered by proof of consent on the part of the person bringing the charge. Thus, if a man strike another with a stick, this is primâ facie an offence, although no real harm be done; if, however, the two had agreed to engage in a match of singlesticks, and in the course of the game, and without transgression of its rules and with no intent to inflict harm, the complainant was struck, his consent to run the risk of receiving a blow is a defence to the charge of assault.

In a criminal prosecution by the wife of O., for assault made upon her in entering her husband's house, the defence was that she had no right to enter, and that her intention was to take away property which she had no legal right to take, but it was held, on a case reserved, that this would not justify the assault, there being no previous request made of her to leave the house, nor any statement of her intention, or of an attempt, to take anything. The Queen v. O'Neill, 3 P. & B. (N.B.) 49.

291. Every one who commits a common assault is guilty of an indictable offence and liable, if convicted upon an indictment, to one year's imprisonment, or to a fine not exceeding one hundred dollars, and on summary conviction to a fine not exceeding twenty dollars and costs, or to two months' imprisonment, with or without hard labour. 55-56 V., c. 29, s. 265. **Common assaults.**

Common assault.]—See sec. 290 for the statutory definition of an "assault" and see also the notes to that section.

Summary conviction.]—Section 732 provides for cases in which a summary conviction may be made for a common assault.

Title to land.]—By sec. 709 it is provided that no justice shall hear and determine any case of assault or battery in which any question arises as to the title to any tenements, hereditaments or any interest therein or accruing therefrom, or as to any bankruptcy or insolvency, or any execution under the process of any court of justice. Rent payable under a lease of land is an incorporeal hereditament. Kennedy v. MacDonell (1901), 1 O.L.R. 250.

If the justice finds the assault complained of to have been accompanied by an attempt to commit some other indictable offence or is of opinion that the same is from any other circumstance a fit subject for prosecution by indictment, he is not to adjudicate thereupon but must deal with the case in all respects in the same manner as if he had no authority finally to hear and determine the same. Section 732.

www.ingramcontent.com/pod-product-compliance
Ingram Content Group UK Ltd.
Pitfield, Milton Keynes, MK11 3LW, UK
UKHW061007110526
12378UKWH00049BA/1383

9 781287 354017